Consciousness and Class Experience in Nineteenth-Century Europe

Edited by John M. Merriman

HOLMES & MEIER PUBLISHERS, INC.

NEW YORK • LONDON

First published in the United States of America 1979 by
Holmes & Meier Publishers, Inc.
30 Irving Place
New York, N.Y. 10003

Great Britain:
Holmes & Meier Publishers, Ltd.
131 Trafalgar Road
Greenwich, London SE10 9TX

LIBRARY OF CONGRESS CATALOGING IN PUBLICATION DATA

Consciousness and class experience in nineteenth
-century Europe.

Bibliography: p.
Includes index.
1. Social classes—Europe—Case studies.
2. Labor and laboring classes—Europe—Case studies.
I. Merriman, John M.
HN380.Z9S6385   1979   301.44'094   79-16032
ISBN 0-8419-0444-8

Manufactured in the United States of America

Contents

Acknowledgments

This book began as a series of lectures on the topic "Social Change in Nineteenth-Century Europe," sponsored by the Council on West European Studies at Yale University. The program, which took place during the 1977–78 academic year, was made possible through the support of the Concilium on International and Area Studies, by William Parker, our council's capable and amiable chairman during that and previous years, and through the efforts of Heather Salome, our very able administrative assistant, and Beth Aumon, our bursary student. In addition to the essays included in this volume, other contributors to the series were Robert Bezucha, Richard Morse, Natalie Zemon Davis, Ted W. Margadant, Roger D. Price, George Grantham, Robert Herbert, Miriam Cohen, William Parker, Eugenia Herbert, Louise Tilly, Patricia Klaus, and Mary Curran, who helped plan the series. We are fortunate to enjoy the continued support of Albert Fishlow, the concilium's director. During that year, we benefited from the encouragement and unfailing good cheer of colleagues Ivo Banac and Paul Bushkovitch. Thanks should also go to Micheline Nilsen, who translated much of the Perrot article, to Carol Payne, who made valuable suggestions and provided good advice, and particularly to Joyce Seltzer, our editor. It has been a pleasure to work with her. My major debt is, of course, to the contributors, who are friends as well as *compagnons*.

Introduction

JOHN M. MERRIMAN

The nineteenth century has been called "the bourgeois century," the "Age of Revolution," and "the rebellious century."[1] It was all three, as each of these characterizations shows one of the century's dimensions. Bourgeois, revolutionary, and rebellious, the nineteenth century in Europe was a period of intense change; in it the economic, social and political structure of the continent was fundamentally altered. Populations rose dramatically as the peaks in mortality disappeared and levels of mortality declined. The populations living in cities increased even more rapidly. Europe urbanized. Governments centralized and bureaucratized their authority and thus expanded their effective power over their citizens—still called subjects in some places—sometimes also over their neighbors as the number of independent states declined, and even over faraway places as colonialism extended into Africa and Southeast Asia and the age of imperialism began. Large-scale industrialization changed the locations of work and residence, separating them from one another and altering patterns of leisure and social life. The railroad visibly, even dramatically improved transportation, expanding horizons and increasing consumption, and facilitated communication despite an unfortunately inauspicious beginning in 1830 when Francis Huskisson, a member of the British cabinet, was, shortly after cutting a ribbon inaugurating the Liverpool to Manchester train, run down and killed by that same train. The train even modernized political repression; some of the National Guardsmen brought from the provinces to put down the insurgents during the June Days of 1848 in Paris arrived by train. For many people and in many ways, the train became a symbol of an age.

These changes began in England but spread through much of the West. Contemporaries could not help but be acutely aware of their changing world. Manchester and Tourcoing grew up in one generation. Some people struggled to adjust to these changes, some profited from them, and some—perhaps even more—fought them; others simply tried to understand them. This was— somewhat self-consciously—the period of the "rising bourgeoisie"—inextricably linked with the "age of liberalism." Although the bourgeoisie hardly formed an undifferentiated bloc, it shared certain economic and psychological attitudes and came to demand political power commensurate with its economic achievements. It was no longer déclassé "to live as a bourgeois." Adeline Daumard has argued eloquently a general unity of response as the bourgeoisie of Paris, having gained access to political information and rights, tried to pull up the drawbridge behind it, and produced the Revolution of 1848.[2] The pace of social change appeared to be most rapid in the cities, where the bourgeoisie was at home, increasingly segregated from the "dangerous and laboring classes." And they were anxious. Middle-class citizens demanded to be made constables in Manchester in 1819 shortly before Peterloo. In England the middle classes, who shared the gentry's positive attitudes toward commerce and mistrust of the lower classes, never contemplated turning loose workers in the streets even to fight for an issues as close to their hearts as electoral reform. In France the bourgeois opposition to the Bourbons in 1829–30 became the *juste milieu* of the July Monarchy, nervously looking back over its shoulder. Later, it embraced Bonapartism as a guarantee of social order and, when that guarantee was no more, most of the bourgeoisie applauded the bloody repression of the Commune. In the Germanies, the Revolution of 1848 was crushed, leading to another reactionary regime. Like Gustave Le Bon, the bourgeoisie was awed by the crowd it feared. The great French caricaturist Honoré Daumier's bourgeois figures often seem more anxious and bewildered than smug and confident; one panics as the wind carries his top hat further and further from his clutching grasp down the Rue des Quatre vents; another proudly dresses his male offspring in a miniature uniform of Bonaparte; while a third admires himself in his uniform of the National Guard, that quintessentially bourgeois institution which was more concerned with defending Paris against internal insurrection than against attack from outside. The forts around the capital built during the July Monarchy (that regime popularly identified with the bourgeoisie) were spaced so that the guns would be effective in reaching the workers' quarters of the capital as well as in holding off foreign attackers. Balzac often describes Paris as a jungle, in which the bourgeois nervously struggled day after day in the hope of making, or maintaining the family fortune.

As the nineteenth century was bourgeois, it was also the time of revolutions and near revolutions, of *journées* and *journées manquées*. The century was, as the Tillys have argued, rebellious. The development of industrial capitalism and the consolidation and professionalization of the centralized state cut deeply into traditional patterns of economic and social life. The process of proletarianization may indeed have been the single most common historical experience in the lives of ordinary people. Many, like the Captain Swing rebels in England in 1830, resisted. Others could not, or did not. A great proportion of the European population was left, as always, with nothing but its labor and guile on which to survive. Industrial capitalism altered the structure of work and entailed considerable dislocation. It also brought in its wake great changes in the collective consciousness of Europeans. Craft and corporate solidarities were very gradually replaced by solidarities of economic class. Migration eroded some neighborhood affinities and created others as a geography of class segregation developed in most industrial cities. A degree of feminism and even political activity among women slowly developed, most noticeably in the aftermath of the Revolution of 1848 and during the Paris Commune. Professionalization accompanied the maturation of certain new occupations, such as those related to technological improvements.

The study of the varieties of collective consciousness—how and when they changed—may hold a key to an understanding of the most significant historical experiences of the nineteenth century, particularly proletarianization. While old solidarities and allegiances were under assault, new ones emerged which made it possible to resist or adjust to the forces of change. People could not help but be aware of the growing power of centralized governments and of industrial capitalism that affected their lives in deeply personal ways as they confronted gendarmes, conscription officers, merchant-capitalists, and foremen. Ultimately they created or came to follow ideologies and doctrines such as socialism, trade unionism, anarchism, or syndicalism which seemed to promise that something could be done by or for them. How, when, and why did people's attitudes and feelings about their situations change? When did various forms of traditional consciousness recede, to what extent did they persist, and what replaced them? How did social groups and individuals defend their interests and adjust to a changing world?

This book offers case studies in the changing historical experience and consciousness of ordinary people. Seven of the essays specifically consider France and two England. These two countries have been taken to be, with reason, the classic cases of the impact of economic, social, and political change. Indeed our knowledge of social change has generally moved from England and France to the east and south, the same direction followed, more or less, by the Industrial Revolution which began in Great Britain. Surprisingly few studies of the variety here presented have been done for areas outside of these two countries. Despite some excellent work, we know relatively little about the experience of German urbanization and industrialization, particularly as they affected ordinary people.[3] The Italian experience is even more obscure. There is little on nineteenth century Spain, with several important recent exceptions.[4] Local archivists have been much busier in England and particularly France, as the weight of the essays in this collection would indicate. But they address crucial questions which are now being or should be asked of other European countries as well; and, enjoying a methodological kinship, they have something to say about how historians will discover what really changed in the nineteenth century.

Charles Tilly contends that the lives of most nineteenth-century Europeans of many social classes were shaped by the historical processes of statemaking and the growth of industrial capitalism. Proletarianization—in many cases spurred on by state policies—was for good or ill, the dominant social experience of the largest part of the continent's population. Tilly estimates the number of proletarians and their families at around three hundred million of a total European population of about five hundred million at the end of the century. Proletarianization, as an objective reality, may have changed the lives of more people than did "liberalism" or "nationalism," at least until World War I.

A central theme of this book is the dynamics of proletarianization, first as an objective, continuous social process and second, as a subjective process involving the erosion of traditional forms of solidarities and the emergence of class consciousness. For the most part, these processes were not sudden, but took place within the context of traditional forms of work and the collective self-perception. Especially outside of England, they may even have had little to do with technological change and the expansion of the factory system. The timing of these changes, then, is crucial. Proletarianization took place earlier and in less sudden and dramatic ways on the continent than in England, and with less regard to sudden change and its "modern" concomitants (factories, machines, railroads).

Three essays specifically deal with the dynamics of proletarianization, defined by Christopher Johnson as "simply . . . the increase, both absolute and proportionate, in the number of wage laborers in a given population and their increasing domination by capitalists"; by Tilly, as an increase in the number of "all people whose survival depended upon the sale of their labor power"; and by Ronald Aminzade as "the process by which direct producers lose ownership and control over the means of production."

Tilly's summary of the proletarianization of the European population and the studies of Johnson and Aminzade make clear that this process was not dependent upon the creation of large units of production. Organizational, and not technological changes first marked the growing power of industrial capitalism. The factory itself, Johnson suggests, may have been a means of industrial discipline rather than the necessary form for a mechanized technology. (This point is salient in Michelle Perrot's essay as well.) Parisian tailors and Lodève woolens workers were proletarianized not because of mechanization, but because of organizational changes implied in the increasing domination of the merchant-capitalist. The organizational antecedents of these two groups of workers and the structure of their trades determined somewhat different possibilities and hopes for resistance. Aminzade emphasizes that the decline of handicraft production in Toulouse and the expansion of the putting-out system and sweated labor deprived workers of control over the production process. Here also factories and machinery had a minimal role. Tilly shows that the proletarianization of the European population, urban and rural, was already well underway at the end of the eighteenth century (as in Lodève) and continued through the nineteenth. Once again, it was not necessarily dependent upon technological advances, mechanization, and the growth of factories. And in Lyon the expansion of the silk industry during the Second Empire involved its *ruralization* (resisted by the master silk weavers) and not its concentration into large factories.

But proletarianization is also a subjective process: how and when did people perceive what was happening to them? These essays take us closer to understanding traditional corporate and craft bonds and solidarities as they were transformed by a commonality of historical experience into ties based upon social class. As Edward Thompson reminds us, consciousness necessarily involves the development of a sense of "collectivity" as well as a sense of "otherness" as class develops in opposition to the interests of powerful outsiders.[5] Aminzade, Johnson, and William Sewell, Jr. document the evolution of different forms of consciousness; Johnson and Aminzade emphasize the fundamental economic changes—the advent of industrial capitalism and changing organization of work which implied loss of control over the means of production—while Sewell emphasizes the cultural implications of changing attitudes toward property. All are interested in how craft and corporate collective experience typical of the *compagnonnage* and traditional guilds served as a basis for resistance to the interests of industrial capitalists, for the evolution of class solidarities based upon perceived shared interest, and ultimately for the growth of socialism. In the nineteenth century there were indeed great changes, but also continuities which facilitated the creation of new solidarities, consciousness, and organization. Unfortunately, the historiography on social change in the period has sometimes tended to emphasize uprooting and upheaval at the expense of an understanding of the evolution and continuities of changing historical experience. Sewell and Aminzade show the continued influence of traditional artisanal organizations, particularly the compagnonnage, which provided organizational experience, a cooperative world view, and solidarity which was transformed by historical circumstance into resistance and a sociopolitical ideology of socialism. Johnson shows the impact of the craft consciousness of Parisian tailors on the evolution of an essentially federalist trade union socialism, while Sewell sees the persistence among artisans of an attitude toward property characteristic of the Old Regime, which fed nicely into a socialism in which the means of production were not privately owned. Perrot demonstrates how workers and their traditional craft and family solidarity resisted the intensification of factory discipline even as the *patronat* moved to try to create a work force which would respond, as Josiah Wedgewood once fantasized, as a single set of hands. My own essay juxtaposes two kinds of consciousness and solidarities within the context of a growing industrial city: those of the butchers of Limoges, who struggled to maintain their patriarchical, corporate, religious, and monarchist traditions and even their neighborhood while Limoges industrialized, grew in population, and expanded; and those of the workers of the faubourgs, which cut across occupational boundaries and became the allegiances of class.

Traditional solidarities and consciousness were not easily broken, and stood as the backbone of the resistance to industrial capitalism. The role of skilled artisans as active participants in insurrections and revolutions has been often demonstrated. Those who fought in the Revolutions of 1830 and

1848 in France were not the uprooted or the dangerous classes, or the bourgeoisie who had the most to win. They were skilled workers whose crafts were threatened by industrial capitalism. In Frankfurt, while lawyers and professors proclaimed liberal generalities, the artisans, drawing up their grievances in a nearby hall, were ignored. Their views of politics and an ideal society derived from the solidarities they enjoyed and their own control over their work.

As Perrot reminds us, evolution of work and work discipline does not move in a straight line; the same is true in the evolution of consciousness and forms of economic and social organization. Only in England and certain areas of cotton spinning or heavy industry on the continent did the industrial revolution imply large units of production and the kinds of proletarianization associated with assembly lines. At many points, the "industrial revolution" meant an intensification of the forms of industry which were already operative. George Sheridan demonstrates that the expansion of the silk industry in Lyon brought an intensification of rural industry, both mechanized and handicraft, leading urban master weavers to adopt strategies permitting them to survive in the trade they had once controlled. Aminzade demonstrates the strength of the putting-out system in Toulouse; and Tilly cites the case of Zurich's hinterland, where industry first expanded into the countryside before finally contracting and reconcentrating in the city. And as Perrot has shown, even within the factory, traditional forms of work organization and discipline survived. Groups of artisans worked near huge machines, and family work teams and collective responsibility survived.

If old forms of consciousness were threatened by the process of proletarianization, how were new solidarities forged? Aminzade shows how new forms of associations, collective action, and new political ideologies reflected the new solidarities of class. Bloody compagnonnage brawls gave way to strikes coordinated between workers in various trades. New mutual benefit societies evidenced wider goals and possibilities; republican socialism developed an allegiance among workers whose fathers, if not themselves, were once proud royalists. Johnson shows that a similar scenario could be found in Lodève. In both cases the middle of the century was the critical period in the evolution of new forms of consciousness in France and probably in Germany as well. My own essay jumps ahead in time to the "heroic age of French labor" and looks at the emerging geography of class segregation in the working-class faubourgs of the city as an essential variable in the creation of class solidarities. The growth of working-class communities thus had and important geographic dimension, whether it be Lodève, Toulouse, Paris, or Lyon (consider the legendary Croix-Rousse, the silk-workers' quarter linked by the narrow *traboules* which permitted silk to be transported in bad weather); or Berlin, London, Essen, or Milan. The emerging social geography of class played an important role in the creation of working-class consciousness. The development of neighborhood solidarities could sometimes mitigate class tensions and could link to the workers many shopkeepers, such as the *cafetiers* and *cabaretiers* dependent on workers' business whom we see in Susanna Barrows' essay. Johnson shows how this worked in a small working-class town where nearly everyone was dependent upon a single industry.

As Johnson and I suggest in our essays, the range of migration is another important variable in the creation of new solidarities. Does migration hinder or aid the creation of working-class consciousness? It depends. We must ask if the kinds of urban villages typical of long range migration patterns identified migrants as outsiders and job competitors sometimes not even speaking the same language. Where the range of migration was quite short (as my preliminary findings would seem to indicate for Limoges) and where many newcomers (as in Lyon, Zurich, and Reims) may have had some industrial experience, migrants may have been integrated rather quickly into the community. Because of the high degree of geographic mobility in much of Europe in the nineteenth century, the question of migration is crucial for an understanding of the class experience of both urban and rural workers.

How important, then, were traditional and long-standing allegiances and consciousness in the formation of new solidarities? When did they conflict? As Sheridan asks, at what point will the boundaries of the solidarities of family, craft, corporation, quartier, or even city be surpassed and become those of class? When will skilled artisans come to enter into coalitions with unskilled laborers against common antagonists? What was the role of new economic and social organizations, such as the French Bourse du travail, in such transformations? When did national solidarities supersede class interests? For example, how was the nationalist revival in France able to transcend the boundaries of class? In 1914 most French workers marched off to fight against German workers believing that they were opposing the Prussian autocracy. When did neighborhood loyalties predominate over class ties?

To understand the impact of proletarianization and large scale industrialization, we must begin to study the total collective experience of European workers, to know, as Lynn Lees puts it, "the structure of the community and family" as well as "economic conditions, ideologies, and cultural norms." Thus varieties of working-class experience must be investigated, for not all workers organized, struck, or participated in politics. For example, Barrows' study takes us into the world of drink immortalized by Emile Zola in his classic *L'Assommoir*. Zola is preoccupied, if not obsessed with the fact that drink became a prodigious problem in France. Reformers and early social scientists were concerned with this demoralization of the French workers and the writings of the early crowd psychologists reflected this preoccupation. Zola portrays a working class which could not have been further from politics and organized economic struggles. Yet his *Germinal* presents a striking contrast. Consider, for example, the changing role of the café and cabaret, sometimes called the church of the working class. To Zola and for Barrows, the café was a window on working-class life, but little political talk could be heard at the many counters described in *L'Assommoir*. Yet in *Germinal*, some of the workers' organizational efforts center on the café. We still need a history of changing patterns of leisure and their influence on politics, as suggested by Maurice Agulhon's study of the role of the Var *chambrées* in the "descent of politics toward the masses" during the Second French Republic.[6]

Clearly, neither the bourgeoisie nor the working class can be studied as an undifferentiated block. Nor can either be studied in isolation. In order to understand the world of working people, we must know something of their relations with other social groups. The study of the city provides such an opportunity. As Tilly stated in a recent review, to study cities one must "begin with the structure of the community, locate your classes within it, make systematic comparisons of class and communities. Reason, in short, from the variables rather than from the constants."[7] One of the reasons we know little about bourgeois relations with the working class—the community study offers a wealth of research possibilities—is that we know very little about the bourgeoisie. Did the Parisian bourgeoisie retain the shared attitudes and psychological preoccupations that they manifested during the first half of the century? How similar was the world of the bourgeoisie of other cities? And, as Peter Gay asks, what about the new bourgeois groups, such as office managers, clerks in train stations, department store personnel, or the white collar factory officials whom Perrot discusses? A.-J. Tudesq's classic study of the French *notables* (noble and bourgeois) offered a model study of collective mentality in the face of social change.[8] Frank Turner considers a much smaller and newer but significant group, Victorian scientists, who also came to share similar attitudes and solidarities and drew together as a professionally conscious and organized body. Schoolteachers, doctors, and lawyers are but three other groups of professionals for whom change meant increased opportunity, prestige, consciousness of themselves as a group, and organization.

Peter Gay offers a deeper meaning of consciousness when he contends that histories of anger, anxiety, and psychological defenses may assist in the quest of historians for an understanding of social change in nineteenth-century Europe. Perhaps it is time to put social groups on the couch and study the relationship between individual and collective behavior and the unconscious. The study of voluntary associations should also provide a means of assessing bourgeois attitudes toward their class inferiors, as well as showing under what circumstances they could join together. How class conscious was the bourgeoisie as a whole? 1848 and 1871 left little doubt in France, though it is doubtful that many bourgeois demonstrated the same degree of collective self-consciousness as those who gathered for the first (and presumably last) "World Congress of the Petty Bourgeoisie" in Antwerp in 1899.[9] Barrows shows how the bourgeoisie came to fear the "drunken commoner" as a result of its perception of the Paris Commune and came to identify all of the most terrifying aspects of the French failure and degradation with the working-class. With the marked development of workers' organizations toward the end of the century, crowds marching with red flags and lists of demands provoked responses of fear and anxiety. If the bourgeoisie was anxious, it was at least partially true that they had much to be anxious about.

Before turning to the essays themselves—and at the risk of some repetition—what should we look for in each of them? How can it help us identify the major historical problems of the nineteenth century? In what ways is it suggestive? Charles Tilly answers the question "What really changed in nineteenth-century Europe?" in his wide-ranging essay entitled "Did the Cake of Custom Break?" The latter takes us from the hinterland of Zurich to Scandinavia, from Flanders to Hungary. Tilly takes as his starting point Eugen Weber's recent provocative book *Peasants into Frenchmen,* which argues that France modernized during the period 1880–1910 as three principal agencies of change—education, improved transportation, and the experience of mass military conscription—transformed peasants into Frenchmen. These changes, Weber argues, led to the integration of rural France into a national, French culture previously limited to the cities, which had stood as oases in the middle of a savage, backward, apolitical, isolated rural world.[10] Tilly finds Weber's interesting account to be another articulate restatement of modernization theory, which seeks to trace the emergence of "recognizable features of 20th-century life." Tilly suggests that the most important changes were related most directly to the process by which national states increased and consolidated their power and the development of industrial capitalism. He suggests that the history of social change in the nineteenth century requires systematic studies of the political, economic, and demographic experience of individuals and groups. Looking at the patterns of changing historical experience—population growth, large-scale industrialization, and patterns of proletarianization—Tilly argues that "immobile societies did not give way during the nineteenth century because they did not exist at the beginning of the century." Indeed, "there was no solid cake of customs to break," which shows the "utter inadequacy of any portrayal of the nineteenth-century rural world as a territory essentially populated by peasants and fundamentally devoted to agriculture." If the complex nature of rural society in nineteenth-century Europe is to be understood, we must grasp the political and social consequences which resulted from "the shift in control" of the interests of rural communities "from local and regional elites to national capital and national state." Tilly provides an agenda for the study of social change, all the more valuable because it accompanies an able summary of a century of change, painted with large brush strokes which lay out the dynamics and implications of the historical experience of nineteenth-century Europeans.

William Sewell, Jr.'s provocative essay discusses the impact of what he sees as a changed conception of property brought by the French Revolution. The strong corporate tradition of the artisanal organizations characteristic of the Old Regime, particularly the compagnonnage, was firmly based in a tradition of "private" property in which rights over property were not absolute, but rather governed by tradition and usage. Sewell uses the example of master artisans, who held the right of property over tools, but whose rights were limited by tradition. The rights of villagers to use lands they did not own was another significant limitation on the property rights of the owner.

However, the legal system that emerged from the French Revolution formed the basis of the new social, economic and political order which supported the bourgeoisie. The Napoleonic code, which was adopted in part or in whole in much of Europe, recognized only the absolute right of private property and did not recognize the kinds of limitations carried by the collective claims which typified the "moral economy." This altered definition of property conflicted with the traditions of artisans and shaped "the profoundly collectivist mentality of the French working-class movement" which cannot be separated from its corporate tradition and attitudes toward private property both of which persisted well into the nineteenth century. Sewell finds the origins of nineteenth-century French socialism in this transformation which, he argues, cannot be understood without coming to grips with the cultural conceptions which underlay the social and political history of the period. The democratic socialists of the Second French Republic (1848–51), while not opposing property per se (in this sense, they were very much in the tradition of the sansculottes of the Revolution, who opposed only unearned property, i.e., property not acquired through labor, came to argue against the private ownership of the means of production.

Sewell's essay offers an interesting contrast to that of Tilly. Both would agree as to *what* changed in the nineteenth century. Yet important differences remain in their assessments of the causes of such changes as the emergence of class-conscious workers. Tilly emphasizes structural shifts in the economy while Sewell's interpretations stress the primacy of cultural factors which preceded fundamental economic change. This is an important issue that is reaffirmed by Sewell's call for "culturally sensitive accounts of social change."

Christopher Johnson's essay, "Patterns of Proletarianization: Parisian Tailors and Lodève Woolens Workers," clarifies the relation between industrial capitalism and the process of proletarianization. He shows how the collective experience of ordinary people was altered well before the advent of large factories and technological changes which are often rather misleadingly associated with the "Industrial Revolution." Johnson takes us into the world of traditional workers during the important transitional period of protoindustrialization between an artisan-based economy and large-scale industrialization. For the purposes of comparison as well as to demonstrate further the objective and subjective accomplishments of proletarianization, Johnson shows how Parisian tailors gradually lost control over their trade. Ultimately their corporate vision lay at the base of their emerging political radicalization and their faith in producers' cooperatives. His central focus is the woolens center of Lodève in the Midi, north of Montpellier, a small and somewhat isolated single-industry town (which peaked as a working-class town relatively early, partially because of wartime demand for woolens). Lodève became a scene of turbulence where striking workers enjoyed the support of many shopkeepers and the bourgeoisie, who were dependent upon the relative prosperity of the town. Using a remarkable census from 1798, which provides information on duration of residence, place of birth, and home ownership, Johnson reconstructs the world of migration, settlement, work, strikes, and political contention. Johnson's research is a significant addition to the history of proletarianization because he has studied his tailors and woolens workers over the *longue durée* and captures the reality and significance of their changing collective experiences.

Ronald Aminzade, a sociologist, is also concerned with the impact of industrial capitalism and the process of proletarianization. Aminzade's city, Toulouse, is in the south of France: unlike Lodève, Toulouse was one of France's largest cities and a regional economic, political, administrative, and cultural capital. Aminzade describes changes in the daily life of the city's workers in the context of regional and national changes in the political economy. He shows how a city with a tradition of popular royalism and the bitter memories of the White Terror after the fall of Napoleon became a center for socialist organization during the Second French Republic. He documents the process by which "the horizontal solidarities and vertical antagonisms of social class gradually replaced the horizontal conflict of trade rivalries and vertical ties of patronage." Aminzade studies the evolving forms of association, changing patterns of collective violence, and the development of republican socialism. He ties these changes in collective historical experience to large-scale economic change. The process was gradual, yet fundamentally revolutionary: capital concentration and the decline of Toulouse's handicraft industry changed the nature of social and political relations as well as the structure of work. Toulousain workers lost control of the work process, and their organizations—principally the compagnonnage—became obsolete. One is reminded of the more than ten thousand *compagnons* who gathered at the Place des Vosges in Paris in April 1848—perhaps the largest such gathering ever—but marking the end of an era. The future lay in new solidarities of social class and political and economic action.

George Sheridan's study of the master weavers of Lyon also illustrates the persistence of traditional forms of economic organization in Europe and the resistance of craftsmen to those changes which have often been lumped together as comprising the Industrial Revolution. Lyon was France's second city, the scene of violent uprisings by the silk workers defending their trade interests in 1831 and 1834 (when they adopted the slogan "Live free or die fighting") and an attempted insurrection in June of 1849. The Second Empire (1852–70) witnessed another kind of resistance. Master silk weavers capitalized on the hesitation of their sometime enemies, the merchant-manufacturers, who emphasized small inventories, small risks, and a tradition of family management and shied away from investing in mechanization; the weavers employed an unskilled and unemployed female labor force and thus preserved their urban trade in an industry vulnerable to shortages of raw materials and the sudden contraction of demand brought about by the

American Civil War and by changes in style. Master weavers therefore adapted their household size, taking in women weavers, whom they housed, fed, and paid very little. In this way the weavers resisted mechanization and the continued "ruralization" of their industry as engineered by the merchant-manufacturers, who capitalized on the availability of cheap rural labor. Sheridan's fine economic history features some thorough quantitative work based upon census samples. Sheridan is able to weave a graphic account of the experiences and alternatives of merchant-manufactuers, master weavers, journeymen and female laborers in the industry. One of the most fascinating parts of this study is Sheridan's portrayal of the mentality of the master weaver and the persistence of a traditional solidarity and heritage of co-operation which contributed to their willingness to defend their trade as it had been long practiced on the hills of Lyon.

My own essay, "Incident at the Statue of the Virgin Mary: The Conflict of Old and New in Nineteenth-Century Limoges," explores geographic and iconographic aspects of the emergency of an industrial center. I contrast two very different kinds of communities, one old and one new, in Limoges; in their experiences we see something of the metamorphosis of a city once known as "Holy Limoges" to "the Rome of socialism." The statue of the Virgin Mary stood before the ancient chapel of the butchers on their street. In April 1905, during a series of violent strikes, the porcelain workers, most of whom lived beyond another statue more relevant to their own experiences, briefly threatened the butchers' statue. This minor incident captured two very different urban experiences. The butchers had retained their corporate control over their trade for centuries, as well as their colorful nicknames and allegiance to the families of butchers, to the king, and to their saints and organized religion. The porcelain workers, the most organized and militant of Limoges's workers, developed solidarities related to their shared experience of work but also to residential geography and relatively common place of origin.

Michelle Perrot's "The Three Ages of Industrial Discipline in France" addresses a problem central to the process of proletarianization. Although proletarianization was not necessarily dependent upon the development of factories in its early stages, ultimately this mode of production became its most salient characteristic. Once urban and rural people began to lose control over the work process, the patronat faced the necessity of disciplining its work force. How was a disciplined work force obtained? Perrot suggests a timing for three general stages of industrial discipline, while recognizing that different forms of discipline could, like different technological stages, be found at the same time, or even in the same factory. Here as in her splendid study *Les Ouvriers en grève* suggestions and ideas leap from every page.[11] She takes us from the *Panopticon* of Jeremy Bentham, where the prison supervisor could see all cells without being seen, and the discipline of eighteenth-century "factories," through the advent of posted factory regulations which with their enforcer, the foreman, sought to break old habits of talking during work, or leaving for drink and fresh air, and on to the problems imposed by Taylorism and the early attempts to create a "science of work" at the beginning of this century. Several aspects of her essay are particularly intriguing: the discussion of the disciplinary function of the family, which continued well into the nineteenth century, her analysis of the concomitants of paternalism and the development of *cités industrielles* which aimed at total supervision of workers' lives, the role of mechanization in factory discipline, the architecture and structure of factory units, and the advent of staffs, managers and, above all, the foreman; and finally to the "mathematical logic" and the "quiet violence" of the computer.

At every stage, workers resisted the regimentation and discipline, and this resistance generated new forms of institutionalized control. One has only to recall the strikes called to protest the arbitrary authority of the foreman during the decades at the turn of this century. Perrot's stages should inspire further research in this area essential to the entire historical problem of proletarianization in Europe and beyond.

Lynn Hollen Lees explores a crucial dimension of the working-class experience with her essay on family budgets in northern England. She here considers workers from essentially large-scale industries at the "end" of the process of industrialization. Lees uses a survey of the budgets of 777 working-class families in 1890, undertaken, oddly enough, by the U.S. Department of Labor. She demonstrates that the families in question were relatively well off. Taking into consideration occupational and life-cycle differences, she shows that over 80 percent could afford some kind of insurance and a good proportion regularly purchased newspapers or books and allocated sums to other leisure activities. The sample, as she recognizes, is almost certainly weighted toward skilled workers and away from the large unskilled, casual, and transient portion of the British working class. Furthermore, the survey was taken during a generally prosperous time for the English economy. Nonetheless, Lees' general conclusion is important: "A complex and relatively self-enclosed working-class culture had developed in English industrial communities, although not all families could afford to participate equally." Increased literacy and educational opportunities helped break down occupational and regional differences, and create a truly national working-class culture. To what extent this is true for other countries or even regions within larger and less integrated nations in Europe remains to be seen. But family, culture, and community, as well as an appreciation of the family economy and developmental cycle, must certainly be considered in the history of the working class. Under what circumstances and to what degree did they mediate between the worker and his or her relationship to the means of production?

Given the profound nature of economic, social, cultural, and political change in the nineteenth century, it is probably not surprising that it was in some ways an uncertain and anxious period. Peter Gay asks if nervousness and anxiety are not keys to understanding the collective historical experience of the European bourgeoisie. Urbanization, migration, the decline of traditional religious adherence, and the challenge of the working class must have been potentially unsettling. How did the bourgeoisie deal with its anxieties? Can the same psychological responses which characterize the individual's response to his private world be found in the bourgeoisie as a whole? Can one apply our knowledge of the defense mechanisms which are essential to every individual's way of dealing with the world to the historian's quest for an understanding of collective behavior? While in no way denying the complexity of the human experience, Gay suggests that four classic psychological defenses against anxiety—denial, projection, regression, and reaction formation—helped social groups respond to a changing world. Gay's essay "On the Bourgeoisie: Towards a Psychological Interpretation" opens new horizons to be explored in psychoanalytic history. He offers fascinating examples of each.

Susanna Barrows' essay, "After the Commune: Alcoholism, Temperance, and Literature in the Early Third Republic," nicely complements that of her mentor, Peter Gay. Her elegant study focuses on the reactions to the Paris Commune of the French bourgeoisie and its projection of France's weakness (and thus its own) onto the workers and the problem of drink. As the consumption of alcohol skyrocketed during the nineteenth century because of improvements in production and distribution, social reformers and bourgeois critics became aware of drink as a social problem, but not their own. The Communards were, they said after the storm had passed, drunken workers, drunk because they were morally weak, not because they were poor. In the savage repression which followed, stifling artists as well as workers, the problem of alcoholism was highlighted and temperance societies sprang up; these included the honorary members typical of such moralizing associations based on traditional patterns of deference. Barrows examines these fascinating relationships, seen particularly through the eyes of Emile Zola, as he planned and wrote his supposedly apolitical novel *L'Assommoir*, which in reality was a scathing and courageous indictment of bourgeois hypocrisy. Like Gay, Barrows is less concerned with the realities of class experience than on the ways it was perceived and social groups responded and were transformed by their convenient misreading of the events of *l'année terrible*.

Frank Turner's "The Victorian Conflict between Science and Religion: A Professional Dimension" considers another type of consciousness that emerged during the course of the nineteenth century. A collective consciousness of interest and identity as scientists, he suggests, led to the professionalization and indeed the institutionalization of the scientific community in Victorian England. Scientists developed a sense of "collectivity" and "otherness" and succeeded in gaining national recognition and prestige. Their sense of exclusiveness as men of science kept outsiders from joining their professional circles and enabled them to challenge successfully the belief in theology as the source of all knowledge and all moral and social values. The development of this self-conscious and increasingly professional elite is seen in the changing composition of the membership of the Royal Society and in the development of other voluntary associations which ultimately were to serve what Francis Galton called a "scientific priesthood." The struggle between science and religion, the theme of some of Turner's earlier work, thus had important implications not only for questions of the relative national prestige of scientists and men of the cloth, but for the development of professional experience, identity, and organizations.

In drawing historical work together and focusing it on the study of the fundamental and pervasive processes which transformed nineteenth-century Europe, our volume of essays seeks to have an influence beyond its specific subject matter. In addition to their substantive contributions, the essays of this book offer a methodological kinship and are therefore intended to suggest approaches to the study of the dimensions of changing consciousness and class experience. The history of these transformations lies in interdisciplinary case studies of social groups, trades, associations, cities, communities, neighborhoods, migration, women, work-structure, and individuals over the *longue durée*. The answers lie "in the field," in the censuses, police records, surveys, architectural plans, judicial reports, memoirs, and photographs available in national, regional, and local archives, and in the stones of the cities, towns, villages, and farms themselves. Such studies will move us closer to understanding the dynamics of change that revolutionized the way people worked, lived, and perhaps even more important, the way they thought of themselves.

Notes

1. E. J. Hobsbawm, *The Age of Revolution: Europe, 1789–1848* (London: Weidenfeld and Nicholson, 1962); Charles Tilly, Louise Tilly, and Richard Tilly, *The Rebellious Century* (Cambridge, Mass.: Harvard University Press, 1975); Charles Morazé, *The Triumph of the Middle Classes* (London: Weidenfeld and Nicolson, 1966).

2. Adeline Daumard, *Les bourgeois de Paris au XIXe siècle* (Paris: Flammarion, 1970).

3. See, in particular, the fine studies of Mack Walker, *German Home Towns* (Ithaca: Cornell University Press, 1971), and Wolfgang Köllmann, *Sozialgeschichte der Stadt Barmen in 19. Jahrhundert* (Tübingen: J. C. B. Mohr, 1960).

4. Raymond Carr, *Spain, 1808–1939* (Oxford: Oxford University Press, 1966); Temma Kaplan, *The Anarchists of Andalusia, 1868–1903* (Princeton: Princeton University Press, 1977); Edward Malefakis, *Agrarian Reform and Peasant Revolution in Spain* (New Haven: Yale University Press, 1970).

5. E. P. Thompson, *The Making of the English Working Class* (New York: Vintage Books, 1963); George Joseph Sheridan, Jr., "The Social and Economic Foundations of Association among the Silk Weavers of Lyons, 1852–1870" (Ph.D. dissertation, Yale University, 1977).

6. Maurice Agulhon, *La République au village* (Paris: Plon, 1970).

7. Charles Tilly, "Peeping through the Window of the Wealthy," *Journal of Urban History* 3, 1 (Nov. 1976): 135.

8.   A.-J. Tudesq, *Les Grands Notables en France*, 2 vols. (Paris: Presses Universitaires de France, 1964).

9.   *Congrès international de la petite bourgeoisie* (Antwerp, 1899).

10.   Eugen Weber, *Peasants into Frenchmen: The Modernization of Rural France, 1870–1914* (Stanford: Stanford University Press, 1976).

11.   Michelle Perrot, *Les Ouvriers en grève*, 2 vols. (Paris: Mouton, 1974).

ONE

Did the Cake of Custom Break?

CHARLES TILLY

Peasants into Frenchmen, Eugen Weber's big book, has caused a stir among historians of France. Many people have called it brilliant, some have called it great, and others have spoken of it as the most important work of the last decade. Considering the competition from such masters as Richard Cobb, Emmanuel Le Roy Ladurie, Pierre Goubert and Maurice Agulhon, a book which receives such praise must be impressive.

Indeed it is. Weber's discussion of changes in rural France from 1870 to 1914 is vivid, rich, witty, and bubbling with insight. (Who else would think to show us how recently twentieth-century necessities had been luxuries by pointing out that in the nineteenth-century Vivarais the visitor's ritual gift had been a package of coffee, a kilo of sugar, or a loaf of white bread?) Weber has found the means of blending folklore, ethnography, and local history into a lively portrayal of a lost world. Every page bears a rich weave of proverbs, customs, couplets, and anecdotes.

Beneath the brocade, however, the shape of Weber's argument is familiar. Until well into the nineteenth century, he tells us, most of rural France lived in near-isolation from the rest of the world, a congeries of diverse, slow-changing and, yes, barbarous little societies barely penetrated by French civilization. The thin, incoherent rural cultures had grown up as devices for coping with desperate poverty. All this, says Weber, changed fast after 1870. As the whole of France grew more prosperous, roads, rail lines, markets, schools, and military conscription cut into the countryside. These national-izing, rationalizing institutions weakened rural particularism, flooded the hinterland with new ideas, goods, and practices, then tied the countryside into an urbane national culture and social life. The crucial changes, in Weber's account, were mental: confronted with new institutions and altered oppor-tunities, peasants converted to rationalism and instrumentalism. The cake of custom, to use Walter Bagehot's famous phrase, broke. From diversity and barbarity emerged homogeneity and civilization. In a word, rural France modernized.

Weber draws his evidence for this view from three main sources: the testimonies of elite observers such as government officials, doctors, school-teachers, and travelers; the reports of the folklorists who swarmed over rural France during the early decades of the twentieth century; and the regional monographs for which French geographers and historians have become justly famous. He avoids two sorts of evidence which would, I think, require him to mend his argument extensively: (1) systematic observations of the geography of "modernization"—income, literacy, mobility, industrial production, poli-tical activity, and so on—for France as a whole; (2) observations on the pace and character of his crucial changes *before* 1870. That makes it possible for him to argue that

> traditional communities continued to operate in the traditional manner as long as conditions retained their traditional shape: low productivity, market fluctua-tions beyond the producer's control, a low rate of savings, little surplus. What surplus the peasant could accumulate was taken from him in taxes or usurious interest, spent on church buildings and feasts, or invested in land. But land did not increase total production until capital investment in improvements became both possible and thinkable. And this did not happen until the market became an accessible reality, that is, until the expanding communications network brought it within reach.[1]

Nineteenth-century agricultural life may have been grim, but the idea that the grimness resulted from lack of involvement in the market is a basic misap-prehension: the French countryside was already heavily involved in pro-duction for regional, national, and even international markets by the end of the eighteenth century.

Weber applies the same notions of isolation and autarky to politics:

> Political dispute, even rebellion, on the national level played its part in diminishing the significance of local solidarities, suggesting new rival ones, like the new-fangled idea of class. At mid-century, local solidarity had reigned supreme. By the end of the century it had lost its exclusive relevance. The autarkies characterizing most of the nineteenth century were breaking down. Great local questions no longer found their origin or solution in the village, but had to be resolved outside and far from it. The peasantry gradually awakened to urban (that is, general) ideas, abstract (that is, not local) concerns.[2]

This time Weber's reasoning contains an element of truth. National issues and interests did begin to loom much larger in local politics during the nineteenth century. Yet the analysis goes wrong in several important ways.

First (although the vocabulary of class was, indeed, chiefly a nineteenth-century creation), the reality of class division was apparent in rural communi-ties early in the nineteenth century, and before. Pierre de Saint-Jacob devoted much of his masterly study of eighteenth-century Burgundian peasants to the conflicts which separated peasants and landlords; the Revolution, in his view, crystallized divisions which had long been forming.

Second, Weber concentrates on issues with respect to which villagers took the initiative. He forgets the innumerable occasions on which country people

reacted to outside challenges: challenges to local Protestant religious practices in the sixteenth and seventeenth centuries; challenges to local fiscal
rights in the seventeenth and eighteenth centuries; challenges to local control
over the food supply in the eighteenth and nineteenth centuries. Religious
struggles, tax rebellions, and food riots had occurred frequently in the French
countryside for three centuries before 1870; they involved "great local
questions." In fact, Yves-Marie Bercé has built a whole series of books
around the theme of a solidaristic, self-interested peasant community responding to outside attacks by means of repeated rebellions. Only with the
nineteenth century, according to Bercé, did the unified interest and solidarity
decline to the point of undermining the basis for peasant revolts.

Third, Weber's timing is off: the shift toward national politics became
noticeable during the French Revolution, and had gone far by the middle of
the nineteenth century. The massive rural participation both in the mobilization of 1848 and in the 1851 resistance to Louis Napoleon's coup demonstrates that nationalization.[3]

Finally, the critical nineteenth-century alteration in the position of rural
communities was not a move from autarky to integration, but a shift in control
of their interests from local and regional elites to national capital and the
national state. The adoption of an image of modernization as the breaking of
the cake of custom makes those changes in organization and interests hard to
see, and harder to understand.

The view of social change as the dissolution of customary, small-scale
social life is familiar. It became the dominant bourgeois analysis of the
nineteenth century. It knits nicely with the notion that wealth, mobility, and
urban experience corrupt virtuous peasants. It fits just as well, paradoxically,
with the call for a civilizing mission on the part of schools, local government,
and military service. The former is the conservative, nostalgic version, the
latter the liberal, progressive version, of the same theory. The delightful
vibrancy of Weber's book results from his deft use of the conservatives'
preferred sorts of evidence in the service of the progressive theory. At bottom,
he finds the old ways barbaric, and the *mission civilisatrice* well worth
undertaking; yet folklore and local history provide him with his materials.

The bourgeois analysis gave rise to the great nineteenth-century dicho-
tomies: *Gemeinschaft* and *Gesellschaft*, status and contract, mechanical and
organic solidarity. It also helped form such presumptuous disciplines as
sociology and anthropology, whose objects were to document, to explain, and
perhaps to guide the transition from one side of the dichotomy to the other.

Nor did the ideas die with the nineteenth century. On the contrary. They
became the basis of standard twentieth-century conceptions, both academic
and popular, of large-scale change. Although the particular set of variants
called "modernization theory" rose and fell in the quarter-century after World
War II, the general idea of modernization through dissolution and integration
has survived from the nineteenth century to our own time. It has survived, as
we have seen, into the fascinating work of Eugen Weber. In one form or
another, it appears widely in North American analyses of Europe, including

those of such widely read authors as Cyril Black, Edward Shorter, Peter Stearns, and John Gillis. The difference between Weber and his colleagues does not lie in the novelty of his basic argument, but in his insistence on the period from 1870 to 1914 and, more important, in his extraordinary use of ethnographic detail to present the argument.

Familiarity is not truth. Is it *true* that the dominant social changes in nineteenth-century Europe comprised (or resulted from) the displacement of traditional, localized, immobile cultures by industrialism, urbanism, and expanding communications? That is doubtful. It is doubtful on two rather different grounds: (1) because many of the most important concrete changes in the social life of nineteenth-century Europe did not follow the paths required by theories of modernization; (2) because the massive industrialization, urbanization, and communications shifts—which did, indeed, occur—grew from the interaction of two deeper and wider processes: the growth of national states and the expansion of capitalism.

My discussion will dwell on the first point: the failure of important processes to follow the courses charted by theories of modernization. That is the easier of the two points to establish. It also leads naturally to consideration of the reasons for the theories' failure, then to reflection on alternative general accounts of social change in nineteenth-century Europe. Those alternatives will easily take us back to capitalism and statemaking.

The issues matter in their own right: we are asking, after all, how the world changes, and how the world we know came into being. The issues also matter in another way: theories of modernization underlie many accounts of nineteenth-century conflict, consciousness, and collective action. Conservative modernization models nest neatly with interpretations of protest, conflict, and collective action as irrational responses to the stresses and strains of rapid change. Progressive modernization models, on the other hand, articulate plausibly with a vision of awakening consciousness, of increasing integration into cosmopolitan world views which guide collective action on a large scale. If the underlying models prove incorrect, we shall have to consider another alternative more seriously: that most of the time ordinary people have an idea, more or less clear, of their short-run interests, but vary enormously in their capacity and opportunity to act on those interests. If that is the case—as, obviously, I think it is—the proper substitute for the study of "modernization" is likely to be the study of the ways in which large social changes alter the interests, capacities, and opportunities of ordinary people.

Notions of Modernization

Whether theories of modernization are worthless or merely cumbersome depends, however, on how much we ask of them. In an undemanding version, the notion of modernization is simply a name for general features of contemporary life: intense communications, big organizations, mass production, and so on. If our program is simply to inquire whether those features of social life were already visible in the nineteenth century, and to search for their origins, then the analysis of modernization is no more misleading than most other retrospective schemes.

In a somewhat more demanding guise, modernization becomes a label for dominant patterns of change. Rainer Lepsius, for instance, breaks modernization into the following elements: (1) differentiation; (2) mobilization; (3) participation; and (4) institutionalization of conflict.[4] The fit between these terms and the main trends in nineteenth-century Europe depends on their specification: which units are supposed to be differentiating, who is supposed to be mobilizing with respect to what end, and so on. It also depends on our vantage point: from the perspective of the national state and the national elite, differentiation, mobilization, participation, and institutionalization summarize many of the changes that occurred in nineteenth-century Europe. From the perspective of the local community, many of the same changes involved dedifferentiation, demobilization, perhaps even deinstitutionalization; rights, rituals, and rounds of life which had previously prevailed now lost their strength. Nevertheless, any model of social change requires us to take some vantage point, and the center is as permissible a vantage point as any other. Thus we can make it a question of fact whether differentiation, mobilization, participation, and institutionalization do, indeed, describe the main trends in nineteenth-century Europe, as seen from its central locations.

The real difficulties with modernization theories only begin when we move from simple inventories of common themes to the analysis of what sorts of structures changed, and why. Did urbanism, industrialism, and expanding communications dissolve previously stable, small, self-contained structures, release people from their control, generate disorder as a consequence, and finally produce a new, complex, large-scale set of connections to replace the old? Such an account, to my mind, has far too little power, interest, and conflict in it. But even if it were sometimes a plausible account of social change, it would be an unlikely model for the European nineteenth century. Its most important weakness as a guide to the nineteenth century is its starting point: a closed, traditional, unconnected, immobile set of social worlds. In the remainder of this essay, I shall spend a major part of my effort in demonstrating the openness, connectedness, and mobility of the European world as it faced the nineteenth century. Because the rural world is the one in which modernization models should apply most clearly, I shall concentrate on changes in Europe's rural areas.

What will we find in the countryside? We will find a mobile, differentiated population heavily involved in different forms of production for the market, and responsive to changes occurring far from home. We will find varying forms of mercantile capitalism penetrating deep into village life. We will find agents of national states intervening actively in local organization in order to extract the men, food, and money required for armies and other expensive governmental activities. We will find a sensitive interplay between economic structure and family life—between the organization of production and of reproduction. We will find few traces of the isolation and autarky which are dear to theorists of modernization.

None of this means that the nineteenth century was a time of stability, or of trendless turbulence. Industrial capitalism took shape in important parts of Europe. Capital concentrated and the scale of production rose. The working population, urban and rural, proletarianized. Firms, parties, trade unions, and other specialized associations assumed much more prominent roles in public life. National states continued to gain power by comparison with any other organizations. Capitalism and statemaking, in short, transformed social life. That includes the social life of the countryside.

We can have no hope of enumerating, much less of analyzing, the full range of nineteenth-century change in one brief essay. After a look at broad patterns of nineteenth-century change over the continent as a whole, let us close in on the nature of employment in Europe's rural areas.

Population Growth and Vital Rates

A glance at the elementary statistics of the period gives an immediate sense of the nineteenth century's dynamism. The European population of 1800 stood in the vicinity of 190 million, that of 1900 around 500 million. The increase of more than 300 million people implies a growth rate around one percent per year. Such a rate is not sensational by twentieth-century standards; as table 1 indicates, Europe is still growing at about that rate, and all other continents are growing faster. But for a whole continent to grow so fast for so long was an extraordinary event in the history of the world up to that time.[5]

The increase occurred, furthermore, despite a probable net loss through migration on the order of 35 million people. For the century as a whole, a reasonable guess is that 45 million Europeans left the continent, and 10 million returned home. Close to half the century's emigrants left from Britain and Ireland, and three quarters of the British and Irish went to North America. The vast majority of emigrants from all parts of Europe sailed to the Americas; the transatlantic movement was one of the grandest migrations of all time. In sheer numbers and distances, it was probably unprecedented in human history.

If the estimates of migration are correct, Europe's excess of births over deaths during the century as a whole totaled close to 350 million. With a plausible crude birth rate of 35 for the whole continent and the whole century, that figure implies a crude death rate in the vicinity of 25. In the world of the later twentieth century, a crude birth rate of 35 and a crude death rate of 25 could only occur in a poor country. For purposes of comparison, table 1 presents continental rates from the 1960s. No continent now approximates the European nineteenth-century situation; all continents now have lower mortality, and the poorer parts of the world all have larger gaps between birth rate and death rate; that means, of course, that the rates of natural increase are higher today than they were in nineteenth-century

Europe. The closest approximations of Europe's situation a hundred years ago are contemporary Africa and Asia.

TABLE 1

Annual Growth Rates and Vital Rates for Major World Areas, 1960–68

Area	Annual Growth Rate	Crude Birth Rate	Crude Death Rate
Africa	2.4%	45	21
North America	1.4	21	9
Latin America	2.9	40	12
Asia	2.0	38	17
Europe	0.9	18	10
Soviet Union	1.3	20	7
Oceania	2.1	26	10
World	1.9	34	15

SOURCE: Annuaire Statistique de la France 1970/71:7*.

Within Europe, the nineteenth century brought pivotal changes in the character and geography of natural increase. Over the continent as a whole, the trend of nineteenth-century fertility was no doubt a gentle decline, as compared with a significant drop in mortality; the difference between the two rates of decline accounted for the continent's large natural increase. Table 2 presents some scattered observations of birth rates and death rates for 1800, 1850, and 1900. In general, the poorer parts of Europe (which were probably also, on the average, the areas of higher fertility and mortality throughout the century) lack data for the early years; there was a rough correlation between prosperity and statistical reporting. As of 1900, the range of variation was large: crude birth rates running from 21.3 in France to 49.3 in Russia, crude death rates from 15.8 in Norway to 31.1 in Russia. As Ansley Coale and his collaborators have shown, a long frontier separated the high-fertility regions of eastern and southeastern Europe from the low- to medium-fertility regions of the north and west. In these statistics, Bulgaria, Hungary, Romania, Russia, and Serbia stand well above other countries.

The national units mask further diversity: fertility and mortality correspond much more closely to economic and cultural regions than to political boundaries. Although Hungary shows up in these statistics as a high fertility area, for example, Hungary actually included some of Europe's lowest fertility regions. Rudolf Andorka and his colleagues have done family-reconstitution studies of several villages in the Ormánság and Sárköz regions of Hungary during the eighteenth and nineteenth centuries; there they have discovered marital fertility plummeting to remarkably low levels. In those areas an arrangement known as the "one-child family system" prevailed; by 1850 actual completed family sizes were running between three and four.[6] Plenty of other studies from elsewhere show significant village-to-village variation as a function of economic opportunity and family structure.[7]

TABLE 2

Vital Rates for Selected European Areas in 1800, 1850, and 1900

Country	Crude Birth Rate			Crude Death Rate		
	1800	1850	1900	1800	1850	1900
Austria		39.6	35.0		32.9	25.2
Belgium		30.0	28.9		21.2	19.3
Bulgaria			42.3			22.6
Denmark	29.9	31.4	29.7	28.5	19.1	16.8
Finland	37.6	35.7	32.6	25.5	26.3	21.9
France	32.9	26.8	21.3	27.7	21.4	21.9
Germany		37.2	35.6		25.6	22.1
Hungary			39.4			27.0
Ireland			22.7			19.6
Italy			33.0			23.8
Netherlands		34.6	31.6		22.2	17.9
Norway	22.7	31.0	29.7	27.6	17.2	15.8
Portugal			30.5			20.3
Romania			38.8			24.2
Russia			49.3			31.1
Serbia			42.4			23.5
Spain			33.9			29.0
Sweden	28.7	31.9	27.0	31.4	19.8	16.8
Switzerland			28.6			19.3
England, Wales		33.4	28.7		20.8	18.2
Scotland			29.6			18.5

SOURCE: Mitchell 1975: 105–120.

Industrialization

One of the factors behind the changing microgeography of fertility in nineteenth-century Europe was the continent's industrialization. Industrialization has two dimensions: (1) a decrease in the proportion of economic activity devoted to agriculture, forestry, and fishing; (2) an increase in the scale of producing units. Our twentieth-century prejudice—compounded by a sloganeering idea of the Industrial Revolution and a fixation on the factory as the vehicle of industrial growth—is to think of the two as tightly correlated. In fact, they have often varied quite separately from each other. Many regions of Europe were already relatively industrialized with respect to the first dimension by the end of the eighteenth century: major shares of the rural and small-town population were involved in various forms of manufacturing. But the scale remained very small; the household and the small shop were the typical producing units. The nineteenth century saw both a substantial decline in the share of agriculture, forestry, and fishing, and a dramatic rise in the average scale of production.

No one has so far assembled comparable accounts of these ninteenth-century changes for all regions of Europe. Some features of the changes, nevertheless, are fairly clear:

1. The areas which experienced major industrialization during the nineteenth century were basically of two kinds:

   a) areas in which small-scale manufacturing had already been important during the eighteenth century—the regions of Manchester, Lille, Milan, Barcelona, Moscow, and so on—and which experienced an urbanization and increase in the scale of that industry during the nineteenth;

   b) areas in which coal deposits combined with water and/or rail transportation to facilitate the development of heavy industry: Yorkshire, much of Belgium, Silesia, etc.

2. As this "implosion" of industry occurred, large parts of the European countryside *de*industrialized, devoting themselves more exclusively to agriculture.

3. In absolute terms, agriculture, forestry and fishing did not decline. They actually grew, but more slowly than manufacturing and services. In sheer numbers, the agricultural labor force probably reached its maximum some time around World War I.

4. Wage laborers—proletarians in both agriculture and industry—increased far more rapidly than the rest of the labor force. One reasonable guess is that proletarians and their families comprised 90 million of Europe's 190 million people in 1800, and had grown to 300 million of the total of 500 million at the end of the century. Most of the increase took place in cities. Urbanization and proletarianization were interdependent processes.

As a result of these changes, regional disparities in industrial activity, wealth, urban concentration, and population density increased through the nineteenth century. Around 1900 the major countries of Europe distributed themselves in the following manner[8]:

over 70% of the labor force in agriculture, forestry, and fishing: Bulgaria 81.9, Romania 79.6
61–70%: Hungary 70.0, Portugal 65.1, Spain 68.1
51–60%: Austria 59.8, Finland 51.5, Italy 58.7, Russia 58.6, Sweden 53.5
41–50%: Denmark 46.6, France 41.4, Ireland 42.9, Norway 40.8, Poland 45.9
31–40%: Germany 39.9, Switzerland 34.2
less than 31%: Belgium 27.1, Netherlands 30.8, United Kingdom 9.1

The proportions rose, broadly speaking, with increasing distance from the English Channel.

The changing geography of wealth shows up in Paul Bairoch's estimates of per capita gross national product.[9] To take only the eight highest ranking areas in 1830 and 1900:

	1830			*1900*
Netherlands	347ª		United Kingdom	881
United Kingdom	346		Switzerland	785
Belgium	295		Belgium	721
Norway	280		Germany	639
Switzerland	276		Denmark	633
Italy	265		Netherlands	614
France	264		France	604
Spain	263		Norway	577
EUROPE	240		EUROPE	455

ªFigures in 1960 U.S. dollars and prices.

Real GNP per capita, according to Bairoch's estimates, rose by about 90 percent during those seventy years. That is slow growth by twentieth-century standards but extraordinary as compared with anything that had happened before. Per capita GNP grew fastest in Denmark, Sweden, Switzerland, Germany, and Belgium—especially, that is, in the areas which saw the development of coal-consuming, metal-processing industries.

The map of urban population conformed more and more closely to the map of large-scale industry. Table 3 summarizes the changes. In 1800, something like 3 percent of the European population lived in cities of 100,000 or more, By 1850, the proportion had risen to around 5 percent. By 1900, 10 percent. That meant a rise from 5.4 million to 12.7 million to 50.1 million inhabitants of big cities—almost a quadrupling in the last half of the century. The combination of substantial natural increase within cities and massive rural-to-urban migration produced thunderous urban growth: about 0.6 percent per year from 1800 to 1850, about 2.1 percent per year from 1850 to 1900.

TABLE 3

Number of Inhabitants and Percentage of Population in Cities
of 100,000 or More, 1800–1900, in Selected Areas of Europeª

Area	Number of Inhabitants in Cities of 100,000 or More (Thousands)			Percentage of Population in Cities of 100,000 or More		
	1800	*1850*	*1900*	*1800*	*1850*	*1900*
Austria	231.9	549.6	2462.4	1.7	3.0	9.5
Belgium	—	326.7	1148.7	—	7.5	17.1
Denmark	105.0	142.0	491.3	10.7	9.4	20.2
Finland	0	0	0	0	0	0
France	852.4	2025.7	6005.4	3.2	5.8	15.4
Greece	0	0	111.5	0	0	4.4
Hungary	0	170.0	837.2	0	1.3	4.3

	Number of Inhabitants in Cites of 100,000 or More (Thousands)			Percentage of Population in Cities of 100,000 or More		
Ireland	165.0	258.0	722.1	3.0	3.9	16.1
Italy	1053.0	1607.5	3206.4	5.8	6.7	9.9
Netherlands	200.0	224.0	1137.5	9.3	7.2	22.0
Norway	0	0	227.6	0	0	10.1
Poland	100.0	160.0	989.8	3.3	3.3	9.9
Portugal	180.0	240.0	529.4	5.8	6.3	9.8
Prussia/Germany	272.0	799.0	9007.3	1.1	2.3	16.0
Romania	0	120.0	282.1	0	3.1	4.5
Scotland	0	490.7	1390.9	0	16.8	30.8
Spain	400.0	450.0	1676.3	3.3	3.1	9.0
Sweden	0	0	452.6	0	0	8.9
Switzerland	0	0	364.7	0	0	11.0
European Turkey	600.0	850.0	1230.0	13.3	15.2	20.0
England and Wales	959.3	3992.1	12806.2	10.5	21.7	39.0
European Russia	470.0	850.0	5012.5	1.3	1.5	5.0
TOTAL EUROPE	5406.6	12656.9	50091.0	2.8	4.8	10.1

SOURCE: Charles Tilly, Karen Fonde, and Ann V. O'Shea, "Statistics on the Urbanization of Europe, 1500–1950," unpublished paper, Center for Western European Studies, March, 1972.

[a]In table 3, many states (e.g., Greece, Finland) did not exist for some or all of the nineteenth century; in those cases, the figures refer to the boundaries at the acquisition of independence. Others (e.g., Prussia/Germany) changed boundaries radically; in those cases, the figures refer to the boundaries at the date shown. The population estimates in Tertius Chandler and Gerald Fox's *3000 Years of Urban Growth* (New York: Academic Press, 1974) yield slightly higher totals and slightly higher percentages, but the pattern is essentially the same as in my compilations. Here are Bairoch's figures for Europe, excluding Russia[10]:

Date	Percent in Cities of 20,000 or More	Percent in Cities of 100,000 or More
1800	7.6	3.2
1850	12.6	6.1
1900	26.2	11.4

The regional disparities were wide in 1800, and widened during the century. In 1800, the presence of giant Constantinople made the European segment of what was to become Turkey the most urban of the continent's major political units: 13.3 percent of European Turkey's entire population lived in that one city of 600,000. Elsewhere, the range ran downward from the 10 or 11 percent for Denmark, England, and Wales to a number of countries with no city of 100,000 or more. By the end of the century, Finland was the only large political unit with no city of 100,000; Helsinki then had about 90,000 residents. But the range ran from under 5 percent in Finland,

Greece, Hungary, and Romania to over 30 percent in Scotland, England, and Wales. The rank orders of urbanization and industrialization had converged. Either because no one with the heroic statistical capacities of a Paul Bairoch has so far compiled the evidence or because the changes involved do not lend themselves to simple numerical summary, other major changes which were undoubtedly happening are harder to document. Roads, then railroads, proliferated; mail and telegraph communications multiplied; newspapers circulated as schooling and literacy increased; voluntary associations, trade unions, political parties waxed; and so on through the inventory of communications, organizations, and everyday routines.

Amid the great swirl of transformation, the expansion and reorganization of European states set some of the main currents of change. Perhaps the most dramatic feature of Europe's nineteenth-century statemaking was the consolidation of the state system into a smaller and smaller set of larger and larger units: about fifty states of various sorts on the eve of the French Revolution; a radical reduction through French conquests to about twenty-five states in 1800 and about twenty in 1812; a temporary reversion to about thirty-five states with France's defeat, followed by a new consolidation process which left twenty to twenty-five independent states (depending on how we define "independent" and "state") at World War I. Although French imperialism cleared the way and nineteenth-century wars took their toll, the chief paths to consolidation passed through semivoluntary unions, notably those of Germany and Italy. Throughout the process, state structures expanded, were centralized, and became the dominant organizations within their own territories. A number of innovations followed: uniformed professional police forces, national elections and referenda, censuses and statistical bureaux, income taxes, technical schools for specialists, civil service careers, and many other pieces of the state apparatus that prevailed into our own time.

Can we reasonably apply the word "modernization" to this ensemble of changes? That depends on how demanding an idea of modernization we adopt. If all we require is that recognizable features of twentieth-century life emerge, then the urbanization, large-scale industrialization, fertility decline, and other changes portrayed by the statistics easily qualify as modernization. If we demand common paths of change—something like Rainer Lepsius' differentiation, mobilization, participation, and institutionalization of conflict—the question remains moot; observations at a national or European scale simply do not tell us how the changes occurred. And if we want to try a causal model of modernization (one in which, for instance, intensified communications produce new states of consciousness which in turn make people more open to rational solutions for their problems), the hopelessness of approaching the analysis with hugely aggregated evidence becomes clear. We must look at evidence which comes closer to the experiences of individuals and small groups. Let us consider how work changed in Europe's rural areas.

Peasants and Proletarians

In order to understand changes in the nineteenth-century European countryside, we must exorcise the ghosts in the word "peasantry." If all we mean by peasants is poor people who work the soil, then in 1800 most Europeans were peasants. Usually, however, we have something more precise in mind: something like agriculturalists organized in households which control the land on which they live, draw most of their subsistence from that land, and supply the bulk of their own labor requirements from their own efforts. By that definition, the bulk of the European rural population was already nonpeasant by the start of the nineteenth century. In much of eastern and southern Europe, large landlords made the basic agricultural production decisions, and used a variety of devices to draw labor from a mass of agricultural workers who controlled little or no land. In much of northern and western Europe, a major share of the agricultural labor force consisted either of day laborers or of live-in servants and hands. Although the serfs of eastern Europe and the day laborers of western Europe often had garden plots or small fields of their own, they depended for survival on the sale of their household labor power. They were, in a classic Marxian sense of the word, proletarians.

Again a little exorcism is in order. Despite Marx's own clear concentration on changes in the rural labor force, the word "proletarian" has taken on an urban-industrial imagery: *Modern Times,* with Charlie Chaplin turning bolts on the assembly line. If we confine the proletariat to people working at subdivided tasks in large units under close time discipline, then that industrial proletariat certainly grew during the nineteenth century, but it probably did not approach a fifth of the European labor force in 1900.

If, however, we include all people whose survival depended on the sale of their labor power—which was, after all, Marx's basic idea of the proletariat—then by the end of the nineteenth century the great majority of the European labor force was proletarian. Agricultural wage laborers were probably the largest category, but industrial and service workers were then competing for the lead. Before the middle of the nineteenth century, most of the large increase in the proletarian population occurred in small towns and rural areas. By a rough computation from the figures presented earlier, perhaps 50 million of the 70 million increase in the European population from 1800 to 1850 occurred in places under 20,000. It is reasonable to suppose that at least 40 of that 50 million increase in smaller places consisted of wage workers and their families. During the second half of the century, the smaller places may have grown by another 140 million, with the great bulk of the increase proletarian. By then, however, the cities were beginning to take over: 100 million of the 240-million increase occurred in places of 20,000 or more, and many of the smaller settlements that grew were actually suburbs and satellites of major industrial centers. To be sure, in the present state of the evidence, any such numbers rest on a tissue of suppositions. Yet the main point is firm: the patterns of urban growth and of total population growth imply a massive proletarianization of the European people during the nineteenth century. Contrary to common impressions, much of that proletarianization took place in smaller towns and rural areas.

The sketchy evidence I have presented leaves open the possibility that the "places of fewer than 20,000 inhabitants" in question were mainly seats of mines, mills, and other large-scale industrial establishments. The hinterlands of Manchester and Lille, for example, were full of smaller industrial centers. Even in those two quintessential manufacturing regions, however, agricultural proletarians and rural outworkers multiplied during the nineteenth century. Away from the major poles of industrial growth, much more of the expansion took place in agriculture and in manufacturing on a very small scale.

The earlier European experience provides numerous examples of proletarianization within rural areas. In fact, the rural versions of proletarianization were so visible at the middle of the nineteenth century that Karl Marx considered them the basis of primitive accumulation: "The expropriation of the agricultural producer, of the peasant, from the soil, is the basis of the whole process" (*Capital,* chap. 26). It would be useful, however, to differentiate types of agricultural regions rather more than Marx did. At a minimum we need to distinguish:

1. areas, such as coastal Flanders, in which peasants specialized in cash-crop production, and nonproducing landlords were unimportant;

2. areas, such as East Prussia, in which large landlords produced grain for the market by means of servile labor, whose subsistence came mainly from small plots assigned to their households;

3. areas, such as southern England, in which large landlords likewise produced grain for the market, but with wage labor;

4. areas, such as western France, in which landlords lived from rents and peasants lived from various combinations of owned, rented, and share-cropped land.

Within category 1, proletarianization tended to occur as a consequence of differentiation within the peasantry: extra children and households losing in the local competition moved into wage labor for other peasants. In category 2, the redistributions of land which commonly accompanied nineteenth-century emancipations produced a temporary movement away from the proletariat, but the substitution of cash payments for access to subsistence plots created a far larger movement toward wage labor. Category 3 began with an essentially proletarian agricultural labor force, and grew by adding more wage laborers. Category 4, finally, sometimes transformed itself into category 1 by means of the increasing involvement of peasants in cash-crop production, sometimes transformed itself into category 3 as the landlords consolidated their control over production, but rarely created proletarians within the agricultural sector. (Category 4 was not, however, a bulwark against proletarianization; it was an especially favorable environment for cottage industry.) The European agrarian structure, then, provided multiple paths out of the peasantry and multiple paths into the agricultural proletariat. Over the nineteenth century, the net shift from one to the other was very large.

In Europe as a whole, the proletarianization of agricultural labor had begun well before the nineteenth century. Great Britain was one sort of extreme; except for some portions of its Celtic fringes, Britain had essentially eliminated its peasantry by the start of the nineteenth century. By the time of the 1831 census, the breakdown of agricultural families in Britain ran as follows:

Occupying families employing labor	144,600
Occupying families employing no labor	130,500
Laboring families	686,000
Total	961,100

SOURCE: 1831 Census Abstract, Vol. I: ix.

Table 4 presents the occupations of males 20 and over for 1831. Both the breakdown for families and the breakdown for adult males show about 71 percent of Great Britain's agricultural labor force to be essentially landless laborers. For England alone, the figure was 76 percent. Although the division between owners and wage workers within the category "Retail Trade or Handicraft" (in which the letter P, for example, includes Paper-maker; Pastry-cook, Confectioner; Patternmaker; Pawnbroker; Poulterer; Printer; Printseller; Publican, Hotel or Innkeeper, Retailer of Beer) is hard to guess, the figures suggest that in 1831 Britain's agricultural labor force was more proletarian than the rest. By 1851, laborers amounted to some 85 percent of all agricultural workers.[11] That was the peak; thereafter, hired labor began to desert British agriculture for industry, and machines began to replace or displace labor as never before.[12]

Although Britain was extreme, it was not unique. Much of eastern Europe began the nineteenth century with the bulk of its agricultural population proletarians of a different kind from their English cousins: servile landless laborers on large estates.[13] Although nineteenth-century emancipations eventually gave some of them title to land, the main trend ran toward the creation of a vast agricultural proletariat. Peasant property may have increased in absolute terms, but the rural population grew much faster. A common interpretation of those trends[14] is that an exogenously generated population increase overran the supply of land; my own view is that proletarianization helped create the population increase; whichever argument is correct, however, the correlation between proletarianization and rural population growth is clear. In such southern European areas as Sicily, likewise, the dispossession of feudal landlords made property owners of some former tenants; but its main effect was to accelerate the expropriation of the land by large farmers

TABLE 4
Percent Distribution of Occupations of
Males 20 and Over in Great Britain, 1831

Category	England	Wales	Scotland	Total
Agricultural occupiers employing laborers	4.4	10.1	4.7	4.7
Agricultural occupiers not employing laborers	3.0	10.3	9.8	4.3
Agricultural laborers	23.3	28.5	15.9	22.5
Employed in manufacturing	9.8	3.2	15.3	10.3
Employed in retail trade or handicraft	30.1	22.2	27.7	29.4
Capitalists, bankers, professionals, and other educated men	5.6	2.7	5.3	5.4
Nonagricultural laborers	15.7	16.2	13.9	15.4
Servants	2.2	1.1	1.1	2.0
Others	5.9	5.7	6.4	6.0
Total	100.0	100.0	100.1	100.0
Number	3,199,984	194,706	549,821	3,944,511

SOURCE: Great Britain, Census Office. Abstract of the answers and returns made pursuant to an act, passed in the eleventh year of the reign of His Majesty King George IV, entituled, "An Act for Taking an Account of the Population of Great Britain, and of the Increase or Diminution Thereof" (Westminster: House of Commons, 1831), Vol. I, p. xiii, "General Summary of Great Britain."

and bourgeois, and thus to hasten the proletarianization of the remainder of the agricultural workers.[15] Again a rapid population increase aggravated the process of proletarianization, and again the causal connections between proletarianization and population increase are debatable.

The cases of eastern and southern Europe are well known. Less known until recently was the extensive proletarianization of the Scandinavian rural population. Christer Winberg sums up the Swedish experience:

> Between 1750 and 1850 the population of Sweden doubled. The increase in population was particularly rapid after 1810. Throughout this period about 90 percent of the national population lived in rural areas. The increase was very unequally distributed among the different social groups of the rural population. The number of bönder (peasants) rose by c. 10 per cent, while the number of landless—i.e., torpare (crofters), inhyseshjon (bordars), statare (farm workers partly paid in kind), etc.—more than quadrupled.[16]

Winberg attributes the rural proletarianization to two main processes: a capitalistic reorganization of large estates which squeezed out the tenants in favor of wage laborers, and an increasing integration of the peasantry into the national market economy, which in turn produced increased differentiation between landed and landless. If that is the case, Sweden combined the paths of category 1 and category 2, and ended with a combination of a small number of capitalist landlords, a larger number of cash-crop farmers, and a very large number of agricultural wage workers.

Protoindustry and Proletarianization

Sweden was unusual in one important regard: unless we count mining and forestry, very few of Sweden's rural workers went into industry. Over Europe as a whole, manufacturing played a large part in the transformation of the nineteenth-century countryside. Economic historians have recently begun to speak of *protoindustrialization*: the growth of manufacturing through the multiplication of small producing units rather than through the concentration of capital and labor. Economic historian Franklin Mendels introduced the term into the literature in order to cope with the way that sections of rural Flanders made large shifts from agriculture to manufacturing without the development of factories, without important changes in production techniques, without large accumulations of capital, without substantial urbanization of the working class.

Older economic historians, back to Marx, knew about cottage industry and allied forms of production long ago. The advantage of the new term is to draw attention to the variety of ways in which European entrepreneurs of the seventeenth to nineteenth centuries organized networks of households to produce large volumes of cheap goods for national and international markets. In the process, they made manufacturing not a mere by-employment for farmers, but the dominant economic activity in important parts of the European countryside. A recent book, *Industrialisierung vor der Industrialisierung*, by Peter Kriedte, Hans Medick, and Jürgen Schlumbohm surveys the growing literature on the subject. The book emphasizes the ways in which protoindustrialization transformed the rest of the rural economy, established its own peculiar patterns of family structure, and cleared the way for large-scale industrialization. It makes clear the utter inadequacy of any portrayal of the nineteenth-century rural world as a territory essentially populated by peasants and fundamentally devoted to agriculture.

As Peter Kriedte sums up the importance of protoindustrialization:

> Proto-industry stands between two worlds, the narrow world of the village and the boundary-breaking world of trade, between the agrarian economy and merchant capitalism. The agrarian sector produces a labor supply, a supply of merchant-entrepreneur knowledge and capital, supplies of products and markets. Merchant capital opens foreign markets to rural crafts, whose personnel thus become aware of the opportunity for expansion if they enter into protoindustrialization. . . . The unified symbiosis of merchant capital and peasant society thereby marks a decisive step on the way to industrial capitalism.[17]

The general line of argument, in terms of "vent-for-surplus," goes back to Adam Smith.[18] But Kriedte and his collaborators go on to point out the irreversible effects of the new symbiosis: commercialization of the entire rural economy, dependence on adjacent agricultural areas for subsistence, transformation of households into suppliers (and breeders) of wage labor, detachment of marriage and reproduction from the inheritance of land, acceleration of population growth, rising rural densities, the growth of an industrial proletariat in the countryside.

Kriedte and others brush against, but do not quite state, a fundamental advantage of protoindustrial production over urban shops and/or factories: in a time of small-scale agricultural production with high costs for the transportation and storage of food, protoindustry kept the bulk of the labor force close to the food sources, and made industrial labor available, in odd moments and peak seasons, for food production. Up to a point, the individual merchant could assume that the workers would feed themselves. The logic of the system, in short: a cheap, elastic, compliant labor force for merchants who are short on capital and technical expertise but long on knowledge of opportunities and connections.

Protoindustrial population and producers multiplied, beginning well before 1800, and did not start to contract visibly until well into the nineteenth century. A labor force consisting largely of dispersed, part-time, and seasonal workers resists enumeration; we are unlikely ever to have precise counts of the rise and fall of protoindustrial workers. Nevertheless, we have enough evidence to be sure that protoindustrialization was not simply one of several known patterns of change. Before the middle of the nineteenth century, when manufacturing increased significantly in some parts of Europe, it normally increased through the multiplication of households and other small, dispersed producing units linked to national and international markets by webs of entrepreneurs and merchants. It increased, that is, not through the concentration of capital, labor, and the scale of production, but through protoindustrialization.

This is notably true of textile production. As Milward and Saul put it:

> It is impossible not to be struck by the extraordinary growth of spinning and weaving in the countryside of many European areas. In some areas the manufacture of iron products, toys or watches developed in the same way, but textiles, whether of linen, wool or the newfangled cotton were the typical rural product. The technological transformations which initiated the Industrial Revolution in Britain, were heavily concentrated in these rural textile industries and their development on the continent may therefore be seen as the true precursor of the Industrial Revolution there rather than the older "manufactures." But setting on one side the developments of the Industrial Revolution itself and looking at the matter simply from the point of view of employment in industrial activities whether those industries were "revolutionised" or not it would still be true to say that the most industrial landscapes in late eighteenth-century Europe, for all their lack of chimneys, were the country areas around Lille, Rouen, Barcelona, Zurich, Basel and Geneva.[19]

The rise of coal-burning and metal-working industries during the nineteenth century eventually changed the picture. But it took a long time. The expansion of manufacturing continued to take a protoindustrial form well past 1800.

Because of Rudolf Braun's rich, intensive analyses of the Zurich region, the Züricher Oberland has become the *locus classicus* for students of protoindustrialization. In the Züricher Oberland, the poor subsistence-farming areas far from the city had been thinly settled exporters of domestic servants and mercenaries until the eighteenth century. Then the growth of an export-oriented cotton industry based in Zurich but drawing the bulk of its labor from the countryside transformed the uplands: farm workers took to spinning and weaving, emigration slowed, population densities rose, and an essentially industrial way of life took over the villages and hamlets of the mountains. A rural proletariat took shape.

During the nineteenth century, as the scale of production in Zurich and its immediate vicinity rose, the process reversed. The hinterland deindustrialized, and migrants flowed toward Zurich. The Zurich region moved from (1) urban manufacturing fed by a largely agricultural countryside to (2) rural protoindustrialization coupled with expanded mercantile activity in the central city to (3) concentration of industry near the center, bringing hardship to rural producers, to (4) deindustrialization of the countryside. Zurich's sequence provides a paradigm for the regional history of protoindustry throughout Europe. The chief variables are when the sequence occurred, how extensive each stage was, and whether a significant industrial nucleus survived the final period of urban implosion and rural contraction.

Urbanization of Industry, Deindustrialization of the Country

Properly generalized, Zurich's experience has significant implications for Europe's nineteenth-century experience as a whole. Protoindustry did finally give way to its urban competitors throughout the continent. If so, the rural workers involved disappeared. But only in the artificial world of statistics can workers simply vanish. In real life, Europe's protoindustrial workers either hung on unemployed, moved into other employment in the countryside, or followed industry to the city. They did all three, although in what proportions we do not know so far. In the region of Lyon, at mid-century, rural workers miles from the city lived in its long shadow. "For if we observe," comments Yves Lequin,

> the concentration of workers in urban centers which were seizing, to their advantage, declining rural industries, the latter held on to a considerable share; in some places, indeed, the spreading of work into the countryside had found its second wind and was promoting the expansion of other more dynamic branches of industry. The large shares of the districts of Saint-Etienne and Lyon should not mislead us: cities without boundaries, they attracted people, to be sure, but even more so they projected their energy into distant villages; rather than men coming to industry, it was work that went to men.[20]

The balance shifted in the next half-century. Despite a decline in the old handicraft manufacture of silk, despite a distinct suburbanization of Lyon's manufacturing, and despite some tendency for mills with power looms to head for the water power of the Alpine slopes, the industrial capital swelled. Lyon grew from 235,000 to 456,000 inhabitants between 1851 and 1906. The depression of the 1870s and 1880s first struck at the manufacturing population of the countryside and temporarily augmented the agricultural labor force. But the depression marked the end of a long expansion for the hinterland. The villages began to leak women and men to the cities, especially to Lyon.

The changing relationship between Lyon and its hinterland had a paradoxical effect: the geographical range from which the city recruited its working population narrowed during the latter half of the nineteenth century. Instead of arriving from Switzerland, from Italy, from industrial centers elsewhere in France, they arrived increasingly from Lyon's own surrounding region. Within the region, however, Lyon and the other industrial cities did not simply attract a cross-section of the rural population; they drew disproportionately from the old centers of rural industry.[21] The incomplete evidence suggests that they also drew disproportionately on the *people* of the hinterland who were already involved in their industrial networks.

The other side of this process was a wholesale deindustrialization of the countryside. Rural areas became more exclusively agricultural than they had been for centuries. Area by area, the homogenization of rural life was even greater, for the specialization in one cash crop or another tended to convert whole regions into vineyards, or wheat fields, or dairy farms. So we arrive at a set of unexpected consequences: an industrialization which recruited, not peasants, but experienced industrial workers from the countryside; a "ruralization" of that same countryside as a consequence of the increasing importance of the city; an increasingly great contrast between the economic activities of city and country.

Rural Exodus

In absolute terms, Europe's rural population kept growing until some time in the twentieth century. Its proportion declined only because the urban population grew faster than the rural. Nevertheless, the cloud of numbers through which we have made our way implies a huge nineteenth-century exodus from the European countryside. Let us take a very conservative assumption: that rates of natural increase were just as high in places above twenty thousand inhabitants as in smaller places. Even on that assumption, the figures imply that the smaller places lost about twenty-five million people to net migration in the first half of the century, and about ninety million in the second half. A substantial number of those migrants went overseas, but the net movement to larger places within Europe must have been on the order of eighty or ninety million migrants.

Who left? That depended on the pattern of opportunities in country, city, and overseas area. Those patterns varied with time and place. As a working hypothesis, I suggest the following rough rank order for departures from the nineteenth-century European countryside: (1) rural industrial workers; (2) agricultural wage workers; (3) tenants and sharecroppers; (4) landowning farmers. I suggest, but with greater hesitation, that their school-leaving children emigrated in roughly the same order: children of rural industrial workers first, and so on. The logic of the hypothesis is simple: having transferable skills promotes migration, but having a stake in the land impedes it. The same logic suggests that in the case of migration to farms elsewhere (as in much of the Scandinavian migration to the American Midwest), agricultural workers headed the list. But that was a secondary stream; most people who fled Europe's rural areas entered urban employment.

The consequence of such an order of departure would be first to deindustrialize the countryside, then to strip it of its remaining proletarians. At the logical end of such a process, family farms would predominate. For Europe as a whole, rural natural increase may well have exceeded outmigration—thus producing continued slow growth in the total rural population—until the end of the century. In the precocious case of rural France, however, large regions were losing population before 1900. In those regions, by and large, the remaining population was becoming more nearly peasant than it had been for centuries. There and elsewhere, deindustrialization and rural exodus had the ironic consequence of creating an agrarian world which resembled the "traditional" countryside postulated by simple models of modernization.

At first view, the rural exodus itself seems to fit one part of the modernization model: the presumed rise of mobility and of urban contacts breaks down rural isolation and opens the countryside to civilization. A closer look at nineteenth-century mobility patterns, however, gives a very different idea of what was going on. In the early nineteenth century and before, local markets for wage labor were very active, generally involved more than a single village, and commonly promoted widespread seasonal, annual, and lifetime migration from village to village. In areas of wage labor, mobility rates comparable to those prevailing in the contemporary United States—a fifth of the population changing residence in an average year—seem to have been common.[22] Temporary migration, over short distances and long, permitted millions of European workers to supplement the inadequate incomes available at their homes by meeting the seasonal demand for labor elsewhere.[23] Some rural regions (upland Switzerland is a famous example) built their economic survival on the exportation of domestic servants and mercenaries, and the importation of remittances from the servants and mercenaries, until the expansion of cottage industry permitted excess hands to remain on the land.[24] Growing cities generated huge migration flows because cities both (1) recruited many of their workers as temporary migrants who moved on or returned home and (2) were deathtraps, especially for the migrants themselves; both factors meant that the total numbers of migrants were far, far greater than the net increases through migration.[25]

All these features were true of European mobility patterns before the nineteenth century, and continued well into the century. Yet the nineteenth century did not simply bring more of the same. Overseas migration, as we have already seen, played an incomparably greater role than it had in previous centuries. The net flows of migrants to cities from rural areas rose far above earlier levels. The average distances people moved undoubtedly increased. The definitiveness of long-distance moves probably increased as well: fewer people spending their lifetimes in repeated migration from one distant location to another. Short-distance migration probably declined, at least relatively, as people began to substitute daily commutation by rail or bicycle for longer-term changes of residence.[26] With one crucial exception—the influence of governments, wars, and political crises on international migration was to become preponderant during the twentieth century—the mobility patterns with which Europeans are familiar today were taking shape. The mistake is to think that those contemporary mobility patterns emerged from a previously immobile world.

Summed up, the nineteenth-century changes in work, mobility, and population distribution have another important implication. The locus of proletarianization was shifting radically. For a long time, most individuals and families who passed into the proletariat had made the fateful transition in villages and small towns. During the nineteenth century, the balance shifted toward cities. Within the city, and in the move to the city, people passed from having some control over their means of production to depending on the sale of their labor power to others. Those others were mostly capitalists of one variety or another. The work they offered consisted increasingly of disciplined wage labor in relatively large organizations: offices, stores, factories, railroads, hospitals, and so on. Capitalists, managers, and large organizations took over the task of creating a compliant proletariat. While the small entrepreneurs who preceded them had relied on cash payments, personal patronage, and community pressure to secure compliance, the nineteenth-century capitalist boldly undertook the creation of new kinds of people: tidy, disciplined, sober, reliable, and uncomplaining. That they did not quite succeed is a tribute to the staying power of the European working class.

Did the Cake of Custom Break?

Much more changed, of course, in nineteenth-century Europe. In order to build a comprehensive analysis of nineteenth-century social change, we would have to follow the expansion and elaboration of capitalism much farther. We would have to deal seriously with the concentration of power in national states. We would have to examine the changes in organization, productive technique, communications, politics, and everyday experience which developed from the interaction of capitalism and statemaking. We would have to take account of the interdependent but distinct trajectories of center and periphery, of north, south, east, and west. The thin slice we have taken from the century is far from a cross-section.

Nevertheless, the evidence we have reviewed is broad enough to make clear what did *not* happen. A congeries of isolated, immobile agrarian societies did not give way under the impact of industrialization, urbanization, and expanding communications. The isolated, immobile societies did not give way during the nineteenth century because they did not exist at the beginning of the century. The European world bequeathed to the nineteenth century by the eighteenth was actually connected, mobile and even, in its way, industrial. There was no solid cake of custom to break.

What *did* change, then? The scale of producing organizations increased greatly. The average range of geographic mobility expanded. National states, national politics, and national markets became increasingly dominant. The population of Europe urbanized and proletarianized. The long transition from a high-fertility/high-mortality world began. Inanimate sources of energy started to play an indispensable role in everyday production and consumption. Capitalism matured. The European way of life we now know took shape.

So is there anything wrong with summing up those changes as the "modernization" of Europe? No, if the name is nothing but a convenient name. The errors only begin with the elevation of the idea of modernization into a model of change—especially as a model in which expanded contact with the outside world alters people's mentalities, and altered mentalities produce a break with traditional forms of behavior. The magic mentalism is not only wrong but unnecessary. The analysis of capitalism and of state making offers a far more adequate basis for the understanding of change in nineteenth-century Europe.

Notes

1. Eugen Weber, *Peasants into Frenchmen: The Modernization of Rural France, 1870–1914* (Stanford: Stanford University Press, 1976), pp. 481–82.

2. Ibid., p. 276.

3. John M. Merriman, *Agony of the Republic: The Repression of the Left in Revolutionary France, 1848–51* (New Haven: Yale University Press, 1978).

4. M. Rainer Lepsius, "Soziologische Theoreme über die Sozialstruktur der 'Moderne' und die 'Modernisierung,' " in *Studien zum Beginn der modernen Welt*, ed. Reinhart Koselleck (Stuttgart: Klett-Cotta, 1977), pp. 24–29.

5. John Dana Durand, "The Modern Expansion of World Population," *Proceedings of the American Philosophical Society* 111 (1967): 136–59.; Thomas McKeown, *The Modern Rise of Population* (New York: Academic Press, 1976).

6.   Rudolf Andorka, "The One-Child Family System in Two Microregions of Hungary in the 18th and 19th Century." Paper in Central Statistical Office, Budapest, 1977.

7.   See, for example, David Levine, *Family Formation in an Age of Nascent Capitalism* (New York: Academic Press, 1977); David Gaunt, "Pre-Industrial Economy and Population Structure: The Elements of Variance in Early Modern Sweden," *Scandinavian Journal of History* 2 (1977): 183–210; Paul G. Spagnoli, "Population History from Parish Monographs: The Problem of Local Demographic Variations," *Journal of Interdisciplinary History* 7 (1977): 427–52.

8.   Brian Mitchell, *European Historical Statistics, 1750–1970* (New York: Columbia University Press, 1975). Paul Bairoch, ed., *La Population active et sa structure* (Brussels: Institut de Sociologie, Université Libre de Bruxelles, 1968), pp. 83–120.

9.   Paul Bairoch, "Europe's Gross National Product, 1800–1975," *Journal of European Economic History* 5 (1976): 286.

10.   Paul Bairoch, *Taille des villes, conditions de vie et développement économique* (Paris: Ecole des Hautes Etudes en Sciences Sociales, 1977), pp. 43–44.

11.   Phyllis Deane and W. A. Cole, *British Economic Growth, 1688–1959: Trends and Structure* (Cambridge: Cambridge University Press, 1967), pp. 143–44.

12.   Eric L. Jones, "The Agricultural Labour Market in England, 1793–1872," *Economic History Review* 17 (1964): 329–44.

13.   Jerome Blum, *The End of the Old Order in Rural Europe* (Princeton: Princeton University Press, 1978), pp. 38–44.

14.   For example, see Blum, op. cit., pp. 435–36.

15.   Salvatore Francesco Romano, *Storia della Mafia* (Milan: Sugar, 1963); Jane Schneider and Peter Schneider, *Culture and Political Economy in Western Sicily* (New York: Academic Press. 1976), pp. 116–18.

16.   Christer Winberg, "Population Growth and Proletarianization: The Transformation of Social Structures in Rural Sweden during the Agrarian Revolution," in *Chance and Change: Social and Economic Studies in Historical Demography in the Baltic Area*, ed. Sune Åkerman et al. (Odense: Scandinavian Universities Press, 1978), p. 170.

17.   Peter Kriedte et al., *Industrialisierung vor der Industrialisierung: Gewerbliche Warenproduktion auf dem Land in der Formationsperiode des Kapitalismus* (Göttingen: Vandenhoeck & Ruprecht, 1977), p. 88.

18.   Richard E. Caves, " 'Vent for Surplus' Models of Trade and Growth," in *Trade, Growth, and the Balance of Payments: Essays in Honor of Gottfried Haberler*, ed. Robert E. Baldwin et al. (Chicago: Rand-McNally, 1965); idem, "Export-Led Growth and the New Economic History," in *Trade, Balance of Payments and Growth: Papers in International Economics in Honor of Charles P. Kindleberger*, ed. Jagdish N. Bhagwati et al. (Amsterdam: North-Holland, 1971).

19.   Alan S. Milward and S. B. Saul, *The Economic Development of Continental Europe, 1780–1870* (London: George Allen & Unwin, 1973), pp. 93–94.

20.   Yves Lequin, *Les Ouvriers de la région lyonnaise (1848–1914)*, 2 vols. (Lyon: Presses Universitaires de Lyon, 1977), 1:43.

21.   Ibid., pp. 239–46.

22.   See, for example, Ingrid Eriksson and John Rogers, *Rural Labor and Population Change: Social and Demographic Developments in East-Central Sweden during the Nineteenth Century*, Studia Historica Upsaliensia, 100 (Uppsala: Uppsala University, 1978. Distributed by Almqvist & Wiksell, Stockholm), pp. 177–239.

23.   See, for example, Abel Châtelain, *Les Migrants temporaires en France de 1800 à 1914: histoire économique et sociale des migrants temporaires des compagnes françaises du XIXe siècle au début du XXe siècle*, 2 vols. (Lille: Publications de l'Université de Lille, 1976).

24. See, for example, Alfred Perrenoud, "Les Migrations en Suisse sous l'Ancien Régime: quelques problèmes," *Annales de démographie historique* (1970): 251–59.

25. See, for example, Alan Sharlin, "Natural Decrease in Early Modern Cities: A Reconsideration," *Past and Present* 79 (1978): 126–38.

26. For a general survey of these trends, see Charles Tilly, "Migration in Modern European History," in *Human Migration: Patterns, Implications, Policies,* ed. William H. McNeill (Bloomington: Indiana University Press, 1978).

References*

Abel, Wilhelm. *Massenarmut und Hungerkrisen im vorindustriellen Europa.* Hamburg and Berlin: Paul Parey, 1974.

Ågren, Kurt et al. *Aristocrats, Farmers, Proletarians: Essays in Swedish Demographic History.* Studia Historica Upsaliensia, 47. Uppsala: Almqvist & Wiksell, 1973.

Åkerman, Sune; Johansen, Hans Christian; and Gaunt, David, eds., *Chance and Change: Social and Economic Studies in Historical Demography in the Baltic Area.* Odense: Scandinavian Universities Press, 1978.

Alapuro, Risto. "On the Political Mobilization of the Agrarian Population in Finland: Problems and Hypotheses." *Scandinavian Political Studies* 11 (1976): 51–76.

Andorka, Rudolf. "The One-Child Family System in Two Microregions of Hungary in the 18th and 19th Century." Paper in Central Statistical Office, Budapest, 1977.

Bairoch, Paul. "Europe's Gross National Product, 1800–1975." *Journal of European Economic History* 5 (1976):273–340.

———. *Taille des villes, conditions de vie et développement économique.* Paris: Ecole des HautesEtudes en Sciences Sociales, 1977.

———, ed. *La Population active et sa structure.* Brussels: Institut de Sociologie, Université Libre de Bruxelles, 1968.

Bercé, Yves-Marie. *Croquants et nu-pieds: les soulèvements paysans en France du XVIe au XIXe siècle.* Collection Archives. Paris: Gallimard/Julliard, 1974.

———. *Fête et révolte: des mentalités populaires du XVIe au XVIIIe siècle.* Paris: Hachette, 1976.

Black, Cyril. *The Dynamics of Modernization: A Study in Comparative History.* New York: Harper & Row, 1966.

Blom, Grethe Authen, ed. *Industrialiseringens første fase.* Urbaniseringsprossen i Norden, vol. 3. Oslo: Universitetsforlaget, 1977.

Blum, Jerome. *The End of the Old Order in Rural Europe.* Princeton: Princeton University Press, 1978.

Braun, Rudolf. *Industrialisierung und Volksleben.* Zurich: Rentsch, 1960. *Sozialer und kultureller Wandel in einem ländlichen Industriegebiet.* Zurich: Rentsch, 1965.

———. "Early Industrialization and Demographic Change in the Canton of Zurich." In *Historical Studies of Changing Fertility,* edited by Charles Tilly. Princeton: Princeton University Press, 1978.

Caves, Richard E. " 'Vent for Surplus' Models of Trade and Growth." In *Trade, Growth, and*

*In addition to items cited specifically in the text, I have added a number of general sources dealing with major nineteenth-century changes. I am grateful to Cecilia Brown for assistance with the bibliography, and to the National Science Foundation for support of the research on social change and collective action that lies behind this paper.

the Balance of Payments: Essays in Honor of Gottfried Haberler, edited by Robert E. Baldwin et al. Chicago: Rand-McNally, 1965.

———. "Export-Led Growth and the New Economic History." In *Trade, Balance of Payments and Growth: Papers in International Economics in Honor of Charles P. Kindleberger*, edited by Jagdish N. Bhagwati et al. Amsterdam: North-Holland, 1971.

Chandler, Tertius, and Fox, Gerald. *3,000 Years of Urban Growth*. New York: Academic Press, 1974.

Châtelain, Abel. *Les Migrants temporaires en France de 1800 à 1914: histoire économique et sociale des migrants temporaires des campagnes françaises du XIXe siècle au début du XXe siècle*. 2 vols. Lille: Publications de l'Université de Lille, 1976.

Coale, Ansley. "The Decline of Fertility in Europe from the French Revolution to World War II." In *Fertility and Family Planning*, by S. J. Behrman et al. Ann Arbor: University of Michigan Press, 1969.

Deane, Phyllis, and Cole, W. A. *British Economic Growth, 1688–1959: Trends and Structure*. Cambridge: Cambridge University Press, 1967.

Dunbabin, J. P. D. *Rural Discontent in Nineteenth-Century Britain*. New York: Holmes & Meier, 1974.

Eriksson, Ingrid, and Rogers, John. *Rural Labor and Population Change: Social and Demographic Developments in East-Central Sweden during the Nineteenth Century*. Studia Historica Upsaliensia, 100. Uppsala: Uppsala University, 1978. Distributed by Almqvist & Wiksell, Stockholm.

Gaunt, David. "Familj, hushåll och arbetsintensitet." *Scandia* 42 (1976):32–59.

———. "Pre-Industrial Economy and Population Structure: The Elements of Variance in Early Modern Sweden." *Scandinavian Journal of History* 2 (1977):183–210.

Gillis, John. "Political Decay and the European Revolutions, 1789–1848." *World Politics* 22 (1970):344–370.

———. *Youth and History: Tradition and Change in European Age Relations, 1770–present*. New York: Academic Press, 1974.

Henning, Friedrich-Wilhelm. "Der Beginn der modernen Welt im agrarischen Bereich." In *Studien zum Beginn der modernen Welt*, edited by Reinhart Koselleck. Stuttgart: Klett-Cotta, 1977.

Jones, Eric L. "The Agricultural Labour Market in England, 1793–1872." *Economic History Review* 17 (1964):322–338.

———. "The Agricultural Origins of Industry." *Past and Present* 40 (1968): 58–71.

Kälvemark, Ann-Sofie. "The Country that Kept Track of Its Population." *Scandinavian Journal of History* 2 (1977): 211–230.

Kellenbenz, Hermann. *The Rise of the European Economy: An Economic History of Continental Europe from the Fifteenth to the Eighteenth Century*. London: Weidenfeld & Nicolson, 1976.

Köllmann, Wolfgang, *Bevölkerung in der industriellen Revolution*. Göttingen: Vandenhoeck & Ruprecht, 1974.

———. "Zur Bevölkerungsentwicklung der Neuzeit." In *Studien zum Beginn der modernen Welt*, edited by Reinhart Koselleck. Stuttgart: Klett-Cotta, 1974.

Kosinski, Leszek A. *The Population of Europe: A Geographical Perspective*. London: Longmans, 1970.

Kriedte, Peter; Medick, Hans; and Schlumbohm, Jürgen. *Industrialisierung vor der Industrialisierung: Gewerbliche Warenproduktion auf dem Land in der Formationsperiode des Kapitalismus*. Göttingen: Vandenhoeck & Ruprecht, 1977.

Kuhnle, Stein. *Social Mobilization and Political Participation: The Nordic Countries, c. 1850–1970*. Bergen Institute of Sociology, 1973.

Landes, David S. *The Unbound Prometheus: Technological Change and Industrial Development in Western Europe from 1750 to the Present*. Cambridge: Cambridge University Press, 1969.

Lepsius, M. Rainer. "Soziologische Theoreme über die Sozialstruktur der 'Moderne' und die 'Modernisierung.' " In *Studien zum Beginn der modernen Welt*, edited by Reinhart Koselleck. Stuttgart: Klett-Cotta, 1977.

Lequin, Yves. *Les Ouvriers de la région lyonnaise (1848–1914)*. 2 vols. Lyon: Presses Universitaires de Lyon, 1977.

Lesthaege, Ron J. *The Decline of Belgian Fertility, 1800–1970*. Princeton: Princeton University Press, 1977.

Levine, David. *Family Formation in an Age of Nascent Capitalism*. New York: Academic Press, 1977.

Lundqvist, Sven. *Folkrörelserna i det Svenska samhallet, 1850–1920*. Stockholm: Almqvist & Wiksell, 1977.

Mendels, Franklin. "Proto-industrialization: The First Phase of the Industrialization Process." *Journal of Economic History* 32 (1972):241–261.

———. "Agriculture and Peasant Industry in Eighteenth-Century Flanders." In *European Peasants and their Markets*, edited by William N. Parker and Eric L. Jones. Princeton: Princeton University Press, 1975.

Merlin, Pierre et al. *L'Exode rural, suivi de deux études sur les migrations*. Institut National d'Etudes Démographiques, Travaux et Documents, Cahier 59. Paris: Presses Universitaires de France, 1971.

Milward, Alan S., and Saul, S. B. *The Economic Development of Continental Europe, 1780–1870*. London: George Allen & Unwin, 1973.

Pellicani, Luciano. "La rivoluzione industriale e il fenomeno della proletarizzazione." *Rassegna italiana di sociologia* 14 (1973): 63–84.

Perrenoud, Alfred. "Les Migrations en Suisse sous l'Ancien Régime: quelques problèmes." *Annales de démographie historique* (1970): 251–59.

Pitié, Jean. *Exode rural et migrations intérieures en France: l'exemple de la Vienne et du Poitou-Charentes*. Poitiers: Norois, 1971.

Redlich, Fritz, and Freudenberger, Herman. "The Industrial Development of Europe: Reality, Symbols, Images." *Kyklos* 17 (1964):372–401.

Romano, Salvatore Francesco. *Storia della Mafia*. Milan: Sugar, 1963.

Runblom, Harald, and Norman, Hans, eds. *From Sweden to America: A History of the Migration*. Minneapolis: University of Minnesota Press, 1976.

Saint-Jacob, Pierre de. *Les Paysans du Bourgogne du Nord*. Paris: Les Belles Lettres, 1960.

Saville, John. "Primitive Accumulation and Early Industrialization in Britain." *Socialist Register* (1969):247–71.

Schneider, Jane, and Schneider, Peter. *Culture and Political Economy in Western Sicily*. New York: Academic Press, 1976.

Sharlin, Alan. "Natural Decrease in Early Modern Cities: A Reconsideration." *Past and Present* 79 (1978):126–38.

Shorter, Edward. *The Making of the Modern Family*. New York: Basic Books, 1975.

Spagnoli, Paul G. "Population History from Parish Monographs: The Problem of Local Demographic Variations." *Journal of Interdisciplinary History* 7 (1977):427–52.

Stearns, Peter. *European Society in Upheaval: Social History since 1750*. 2d. ed. New York: Macmillan, 1975.

Sundbärg, Gustav. *Aperçus statistiques internationaux*. Stockholm: Imprimerie Royale, 1908. Reprint. New York: Gordon & Breach, 1968.

Tilly, Charles. "Migration in Modern European History." In *Human Migration: Patterns, Implications, Policies*, edited by William H. McNeill. Bloomington: Indiana University Press, 1978.

Tilly, Louise A., and Scott, Joan W. *Women, Work and Family*. New York: Holt, Rinehart & Winston, 1978.

Tilly, Richard, and Tilly, Charles. "An Agenda for European Economic History in the 1970s." *Journal of Economic History* 31 (1971):184–97.

Tortella Casares, Gabriel. *Los orígenes del capitalismo en Espanā: Banca, industria y ferrocarria en el siglo XIX*. Madrid: Editorial Ternos, 1973.

deVries, Jan. "Barges and Capitalism: Passenger Transportation in the Dutch Economy, 1632–1839." *A.A.G. Bijdragen* 21 (1978):33–398.

Walle, Etienne van de. *The Female Population of France in the Nineteenth Century: A Reconstruction of 82 Departments*. Princeton: Princeton University Press, 1974.

Weber, Eugen. *Peasants into Frenchmen: The Modernization of Rural France, 1870–1914*. Stanford: Stanford University Press, 1976.

Winberg, Christer. "Population Growth and Proletarianization: The Transformation of Social Structures in Rural Sweden during the Agrarian Revolution." In *Chance and Change: Social and Economic Studies in Historical Demography in the Baltic Area*, edited by Sune Åkerman et al. Odense: Scandinavian Universities Press, 1978.

TWO

———————●———————

Property, Labor, and the Emergence of Socialism in France, 1789–1848

WILLIAM H. SEWELL, JR.

In 1789 the National Assembly declared that property was a "natural, inalienable and sacred" right of man. Ever since then, property has been seen as one of the central issues of the French Revolution. But while nearly all historians have recognized that the Revolution definitively secured the rights of private property, few have recognized how thoroughly the meaning and nature of property were transformed in the Revolution, and how far-reaching the consequences of this transformation were for the subsequent history of France. This paper has two objectives: first, to show how the French Revolution changed not only the system of property but the conception of property that had existed under the Old Regime; and second, to show how the new conception of property, embodied in a new system of laws, gave rise to a new set of social conflicts that culminated in an attempt to abolish private property in the Revolution of 1848.

Under the Old Regime, the term *property* referred to a much wider variety of rights than it came to refer to after the Revolution. Property was a thing or a right, usually of some material value, that belonged to a person by clear and indisputable legal title. Sometimes having property in a thing meant that one had free and absolute dominion over it—as came to be the case for all property after the Revolution. But this was by no means always true. For the sake of clarity, we can distinguish three different types of property that were . recognized by the Old Regime.

The first type was absolute private property of the kind that was recognized as the only valid form of property under the Revolution: something, to quote one seventeenth-century definition, over which "one is absolute master, that one may sell, pledge, or dispose of at one's pleasure."[1] Most personal property and a significant amount of real estate and commercial property in Old Regime France were of this type. But there were also many other legitimate properties, held by all classes and orders of the population, that simply did not fit this description.

A second type of Old Regime property belonged unquestionably to its owner, but by no means lay under his absolute dominion. Rather, it was held by the owner under the supposition of detailed regulation by the community for the public good. This second type was very widespread, including a vast amount of the productive property employed in agriculture, in commerce, and in industry in Old Regime France. For example, a piece of land held in the regions of France where open-field agriculture was practiced was subjected by the local village community to a compulsory rotation of crops and to the practice of *vaine pâture*—letting cattle loose to graze on the stubble after the harvest. A proprietor in these areas did not have the right to determine what crops he would plant in his own fields or when he would plant them, and if he tried to plant another crop on his field after the harvest, it would be devoured—quite legally—by his neighbor's beasts.[2] In a similar way, a master in the corporate trades of the cities, although the unchallenged proprietor of his stock, tools, and raw materials, could use these only in the restricted ways specified by the statutes of his corporation. The number of journeymen and apprentices he might employ, the wages they were paid, the techniques of manufacture, the type and quality of raw materials he could use, the price and mode of sale: any and all of these might be determined by the corporation and its statutes rather than by the man who owned the means of production.[3] In short, the rights of the proprietor over this second type of property were sharply restricted by the prior rights of the public and the community.

The third category of Old Regime property not only was regulated for the public good but was derived from and had no existence apart from public authority. This was property in public functions. The most obvious and notable example was venal office. Officials ranging from members of the Parlement of Paris to municipal magistrates in third-rate provincial towns possessed offices they had bought from the king, offices that carried the obligation to perform certain public functions in return for an annual income. These offices, like other forms of property, were passed on from generation to generation; legally, they even became assimilated to the forms governing inheritance of landed property.[4] Besides venal office, two other examples of property in public function were seigneuries and masterships in the corporate trades of the cities. By the seventeenth or eighteenth century, the seigneury had become an extremely diverse bundle of specific legally enforceable dues and obligations which the peasants of a jurisdiction owed to the seigneur: quitrents, fees paid at inheritance or transfer of land, assorted personal services, *banalités*—the obligation to press one's grapes at the lord's wine-press or bake one's bread in the lord's oven—and the like. All of these dues and obligations derived from the lord's quasi-public power of dispensing justice, and were regarded as the property of the lord; as such they could be inherited, farmed out to collectors, and occasionally—under certain circum-stances—sold outright.[5] Masterships were required of all who wished to do business in any of the vast array of urban commercial or industrial trades that were regulated by corporations. Corporations were established by public authority and granted the power to regulate a particular trade in a particular city. In order to practice one of these trades, a man had to obtain a mastership by, among other things, paying a fee to the corporation.[6] The mastership, which was essentially a share in the quasi-public authority granted to the corporation by the crown, then became his property and could be passed on to his sons or to his widow. Under certain very restrictive conditions, it could even be sold.

The meaning of property in the Old Regime can be clarified by considering a fourth type of rights that were considered to be a kind of quasi property, or at least analogous to property. These were privileges, prerogatives, and hereditary distinctions of various kinds. The similarity between privilege and property was invoked, for example, by the Parlement of Paris in a remon-strance of 1776: "The first rule of justice is to preserve for every man what belongs to him . . . , a rule that consists not only in maintaining the rights of property, but also in preserving rights attached to the person and those which derive from the prerogatives of birth and estate.[8]" This parallel was far from spurious: for while the privileges and prerogatives of the Old Regime usually could not be sold, they belonged to a person no less securely than his land or buildings. Moreover, many of them were also of material value, since they carried exemption from taxation, access to lucrative office, and the like. Under the Old Regime, privilege and property were members of the same family of rights. It was only when the French Revolution drastically simpli-fied and narrowed the definition of property that privilege and property became antithetical categories—the one a "natural and imprescriptible right of man," the other an odious usurpation. This the Revolution did by either abolishing or transforming all property that was not under the absolute dominion of the proprietor. Both privileges and property in public function—our property of type three—were abolished outright: seigneuries, venal offices, and the assorted privileges of nobles and clerics were annihilated on the night of August 4, 1789, and trade corporations with all their attendant masterships disappeared in 1791. Meanwhile, all property of type two was freed of community regulation and thereby assimilated to property of type one. Henceforth the right of property became, in the words of the Civil Code of 1804, "the right to enjoy and to dispose of goods in the most absolute manner."[8]

In the eyes of its makers, the French Revolution was above all an attempt to construct a social and political order that was derived exclusively from natural law. The political theory of the Old Regime derived the French state from divine ordinance: the king was a minister of God, annointed with holy chrism at his coronation, and he ruled—as the cliché put it—"by divine right." The state was conceived of as a body with the king as its head, and was in turn composed of a hierarchy of subordinate bodies or estates united in common subjection to and reverence for the will of the king. The constitution of the kingdom was made up of the particular obligations and privileges of these manifold bodies—privileges and obligations deriving originally from the divine power vested in the sovereign and made venerable by long usage. In regenerating the French nation in 1789, the revolutionaries sought to eschew what they regarded as these superstitions supporting tyranny, and to erect the state on the unchanging truths and pristine simplicity of Nature.

Property, in the theory adopted by the National Assembly, stood at the very origins of the social and political order. Property was created by man's labor on the physical world. By laboring, man annexed to his person as his property those pieces of nature which his labor removed from their natural state. He thereby gained the right to enjoy and to dispose of his property as he saw fit. Property was thus prior to the state; indeed, it was partly to protect their property that men formed civil societies in the first place. In civil society as in the state of nature, property was an extension of the individual person; it was property that made the citizen a complete and independent individual, capable of resisting private or public oppressions. It was therefore a domain of the strictest individual liberty. "The exercise of the natural rights of each man," the Declaration of the Rights of Man and Citizen put it, "has no limits except those which assure to other members of society the enjoyment of the same rights." In the new, naturalistic constitutional theory of the National Assembly, free individual citizens surrounded by their property—rather than corporate bodies—became the constituent units of the nation. And their will, rather than the will of the king, became the only valid source of law.

Given this theory of the origins of property, only property of an absolute and individual kind could possibly be accepted as legitimate. If property was prior to the state, then property in public function or in honors and privileges bestowed by the king were nonsensical—since property existed before public functions or kings—and public or community tyranny over the disposition of private property was a breach of the very terms of the social contract. Moreover, if property was created by labor, then property could only refer to physically palpable objects removed from the state of nature by human labor—not to publicly created rights, functions, or privileges. Hence the Civil Code's definition of property—"the right to enjoy and to dispose of *goods* in the most absolute manner"—expressed perfectly the intentions of the French revolutionaries.

By recognizing and securing property rights, the Revolution was also recognizing the persons who performed society's labors, and was assuring them of the place they had earned in the social order. It was a commonplace of revolutionary discourse that men had a claim to citizenship in part because they performed useful work. This was one of the major themes of the Abbé Sieyès, who demonstrated in his famous pamphlet that the Third Estate was actually the entire nation because only its members performed "the labors that support society," while the nobility "is foreign to the nation because of its idleness."[9] Property, in the eyes of the revolutionaries, was a manifestation of a man's useful labor, both its token and its reward, and the guarantee of a man's continuing existence as a citizen. With this conception in mind, the revolutionary constitutions tended to use possession of property as a qualification for full citizenship. In the constitution of 1791 and, for that matter, in all but two of the nine constitutions of France that were in force between 1791 and 1848, there was some kind of property qualification either for suffrage or for holding elective office.[10] In other words, under the new political system property was not only recognized and secured but also became a condition for exercise of the full rights of citizenship.

It would be no exaggeration to say that the French Revolution made private property the basic institution of the social and political order. This is why the idea that the French Revolution was a "bourgeois" revolution continues to have such a strong appeal. Of course, since Alfred Cobban, Elizabeth Eisenstein, George V. Taylor and others launched their attack on the idea of the "bourgeois revolution" over a decade ago,[11] this may be the only respect in which the Revolution still seems unproblematically bourgeois. The idea that the Revolution was made by a "revolutionary bourgeoisie," for example, is no longer tenable. Taylor and Cobban have effectively shown that the so-called "revolutionary bourgeoisie"—whether one defines it as the whole of the politically active Third Estate or as the representatives of the Third Estate in the National Assembly—actually had economic interests and styles of life that were scarcely distinguishable from the aristocracy. Like the nobles, their investments were overwhelmingly in land and other forms of low-yield but highly secure wealth that Taylor dubs "proprietary," as opposed to "capitalist."[12] And Elizabeth Eisenstein has noted that many— perhaps most—of the prominent leaders of the "patriot party" that guided the fortunes of the Revolution in this period actually had their origins in the privileged orders. This was notably true of the three great leaders of 1789— the Marquis de Lafayette, the Abbé Sieyès and the Comte de Mirabeau. But it was also true of lesser figures such as Adrien du Port, d'Aiguillon, Talleyrand, Hérault de Sechelles, Condorcet, La Rochefoucauld-Liancourt and Le Pelletier de Saint-Fargeau.[13] In short, it has been clear for some time that the Revolution of 1789 was not made by a distinct and unified bourgeois class. But given the revolutionaries' extraordinary interest in the rights of private property, perhaps one could argue that it was a revolution *for* the bourgeoisie, even if it was not bourgeois who guided it. Perhaps the revolutionary redefinitions of property and the Enlightenment theories on which they were based were a recognition—either conscious or unconscious—of the rising power and importance of the commercial and industrial bourgeoisie of the cities.

But when we look at Enlightenment discourse on property, which was the undoubted guide of the revolutionaries, we find that it virtually ignored urban, commercial, and industrial forms of property. In other words, when the revolutionaries secured the rights of absolute private property, it was absolute property in land, not commercial and industrial property, that they had in mind. This fixation of attention on landed property was a ubiquitous feature of Enlightenment thought. The Physiocrats, for example, held that only agriculture, not commerce or industry, was productive of wealth. Thus Turgot, often hailed by historians as a prophet of the bourgeoisie, drew up a memoir to the king—the *Mémoire sur les municipalités*—proposing a system of representation that would have alloted votes in strict proportion to landed property holdings, entirely denying suffrage to those who possessed only mobile wealth. Had Turgot's scheme been enacted, the most mediocre peasant proprietor would have been given more weight in the state than a prosperous bourgeois whose wealth was solely commercial or industrial in character.[14] Indeed, so exclusively did Turgot think of property in terms of land that he characterized masters in the urban trades, who were nothing if not small proprietors, as "that class of men . . . having *no property* except their labor and their industry.[15] Because they owned no land, Turgot saw them as having no property beyond their own persons.

If not all Enlightenment thinkers were as extreme as Turgot in denying forms of property other than land, they were like him to this extent: when they thought of property, it was land that they envisioned. This was as true of those who made the Revolution as of those who came before it, and as true of those who wished to redistribute property as of those who wished to make it inviolable. For example, when Saint-Just concluded at the height of the terror that division of property was a necessary precondition for establishing the public good, he formulated this conclusion exclusively in terms of land. "To reform morals," he wrote, "we must begin by satisfying need and interest; we must give some land to everyone."[16] Thus, while it is true that the revolutionaries' ideology laid heavy stress on the rights of private property, it also tended to assume a simple, abstract, and rural model of society in which landed property was taken to epitomize all property. This does not mean that the revolutionaries denied protection to commercial and industrial property. Their legal formulae, after all, were abstract and general, and therefore applied to property of all kinds: to stocks of goods acquired only to be sold, to raw materials to be processed and placed on the market, to commercial credits and bank deposits, to diversified portfolios of investments. But it was land, not these volatile and evanescent forms of wealth, that the revolutionaries envisaged as the permanent foundation of the state.

In this connection, it should be noted that the revolutionaries' emphasis on rural property fits rather well with some important characteristics of post-revolutionary French society. First, while urban property relations were not visibly altered by the Revolution, property relations in rural France were palpably and immediately transformed. Seigneuries were abolished, interlocking claims of landlords and peasants were sorted out and simplified into either rental contracts or freehold properties, and vast tracts of land belonging to the Church and to émigré nobles were seized by the State, divided, and sold. By the end of the 1790s, French rural property had acquired the physiognomy it would wear through the nineteenth and much of the twentieth century. Second, French political life through the first half of the nineteenth century was dominated not by urban capitalists, but by the great landholding "notables" made familiar to us by A.-J. Tudesq.[17] In politics, at least, rural rather than urban property holders seem to have been pushed to the fore by the French Revolution. Finally, the French Revolution's liberation of property from "feudal" constraints did not result in rapid industrialization. French industry, which had already begun its sustained growth well before the Revolution, continued to grow very gradually right through the nineteenth century. But it long continued to be dominated by small-scale firms and artisan techniques, and it never underwent the prodigious transformations that took place in contemporary Britain.[18] As Alfred Cobban has pointedly suggested, France in the century following the French Revolution remained in many respects an agrarian and deeply conservative society.[19]

But in spite of all this, it would be perverse to conclude that the French Revolution was in no sense a bourgeois revolution. For while it was not made *by* the bourgeoisie or *for* the bourgeoisie, it nevertheless did create in France what has since come to be called a bourgeois (or alternatively a liberal) form of society—that is, one in which private property and individual liberty are considered to be the foundations of the social and economic order. The Revolution was carried through by a shifting coalition of men of letters, lawyers, and landowners whose vision of the social order was basically agrarian, not by a commercial or industrial bourgeoisie. Moreover, the Revolution did not bring a new class to power, if we mean by class a group of people with a common relation to the means of production. Both before the Revolution and after, those who held ranks of honor and authority in France were nearly always landowners. But before the Revolution, their honor and authority arose not from their possession of land per se, but from their possession of offices or seigneuries, or from their membership in privileged orders, bodies, or companies. After the Revolution, their public standing arose directly from their possession of property—initially of landed property, but with the role of commercial and industrial property increasing gradually as the country urbanized and industrialized. Where the Old Regime produced an elite whose position rested on privilege, the new regime produced an elite whose position rested on property. If a bourgeois society is defined as one in which domination is based on ownership of property, then Colin Lucas was right to conclude that "the Revolution made the bourgeoisie even if it was not made by the bourgeoisie."[20]

Thus, in spite of the many continuities between prerevolutionary and postrevolutionary society, the French Revolution was a social revolution in the deepest sense, one that transformed a hierarchical corporate society based on privilege into a fundamentally different liberal and individualistic society based on private property. The Revolution changed the definition of social order and the terms of social action; above all, it made private property the pivot of social life.

One important sign of the centrality of property rights in the new bourgeois or liberal society is that private property came to be contested as it never had been before. While there was no absence of disputes about property in rural areas, the contestation was far more intense and far more radical in urban industry—in part, one suspects, because the revolutionaries gave less careful thought to the consequences of the new property system for industry than for agriculture. In any case, it is a remarkable fact of nineteenth-century history that France, for all its domination by landowners and its slow industrialization, was also the homeland of socialism. With the exception of Robert Owen, nearly all the great early pioneers of socialism were French: Babeuf, Saint-Simon, Fourier, Proudhon, Cabet, Blanqui, Louis Blanc. (The Germans, for all their brilliance, were later entries; Marx was only really known by the end of the 1840s.) Nor was this only a matter of intellectual precocity. It was also in France that socialism first became a mass movement. By 1848 socialist ideas were so widespread in the French working class that the revolution of that year quickly became a life-and-death struggle between working-class socialists and bourgeois liberals. And in June of 1848, the workers of Paris staged the world's first self-conscious workers' uprising. It was the French workers' movement of 1848 that made socialism a serious alternative in European politics—an ominous threat for some, a bright hope for others, but a force to be reckoned with for all. The fact that socialism arose in France so early and with such strength is itself powerful evidence that France had become a "bourgeois" society by 1848, at least in that private property had become the essential pivot of the social order.

Most historians have attributed the rise of a socialist working class to the development of an industrial economy. But this explanation clearly cannot account for the French case, where socialism developed early even though the industrial revolution was unusually gradual. I shall argue instead that the precocious development of socialism in France resulted above all from the transformations in property that took place in the French Revolution. These transformations, I believe, set in motion two dynamics that eventually led to the rise of a socialist working class. The first of these dynamics—a movement of critical speculation about the role of labor and property in the social order—began above all as a dynamic of thought. The second—the development by workers of organizations intended to bring relations of production under control of the collectivity—originated entirely independently of socialist ideas. But beginning with the Revolution of 1830, these two dynamics became more and more intertwined, and by 1848 they became almost impossible to distinguish.

The history of French socialist thought is well known and amply documented, so I will limit myself here to a sketch of the specific links I see between socialist speculation and the Revolution's redefinition of property.

The French Revolution's conception of property placed the origin of property in human labor on nature. By recognizing the centrality of property in the social and political order, therefore, the Revolution was also recognizing the centrality of labor. But this concept of property had a pregnant ambiguity. On one hand, man's title to private property was ultimately created by labor; on the other hand, many men labored a whole lifetime without accumulating property, while others possessed vast amounts of property without performing any significant labor. As long as Enlightenment discourse about property was essentially a discourse of political opposition, a way of demonstrating the inequity, the oppressiveness, or the irrationality of the institutions of the Old Regime, this ambiguity was not noticed—indeed, one ought perhaps to say it did not exist. It was only after the French Revolution, when Enlightenment discourse about property came to have a different function and meaning, when it became the dominant language of social order, that the ambiguity came to be visible. Even then, the conception of property imposed by the French Revolution was not necessarily self-contradictory; whether it was or not depended on precisely what one meant by labor and by property, and on how one interpreted the links between them. But by building this concept of property and labor into the foundation of the society and the state, the French Revolution ensured that the nature, the functions, the significance, and the relationships of property and labor would be the subject of intense and extensive speculation. In my opinion, it was this deep ambiguity about central concepts of the new social and political order, and not the growth of a new industrial economy, that made French thinkers the pioneers of socialist thought.

My remarks on the French labor movement—the second dynamic set in motion by the French Revolution—will be longer and considerably more complicated. The classical Marxist account of the labor movement had the merit of connecting the rise of labor to the French Revolution indirectly—the Revolution, it claimed, cleared the way for the rise of industrial capitalism, and the growth of modern industry in turn created the labor movement. But because recent research has found that the early labor movement was dominated by skilled artisans in small-scale industry, neither the growth of factory industry nor the French Revolution has figured much in recent accounts. Rather, the rise of the labor movement has recently been attributed mainly to economic changes and intensified exploitation *within* the confines of small-scale industry: to increased division of labor, to replacement of made-to-order by ready-to-wear items, to skill dilution and production of shoddy goods, to increased use of "putting-out" arrangements in urban trades, to the multiplication of subcontractors between capital and laborers—in short, to changes in the organization of production and marketing that eroded the status, the security, and the incomes of skilled artisans.[21] These practices were, of course, a response to rising demand—which in turn resulted from population growth, increased urbanization, and an expansion of national and inter-regional markets. As the economists would put it, rising demand made it possible for entrepreneurs to take advantage of economies of scale. But neither the extent and shape of these exploitative practices nor the workers' responses to them can be understood in purely economic terms. Both the practices and the workers' responses to them are inseparable from a whole set of decisive changes in relations between workers and masters that were imposed by the French Revolution's redefinitions of property.

What were these changes and what were their effects? Under the Old Regime, the artisan trades of French cities had been governed by corporations. These corporations held monopolies in the local market, and were regulated by their own statutes. Each corporation was considered to be a single legal person, empowered to initiate lawsuits or to own property like any other subject of the king. The corporation was composed of masters, journeymen, and apprentices, with the latter under the paternal discipline and solicitude of the masters, and its members were bound to one another as part of the same legal and moral body. The corporation was also a religious unit; each trade venerated its own patron saint and maintained a confraternity for this purpose. The ethic of corporations was in principle broadly collective: corporations were to maintain the good order of the trade for the benefit of the trade community as a whole—including the journeymen and apprentices—as well as for the benefit of the public at large. In order to do so, as we have seen, corporations imposed strict limits on the masters' use of their property. Of course, corporations were utterly dominated by the masters, and in practice they often used this domination to squeeze their journeymen, to limit access to mastership, to hold down competition so as to drive up prices, and to engage in endless boundary disputes with the corporations of neighboring trades.[22] Yet in spite of all these abuses, workers were no less insistent than masters that the trade was a moral community. When journeymen formed their own organizations to challenge the masters' tyranny, they always claimed to be acting for the trade as a whole, not for the journeymen alone. As one sixteenth-century journeymen's brotherhood put it, "the Masters and Journeymen are or ought to be only one body together, like a family or a fraternity."[23] Journeymen and masters might engage in the bitterest of struggles, but even their struggles testified to a shared ideal of the moral community of the trade.

The French Revolution dissolved corporations when it redefined the rights of property. Masters, as we have seen, were deprived of property in their masterships. Meanwhile, their productive capital was freed of collective constaint and was thereby transformed into absolute individual property. As a result of these changes, masters lost their collective authority as a corporation, but in return they became sovereign proprietors in their workshops; workers, on the other hand, gained a certain legal freedom, but they also lost their moral claims to fraternal solicitude and to collective regulations for the good of the trade community as a whole. According to the revolutionary legal code, both masters and workers were now fully autonomous and equal individuals who came together in a free market, and who contracted on a one to one basis to collaborate in the production of some commodity.[24] But in practice, workers were almost invariably at a severe disadvantage in this collaboration. They entered the market with nothing but their labor power, while the masters, as proprietors of the means of production, were in a vastly superior bargaining position. As a result of this disparity, workers sought ways to gain by association the strength they lacked as individuals, and by doing so to reassert the moral claims of the collectivity against the unchecked cupidity and licence of individual masters.

Among the workers' most important grievances were changes in the organization of production of the type we noted above; changes that standardized products, reduced the skill level required of workers, reduced their autonomy on the job, and threatened their dignity as skilled artisans. Before the Revolution, changes of this sort were contrary to the statutes of the corporations—although, of course, they sometimes occurred anyway. Some urban corporations of the Old Regime were bothered by competition from *chambrelans,* as they were called—workers who were not members of the corporation and who produced low-quality standardized goods in hiding in their own rooms. And in many textile trades the entrepreneurs avoided the corporations altogether by putting their weaving out to rural weavers who lived beyond the jurisdiction of urban corporations. But the existence of corporations certainly inhibited changes in the organization of production in the vast majority of urban trades under the Old Regime. In the nineteenth century, by contrast, all these changes ceased to be abuses and became perfectly legal exercises of the entrepreneur's right to dispose of his property as he saw fit. They could not be limited by statute, but only by collective action on the part of the workers.

The idiom workers adopted for their collective action was—not surprisingly—a modified version of the corporate idiom of the Old Regime. Workers attempted to counterbalance the new power of masters as absolute individual proprietors and to combat what they saw as destructive and chaotic innovations in the organization of production by reasserting the existence of a single, unified corporate trade community. In doing so they were not attempting to restore the corporations of the Old Regime—they had no reason to wish for the reestablishment of privileged hierarchical corporations governed by the masters. Rather, they created their own workers' corporations that used the familiar language, rituals, and organizational forms from the Old Regime to assert the continuing existence of a moral community of the trade, and to maintain vigilance over conditions of labor in the workshops.

The most common institutional forms assumed by these workers' corporations were *compagnonnage* and mutual aid societies. Compagnonnages were national federations of secret journeymen's brotherhoods that dated back to the fifteenth or sixteenth century, and had grown up around the Tour de France. Their constituent units were tightly organized groups of itinerant journeymen who took room and board at a common lodging house (called the *mère*) and undertook to find jobs for new arrivals—or to help with the journey to the next town on the tour if no jobs were available. The compagnons borrowed many of the key rituals and practices of the masters' corporations—detailed regulations or statutes, a requirement that members produce masterpieces, celebration of the festival of the patron saint, corporate funerals, practices of mutual aid—and supplemented these by elaborate myths and ritual practices of their own. Moreover, like the masters' corporations, they were concerned with maintaining the good order of the trade as a whole, and when masters acted so as to threaten the well-being of journeymen, compagnonnage would counter with partial or industry-wide work stoppages. Compagnonnage came through the French Revolution more or less intact, and was probably the most important single form of journeymen's organization throughout the Restoration. It seems to have begun to decline in the 1830s, and declined more sharply in the 1840s. But it remained important right up to the Revolution of 1848.[25]

Mutual aid societies probably had surpassed compagnonnage as the most important form of workers' organization by the 1830s. Legally, mutual aid societies were purely secular and utilitarian associations formed to provide mutual insurance benefits in case of sickness, death, and disability. But in practice, they were also postrevolutionary versions of confraternities—the devotional subsidiaries of trade corporations which had performed these same mutual aid functions under the Old Regime. Particularly after the restoration of the Bourbons in 1815, when both State and Church patronized mutual aid societies as part of the campaign to win the popular classes back to the true faith, workers could use these associations to organize themselves under the banner of their trade's traditional patron saint and to practice precisely the same kinds of mutual charity that had marked trade corporations of the Old Regime. At the same time, the mutual aid society could and did—though not legally—act as the organizational center for maintaining vigilance over wages and working conditions in the trade as a whole and for organizing strikes or boycotts when necessary.[26] By means of these organizations, which the workers tended to call *sociétés* and *corporations,* nineteenth-century French workers managed to assert the moral claims of the laboring trade community against the legal claims of absolute private property.

Some of these corporations were extremely complex, ambitious, and powerful. The Parisian hatters are a good example. An old compagnonnage trade, the hatters continued to maintain mères, to regulate job placement, and to provide travel payments for those unable to find work. But they also formed two legally registered mutual aid societies: one with the usual benefits for death and sickness, and a second "auxiliary" society to provide aid in case of unemployment. Besides the statutes of these legally registered societies, the hatters also had an "interior regulation" empowering a commission of workers to draw up wage schedules and to call strikes against workshops where these wage-rates were not observed. It also granted unemployment benefits to workers who went on strike or were fired for legitimately resisting their masters. The hatters' corporation also maintained high standards of workmanship and good behavior in the workshops, requiring workers to pass tests of their skill, imposing fines for drunkenness, and denying unemployment aid to workers fired for "grave faults" of any kind. Moreover, the solidarity of the trade was ritually celebrated in banquets, funerals and processions in honor of the patron saint, and it was practically realized in arrangements to equalize incomes: workers who made over forty francs a week were required to put the excess in a common fund to be distributed to less fortunate workers. In short, the hatters' corporation was a comprehensive practical and moral community encompassing all aspects of the trade.[27]

Of course, not all workers' corporations were as complex or as powerful as that of the Parisian hatters. Some had only the most rudimentary organization, and some probably had to content themselves with little more than the mutual insurance functions specified in their legally registered statutes. We have very little evidence for most trades, and often know only whether some sort of organization existed or not, and even that is sometimes uncertain. Yet the available evidence points to the existence of some kind of corporation in most of the skilled trades of the cities. My own research in Marseille, for example, has uncovered positive evidence of organization for no fewer than forty-three trades, comprising all but four of the skilled trades in the city that occupied one hundred or more men, and several of the smaller trades as well.[28] These corporations, both in Marseille and elsewhere in France, varied widely in structure, in aggressiveness, in power, and in effectiveness. But whatever form they might take, workers' corporations were a ubiquitous feature of nineteenth-century French cities.

In forming these corporations, workers initially had no thought of supplanting private property with collective property; they merely wished to reassert a certain measure of collective control over the individually held property of the masters. But in a legal system that recognized only the absolute and individual rights of proprietors, collective control could be maintained only by constant effort. In practice, the masters in a given trade were sometimes willing—at least tacitly—to negotiate some sort of collective agreement with the workers. After all, many of them had spent time as journeymen themselves, and shared some of the workers' corporate views of the trade. Besides, by cooperating with the workers' attempts to maintain uniform standards in the trade, small masters could sometimes inhibit threatening innovations by their larger and more dynamic competitors. But the tacit agreements reached by workers and masters were always fragile. They had no legal validity, and could be destroyed by a single entrepreneur who was determined to bring matters to a head. For when it came to a test of strength—a strike or a boycott—the authorities had little choice but to recognize the rights of the proprietor, and the workers' leaders were liable to be jailed and fined for the crime of illegal coalition. The legal system recognized only the rights of private property; it was stacked against collective claims of any kind.

This fact was revealed most dramatically in the years following the Revolution of 1830. The establishment of a regime ostensibly dedicated to liberty and the widely felt sense that it was "the people" who had conquered liberty on the barricades encouraged workers to act far more openly than before, and to make more ambitious claims of control over their trades. The result was a dramatic wave of strikes and agitation that climaxed in major workers' uprisings in Lyon and Paris in 1831, 1832, and 1834—followed by intensified government repression, tougher laws against associations, and an ever more dogmatic defense of the rights of private property.[29] These struggles, and the continual reassertion of the sanctity of private property which they provoked from the authorities, propelled a significant minority of the workers toward the conclusion that collective control of their trades was impossible without collective ownership of the means of production.

In fact, workers did not reach this conclusion entirely on their own, but in collaboration with republicans and socialists. It was in the early 1830s that the workers' movement and socialism discovered one another, that these two initially independent responses to the French Revolution's redefinition of property came to be intertwined. To the socialists, the workers' practical struggles against laissez-faire individualism seemed to confirm their own analysis of the evils of current society, and to workers, who began to encounter socialism in republican political societies and in the new radical press, the socialists' ideas seemed to explain and clarify many of their own experiences. Meanwhile republican militants, most notably in the Friends of the People and the Society of the Rights of Man, found themselves drawn increasingly to socialist themes and language in their attempts to recruit a working-class following. The main product of this encounter was a variety of schemes for replacing private production with cooperative producers' associations, thereby solving the problem of collective control by making the workers collective owners of the means of production. It is impossible to attribute principal responsibility for this idea either to republicans, or to socialists, or to workers. It developed at once out of the republicans' concern with the right of free association, out of the socialists' attempts to overcome the destructive effects of economic competition, and out of the workers' practical experience of collective organization. It was a kind of simultaneous invention that arose spontaneously out of their joint agitation.[30]

This idea of associative production—what one scholar has dubbed "the utopia of association"[31]—lay at the center of most socialist discourse of the 1830s and 1840s, and of the socialist projects undertaken by workers in 1848. Until the Revolution of 1848, however, adherence to socialism in any form was strictly a minority phenomenon among French workers. Corporate forms of labor organization were still ubiquitous, and their practical goals were still limited to establishing collective constraints on the masters. But the thought and agitation of the early 1830s had established cooperative ownership of property as a thinkable alternative, and the great burst of socialist writings of the 1830s and 1840s elaborated this alternative more fully: not only the works of Proudhon and Louis Blanc, but a host of works by such lesser figures as Philippe Buchez, Pierre Leroux, Victor Hennequin, Pierre Vinçard, and dozens of other more or less obscure writers and publicists. But it was only in the spring of 1848, when the workers seemed to be the victors of a new revolution, that collective ownership of productive capital became a ubi-quitous goal.

The focus and organizational center of the workers' movement in 1848 was the Luxembourg Commission. Established by the provisional revolutionary government in March of 1848 under the chairmanship of Louis Blanc, the commission was a kind of parliament of labor, composed of two elected deputies from each worker's corporation in the capital. Although its official function was only advisory, revolutionary workers saw its role in much loftier terms. In the words of the cabinet makers' delegates, its task was nothing less than elaborating "the constitution of labor," and Louis Blanc himself characterized the commission as "the Estates General of the people."[32]

The commission was abolished long before it could complete its "constitution of labor," but the general outlines of the project are nevertheless clear. Labor was to be recognized explicitly as the sole foundation of the social and political order. As a "Manifesto of the Delegates of the Corporations (Who Sat at Luxembourg)" put it in June of 1848, "the state . . . is the producer. . . . Is it not sovereign, the producer of all riches?"[33] This sovereignty of the producers was to be based not on laborers as individuals, but on workers' corporations, the collective units in which production was actually carried out. Workers' corporations, aided by state-supplied credit, would be transformed into democratic associations of production, with the former workers and the former masters alike becoming equal "associates" who would jointly own and control the means of production. These democratic corporations would become the constituent units of the "Democratic and Social Republic," represented, as at Luxembourg, by elected delegates. In this way, the tyranny of wealthy proprietors would cease at last, and the gentle passions of cooperation and harmony would finally rule in the social world.[34]

This, of course, never came to pass. National elections held in April 1848 showed that the workers and socialists, for all their rhetorical dominance of Paris, were still a small minority in the country at large, and the new Constituent Assembly quickly snuffed out the socialists' schemes—most dramatically by ruthlessly suppressing the workers' rebellion of June 1848. Struggles for a "democratic and social Republic" continued, despite the repression, right down to December 1851, when they were finally stilled by Louis Napoleon's coup d'état. The events of 1848 and the Second Republic left a permanent mark on French politics and class relations. From that time on, some form of collective ownership of the means of production has been a constant goal of the labor movement. Since 1848, the absolute private property established by the French Revolution has been under constant—if often not terribly perilous—challenge by a socialist working-class movement.

The account I have presented here is brief and synthetic, and it makes a number of unconventional claims: that the French Revolution's obsession with private property can be understood better as an attempt to construct a social order on "natural" foundations than as an attempt to secure the interests of the rising commercial and industrial classes of the cities; that the French Revolution created a bourgeois society even though there was no revolutionary bourgeoisie on hand to preside over its creation; that the rise of socialism in France must be attributed in large measure to transformations in property that took place during the French Revolution; that the emergence of working-class consciousness in France took place in advance of the rise of an industrialized economy; and that the profoundly collectivist mentality of the French working-class movement owed at least as much to corporate traditions of moral community as to the thought of Saint-Simon, Fourier, Proudhon, and Louis Blanc. These claims are in some degree polemical, and I cannot expect others to accept all of them without more evidence than I have been able to offer here.

But even if some of these specific interpretations are open to dispute, I hope to have demonstrated the value of a certain *mode* of interpretation, of a certain approach to the problem of social change—one that pays as close attention to the cultural conceptions encoded into the social and political order as it does to economic life, or demography, or technological change, or the relative power of different social groups. For I am convinced that understanding such major shifts in society as the formation of a bourgeois pattern of social relations or the rise of a socialist working class requires us to read, to analyse, and to interpret these cultural conceptions and to trace out their effects—both intended and unintended—on society as a whole. And in working out culturally sensitive accounts of social change, I suspect that we will continually be drawn to such major political events as the French Revolution, the Restoration, the Revolution of 1830, or the Revolution of 1848—events marked by explicit efforts to reorder the cultural constitution of society. In this sense, at least, social history turns out to be inseparable from the history of political action.

NOTES

1. Antoine Furetière, *Dictionnaire universel* (The Hague, 1691).
2. The classic account is Marc Bloch, *Les Caractères originaux de l'histoire rurale française.* (Paris, 1964), esp. chaps. 3 and 4.

3.   The best work on the legal history of corporations is François Olivier-Martin, *L'Organisation corporative de la France d'ancien régime* (Paris, 1938), esp. pp. 81–230. See also Etienne Martin Saint-Léon, *Histoire des corporations de métiers, depuis leurs origines jusqu'à leur suppression en 1791* (Paris, 1899), and Emile Coornaert, *Les Corporations en France avant 1789* (Paris, 1941).

4.   See the brief but illuminating discussion in Ralph E. Giesey, "Rules of Inheritance and Strategies of Mobility in Prerevolutionary France," *American Historical Review* 82, no. 2 (April 1977), esp. pp. 281–85. The standard work on venal offices is Roland Mousnier, *La Vènalité des offices sous Henri IV et Louis XIII*, 2nd ed. (Paris, 1971).

5.   Once again, the classic account is Bloch, *Les Caractères originaux*, esp. chap. 3 and 4.

6.   For figures on the level of these fees in eighteenth-century Paris, see Martin Saint-Léon, *Histoire des corporations*, pp. 590–93.

7.   Jules Flammermont, *Remontrances du Parlement de Paris au XVIIIe siècle*, 3:278.

8.   André-Jean Arnaud, *Les Origines doctrinaires du Code civil français* (Paris, 1969), p. 179.

9.   Emmanuel Sieyès, *Qu'est-ce que le Tiers état?* (Geneva, 1970), p. 125.

10.   The exceptions were the "Jacobin" constitution of 1793 and the first Napoleonic constitution of 1799; both were ephemeral even by French standards. The first lasted only two years and the second only three. See Jacques Godechot, ed., *Les Constitutions de la France depuis 1789* (Paris, 1970).

11.   Alfred Cobban, *The Social Interpretation of the French Revolution* (Cambridge, Eng., 1964); idem, "The Myth of the French Revolution," in *Aspects of the French Revolution* (New York, 1968), originally delivered as a University of London inaugural lecture in 1954; George V. Taylor, "Noncapitalist Wealth and the Origins of the French Revolution," *American Historical Review* 72, no. 2 (January 1967):469–96; and Elizabeth Eisenstein, "Who Intervened in 1788?: A Commentary on the coming of the French Revolution," *American Historical Review* 71, no. 1 (October 1965):77–103. An excellent summary and commentary on the problem of the "bourgeois revolution" is provided by Colin Lucas, "Nobles, Bourgeois and the Origins of the French Revolution," *Past and Present*, no. 60 (August 1973):84–126.

12.   Taylor, "Noncapitalist Wealth," pp. 487–90; Cobban, "The Myth of the French Revolution," esp. pp. 99–101.

13.   Eisenstein, "Who Intervened in 1788?" esp. pp. 99–100.

14.   E. Daire and H. Dussard, eds., *Oeuvres de Turgot et documents le concernant*, vol. 4 (Paris, 1922), pp. 582–89, 599–603.

15.   The quotation is from Turgot's decree suppressing corporations in 1776 (my emphasis). M. Jourdan, *Recueil général des anciennes lois françaises*, vol. 23 (Paris, 1826), p. 371.

16.   The quotation is from Saint-Just's "Fragments sur les institutions républicaines," in *Oeuvres complètes de Saint-Just*, vol. 2, ed. Charles Vellay (Paris, 1908), p. 513.

17.   A.-J. Tudesq, *Les Grands Notables en France (1840–1849): etude historique d'une psychologie sociale*, 2 vols. (Paris, 1964).

18.   Recent research indicates that France never had an industrial takeoff of the sort identified by W. W. Rostow in *The Stages of Economic Growth* (Cambridge, Eng. 1961). French industry began its sustained growth around the middle of the eighteenth century and expanded steadily but gradually throughout the nineteenth century. While French industry grew much more slowly than British industry, rates of growth in income per capita were virtually the same since the French population was growing much less rapidly than the British. The most cogent recent examinations of French industrialization are Jean Marczewski, "The Take-off Hypothesis and the French Experience," in *The Economics of Take-off into Sustained Growth*, ed. W. W. Rostow, (London, 1964), pp. 119–33; M. Lévy-Leboyer, "Le Processus d'industrialisation: le cas de l'Angleterre et de la France," *Revue historique* 239 (1968): 281–98; Richard Roehl, "French Industrialization: A Reconsideration," *Explorations in Economic History* 13

62   William H. Sewell, Jr.

(1976):233–81; Patrick O'Brien and Caglar Keydar, *Economic Growth in Britain and France, 1780–1914: Two Paths to the Twentieth Century* (London, 1978).

19. Cobban, *Social Interpretation*, pp. 89–90.

20. Lucas, "Nobles, Bourgeois and the Origins of the French Revolution," p. 126.

21. The classic description of such a process remains E. P. Thompson, *The Making of the English Working Class* (New York, 1963), chap. 8. For analogous developments in France, see Christopher Johnson, *Utopian communism in France: Cabet and the Icarians, 1839–1851* (Ithaca, N.Y., 1974), esp. chap. 4; idem, "Economic Change and Artisan Discontent: The Tailors' History, 1800–48," in *Revolution and Reaction: 1848 and the Second French Republic*, ed. Roger Price (London, 1975), pp. 87–114; and Bernard H. Moss, *The Origins of the French Labor Movement: The Socialism of Skilled Workers* (Berkeley and Los Angeles, 1976), esp. chap. 1. See also Ronald Aminzade's essay in the present volume.

22. In addition to the works by Olivier-Martin, Martin Saint-Léon, and Coornaert cited in note 3, see Pierre Deyon, *Amiens, capitale provinciale: étude sur la société urbaine au XVIIe siècle* (Paris, The Hague, 1967), pp. 200–203, 243–46, Maurice Garden, *Lyon et le lyonnais au XVIIIe siècle* (Paris, 1975), pp. 311–30, and Jean-Claude Perrot, *Genèse d'une ville moderne: Caen au XVIIIe siècle* (Paris, 1975), 1:327–40.

23. Natalie Zemon Davis, "A Trade Union in Sixteenth-Century France," *Economic History Review*, 2nd ser., 19, no. 1 (April 1966):53.

24. The classic statement of this doctrine was made by Le Chapelier when he introduced the law bearing his name in the Constituent Assembly in June 1791. See P. J. B. Buchez and P. C. Roux, *Histoire parlementaire de la Révolution française*, vol. 10 (Paris, 1834), pp. 193–195.

25. The best recent work on compagnonnage is by Cynthia Truant, "Compagnonnage: Symbolic Action and the Defense of Workers' Rights in France, 1700–1848" (Ph.D. diss., University of Chicago, 1978). See also Emile Coornaert, *Les Compagnonnages en France du moyen âge à nos jours* (Paris, 1966) and Etienne Martin Saint-Léon, *Le Compagnonnage* (Paris, 1901).

26. There is no adequate general discussion of mutual aid societies in nineteenth-century France. See, however, E. Labrousse, *Le Mouvement ouvrier et les théories sociales en France de 1815 à 1848* (Paris: Cours de Sorbonne, 1948), pp. 79–84; Maurice Agulhon, *Une Ville ouvrière au temps du socialisme utopique: Toulon de 1815 à 1851* (Paris, 1970), pp. 113–95; Paul Chauvet, *Les Ouvriers du livre en France de 1789 à la constitution de la fédération du livre* (Paris, 1964), passim; Robert J. Bezucha, *The Lyon Uprising of 1834: Social and Political Conflict in the Early July Monarchy* (Cambridge, Mass., 1974), pp. 100–112.

27. Jean Vial, *La Coutume chapelière: histoire du mouvement ouvrier dans la chapellerie* (Paris, 1941), pp. 32–78.

28. William H. Sewell, Jr., "The Working Class of Marseille under the Second Republic: Social Structure and Political Behavior," in *Workers in the Industrial Revolution: Recent Studies of Labor in the United States and Europe*, ed. Peter N. Stearns and Daniel J. Walkowitz (New Brunswick, N.J., 1974), p. 84.

29. The classic accounts of this period are by Octave Festy, *Le Mouvement ouvrier au début de la monarchie de juillet (1830–1834)* (Paris, 1908) and Edouard Dolléans, *Histoire du mouvement ouvrier* (Paris, 1936–39), I:51–107. For Paris, see Alain Faure, "Mouvements populaires et mouvement ouvrier à Paris (1830–1834)," *Le Mouvement Social*, no. 88 (July-September 1974):51–92. For Lyon, see Bezucha, *The Lyon Uprising of 1834*, pp. 134–48.

30. This conclusion is very close to that of Festy, *Le Mouvement ouvrier*, esp. pp. 131, 336–38. See also Bernard H. Moss, "Parisian Workers and the Origins of Republican Socialism, 1830–1833," in *1830 in France* ed. John M. Merriman (New York, 1975), pp. 203–21.

31. Moss, *Origins of the French Labor Movement*, pp. 31–70.

32. Rémi Gossez, *Les Ouvriers de Paris: l'organisation, 1848–1851*, vol. 24 of the *Bibliothèque de la révolution de 1848* (La Roche-sur-Yon, 1967), pp. 129, 225.

33. A facsimile of the manifesto appears in Gossez's *Les Ouvriers de Paris*, pp. 292–93.

34. For a fuller analysis of the corporate theme in 1848, see William H. Sewell, Jr., "*Corporations républicaines*: The Revolutionary Idiom of Parisian Workers in 1848," *Comparative Studies in Society and History* 21, no. 2 (April 1979); idem, *Labor and Revolution in France, 1789–1848: From Corporate Community to Socialist Republic* (Cambridge University Press), forthcoming.

THREE

Patterns of Proletarianization:
*Parisian Tailors and Lodève Woolens Workers**

CHRISTOPHER H. JOHNSON

At 11 P.M. on the night of lundi gras, 1749, Henri Sauclières, the royal inspector of manufactures in Lodève, was disturbed on his evening prome-nade by three woolens workers, Joseph Alias, a weaver; his brother, a fuller from whom the inspector had recently seized a bolt of cloth; and another man. Words were exchanged—no doubt stimulated by time-honored customs of social inversion during the days of Carnival—and the infuriated Sauclières ran Alias through with the sword that his office privileged him to carry. Alias died the next morning. Sauclières fled to his familial home in Gignac, cashed in some bonds, and proceeded to slow the process of justice in Lodève with some well-placed bribes. But the widow of Alias was not easily forestalled. Through the intermediary of a curé at the parish church of St. Pierre, where the *confrérie* of the weavers held their ceremonies, she communicated her distress to the Intendant, pointing out that two witnesses—her husband's companions—had not been called to testify. In August a notarial entry shows widow Allias receiving 2,000 livres in compensation for abandoning all further action against Sauclières—who in turn would "henceforth fix his domicile elsewhere." Sauclières was happy to oblige: he had just received an appointment as a royal inspector of manufactures in the Auvergne.

Precisely one hundred years later, Lodève witnessed another famous murder, but the terms of trade in human life had changed dramatically. For on May 19, 1849, again at 11 P.M. in the ill-lit streets of the old city, the main judicial official in the town, Paul Adam, recently appointed to enforce the

*I wish to express my thanks to the National Endowment for the Humanities for making the research for this paper possible.

reaction in the wake of the upheaval of 1848, died of multiple stab wounds administered by a small band of woolens workers. And they got away with it, too. Not due, however, to the power of money, position, and privilege, but to the power of a proletariat united. It became quickly apparent to officials that two brothers named Balp—both weavers— had been the principal agents of the crime, that it was planned in advance and very probably blessed by the chief of the democratic socialist movement in Lodève, Moïse Lyon, but no witnesses to the crime nor to the circumstances leading up to it could be found. The popular classes of this ancient woolens city in Languedoc simply clammed up. Officials were hesitant to indict on circumstantial evidence not so much, it would seem, because of legal scruples, but because of the storm that arrests without solid evidence might unleash.[1] By that time they had three decades of experience with this working class upon which to base their prudence. What had happened in the century between these two events—so similar in nature, so totally different in the historical circumstances they symbolize—will be the main focus on this essay.

Let us switch to Paris—and to another death. In November 1831 a thirty-year-old German-born master tailor named Joseph Cornély died in the insanity ward of the Bicêtre prison shortly after final action had been taken on his bankruptcy proceedings. The *Journal des Tailleurs*, the trade journal reporting his obituary, remarked that the real cause of his dementia and death was the collapse of his reputation, the destruction of his pride as a skilled and honorable artisan. Cornély came to Paris in 1819, quickly gained attention as a marvelous journeyman to whom "several master tailors today owe their fortunes," and set up his own shop in 1825 on borrowed money. But the crisis of the late twenties took its toll, and the glorious expectations of this young life were dashed.

Seventeen years later, on the night of June 23, 1848, the warehouse and cutting shop in the Rue Rocquette belonging to Adolphe Parissot, owner of the ready-made clothes business and department store still known as La Belle Jardinère, was burned to the ground. Specific responsibility for this act was never determined, but Parissot assumed it was the work of journeymen and small master tailors. Two incidents that again dramatically characterize a process: a petty half-capitalist half-artisan dying with his head between his knees in debtors' prison, destroyed by the power of money (if not position and privilege), and two turbulent decades later an enterprising capitalist in the clothing industry seriously wounded by people who might well have been Cornély in 1831.[2] The story of those intervening years and a good number preceding them provides my second focus.

These are vivid tales in the history of proletarianization and help to define the temporal and contextual dimensions of the problem to be explored here. I shall be examining aspects of working-class formation typical of the transitional era between the stages of industrial development popularly termed protoindustrialization and the industrial revolution. In general, it is a phase of rapid acceleration of objective proletarianization, simply defined as the increase, both absolute and proportionate, in the number of wage laborers in a given population and their increasing domination by capitalists.

But proletarianization is also a *subjective* process: one must ask questions about what it means to be a proletarian, about class unity, about social conflict, about consciousness, in short, about proletarian behavior. And it is the dialectical interplay between objective conditions of change and subjective reactions to change that provides the real fascination of the entire process.[3]

Few would maintain today that proletarianization has been merely a function of technological development. The imposition of the division and specialization of labor, the wrenching of control over the means and, indeed, the knowledge of production, the disciplining of the labor force, and the creation of replaceable labor units: such capitalist strategies predate the rise of modern industrial technology and prepare the way for it. It is not absurd to argue, in fact, that machine production, the factory system, Taylorism, and the assembly line must be viewed as much as elements in the further disciplining and controlling of the labor force as devices to achieve greater technical efficiency.[4]

The crucial point is that the evolution of industrial capitalism must be understood in terms of *structural* change—from the structure of the world economy at the broadest and most abstract level down to business organization, community structure, and the structure of work in home, shop, or factory. It is at this lowest level that the daily reality of proletarianization was played out. The local focus is particularly relevant when dealing with the transitional age between the stages of protoindustrialization and machine production. One can view the process of proletarianization in a detailed and concrete fashion and, given the relatively severe decentralization of the economy, feel assured that he is at the core of the problem.

The case studies that have occupied my research interests for several years concern two patterns of proletarianization during this transitional phase. The first fixes upon the path of large-city artisans as structural change engulfs their handicraft industries, the second upon small monoindustrial towns whose industrial character was set well before the machine revolution. In my earlier work on the appeal of radical ideas among French working people and on the incidence of militance expressed through strike activity and sociopolitical protest, I was consistently struck by the fact that, along with large-city artisans, the worker populations of old, small, industrial cities known for a particular kind of manufactured product, crop up again and again: places in France like Vienne, Reims, Niort, Rive-de-Gier, Elbeuf, Mirecourt, Troyes, and Lodève, as well as its nearby sister cities in woolens, Clermont l'Hérault and Bédarieux.[5] For such cities as for the large-city artisans, the Revolution of 1848 was more an end of an era than a beginning. Thereafter, the focus of industrialization, proletarianization, and militance tends to shift to the industrial *villes-champignons*, such as the Lille-Roubaix-Tourcoing complex or Clermont-Ferrand and to thriving port cities such as

Marseille or LeHavre. Paris and Lyon, of course, hardly fade from the scene, and their proletarianized artisans continue to play a leading role in the working-class movement, but they increasingly share the stage with workers, especially skilled workers, from the "modern" sector.

Thus the scene is France, 1750 to 1850, the problem urban proletariani-zation, and the examples a single Parisian craft, tailoring for men, and an old, small, essentially monoindustrial manufacturing town, Lodève.

Journeyman tailors stood at the forefront of the Parisian class struggle during the 1830s and 1840s.[6] Their craft union organization became a model for others, they initiated the great strike of 1840 that included dozens of other trades, they flocked to radical political movements of all sorts, and above all, they pioneered the development of producers' associations, especially through their highly successful cooperative set up in 1848 in the former debtors' prison of Clichy. The search for the causes of such behavior led me to the careful study of the changing structure of the tailoring industry during the first half of the century. What had occured was the full swing from a corporative, or guild, mode of production to an industrial capitalist one over the fifty years after the French Revolution. And this change had unfolded without the least mechanization of the industry. Two broad stages in the process can be identified. The first involved personnel within the old corporate structure of prerevolutionary France as larger master tailors expanded their operations in two basic ways. First, they began to maintain large stocks of cloth and developed elaborate credit arrangements with their suppliers, the cloth mer-chants. Secondly, they profoundly altered the relations of production by increasing the size of their work force, dividing specific tasks according to a hierarchy of skills, and most ominous of all, by hiring unapprenticed home workers, largely women, to sew simpler garments, such as trousers and vests, at half the wage of a journeyman. In the shops of these merchant tailors, as they came to be called, the live-in journeyman became a thing of the past. The abolition of the guilds during the Revolution, of course, had been the fundamental legal base for this development. By the mid-twenties, out of approximately 1,800 tailoring shops operating in Paris, perhaps 200 were run by merchant tailors. But most of the smaller traditional masters were also prospering due to lower costs of cloth, Paris's growing population of middle-income people, and her reputation that attracted flocks of provincial and foreign bourgeois to her shops. Journeymen also benefitted: real wages rose an estimated 15 percent from 1800 to 1825. In short, tailoring experienced a "golden age" in the first twenty-five years of the nineteenth century. But storm clouds were beginning to gather.

The industry became overcrowded, and with the depression of the late twenties, the scene was set for the second stage in the structural change that transformed Parisian tailoring for men. This was the rise of *confection*, ready-made clothing produced in standardized sizes and marketed through depart-ment stores. Here the thrust came from outside the craft as large cloth merchants brought their capital, market connections, and entrepreneurial skills into the business. Their basic strategy was to hire cheap, unapprenticed labor who worked for them or their subcontractors at home. Only the highly skilled cutting operations were carried out on their premises. But journeymen in bespoke tailoring also did homework for them, especially during the slack season of the made-to-order industry. Confection, producing for anonymous sale, could work the year 'round.

A few simple figures from the inquiry on Parisian industry in 1847 tell the story of what happened during the July Monarchy. In that year, Parisian tailoring as a whole had gross sales of over 80 million francs, and confection accounted for a third of it. The share of the bespoke tailors was 60 percent. Another 7 percent derived from the activity of subcontractors called *appiéceurs*, many of whom also worked for the ready-made magnates. The work force in bespoke tailoring was 9,765 people, while ready-made employed a disproportionately high number, 7,445, indicating an important fact: ready-made was labor-intensive and relied on cheap labor for its success. The number of confectionneurs in Paris was a mere 223 while that of master bespoke tailors was 3,012. The confectionneurs' gross sales averaged 125,000 francs and the bespoke tailors only 16,000. But the *merchant*-tailor was not the one who paid with the rise of ready-made. Among all tailoring firms exceeding 100,000 francs of business per year, 56 bespoke tailors were represented, and the total number of merchant tailors had increased by 250 percent since 1830.

But the vast majority of bespoke tailors were very small operators. Three-fifths had gross sales of less than 5,000 francs. Even figuring a profit margin of 20 percent, the yearly income of a majority of bespoke master tailors in Paris was about the same as a steadily employed journeyman in the trade.[7]

Finally, the volume of business in the whole industry had just about doubled since 1825. The lion's share of this went to the ready-made business to be sure, but the big merchant tailor in bespoke tailoring got his due as well.

Revolutions in marketing and industrial structure had occurred. The small master either fell into the ranks of the wage earners or eked out an existence against insurmountable odds. Or he became a subcontractor of sweated labor. On the other hand, the merchant-tailors survived by accentuating trends they had begun and by copying the capitalist practices of the confectionneurs. By 1848 over half of their work force worked at home and around 40 percent of their workers were women. They also took on subcontracted labor as heavily as the ready-made people. The great new force, then, in the wage-earning categories of tailoring was sweated labor. Their wages were 60 percent of that of the in-shop journeyman, they were totally unorganized, and their hours totally unregulated.

What happened to the work life of the journeyman tailor? First, his skill level deteriorated. The old system called upon the shop journeyman to learn every aspect of the trade, but the new one led to specialization and an elaborate division of labor. Only an elite of cutters maintained the old diversity of knowledge. Rationalization, efficiency, lower costs—and, for the worker, monotony and, above all, *partial* training—became the hallmarks of the trade. Only the small shops retained the tradition of multiskilled activities, but they were being crushed. Then there was the insecurity of employment. Tailoring had always been seasonal—heavy demand in the spring and fall. But the competition of ready-made goods caused *bespoke* employers to push harder in rush times, lay off more and earlier in slack. Finally, journeyman's wages declined after 1830 under the inevitable calculus of labor competition. The misery of sweated labor produced the hardship of the journeyman shopworker.

Whom did the journeymen attack? At first, their direct employers, the bespoke masters. They did so largely through typical trade union activity. Around 1846 and especially in 1848 they increasingly turned their wrath toward confectionneurs such as Parissot and were joined by many small masters as well. Spurred on by dreams of a past independence they never really had, tailors fused together in struggle. They were artisans whose work and beings were being de-artisanized. With their corporate traditions, long urban experience, a strong sense of self-worth, and—not incidentally—a high level of literacy, they joined one army in the working class war against emergent industrial capitalism.

Tailors fought beside cabinetmakers now forced to sell cheap goods to jobbers or peddle their finer products on the streets; beside shoemakers chained to subcontractors of leather merchants, waiting in houses on call for orders or simply roaming the streets in search of customers; beside masons, carpenters, and joiners no longer called to work by customers who wanted a building put up, but by building-trade entrepreneurs, or rather their sub-contracted agents in the trade.

The large-city artisans of France, proletarianized by structural change, thus formed one wing of the working class movement. But the form and ideology of their struggle reflected the peculiarities of their artisan past and the rather isolated experiences of their proletarianization. The consequence was the development of powerful and militant, yet essentially limited *craft consciousness*, seen especially in their orientation toward producers coopera-tives. The ideological outcome, analyzed with precision in a recent book by Bernard Moss, was a federalist trade socialism, or in Moss's words, "a form of socialism that would preserve the autonomy and integrity of the trade."[8]

Let us now turn to another world of struggle against industrial capitalism in mid-nineteenth-century France, the small, old, monoindustrial city. Here, the pressures of structural change often went deep into the eighteenth century and resulted in the meshing together of functionally separate crafts as their traditional corporative autonomy was destroyed. In contrast to the large city artisans, workers in such towns were thrown together by objective forces of industrial change and forged a unity of purpose which emphasized intercraft cooperation and the struggle for control of the entire community. They were, I suppose one might say, "truer"proletarians than the Parisian tailors and their kin; they might be viewed as more exact prototypes of the modern industrial proletariat, harbingers as they were of industrial unionism and class-conscious socialism. But if large city artisans operated in relative craft isolation, they did so in relative geographical isolation. Lodève provides an excellent laboratory for assessing the various processes at work. Some of my preliminary findings about this Languedoc city may prove useful in stimulating further thought on this pattern of proletarianization.

The main center of woolen cloth production for the army, which ensured a secure if highly fluctuating market, Lodève was a bustling town of 12,000 people in 1851. Fully 45 percent of the city's active population found employment in the woolens industry, another 2 percent owned it, and most of its artisans, shopkeepers, and professionals owed their livelihood to it. Lodève had a large agricultural population that also had various ties with the industry. Lodève was and is a physically small city—one can walk across it in any direction in ten minutes. Its housing is densely packed together, opening up only along the quays of the Lergue and Solandres rivers, the lifeblood of the industry with their clear waters and rapid flow, and in the Place St. Fulcran before the ancient cathedral and the episcopal palace that became the city hall during the French Revolution. In the mid-nineteenth century the town was socially segregated. The large houses of the *fabricants* (the owners) and professionals were located in the upper town near St. Fulcran. The workshops and shops of the artisans and retailers dotted the central city. Woolens workers were concentrated in the lower city—the old parish of St. Pierre—and especially in the faubourgs across the rivers, Montbrun and Carmes. The agricultural workers and the small number of peasant proprietors tended to be located in the peripheral areas of the city, though they were found in significant numbers in all *quartiers*.[9]

Such was the general look of Lodève in the mid-nineteenth century. What went on inside its confines? Essentially, a class struggle of epic proportions. Which brings us back to why the Balp brothers got away with murder. Space prevents a full presentation of the evidence proving the proletarian character of this city. But a few key points should be stressed. Hardly a year passed between 1821 and 1848 in which *some* kind of collective working class action did not occur. Full-fledged work stoppages in the woolens industry occurred in twelve of those twenty-seven years. These strikes share several important characteristics.[10] First, all occurred when the *fabrique* was besieged with orders. Woolens workers did not strike defensively. Second, strike activity, while generally initiated by workers in a particular craft (such as the croppers in 1821 or the spinners in 1831 or the weavers in 1834 and 1845) won universal support in the other woolens crafts. Moreover, women workers often stood at the forefront of the movement—as in 1821, when women pelted gendarmes and scabs with stones. And nonwoolens workers were involved in crowd manifestations associated with the strikes, while retail merchants were generous with credit during strike periods. If scabs were to be found, they had to be imported. Third, if Luddism, the struggle against the machine, went on, it occurred in the context of a complex of other issues. In 1821, croppers and their allies actually managed to stop the introduction of the first *tondeuse,* or cropping machine, into Lodève, but the action also led to demands by spinners and weavers for pay increases, which came the following year with a new strike. The tondeuse arrived successfully in 1823 and provoked a strike, the outcome of which guaranteed no layoffs, past wage levels, and worker training in the operation and maintenance of the machine. The strikes of 1831–34 and 1839–40 had nothing at all to do with machinery, being focussed instead on regaining earlier piece rates, equalizing pay from work-shop to workshop, and bettering working conditions among weavers and spinners. The great 1845 strike *began* as a reaction to the introduction of the power loom, but soon gave way to a general struggle over piece rates, fine systems, and a host of work-related grievances. The king's prosecutor (*procureur du roi*), hardly a friend of the workers, finally declared after a long discussion with the bosses that the real goal of the fabricants in their massive efforts to break the strike was not specifically to protect or enhance their profits, but that for them "it was a question of *mastery,* that it was necessary for a master to govern his workers, failing which the latter would not work." And machinery was a means more surely to effectuate that end. For Lodève workers, then, the struggle against the machine was not the last gasp of dying artisans, but a sophisticated and variegated response to their employers' efforts to enhance their dominant position. Fourth, and perhaps most important, throughout this period, the Lodève woolens workers main-tained associational links, the concrete dimensions and structures of which completely eluded police surveillance. As with the Adam assassination, officials *knew* they were there but could not prosecute. The subprefect lamented in 1834 that "the workers employed in woolens manufacture are associated by *corps d'état* or profession." Moreover, "they are associated as a mass in ways impossible to determine."[11] One has the impression of an incredible network of professional, social, and familial links, all intertwined, that produced virtually instantaneous action when needed.

Strike strategy indicated an elaborate organizational base. For example, the strike of 1834, begun by handloom weavers objecting to an uncom-pensated increase in the size of the cloth, quickly turned to demands for increases beyond the compensation. A single, twenty-four-loom weavers' shed, that of Jourdan, was selected as the focus, and its strikers were monetarily supported by the rest of the weavers. As Jourdan, pressed with heavy orders, began to waver, his machine spinners and carders went out, and the weavers upped their demands to include an *indemnity* for the time they had lost while on strike! This was followed by another selective strike of spinners at Pascal's. The subprefect was convinced that this intercraft action was planned in advance and supported by the bulk of the town's woolens workers, who would then seek to generalize the wage standards set at Jourdan's. This became clear when, on January 27, 1834, a huge demon-stration of seven hundred Lodève workers was organized to protest the failure of the mayor to validate work passports of four Jourdan weavers who wanted to go to Bédarieux to seek work. What occurred at the end of the march, on the route to Bédarieux, symbolizes the dimensions of the class struggle in Lodève. The National guard had not been called out because it was unreliable; as a police report noted, the guardsmen "are mostly proprietors and artisans who are little disposed to show favor to the fabricants against the workers." Thus only the subprefect Brun and a few gendarmes were there to meet the crowd. Brun declared the entire body of marchers under arrest, to which their leader, the weaver Jacquesjean, responded that they were merely exercising their historic rights as compagnons to see their brothers off on the Tour de France! The humor of it all escaped Brun, as did the next incident: a spinner named Ollier dashed from the crowd, grabbed one of the *garde champêtre*'s sword, and scurried back, waving it over his head to the laughter of seven hundred voices. The chief of police, a squat retired army captain and relative of the powerful Fabreguettes fabricant family, saved some face for the other side by wading into the crowd and retrieving it. Brun then proceeded to try to arrest the front row of demonstrators, who quickly pinned his arms to his sides and then quietly disarmed the motley band of justice's defenders. The farce was over. Brun and his companions were left sputtering in the twilight as the crowd disappeared into the streets, courts and doorways of the city.

The effect of this action was twofold. First, the fabricants caved in, for the rush of orders was too great. They even promised that no arrests would be made in connection with the demonstration. But, second, Brun and his superiors in Montpellier and Paris refused to submit to such intimidation. Thus, on February 5 an attempt to arrest the four weavers now back at work chez Jourdan resulted in a two-day, clearly political strike in which the entire woolens industry was closed down in a stroke. It was now a struggle for the very soul of the town. In the dénouement, the woolens workers did not win, as the town was infested with troops. But neither did they lose. Their economic strike demands had been met, their collective strength in the community was made obvious, and they had gained an important psychological edge.[12] A working-class presence was manifest.

And this manifestation went well beyond strikes: anticlerical demonstrations, July Revolution festivals, political meetings in the countryside, constant cafe gatherings, numerous examples of in-shop protests under the clear direction of shop stewards, and dozens of other activities demonstrated the unified and determined struggle for power unfolding under the July Monarchy.[13] And during the Second Republic, the Lodève proletariat came to democratic socialism en masse, became the only working class in France simply to take over the writing of the cantonal inquiry on agricultural and industrial work, and then defied the reaction through outright murder, secret societies, and finally resistance to the coup d'état.

The central question is how did it get that way? This is a more complicated problem than locating the foundations of craft consciousness among proletarianizing artisans, for while changing work structures stimulated the process of proletarianization and impelled this working class toward unity, sociodemographic, ecological, and general community structural considerations played just as important a part. But there was a clear chronology. The years from 1740 to around 1800 comprised the main period for changes in work structure and the power relations on the job. This transformation occurred before machine technology had made any significant impact at all and largely in the political context of the Old Regime. The second set of factors, those relating to community structure, seem to date from around 1780 and continue to function in the making of this working class down to the Second Republic.

Let us briefly outline the first.[14] Seventeen twenty-nine is probably the key date in the history of Lodève, for in that year Cardinal Fleury, her most famous native son, directed the bulk of the army orders for woolen cloth to this little city of about four thousand souls, and the peculiar rhythm of the city's industrial life was established. The sharp ebb and flow of orders, which followed the military situation, created constant boom and bust alterations.

In the first years of the eighteenth century, before the new army demand, the structure of production in Lodève was typically corporative: the main stages of manufacturing were controlled by guilds whose regulations were recognized under public law. And by law, all processes were to take place within the city. The merchant-manufacturers, or fabricants, formed the first and most influential guild. They had already gained full control over the materials of production and, in typical fashion, put out the wool and carried it through all the stages of manufacture, finally marketing the finished cloth. The first steps of production—degreasing, washing, fluffing, and sorting—were carried out by wage-earning employees of the fabricants (mainly women) who worked in the fabricants' warehouses and in the shallow beds in the rivers nearby. The prepared wool was then put out on a contractual basis to carders whose guild structure was already weak at the opening of the century, having been unable to prevent nonguildsmen from entering the trade. The fabricants had paved the way by offering to supply expensive carding tools and oil to the interlopers. Both guild and nonguild carders subcontracted almost exclusively female home labor for spinning, generally providing them with their wheels. This large labor force worked for piece wages.

The weaver's guild commanded the next step in the process. Master weavers maintained their own shops, generally owned their looms, and usually kept one journeyman and one apprentice. It was a male craft. They often contracted with specialists who had rights, through the guild, to string the warp of the loom and bathe the finished warp in light glue. Such operations, however, might also be done by family members. An efficient shop would have at least two looms. Weavers were never wealthy, but were without question the hub of the industry. The legal support of their guild regulations, control over access to mastership, and the maintenance of monopoly rights over cloth bearing the *marque de Lodève*—these were the keys to their independence and power. Their confrérie, with its patron saints, processions, ceremonies, and social events, cemented their bond of brotherhood.

The cloth was then returned to the fabricants' warehouses and submitted to *épotoyage,* the pulling of woof threads to remove irregularities, done by women who doubled as sorters and were in the direct employ of the fabricant. Fulling came next and was carried out in water-powered mills generally owned by the fabricants. These mills were manned by skilled managers whose contractual relations with the fabricants varied widely.

The finishing processes were turned over to the true elite of producers in Lodève and members of the strongest guild beneath that of the fabricants, the *pareurs* or teaselers. They took the rough cloth from the fulling process through the final stages of teasing, cropping, squaring, and folding. The cloth was then returned to the warehouse for the final pressing. All the skilled men associated with the finishing process contracted with master pareurs and were associated in their guild. They tended to be richer than weavers and like them, were protected through their guild regulations and their confrérie. Dyers, less prominent in Lodève because of the nature of its product, shared the characteristics of the fullers.

Prices of all work involving guild interrelationships were set by elaborate codes agreed upon by the guilds through the arbitration of the royal inspector. Workers outside guild protection were paid according to the laws of supply and demand, as was subcontracted labor. Agreement between fabricants and fullers and dyers responded to market conditions as well. Final quality control was exclusively in the hands of the *jurés-gardes,* a six-man elected board of fabricants who reported to the inspector.

Lodève's woolens industry thus operated on the basis of a hodgepodge of market and corporative principles in which the proletarian characteristics of its work force were minimal.

The transformation of the eighteenth century was decisive. It evolved in two basic stages: (1) the drastic alterations accompanying the initial impact of large army orders and most keenly felt during the war of Austrian succession, which obliterated the authority of the weavers' and pareurs' guilds, and (2) the more subtle changes occuring during and after the American War for Independence that commenced the trend toward a factory system without machines.

The first was marked by the collapse of the legal buttresses supporting the position of the two key producers' guilds. The 1730s witnessed the proliferation of rural carding and spinning, which was then followed by rural weaving. The latter developed especially in the early forties when orders doubled virtually overnight. It was illegal, but the law turned a deaf ear to the Lodève weavers. Next came the push by fabricants to get individual master weavers to work for only one manufacturer, which they contrived by offering generous advances and catching many weavers in a form of peonage. Significant pay differentials began to emerge. Then came the inevitable—the hiring of nonguild weavers in Lodève itself, largely migrants from weaving villages. One can imagine their reception in the weavers' community at the time, but the law—ultimately validated by the Estates of Languedoc—supported the fabricants' drive for free enterprise. At the same time, entrance into the fabricants' guild became increasingly difficult, above all due to the skyrocketing cost of the mastership fee: 300 livres in 1708, it rose to 1,050 livres by 1749, but with the crucial proviso that the sons of fabricants would be required to pay a mere 200.[15] The fabricants were becoming a closed caste. The merchant-manufacturers' struggle against the pareurs followed a pattern similar to that against the weavers, but since rural competition was largely impossible given the skill requirements of the finishing crafts, the path was more difficult. Nevertheless, during the forties, the same policies of entrapment and hiring nonguild workers ensued. To a vociferous protest by the pareurs, the inspector general in Montpellier issued this chilling decision: "Contract, day, and pieceworkers of his province would like to lord it over those who give them subsistance. It would not be convenient to send their request further, a request that must only be answered by a resounding no!"[16] Lyonnais silk weavers had a similar experience at about the same time. Maurice Garden's comments regarding the changing face of the law under the impact of economic expansion in the eighteenth century are well taken.[17]

The guilds were broken and the logic of industrial capitalism took hold in Lodève. Stage two added at least four new ingredients. First and above all, was the drive to concentrate carders, weavers, pareurs, and their adjunct crafts into factory-like contexts under the eye of the boss and operating on his time schedule. The process was nearing completion by the time of the Revolution, as indicated by a petition to the Convention from distraught home workers.[18] Second was the employment of female workers in weaving. The word *tisserande* would have been a contradiction in terms in 1740. By 1800 approximately one-fourth of the weavers of Lodève were women, although they may not have put in the same hours annually as the men. Third, the segregation of housing accentuated during the second half of the century, especially since the population of Lodève had increased by about three thousand. In 1798, 34 percent of Lodève's population were migrants, the vast majority of whom came to the city as young adults. They located where rentals were cheap—in the teeming parish of St. Pierre and especially in the faubourgs. The patterns of human ecology of 1851 were well in place by 1800. Fourth, the origins of migrants who are found in the woolens trade in 1798 changed significantly from the time of the American Revolution on, while the rural putting-out system in the Lodève area declined. A *reurbanization* of the industry was occurring. Manufacturers, having broken the guilds, now reduced their reliance on the more distant and less stable rural work force and increasingly sought experienced urban weavers willing to accept proletarian status. These they found: 70 percent of the migrant weavers who arrived in Lodève after 1778 came from *depressed* woolens centers still operating under modified corporative structures—towns such as St. Pons,

Riols, St. Chinian, Lacaune, and St. Affrique, or from towns which were themselves following the Lodève pattern, such as Clermont and Bédarieux. Migrants from distraught outworking villages arrived as well, but their success rates as measured by home ownership were not nearly that of the previous generation. Lodève belonged to the fabricants; they had a proletarianized population to do their bidding.[19]

But by the 1820s, and particularly by the 1830s, this population increasingly refused to do their bidding. Bear in mind that during the Napoleonic years, Lodève prospered. Army orders were naturally high, but manpower relatively scarce. This improved the bargaining position of the woolens workers, especially in terms of wages, but it also stimulated further efforts on the part of the fabricants to rationalize production. During this era, carding and spinning underwent significant mechanization and the use of female labor in handloom weaving sheds accelerated. Neither trend appears to have provoked much protest for two interconnected reasons: the manner in which labor was redeployed and the maintenance of levels of family earnings. Hand carders, already more proletarianized than any other craft, became carding and spinning machine tenders, indeed foremen, often for the same fabricant for whom they worked as hand carders. The female hand spinners also found work in mechanical spinneries, as did their children. In many cases it must have been simply a matter of whole families moving from nonmechanized to mechanized work. The spinning factories were small, and the machines carried a low number of spindles and were crude devices in need of constant attention from workers. Redundant female hand spinners, moreover, could easily move into handloom weaving jobs. The central fact, I think, was that the operation of the workers' family economy could remain intact. Overall—the second point—what we are witnessing is the historic trade-off of pay, on the one hand, for job reclassification involving greater domination by the boss, on the other. In general, then, the empire saw some fairly severe alterations of work structure, but also, because of the constancy of employment and decent pay, took on the allure of a kind of "golden age." It was followed by severely depressed conditions, from 1814 to 1821, which carries us up to the beginning of Lodève's age of proletarian revolt.[20]

But the proletarian character of this city was for all intents and purposes fixed before these two decades of mechanization, prosperity, and collapse. Let me lay out some of the evidence demonstrating the level of working-class integration—bases for the subjective unity of this proletariat—that I have been able to draw from the remarkable census of 1798. This census, taken for unknown local reasons, is to my knowledge without parallel in France at this early date and includes (besides normal information such as age, sex, occupation, family relationships, household and house data) home ownership, precise birthplace, *and* the number of years migrants had been in Lodève at that date. It is a gold mine, and I am still in the process of analyzing the mass of information that it can yield.[21]

The central question here is this: To what extent was the in-migrant population of Lodève integrated into its working class? All the evidence in the world proving that changing structures of work and industrial organization were pushing toward the formation of a proletariat does not necessarily demonstrate that proletarian unity occured. People might face precisely the same objective conditions on the job, be thoroughly similar in their income status, and hate each other's guts. Just talk to Black and Polish workers in Detroit's Dodge Main. Migrants, the circumstances of their arrival, their role in the economy, their cultural peculiarities, their manner of living and relating to the host population, and many other factors, can and have historically muddied the clearest of objective analyses of why a conscious proletariat *ought* to exist in any given context. Migrants can also have a positive effect on class formation and emergent consciousness, as Sewell has shown for nineteenth-century Marseille and Agulhon, for Toulon. But the more typical situation is that described by Pierre Guillaume working on nineteenth-century Bordeaux: the large flow of in-migrants came from backgrounds alien to old Bordeaux working people; they settled in clusters, developed self-sustaining communities, and were seen as job competitors. This provides one of the bases for his explanation of the low level of labor militance in the city. I have been impressed with the same kind of thing in studying a much smaller city, Mazamet in the Tarn.[22]

It seems to me that in-migrants can negatively effect proletarian unity in two basic ways: that they form self-insulated colonies in a city in which their village or home cultures are significantly maintained and where the focus of their attention is "back home." Chain migration, kin and regional ties in the host city, housing segregation, and lots of coming and going between city and place of origin are some of the indicators of their situation. The other situation—although now proved much rarer—is that of the marginal migrant without these kinds of ties, but also without any real ties to the host city either—floaters, distracted and distraught, whom the liberal social patholo-gists of a generation ago erroneously thought were the real troublemakers in the urbanization process.[23] But neither the insulated nor the marginal in-migrant is integrated into the working class of the city as a whole, and the larger their numbers, the less likely is that city to manifest proletarian unity and class consciousness. How does the Lodève worker population meet the test of migrant absorption? We are talking about people who comprise one-third of the city's population of 7,200 in 1798. The answer is very well indeed. Rural migrants, at least woolens workers, may well have been received with antagonism in the mid-eighteenth century: the fact that they tended to marry other migrants, often from their home areas, is one indi-cation of their reception. But this flow slowed down and gave way to the arrival of more urban woolens workers; in any case, the work framework in Lodève had changed sufficiently so that migrants were no longer being used to break the corporative industrial structures. Another indication was that migrants in woolens lived thoroughly intermingled with all the other Lodève-born woolens workers. Artisan and retailer migrants lived with their kind and professionals and the few migrant manufacturers with theirs. Sociooccupational segregation in housing was clearly a more prominent feature of turn-of-the-century Lodève than place-of-origin colonies—*except,* perhaps, for the agricultural workers, to whom we shall return.

The following facts further demonstrate the integration of migrants into Lodève's working class population. Chain migration, either in the form of kin following kin or of people from the same village following each other, is little evident. The three Cunienq brothers, all weavers from Riols who came in 1782, 1784, and 1792, are interesting because they are so exceptional. Michael Anderson's famous examples of migrant sibling or kin living in with working-class families already established is virtually unknown in Lodève in 1798. The only tendency of this order of statistically relevant proportions is the case where widowed parents, usually women, come to live with their children's families long after the children have migrated. Extended family structures in general are rarer among households of migrant heads of all occupations than among Lodèvois unless the migrant has become a home-owner. Again, the only occupational group where the vaguest indications of chain migration are discernable is among agricultural workers.[24]

The age, character, and marriage patterns of migrants, however, provide the surest evidence of my thesis. Migrants to Lodève, male or female, wherever they came from, whenever they came, overwhelmingly arrived as single young adults. They migrated for work-related reasons and they married in Lodève generally after several years of residence. Whom did they marry? Men and women from back home? Almost never. At least other migrants? No—not normally—and here is the central point. Migrants, male and female, tended to tie themselves to established Lodève families through the process of marriage, except again among agricultural workers. Special attention should be drawn to male woolens workers. Out of ninety-eight migrants in the trade who were married (another seventy were not), seventy-five had married Lodève women, and only two of those who married migrants had wed a woman from "back home." Moreover, marriage records indicate a strong tendency among migrant woolens workers to marry daughters of Lodève woolens workers.[25] Finally, female migrants were perfectly acceptable wives for Lodève-born woolens workers. One-third of their marriages were contracted with migrants.

These figures take on greater significance when compared with other occupational categories. If 76 percent of migrant woolens workers married Lodèvoises, the figures are 66 percent for building trade artisans and 58 percent for other artisans and retailers. In other words, the last fell somewhat below the figure of simple random choice of all available partners. But the majority of agricultural workers (*brassiers*) were migrants, and these men overwhelmingly tended to marry other migrants: only 34 percent of all migrant brassiers found Lodève wives, exactly reversing the random expectation.

In general, the situation of agricultural workers differed from that of woolens workers. They appear in this census as the proletarian element least integrated into the life of the city. In 1798, they made up a larger percentage of the active population than they would in 1851: 26 percent as opposed to 21 percent. Their migrant wives, especially, tended more to cluster in Lodève neighborhoods with fellow villagers, and evidence of family chain migration among agricultural workers is stronger as well. Although they had the least access to home ownership of any major occupational group, if they *did* buy a house or part of a house (which was more normal), they maintained extended families at about double the rate of migrant woolens workers, thus exhibiting similarities to practices in this regard of the small peasant proprietors in the rural areas of the Causses, or uplands, from which most of them had come.[26] In short, if Lodève had "urban villagers," whose life-style and situation differed from the rest of the proletarian population, they were, not surprisingly, the agricultural workers.

But this tended to change as the decades passed. Most important, marriage documents examined each decade after 1806 showed that sons of agricultural workers were becoming woolens workers with increasing ease and that intermarriage between agricultural and woolens families was common.[27] Moreover, the census of 1851 reveals that over half the wives of men listed as agricultural workers held jobs, at least part-time, in the woolens industry.[28] Still, a caveat should be registered: in expressions of worker militance through the nineteenth century, the role of agricultural laborers was modest. They do not appear to have served as a force limiting the rise of working-class consciousness in Lodève, but neither did they contribute to it.

The place of Lodève's artisan and shopkeeper population provides fewer difficulties. Although they tended to live in the central parts of the city, largely for commercial reasons, a variety of factors tied them increasingly to the woolens workers. Most obviously—and already stressed—their principal customers, save for an elite few, were woolens workers. Their shops were often gathering places for socializing and discussion among woolens workers.[29] Moreover, as the nineteenth century progressed, intermarriage between members of the lower levels of the artisan and shopkeeper community (tailors, shoemakers, masons, street-stall operators, mule-train men and the like) and woolens workers increased. They were notoriously unreliable National Guardsmen during the July Monarchy, and in 1848 and after, large numbers of them were to be found in the ranks of protesters. For example, among those arrested in the wake of the coup d'état, they comprise a proportion almost exactly the same as their proportion in the active population of the city at large, with tailors being especially prominent.[30] Overall, the artisans and shopkeepers of the city tended to throw their weight to the side of the woolens workers as the class struggle in nineteenth-century Lodève unfolded.

This comparative analysis of two early patterns of proletarianization suggests several conclusions. In both cases, we are dealing with the collapse of corporative modes of production as capitalist practices pervade the manufacturing process. The structural change in the organization of production precedes any major technological change and indeed paves the way for it. And the legal framework in which such changes occur is crucial—for Parisian tailoring, it was the licence given to laissez-faire resulting from the French Revolution, but for Lodève, an earlier, more subtle process involving a series of specific decisions in the mid-eighteenth century. In general, then, the structural transformations in both cases bear marked similarities, although they operate on a different timetable. But this difference is fundamental, as is the totally different social and geographical context in which the transformation occurs. Both the tailors' and the Lodève movements reached a climax at roughly the same time—the mid-nineteenth century. Yet the tailors were at that point in the full throes of de-artisanization in a context in which their corporate traditions continued to play a basic role in their mentality. They did not try to organize their entire industry against capitalist exploitation. In fact they regarded the sweated labor produced by merchant-tailors and ready-made entrepreneurs as their enemies. More telling still is the fact that as the Clichy producers' cooperative achieved success in 1849, it too began to *hire* sweated labor. Suggestions of antagonism against new workers outside the corporation were certainly there in eighteenth-century Lodève, but by the mid-nineteenth century virtually all vestiges of corporate exclusivism had disappeared. Thus, on the one hand, the tailors and other large-city artisans undergoing proletarianization bequeath to the later nineteenth-century labor movement a powerful ideology of craft-conscious trade socialism, whereas, on the other, Lodève workers and their bretheren in small, old industrial towns leave an inheritance of vociferous class consciousness, industrial unionism, and democratic socialism broadly conceived. But all this existed in miniature. The established, intensively interactive, and industrially integrated city that produced this true proletariat was, after all, very small and relatively isolated. The final irony was that Lodève did not survive as an industrial city in the later nineteenth century. One can argue that the specialized nature of its market, the developing obsolescence of its technology, the competition of the north, the advance of the vine in the south, and even the betrayal of its governmental patron, Michel Chevalier, were responsible for this collapse. But figuring into every aspect of such arguments was an overriding fact: this was a proletarian city and its proletariat was *too* powerful.

I would like to conclude with a methodological comment. In recent years, considerable attention has been devoted to the study of work structure in analyzing the process of proletarianization. Such analysis has been used to explain (or at least clarify) aspects of worker behavior that otherwise seem problematic. It has been an important trend in historical study, and I have been party to it. But we must avoid becoming entrapped by such an approach, for it is very inviting to think that if one has understood the working world of workers, their changing relations with their bosses, and the forms of organization that arise out of work situations, one has understood the working class. But clearly that is not enough, any more than an earlier generation's focus on "the standard-of-living question," trade union development, or labor politics was enough. Nothing short of an attempt to grasp the *whole* of the working class experience in its manifold variety is called for. Two books—Maurice Agulhon's *Toulon* and John Foster's work on Oldham—come to mind as examples of this kind of total history, and it is significant that they are based in local study. With all due consideration for the tradition of Georges Duveau and E. P. Thompson, there is little question that most new insights into the problems of class formation and the development of class consciousness will derive from intensive local or industry-specific study that utilize the cumbersome but richly rewarding social data which have come to be the backbone of labor history.

Notes

1.   Emile Appolis, *Un Pays languedocien au milieu du XVIIIᵉ siècle: le diocèse civil de Lodève, étude administrative et économique* (Albi, 1951), pp. 556–58, and Archives départementales de l'Hérault, C 148. Mairie de Lodève, Etat civil de Lodève, Déclarations de décès, 1849, no. 98, Paul Louis Adam, celibataire; Archives départementales de l'Hérault, 39M139; Archives nationales, BB³⁰401.

2.   *Journal des Tailleurs*, Nov. 21, 1830. P. Parissot to the Ministre de l'Agriculture et du Commerce, July 11, 1848, A.N. F¹²2337.

3.   See Charles Tilly, "The Formation of the European Proletariat." (Paper delivered at the American Historical Association annual meeting, December, 1976.) Harry Braverman seems interested only in objective proletarianization, thus exhibiting a rather mechanical view of the process (*Labor and Monopoly Capital* [New York, 1974], Part I). See also the perceptive remarks on Braverman by Thomas Dublin in his paper entitled "Technology, the Organization of Work, and Worker Solidarity: A View of Women in the Early New England Textile Mills," presented in a session of the Social Science History Assn., Ann Arbor, 1977.

4.   This paragraph summarizes a decade of research and theorizing. The essence of the argument, however, is perhaps best presented by Stephen A. Marglin, "What Do Bosses Do?: The Origins and Functions of Hierarchy in Capitalist Production," *Union of Radical Political Economists* 6 (Summer 1974): 60–112. On protoindustrialization, the recent studies of Franklin Mendels are important, but the best summary of the problem and the most extensive bibliography may be found in Jürgen Schlumbohm's "Productivity of Labour, Process of Production, and Relations of Production: Some Remarks on Stagnation and Progress in European Rural Industries (17th–19th Centuries)," a working paper available from the Max Planck-Institut für Geschichte, Göttingen, W. Germany.

5.   See Christopher H. Johnson, *Utopian Communism in France* (Ithaca, N.Y., 1974), especially chap. 5.

6.   See C. H. Johnson, "Economic Change and Artisan Discontent: The Tailors' History, 1800–48," in *Revolution and Reaction*, ed. Roger Price (London, 1975), pp. 87–114, for a detailed examination of the process outlined here. The reader is referred to that article for complete source citations.

7.   The main statistical sources are: Chambre de Commerce de Paris, *Statistique de l'industrie à Paris résultant de l'enquête faite par la Chambre de Commerce pour les années 1847–1848* (Paris, 1851), pp. 285–305; and Lémann, confectionneur, *De l'industrie des vêtements confectionnés en France* (Paris, 1857), passim.

8. Bernard H. Moss, *The Origins of the French Labor Movement: The Socialism of Skilled Workers* (Berkeley, 1976).

9. These general remarks are drawn from a wide range of sources and personal experience, but the census of 1851 (A.D. Hérault, 115M28/1) is the main base of the figures.

10. All relevant archival citations relating to this section would occupy several pages. Thus only the most voluminous and comprehensive cartons are noted here. A.N., BB[18]1221, 1376, 1389, and 1429; A.D. Hérault, 39M119 and 125 (some eight hundred pieces, "Grèves de Lodève") and 20X16; Archives communales de Lodève 7F1 ("Grèves, coalitions").

11. A.D. Hérault, 39M125.

12. This facinating story is drawn from copies of police reports, the mayor's report, and various detailed reports from Brun, the procureur de roi in Lodève, to his superior in Montpellier, and provides a sample of the incredible detail that my documentation can yield. The relevant sources are A.D. Hérault 39M125 and A.C. Lodève 7F1.

13. A. C. Lodève 7F1, 1I1, 1I6, 1I12, Q22; A. D. Hérault, 39M8, 33, 53, 107, 109, 114, 115, 121, 125, 127, 128, 132, 134, 140, 141.

14. Unless otherwise noted, the following analysis of mid-eighteenth-century Lodève is based on information drawn from Appolis (see note 1); Ernest Martin, *Histoire de la ville de Lodève* (Montpellier, 1900), vol. II; E. Martin, ed., *Le Cartulaire de Lodève* (Montpellier, 1900); and Léon Dutil, *L'Etat économique du Languedoc à la fin de l'ancien régime* (Paris, 1911), pp. 277–444.

15. A.D. Hérault C2792.

16. A.D. Hérault C2424.

17. Maurice Garden, *Lyon et les lyonnais au XVIIIe siècle* (Paris, n.d.), esp. pp. 582–92.

18. "Les Tisserands de Lodève aux citoyens composants la Commission des subsistances à Paris," (n.d., but sometime in the Year II), A. N. F[12]1389–90.

19. The key source for the foregoing section is a census taken in the Year VI (described in the text below) that I discovered in the Archives communales de Lodève (1F2). Also important, however, are *plaintes et placets*, A.D. Hérault C6766 and C6767.

20. A.D. Hérault, 132M1-6; 131M19. A.C. Lodève, 1G2–7, 64–73 (Patentes).

21. What follows is based, to a significant extent, on this census (see note 19). At the time of this writing, the calculations were done by hand. This census is currently being put in machine-readable form. My thanks to Louise Tilly for help in coding procedures.

22. William Sewell, "Social Change and the Rise of Working-Class Politics in Nineteenth-Century Marseille," *Past and Present*, 65 (Nov. 1974): 75–109; Maurice Agulhon, *Une Ville ouvrière au temps du socialisme utopique; Toulon, 1815–1851* (Paris, 1970); Pierre Guillaume, *La Population de Bordeaux au XIXe siècle* (Paris, 1972); and André David, *La Montagne noire* (Carcassonne, 1924).

23. For a general survey and a good bibliography on problems relating to migration, see Charles Tilly, "Migration in Modern European History," in *Human Migration: Patterns, Implications, Policies*, ed. William H. McNeill (Bloomington: Indiana University Press, 1978).

24. See Michael Anderson, *Family Structure in Nineteenth-Century Lancashire* (New York, 1971). The lack of chain-migration evidence for Lodève is perhaps the most significant finding for the argument of this essay. I am not yet prepared to claim it is the pivotal factor in the rapid growth of class-conscious behavior among this working class, but neither will I say it is not.

25. Etat civil de Lodève, Registres de mariage, 1802–1806. (No classification: Mairie de Lodève).

26. See Paul Marres, *Les Grands Causses* (Tours, 1936), vol. 2.

27. Etat civil de Lodève, Registres de mariage, 1806, 1816, 1826, 1836, 1846, 1856.

28. A.D. Hérault, 115M28/1.

29.   A.D. Hérault, 58M45: an 1846 application for a *Société des Arts* for shopkeepers and artisans was well received by the prefect because he hoped that it might help develop social distance between them and the workers. They were viewed by the mayor as "the second class of citizens."

30.   A.N. BB 401 (Commissions mixtes).

FOUR

The Transformation of Social Solidarities in Nineteenth-Century Toulouse*

RONALD AMINZADE

Nineteenth-century French cities witnessed a transformation of the structure of urban social solidarities and of the day-to-day cultural patterns and associational life of urban workers. During the course of the nineteenth century the horizontal solidarities and vertical antagonisms of social class gradually replaced the horizontal conflicts of trade rivalries and the vertical ties of patronage.[1] The following study of nineteenth-century Toulouse reveals the changing structure of working-class solidarities by analyzing changes in associational forms, collective actions, and political ideologies. The central argument is that a transformation of the political economy lay beneath these crucial changes which altered life and politics in this regional capital of the southwest of France.

During the first half of the nineteenth century the growth of class solidarities among urban workers is evidenced by the gradual disappearance of certain associational forms, particularly the *compagnonnage*, and the emergence of new forms of association, like the mutual benefit society. During the early nineteenth century, workers were organized by trades (*corporations* or *corps d'état*) into status-conscious and highly ritualistic associations with admission rites, status symbols, and internal hierarchies. During this period the compagnonnage was the most important working-class organization in France.[2] These secret brotherhood fraternities of bachelor journeymen

*I would like to thank the archivists at the municipal and departmental archives at Toulouse, the Social Science Research Council, the Center for Research on Social Organization of the University of Michigan, and the Center for Research on Politics and Society of the University of Wisconsin.

helped their members exert control over the local labor market by withholding labor from artisanal masters who refused to acknowledge accepted conventions governing wages, hours, and working conditions. The compagonnages sponsored the Tour de France, a network of arrangements throughout France designed to provide temporary employment and housing for young journeymen traveling from city to city to learn their trade. The Tour de France provided a local bureau of employment and a place of lodging for journeymen artisans. It served a training as well as a regulative function, distributing skilled labor to towns where it was in demand and providing the institutional basis for geographic mobility among skilled workers of certain traditional trades. Compagnonnages were organized into three rival orders (*devoirs*), each of which followed different ceremonies and rituals. Although each devoir included several different trades, the compagnonnage was organized by occupation, with each trade responsible for the training and supervision of its members. Each trade had its own ritual vocabulary and songs and the compagnonnage fostered strong craft pride. The compagnonnage also promoted hierarchical status distinctions among trades, which were legitimated by tradition and even legends. These status distinctions were reflected in the refusal to admit those who exercised what were considered to be less noble crafts, in the frequent roughing up of subordinate members (*aspirants*), and in the violent street brawls between members of rival devoirs. Agricole Perdigier, a prominent working-class writer who had been a member of the compagnonnage, described the trade rivalries and violent hostilities which divided skilled workers at the beginning of the century as follows: "The compagnons were warriors, compagnonnages were enemy armies, rival nationalities who dreamed only of crushing one another."[3]

The disappearance of street brawls between workers from rival trades or devoirs (the *rixe de compagnonnage*) reveals the changing solidarities of French workers. Violent street fights pitting worker against worker over symbolic issues were quite common in Toulouse and throughout France during the 1830s. The bakers and shoemakers of Toulouse, excluded from the compagnonnage because of their low status, often became the target of attacks by workers in other trades when they adopted traditional compagnonnage symbols and rituals. In May 1839 Toulousain workers confronted one another in bloody street fighting that left one worker dead and many more seriously wounded. Determined to avenge the bakers' wearing of certain compagnonnage emblems, local carpenters, locksmiths, joiners, blacksmiths, stonecutters, and tanners attacked a group of around two hundred bakers during a procession to the St. Sernin church in celebration of their patron saint's day. In spite of the presence of local police and fifty infantrymen, a bloody street fight ensued which resulted in the arrest of twenty-eight workers.[4] By the end of the 1840s such violent confrontations among workers had disappeared from the scene, not only in Toulouse but throughout France. The disappearance reflected the changing organizational structure of French working-class life as well as the emergence of a spirit of class solidarity among workers in all trades.

The growth of class solidarities among workers could also be seen in strike activities, which, even when centered around the defense of trade interests, increasingly displayed a more general class character and a growing cooperation among workers of different trades. The first attempt at coordinating strikes by workers of different trades in Toulouse was made in September 1850 when shoemakers, tailors, hatmakers, joiners, stonecutters, plasterers, and carriage workers met separately to discuss the possibility of a general strike. According to police, workers decided instead to launch a series of successive strikes, out of fear that a general strike might provoke the government to declare a state of seige.[5] The joiners' strike, however, was broken by the use of troops as strikebreakers. This defeat put an end to plans for further strikes. During the 1860s local workers fighting for a ten-hour day were more successful in coordinating their resistance to employers. The strike wave of 1868 began with a victorious strike for a shorter workday by stonecutters, and was soon followed by successive strikes of the other building trades over the same issue.[6] Although the masons initially lost a seventeen-day strike in May 1868, that summer subsequent strikes for a shorter day by the city's house painters, locksmiths, carpenters, and joiners enabled the masons to win their struggle for a ten-hour day with a one-day partial strike in July 1868. Such experiences helped workers to realize that the actions of workers in other crafts had an important effect upon their own trades. This realization is reflected in the increasing exchange of strike funds across local and occupational boundaries and even across the traditional barrier between skilled and unskilled workers. During the joiners' strike of 1850, five bakers were arrested for soliciting money to aid the strikers. During the hatmakers' strike of January 1865, strikers circulated a resolution in the city to publicize their plight and gain the support of workers in other trades. In May 1868, striking carriage smiths received 100 francs in aid from local hatmakers, and striking foundry workers received 77 francs from workers at the Arsenal as well as promises of aid from foundry workers in other cities. Unskilled factory workers appealed for aid from artisanal workers in June 1866 when striking cotton print workers circulated pamphlets in the city to raise funds for their strike, and in May of 1870 when striking tobacco workers solicited money for their strike fund in the workshops of various trades.[7]

Strike activities, and the support they generated among workers from other trades and other cities, fostered direct personal ties to the symbols, history, and culture of the working class rather than to those of any single occupational group. The exchange of aid between skilled handicraft workers and unskilled factory workers, and the increasing interest shown in the strikes and struggles of workers in other cities in France reflected a shift in consciousness. The personal identities of workers gradually became linked not simply to the localized interests of their trade, but to the collective fate of their fellow workers throughout France.

Changes in working-class associational forms also reflected the growth of new solidarities. The decline of the compagnonnage was accompanied by the emergence of a rival form of organization, the mutual benefit society. These societies rejected the strict hierarchy, the often oppressive initiation rituals, and the status-conscious spirit of the compagnonnage. In Toulouse, dissident compagnons abandoned the organization in favor of the rapidly growing mutual benefit societies, which took hold in the very handicraft trades that had once been compagnonnage strongholds. These societies arose either in direct opposition to the compagnonnage or as secularized versions of church mutual aid groups (*confrèries*). The earliest request for prefectoral authorization to form a mutual benefit society in Toulouse came in 1821 from a group of joiners, masons, tinsmiths, smelters, roofers, shoemakers, carpenters, glaziers, and cabinetmakers. All of the trades from which members were drawn had compagnonnages. In June 1821 the mayor of Toulouse stated that the recently formed joiners' mutual aid society "may be an attempt to destroy the compagnonnage...."[8]

Mutual benefit societies provided many of the same services offered by the more exclusive and ritualized compagnonnages, including aid for the sick and needy and the financing of funeral services. Unlike the compagnonnage, mutual benefit societies did not control occupational training or job placement, did not require a Tour de France training program for their members, and were not based upon the need to protect trade secrets, defend trade privileges, or pass on the trade to succeeding generations. By the end of the 1840s the compagnonnage was an institution in crisis, and by mid-century most of Toulouse's trades no longer had a compagnonnage. Mutual benefit societies had, in contrast, grown rapidly, with ninety-six of them providing unemployment, sickness, accident, and old age insurance to an estimated 18,000 Toulousain workers by 1862.[9] Although trade and neighborhood boundaries often formed the basis of recruitment into mutual benefit societies, these societies were usually, but not always, composed of workers from a variety of occupations. Mutual benefit societies were typically dominated by artisans in handicraft industry, but, unlike the compagnonnages, they often included nonmanual workers and unskilled factory workers.[10] Many of them initially began with close ties to the Catholic church and then gradually took on an increasingly secularized, politicized, and militant character. Associational statutes reveal a growing number of mutual benefit societies in Toulouse which did not include religious observances or a rule limiting membership to Catholics in their statutes, and a declining number that used church buildings as their meeting place. Although by mid-century most societies retained the old custom of taking on the name of a patron saint, the custom of naming a cleric as president of the society had completely disappeared.[11]

Not only did mutual benefit societies become more secularized during the 1840s and 1850s; many also became politicized agents of class struggle. During the Second Republic, democratic socialist militants encouraged workers to form mutual benefit societies, and local police commented upon the political activity of these associations. "Various trades," observed the police commissioner in November 1850, "are planning to form mutual aid societies. These societies are really socialist societies that better disguise their revolutionary schemes."[12] Police cited several prominent Republican socialist shoemakers, tailors, hatmakers, and metal smiths as active in efforts to create these new mutual benefit societies, and labeled the efforts an attempt to create "a new system of secret societies."[13] Mutual benefit societies also came to play an important role in the organization of strikes and strike threats during the 1850s and 1860s, serving as a cover for the collection of strike funds and as a means of surveillance of employers after a strike was settled. The joiners' mutual aid society (La Société des ouvriers menuisiers) was founded in 1850 in the aftermath of an unsuccessful strike, while the housepainters created the Société de secours mutuels des ouvriers peintres en bâtiment after a successful strike of May 1860. The printers' and hatmakers' associations in 1861, the bakers' association in 1868, and the shoemakers' and tobacco workers' societies in 1870 were all active in organizing strikes. In January 1865 the Imperial Prosecutor summarized the role of these organizations as follows: "I must once again point out the danger posed by working-class trade associations which, under the cover of mutual aid, have organized the trades, subjected workers to rigorously enforced clandestine regulations, and often placed employers at the mercy of their workers. These numerous associations have treasuries which, in the event of a work stoppage, can serve to support a strike."[14]

The growth of class solidarities in Toulouse was also visible in the emergence of interoccupational political associations among workers and in the accompanying calls to unity among workers in all trades. By the end of the 1840s Toulousain workers had organized their own newspapers, electoral organizations, and political clubs in an effort to promote common identities among members of different trades. In Toulouse as in much of France, the Revolution of 1848 brought a proliferation of working-class associations. The largest working-class electoral association, the Société des travailleurs, was founded in early March 1848 in an attempt to guarantee the selection of workers as candidates in the National Assembly elections of that year. This association had as its stated goal "the prompt and complete fusion of all trades (corps d'états) into a general association of workers."[15] The city's first working-class newspaper, *Voice of the People*, founded in February 1847, issued calls for working-class unity as the solution to the social question. "Unemployment, inequitable taxes, clerical education, and all abuses," argued the newspaper's editors, "have occurred because the children of the people, isolated and without ties, don't think to associate. If workers came together and organized in a truly fraternal manner, nothing would be able to stop them. Union is our greatest need."[16] Such appeals to working-class unity were quite common during the 1840s, even among those who retained a strong commitment to older forms of organization like the compagnonnage but sought unsuccessfully to reform them and to eliminate the divisive aspects of their rituals. During the early 1840s numerous prominent French working-class leaders denounced in writing the rivalries that divided workers, as did the locksmith Achille François in the following lyrics of a song he wrote: "Proletarians, Why these hatreds? Aren't we all Equals? Don't we have the same problems? Don't we carry the same chains?"[17]

The working-class political ideologies and social movements of the early 1840s reflected the emergence of class solidarities. Republican socialism and Icarian communism were the most important working-class social movements during the early 1840s. Both had their greatest appeal among artisanal workers in handicraft industry. Collective biographies of political militants in Toulouse, compiled from police, judicial, prison, and administrative records reveal that artisanal workers in handicraft industry, especially building joiners, shoemakers, metal smiths, printers, tailors, hatmakers, and foundry workers, were the most active militants in both the Icarian Communist and Republican Socialist movements.[18] Republican socialism envisioned the cooperative ownership of the means of production by workers and asserted that employment was a basic right (*le droit du travail*). In doing so, it responded directly to the daily concerns of artisanal workers faced with periodic unemployment, a growing inability to control entry into their trades, and a growing loss of control over their work processes. The call for political equality also played an important role in attracting workers to the cause of Republican socialism, which urged the extension of the suffrage to all workers regardless of their skills or literacy.

Along with Republican socialism, the other major political ideology and social movement which initially gave collective expression to newly emerging class solidarities and antagonisms in Toulouse was Icarian communism. Etienne Cabet elaborated his vision of an egalitarian society in the book *A Voyage to Icaria*, published in 1840. In the fictional Communist society of Icaria described by Cabet, all production was centrally planned but democratically managed, workers collectively owned all (productive) property, and goods were distributed on the basis of human needs.[19] Icarian communism translated the pressing economic problems facing workers in handicraft industry into clear ideological and political issues, defined in the language of social class. ᵀt fostered a sense of dignity among all workers, regardless of their trade, by portraying workers as the sole producers of all that was necessary. Although Cabet preached class collaboration, and the movement he led included bourgeois and petit bourgeois sympathizers, the largely working-class composition and orientation of its activists gave the Icarian movement a class character. The emergence of the Icarian movement in Toulouse marked the initial appearance of a small group of working-class leaders claiming to speak for more than the narrow interests of their respective trades. In February 1843 Toulousain police arrested twelve Icarian Communist leaders for their participation in a banquet which the authorities claimed was a conspiratorial session to draw up plans for an armed insurrection.[20] Cabet appeared at the trial of the alleged conspirators in August 1843 after the defendants refused to accept the Republican party leader Joly as their defense attorney. The defendants denied the charges of revolutionary conspiracy, insisting that their sole purpose was to aid the cause of the working class. One of the defendants, Balguerie, had been convicted in July 1841 to a year in prison for the crime of "attacking [the institution of] property and inciting hatred against a class of society."[21] The response of the prosecuting attorney to the acquittal verdict—"Oh, the poor French bourgeoisie!"—recognized the class antagonisms that animated the Icarian movement.[22]

The importance of class solidarities in changing political sentiments and attitudes in Toulouse was emphasized by the police comissioner for the center city district when he evaluated support for the Second Republic in November 1849. The commercial bourgeoisie, he wrote, are not

> very devoted to the Republic, but they want it to be sensible and stable; they too fear the political upheavals which sometimes disrupt commerce and cause irreparable losses. Master-artisans (*maitres-ouvriers*) don't share the same fears, and they are more solidly Republican, because all pretentions of superiority offend them, and they envy and slander the wealthy from whom they receive their incomes. The worker has different opinions than his employer and is naturally socialist. I have made this observation after visiting several workshops, especially those of printers, bookbinders, hatmakers, and tailors . . . where workers speak enthusiastically of 1793 and of the need to renew the terrors of this period in order to improve the condition of the working class.[23]

The transformation of Toulouse from a city in which social relations were characterized by status distinctions and trade loyalties into a city in which social relations were characterized by social class was a long and slow process. Old norms and behaviors disappeared slowly while new ideas and associations generated by emerging class solidarities were shaped by traditional trade loyalties. The persistence of traditional patterns of organization in the context of class-based activities is illustrated in the case of the working-class political association, the Société des travailleurs. Founded shortly after the Revolution of 1848, this electoral association sought to transcend narrow occupational interests and rivalries, yet it was organized along trade lines. The Société organized a mass electoral rally on April 2, 1848. The initial gathering took place on the Place Lafayette, where groups of workers from forty different trades met, each with their own flags and the names of their respective trades printed on them, and then marched alongside workers of their own trades to an outdoor meeting on the Prairie des Filtres. There each trade formed a circle, with their flags in the middle, and chose delegates to represent them in the selection of electoral candidates. Although trades (*corps*) remained an important basis of working-class political organization in 1848, the issues and grievances raised by working-class political associations appealed to a broader class-based constitutiency and transcended the specific interests of any one trade. Emerging class solidarities among workers were filtered through the prism of traditional social organization. Traditional trade loyalties were not abruptly abandoned in favor of class solidarities; they were transformed to meet the new needs and aspirations of workers.

By the middle of the nineteenth century the solidarities of social class were quite apparent in French working-class associations, ideologies, and collective actions, while the rivalries and divisions that had once generated intense hostilities among workers from different trades had greatly declined. The growth of class solidarities involved far more than the organizational, political, and attitudinal changes documented above. It was the product of the transformation of the political economy of France. The disappearance of the compagnonnage, the growth of mutual benefit societies, the decline of trade rivalries, and the growth of class solidarities were all related changes brought about by the rise of industrial capitalism and the accompanying crisis of handicraft industry.

The transformation of the political economy of nineteenth-century France included more changes than simply the growth of factories. Although the development of factory industry was the central feature of the rise of industrial capitalism during the early and middle nineteenth century, the decline of handicraft production and the growth of urban putting-out, or "sweated," production were important socioeconomic changes which played a role in the transformation of social solidarities. The three major forms of nineteenth century industrial production—handicrafts, putting-out, and manufacturing—differed in terms of the type of labor they employed as well as in the social organization of the production process. Handicraft industry relied exclusively upon artisanal labor, that is, skilled workers who exercised collective control over the training and recruitment of workers. Putting-out and manufacturing production employed semi- and unskilled labor, although artisanal labor also participated in putting-out production as well as in early factory industry. Handicraft industry, distinguished by its small scale, a limited division of labor, and the fact that employers worked alongside the artisanal journeymen and apprentices they employed, provided artisans with a high degree of autonomy and independence. It allowed them to organize their own work, set their work rhythms, and work cooperatively according to the traditions of their trade. The work process in manufacturing industry was organized very differently, with employers rather than workers controlling the pace and organization of work. Semi- and unskilled workers in factories performed subdivided tasks and produced not a finished product but a portion of it. They repeated a small number of simple tasks requiring little training or skill and exercised little or no control over the rhythm or organization of work. Artisans in early factories did retain their skills, but these workers exercised less control over the pace and organization of production than workers in handicraft industry, and they did not participate in the production of a total product. The social organization of the factory, with its large scale, increased division of labor, work discipline, and what was by and large a later development, mechanization of work, provided workers with less autonomy and creativity than did work in handicraft industry. "Sweated" home labor engaged in urban putting-out production did not eliminate workers' control over the rhythm and organization of their work, but it did involve subdivided tasks, some of which required minimal skills and the production of pieces rather than finished products.

The social organization of work, as well as the type of capital, differentiated manufactures from older forms of industrial production. Putting-out and handicraft industry, unlike manufactures, were organized by merchant rather than industrial capital. Merchant-capitalists provided raw materials and collected finished products for rural and urban putting-out production and often played a similar role in handicraft production. Small artisanal masters often owned a shop where they sold finished products to local consumers, but if the goods produced were distributed beyond the locality, the master artisan relied upon a merchant-capitalist for distribution. Handicraft industries which produced for a regional or national market, like textiles, metallurgy, and hatmaking, as well as other industries which required the assembling of diverse groups of workers with different skills and trade organizations, such as carriage making or construction work, typically relied upon merchant capital for credit or for the distribution of goods. Handicraft industries requiring minimal amounts of capital, producing for a local market, and employing workers with the same skills and trade organizations, such as the local baking and shoemaking industries in 1830, often utilized only the capital of small master artisans. However, these industries witnessed the increasing incursion of merchant and industrial capital during the course of the century. Merchant-capitalist entrepreneurs, unlike industrial capitalists, did not exercise control over the organization of the work process and were primarily interested in conquering markets and finding outlets for their goods rather than in more efficiently organizing production.[24]

Manufacturing production offered employers a number of advantages over handicaft production. It involved less time and effort spent on the transportation of raw materials, which could be shipped to a central point rather than to numerous dispersed households or workshops. The hierarchical organization of work in large-scale factory settings had the additional advantage of offering manufacturing employers greater control over the labor process and greater uniformity in the goods produced. The social organization of manufacturing and urban putting-out industry involved a relatively advanced division of labor. The increased division of labor made manufactures and urban putting-out more efficient than handicrafts because it increased the productive power of labor, since a worker engaged in the same, simple, repetitious task took less time to perform it than a worker performing a diverse series of operations in succession. It also perfected tools and implements to fit each fractional operation, thus creating the conditions for the application of machinery.[25] Early manufactures and urban putting-out industry routinized and subdivided work tasks more than it mechanized them. It was not so much the introduction of new technology which gave factory and sweated industry a competitive edge over handicraft industry, but a new social organization of production, involving larger concentrations of capital and an intensified division of labor.

Despite the preponderance of small-scale handicraft production in France, manufacturing industry made impressive gains during the first half of the nineteenth century. The percentage of the French labor force employed in manufactures remained very modest by mid-century, but manufacturing production accounted for a rapidly growing share of the market for industrial goods. The percentage of French industrial output generated by manufacturing rather than handicrafts rose from around 15 percent during the begining of the century to 35 percent by mid-century.[26] Handicraft production dropped from 68.5 percent of total industrial production in 1835–44 to 58.9 percent in 1855–64.[27] The development of manufacturing industry in France took place at very different rates in different regions, with the north of France leading the way. The leading sectors of French manufacturing industry—textiles and metallurgy—were centered north of the Loire River, where transport costs of coal and iron were low and where cheap foreign supplies of raw materials were readily available. Manufacturing industry developed in areas well connected by railroads, near coal and iron deposits, or near international ports. Toulouse failed to become an important center of French manufacturing industry because the city was not located close to any major iron or coal fields, nor was it located close enough to an Atlantic or Mediterranean port from which cheap foreign raw materials could be acquired, nor were its transport routes and costs relatively superior to those of other cities.

The city of Toulouse served as a commercial, administrative, military, religious, and academic center for the entire southwest of France, more than as an important center of manufacturing industry. Throughout the period from 1830 to 1870 industrial production in Toulouse remained largely handicraft and small scale in character. In 1830, 38.7 percent of the labor force was engaged in handicraft production and only 4.6 percent in manufacturing and urban putting-out.[28] Toulousain manufacturing industry grew during the 1850s and 1860s, but local industry maintained its largely handicraft character, with manufactures and urban putting-out production employing only 7.1 percent of the labor force, or 13 percent of the industrial labor force, by 1872.[29]

Yet the transformations of the political economy of France resulting from the rise of industrial capitalism, especially the crisis of handicraft industry, had a great impact upon the city. In Toulouse the crisis and decline of handicrafts was brought about by the emergence of manufactures in industries which had previously been the realm of handicrafts as well as by growing competition to local urban handicrafts from northern manufacturing industry. The most important growth of manufactures in Toulouse took place in metals and textiles, which employed 43 percent of all the city's manufacturing workers in 1859. In the textile industry the growth of manufactures led to the replacement of flax, wool, and hemp by cotton. Unlike the woolen textile industry, in which the weaving, combing, and carding of wool was organized in a rural putting-out system dependent on the role of the merchant-capitalist, cotton textile production developed as a large-scale manufacturing industry. By 1860 there were 2,079 Toulousain workers engaged in various aspects of cotton textile production, including spinning, weaving, throwing, dying, and printing.[30] Large-scale urban textile factories slowly eliminated the rural putting-out spinning and weaving of flax, hemp, and wool by producing cheaper cotton cloth. In the metal industry the small artisanal ironworks scattered throughout the Ariège countryside and mountains south of Toulouse, powered by wood, charcoal, and water, could not compete with the large-scale urban blast furnaces fueled by coal imported by railroad. The last artisanal furnaces in the Ariège disappeared after twenty years of decline during the 1870s, unable to compete with the large coal-powered blast furnaces at Pamiers, Tarascon, and Toulouse.[31]

The growth of manufactures in Toulouse was not limited to textiles and metallurgy. By the end of the Second Empire (1851–70), hatmaking, shoe-making, and cabinetmaking, trades in which production had been almost exclusively handicraft in character and small in scale in 1830, had acquired sizable manufacturing components. During the 1830s and 1840s the proliferation of ready-made, standardized consumer goods, including clothes, hats, shoes, and furniture, was the product of both the growth of manufacturing production and of urban putting-out or sweated production organized by merchant capital.[32] Custom-made clothes, shoes, and hats produced and sold in small artisanal workshops were increasingly being challenged by both the factory and the sweated production of cheaper ready-made goods. Although many local workers remained employed in the handicraft production of these consumer goods, the threat posed to handicraft industry by the incursion of new forms of industrial production was visible at the local level.

The crisis of local handicraft industry, however, was not chiefly a product of competition from the growth of Toulousain manufacturing or from the emergence of local, urban putting-out production; it was more the result of competition from northern factory-produced goods which were flooding the local and regional market. During the July Monarchy (1830–48), high tariffs protected northern French industry from the competition of more industrialized areas, particularly England. No such barriers existed to protect southern France from the industrial competition of northern France. During the 1840s, when increasingly factory-based northern cotton production exceeded the consuming capacity of northern markets, southern France provided an attractive market which was gradually conquered. Regional flax, hemp, and woolen textile production suffered. The Chamber of Commerce of Toulouse repeatedly blamed foreign and northern imports for problems in local manufacturing and handicraft industry, and many local political officials agreed with this assessment of the situation.[33] In 1848 a Republican city councilman, E. Laujoulet, argued that northern manufacturing industry was largely responsible for the widespread unemployment plaguing Toulouse. He suggested that fulfillment of the new Republican government's pledge of full employment would necessitate restrictions on the influx of northern industrial goods. "Perhaps it would be advisable," he wrote, "in order to defend local industry against Parisian competition, which is now so dangerous because of its superabundant and low-priced products, to provisionally impose an import tax upon luxury goods, including furniture and carriages. . . . This tax should equally apply to all ready-made articles (clothing, clothing accessories, millinery, shoes, etc.). . . . The local importation of these diverse articles, which has increased greatly over the past few years, is destroying, to the benefit of outside capitalists and workers, a large group of workers (tailors, shoemakers, milliners, lingerie workers, etc.) who have a right to be guaranteed work by the city."[34]

The decline and crisis of handicraft industry did not affect only industrial workers; it had an important impact on the commercial and banking activities of the city as well. Just as Holland in the eighteenth century had gradually been eclipsed by the more industrialized England as the central trading nation in the world capitalist system, Toulouse gradually lost its position as the commercial center of the southwest of France to the industrialized manufacturing cities of the north. The subordination of mercantile to industrial capital gradually led to the commercial as well as the industrial decline of the city. French commerce increasingly took on a national and international scope as it was transformed to meet the needs of the new organization of production. By 1870 most of the small towns and villages around Toulouse, which had once relied upon peddlers and regional fairs for supplies of various goods, had become linked to a more regularized national and international distribution network based upon the circulation of standardized products for a mass market.

The rise of manufacturing industry and the integration of the French grain trade into an international market spatially restructured the flow of commerce in France, altering Toulouse's commercial position in the national economy and generating a crisis of local commercial capital. In 1836 the city's Chamber of Commerce suggested to the Minister of Commerce and Public Works that the national government respond to the city's commercial crisis by "placing some obstacles in the way of this ruinous emigration of capital or by reducing the flow of tax revenues to Paris." The Prefect soon appeared at a Chamber of Commerce meeting to explain that "the government has no right to interfere with the natural, and undoubtedly profitable, movement [of capital]." "To complain about the movement of capital attracted by commerce with surrounding areas," he argued, "is to reveal that the Chamber of Commerce is making claims for the city's role not as a center of commerce but as a center of banking. . . . Will not exported capital provide benefits elsewhere, and isn't it the same blind spirit of locality that is behind this complaint?"[35]

Complaints about the city's capital crisis continued during the 1850s and 1860s, as control over the allocation of capital became increasingly dominated by the industrial and financial elite of the north and as capital increasingly flowed into the profitable manufacturing industries of the north. According to the prefectoral reports of the 1860s, local merchant-capitalists were experiencing great difficulty obtaining credit. In December 1865 the Prefect reported that textile merchants faced "growing competition which often, as a result of insufficient capital, leads to bankruptcies." "The bankers," he added in the same report, "do not readily assist [local] merchants, especially the smaller ones, and there is no established interest rate in the financing of commercial transactions. They do not extend unsecured credit and demand such unsecured credit more readily than they extend it."[36]

High interest rates and difficult access to credit were accompanied by the increasing flight of capital, as the financial speculation of the stock exchange drained large quantities of capital away from Toulouse. Stock market speculation centered around European central state bonds and foreign and northern industrial investments, not around Toulousain commerce and industry. In October 1859 Toulouse's Chamber of Commerce cited as one of the major causes of the industrial and commercial crisis facing the city, "the flight of capital, which increasingly flows toward the rapid, but often very disappointing, speculation of the stock exchange. Long-term investments that immobilize capital, which are necessary for agricultural and industrial development and commercial transactions, do not satisfy quickly enough the desire to get rich; money flows toward speculation. . . . A mass of liquid capital has left our city in a short period of time for other areas. . . . These losses are painful, and agriculture, industry, and commerce have felt the inevitable repercussions."[37] The opening of a local stock exchange (*bourse des valeurs*) in 1856 generated intense financial speculation, which only further aggravated Toulouse's capital crisis by drawing more money away from local industry and commerce. After the drop in stock prices which followed the Imperial colonial debacle and troop withdrawal from Mexico in 1867, the Procureur Impérial observed, in April 1867, that "it is in the millions that one must estimate the cost to the city of the decree establishing a stock exchange."[38] The crisis of commercial capital, the flight of industrial capital to centers of northern manufacturing, and the crisis of handicraft industry were central aspects of the declining economic fortunes of the city of Toulouse during the nineteenth century. The central question that remains is how these large-scale structural changes in the political economy of France directly or indirectly played a role in the transformation of the social organization and solidarities of Toulousain workers.

The compagnonnage was firmly rooted in a political economy based upon the social organization of work provided by handicraft industry. The decline of the compagnonnage and the growth of class solidarities in Toulouse were the products of changes wrought by the rise of industrial capitalism and the accompanying crisis of handicraft industry. These changes, which made the compagnonnage increasingly incapable of providing valuable services to either journeymen or their employers, included the reduced mobility of journeyman to mastership that resulted from growing capital concentration and the disqualification of journeymen's jobs produced by an intensification of the division of labor. Growing capital concentration and an increased division of labor—both of which characterized newer forms of industrial capitalist production—were made possible by a decline in workers' collective control over the production process and labor market. Prior to the French Revolution, guilds, which exercised control over the labor market and production process, enforced regulations which prevented capital concentration and an increased division of labor in French industry. Old Regime guild regulations placed restrictions upon whom employers could hire. Guild regulations limited the number of apprentices and journeymen a single master could employ and forbid a master from hiring a worker from any trade other than the one in which he was a master. The Le Chapelier Law of 1791 outlawed the guilds and eliminated these restrictions upon capital concentration and the division of labor. During the nineteenth century, after these Old Regime "fetters" upon the social forces of production had been eliminated, new forms of industrial production grew rapidly. These new forms of production, manufacturing and urban putting-out, involved capital concentration, a consequent alteration in the mobility experiences of artisans, an increased division of labor, and a resultant reduction of skill requirements in industry.

Increased capital concentration and the crisis of handicraft industry made it less likely that a journeyman would acquire the capital necessary to set himself up as a master or survive in business once he did so. During the course of the nineteenth century, small master artisans found it increasingly difficult to compete with larger merchant-capitalists or with industrial entrepreneurs. The growth of manufacturing and sweated industry made it more unlikely that workers could become or remain small artisanal masters. Manufacturing industry, by virtue of its increased scale and the larger number of workers typically employed by any one enterprise, required greater amounts of capital than did handicraft industry. The centralization of mercantile capital which accompanied the urbanization of putting-out production also entailed greater capital concentration. Periods of economic crisis fostered capital concentration, as low-priced ready-made goods flooded the market, driving many small producers and shopkeepers out of business. During the period from 1856 to 1865 there were 148 bankruptcies in Toulouse, and from 1844 to 1848 there were 214 bankruptcies. The major victims of these bankruptcies were small retailers of food and clothing and small artisanal producers of consumer goods.[39]

The listings of the departmental directories of 1840 and 1872 document the increasing capital concentration in Toulouse's clothing and hatmaking industries.[40] Three different types of tailors are listed in these directories: (1) small-scale master artisans (*tailleurs à façon*), shopowners with little capital who typically produced custom-made clothing out of cloth provided to them by their customers; (2) merchant tailors (*marchands tailleurs*) who had larger capital investments, including stocks of cloth which they usually bought in volume from suppliers on credit; and (3) large-scale producers of ready-made clothing (*maisons de confection*). The 1840 listing of Toulouse's tailoring enterprises included forty-four small-scale master artisans, thirty-three merchant tailors, and eighteen establishments producing ready-made clothing, for a total of ninety-five listings. In the 1872 directory, there were listings for forty-nine small artisanal shops, ninety merchant tailors, and twenty-seven ready-made producers. These figures indicate the decline of small custom-made tailoring, from 46 percent to 30 percent of all local enterprises, and the growth of large-scale merchant tailors and ready-made producers. The directories indicate a similar trend toward capital concentration in the city's hat making industry. The directory lists two types of enterprises, small-scale handicraft producers (*marchands-chapeliers*) who typically sold custom-made hats in a small store adjoining their workshops, and larger scale producers of ready-made hats (*fabricants*). The 1840 directory lists thirty-five handicraft enterprises and only four large-scale ready-made producers, while the 1872 directory lists forty-three handicraft shops and twenty-five fabricants.

Capital concentration reduced the mobility of working-class journeymen into the ranks of petit bourgeois masters. This change was reflected in the organizational life of Toulousain artisans. In July 1834 a group of former compagnon joiners founded a Société des maitres anciens compagnons, composed of twenty-seven master joiners. In 1837 the association became a mutual benefit society and in 1845 membership rules were changed to admit former compagnons who were married but had not established themselves as masters. By 1848 the association did not even have enough money to pay fifty francs to its doctor and it cancelled its annual banquet.[41] Like the journeymen's compagnonnage, masters' associations, founded by those who had undergone the shared experience of completing a Tour de France prior to attaining mastership, declined during the 1840s. Hard-pressed masters in handicraft industry, whose ranks were growing thinner as access to mastership became less of a routine reward of the compagnonnage experience, faced a growing challenge from urban putting-out and factory production. They were unable to sustain an organization based upon a shared experience that was slowly disappearing. Instead of looking forward to increased status, improved living conditions, and eventual ownership of the means of production as they grew older, journeymen artisans increasingly faced the prospect of remaining wage laborers for the rest of their lives. As mobility into the ranks of mastership declined, the vehicle for providing that mobility, the compagnonnage, also declined.

The increased division of labor which marked the rise of manufacturing and sweated industry altered the composition of the urban industrial labor force by introducing large numbers of women, children, and semi- and unskilled workers as wage laborers in urban industry. During the Old Regime, women and children often played an important role in handicraft and putting-out production as family members, but that role was restricted by the guilds, which typically excluded women and children from journeyman status and guild membership. As we have seen, during the nineteenth century the growth of manufactures and urban putting-out entailed a greater division of labor and a consequent reduction of skill requirements. These newer forms of industrial production utilized cheap, semi- and unskilled workers, including many women and children. Work in the city's cotton spinning, tobacco, and cotton print factories required subordination to the discipline of factory life, not long years of training and proudly acquired skills. By 1840 Toulouse's 18 large-scale manufacturing firms employed 230 women (16 percent) and 233 children under sixteen (16 percent) out of a total of 1,415 workers.[42] Wages for women and children were far below those of men.[43]

An increased division of labor and the influx of female and child labor also marked the transformation of local shoe- and garmentmaking from handicraft to sweated industries. In these two consumer-goods industries, the shift from small artisanal workshops to an urban putting-out system of home production introduced a subdivision of the work process into separate, semiskilled tasks easily performed by women and children. A similar transformation accompanied the growth of factories in the local hat industry. The increased subdivision of labor in local garment, shoe, and hat production is revealed by the different occupational titles listed in the 1830 and 1872 census manuscripts (see table 1). The presence of several occupations in the 1872 manuscripts that did not appear in the 1830 manuscripts (for example, garment cutter, shoe stitcher, hat trimmer) shows the growing number of local workers engaged in piecework rather than in the production of an entire finished product.

The compagnonnage trained skilled workers, and lengthy periods of training regulated entry into the trades and limited the size of the industrial labor force in France. The increased division of labor that marked the growth of factory and sweated industry in trades like tailoring, hatmaking, and shoemaking, made apprenticeship and training less necessary and threatened the control over the labor market exercised by the compagnonnage. The Tour de France was based upon control over the labor supply by workers, not employers. A relative scarcity of skilled labor in urban areas ensured that a compagnon arriving in a particular town would be able to find work during his stay. The increased division of labor that characterized new forms of industrial production, combined with the massive influx of rural inhabitants into urban areas, meant an oversupply of skilled and unskilled labor. This oversupply of labor made it increasingly difficult for the compagnonnage to control entry into and practice of the trade. Employers' growing control over the labor market was accompanied by the rapid expansion of the urban labor force by rural-urban migration, which was greatly stimulated by the decline of rural putting-out industries that once provided subsidiary incomes to inhabitants of the countryside. The ability of rural migrants to find jobs in the city was enhanced by the weakening of workers' collective control over access to employment in many trades and by the growth of semi- and unskilled jobs. Jules Michelet, historian of the French Revolution, observed *le peuple* in his own time. Writing in 1845, he noted:

> In the past, in addition to the tolls at the town gates, there was another obstacle which barred the peasant from the towns and prevented him from becoming a worker. . . . This barrier was the difficulty of entering into any trade, due to the length of appreticeship and the spirit of exclusiveness in guilds and corporations. Families in craft industries took few apprentices, and those, for the most

TABLE 1

The Division of Labor and Female Labor, 1830 and 1872ᵃ

	1830		1872	
	Women	Total	Women	Total
I. CLOTHING				
Tailor (*tailleur*)	130	610	1160	1630
Garment cutter (*coupeur d'habits, coupeur-tailleur*)	0	0	0	20
Seamstress (*couturière*)	1340	1350	2580	2600
Stitchers (*brocheuse*)	0	0	40	50
Sewing machine operator (*piqueuse à la mécanique*)	0	0	10	10
Waistcoat maker (*giletier*)	0	0		240
Trouser maker (*culottier*)	0	10	340	340
Shirtmaker (*chemisier*)	0	0	80	110
II. SHOEMAKING				
Shoemaker, Bootmaker (*cordonnier, bottier*)	30	730	0	1500
Cobbler (*savetier, sabotier*)	0	10	0	90
Boot stitcher (*piqueuse de bottines*)	0		350	360
Shoe stitcher (*piqueuse de chaussures*)	0	0	40	40
Shoe edger (*bordeuse de souliers*)	0	0	10	10
III. HATMAKING				
Hatmaker (*chapelier*)	10	150	190	470
Hat workers (*ouvrière en chapelierie*)	0	0	10	20
Hat trimmer (*garnisseuse en chapelerie*)	*0*	*0*	*10*	*10*
Hat dyer (*teinturier en chapelerie*)	0	0	0	10
Hat ironer (*repasseur de chapeaux*)	0	10	0	0

SOURCE: Archives Municipales de Toulouse: *Recensements de 1830, 1872.*

ᵃThis table is based upon a systematic sample of every tenth individual listed in the manuscript censuses of 1830 and 1972.

part, were their own children, whom they exchanged among themselves. But new occupations have been created which require scarcely any apprenticeship and welcome any man."[44]

Employers' increased control over the production process and labor market meant that the important decisions and functions once carried out collectively by workers through organizations like the compagnonnage, including the recruitment of skilled labor, the enforcement of standards regarding finished products, and labor discipline, were gradually becoming the exclusive prerogatives of the employer. Although some abuses, such as the oppression of journeymen during the early stages of learning the trade, characterized the compagnonnage, it did provide artisans with social support, training, and a high degree of job security made possible by the organization's control over labor recruitment. The job security and collective control over conditions of work that members of the compagnonnage once enjoyed was increasingly challenged by the rise of industrial capitalism and the corresponding decline of handicraft industry. As artisans faced a growing threat to their control over access to their trades and over the pace and process of their work, they no longer found their self-identities in the status and privileges of their occupational group and its ritualized exclusivism. Socioeconomic changes fostered the growth of new self-identities based upon the common position as wage laborer, rather than upon divisive forms of status or rank.

The rise of manufactures and of sweated industry in France resulted in the proletarianization of the industrial labor force. Proletarianization refers to the process by which direct producers lose ownership and control over the means of production. This long-term process of separation from the means of production, which transforms direct producers into wage laborers, encompasses the separation of cultivators from the land (as was the case with rural enclosures) as well as the separation of master artisans from the small amounts of capital they owned. The overall process involves growing numbers of laborers working on premises or land they do not own, using tools they do not own, and producing goods or services under conditions over which they have little or no control. During the course of the nineteenth century, the process of proletarianization in France included changes in control over the labor process as well as changes in access to ownership of the means of production. Journeymen in handicraft industry often owned their own hand tools, but they typically did not own buildings, raw materials, or larger tools, which usually remained the private property of the master artisan, who employed them, who worked alongside them, and whose position as a master they usually hoped to someday attain. Artisanal journeymen did exercise substantial control over the labor process, a collective control which newer forms of industrial capitalist organization threatened to deprive them of. The rise of industrial capitalism and crisis of handicraft industry not only threatened to alter the work experience of Toulousain artisans, by taking away the autonomy, independence, and collective control over work organization that handicraft industry offered; it also constituted a threat to their entire way of life, to a traditional culture and structure of solidarities that was rooted in a precapitalist form of industrial production.

The strikes and political class struggles of Toulousain workers were produced by the transformation of the political economy of nineteenth-century France. Although the proletarianization that marked the rise of new forms of industrial capitalist production during the nineteenth century played a key role in changing working-class solidarities, it was not among the most proletarianized workers that the solidarities of social class were strongest. Artisanal workers in crisis-riden handicraft industry, who faced the threat of proletarianization from the emergence of new forms of industrial capitalist production, were the most class-conscious workers and the most actively involved participants in the class struggles of the period. Class solidarities were not the direct outcome of the rise of factories or of sweated industry. These new forms of industry arose alongside an older preexisting form of industrial production and had important consequences for workers in handicraft industry. The work structure of handicraft industry, and the artisanal culture that it gave rise to, provided the organizational and cultural basis for workers' collective resistance to the social consequences of the rise of industrial capitalism and the crisis of handicraft industry. This collective resistance to the threat of proletarianization, rather than the final consequences or end product of the process, was central for the formation of class solidarities among nineteenth-century French workers.

This essay suggests that the equation of the rise of industrial capitalism with the growth of factories is mistaken and overlooks some of the major structural transformations and social consequences of the "industrial revolution." Many historians have thus ignored the existence, or misconstrued the character, of the class struggles which took place in cities, like Toulouse, which did not become important centers of factory industry.[45] The consequences of the rise of industrial capitalism were not limited to the factory labor force, which remained a very small segment of the French population during the middle decades of the nineteenth century. The rise of industrial capitalism did not involve simply a rapid acceleration of economic growth but a social transformation as well, which undermined and destroyed traditional ways of working, living, and thinking, and in doing so generated tremendous resistance on the part of ordinary people. This transformation not only affected those who came to work in the new factories that developed during this period. It also had profound consequences for those workers who remained in the "traditional" sectors of industrial production, such as handicraft and putting-out industry, as well as those engaged in the provision of services and distribution of goods. Structural changes in the political economy of nineteenth-century France changed the social, economic, and political realities facing the working class of Toulouse and in altering the day-to-day experiences of workers provided the foundation for the emergence of class-based solidarities. These new solidarities of social class were the basis for the emergence of new associational forms, political ideologies, and collective actions, all of which altered the character and content of class struggles in France.

Notes

1. For a discussion of the decline of patronage politics in Toulouse, see Ronald Aminzade, "Breaking the Chains of Dependency: From Patronage to Class Politics, Toulouse, France, 1830–1972," *Journal of Urban History* 2 (Summer, 1977):485–506.

2. For discussions of the compagnonnage, see Luc Benoist, *Le Compagnonnage et des métiers* (Paris, 1970); E. Coornaert, *Les Compagnonnages en France du Moyen Age à nos jours* (Paris, 1966); E. Levasseur, *Histoire des classes ouvrières avant 1789* Paris, 1900–1901); and E. St. Léon, *Le Compagnonnage* (Paris, 1901).

3. Agricole Perdiguier, *Mémoires d'un compagnon* (Paris, 1964).

4. Archives Nationales, Paris [hereafter cited as A.N.]: BB¹⁸1260.

5. Archives Départementales de la Haute Garonne, Toulouse [hereafter cited as A.D.]: 4M66.

6. Strike activities in Toulouse during this period are documented in the archival sources: A.N.: BB¹⁸1395C, 1398, 1453, 1531, 1543, 1699, 1769; BB²⁴715; BB³⁰389, 390; F¹²4503; F¹ᶜ1119, 14. A.D.: M196; 4M66, 67, 87; 12M32; 223U10, 19, 22, 24, 27; wU72. Archives Municipales, Toulouse [hereafter cited as A.M.]: epi 43; 1I60; 2F4.

7. A.D.: 4M87.

8. Louis Claeys, "Le Compagnonnage à Toulouse de 1800 à 1850" (Mémoire de Maîtrise, Université de Toulouse, 1969), p. 164.

9. Jules Delaye, *Rapport sur les sociétés de secours mutuels d'ouvriers* (Toulouse, 1862); A.N.: BB³⁰388.

10. A.M: 2Q6, 2Q7.

11. Paul Droulers, *Action pastorale et problèmes sociaux sous le Monarchie de Juillet chez Mgr. d'Astros* (Paris, 1954); A.D.: 4M55.

12. A.D.: 4M66.

13. A.D.: 4M66.

14. A.N.: BB³⁰389.

15. *Le Journal de Toulouse*, Avril 1848.

16. *La Voix du Peuple*, Février 1847.

17. J. Bruhat, "Le Mouvement ouvrier français au début du XIXe siècle et les survivances d'ancien régime," *Ordres et Classes* (Paris, 1972), p. 239.

18. The collective biographies of political and strike militants were compiled from the following sources: A.N.: BB¹⁸1543, 1699. A.D.: 223U9, 10, 17–19, 22, 24, 27; M196; wU72; 4M60, 62, 64, 66, 67, 69, 71, 73, 74, 76, 82, 83; 54Y42. A.M: epi 43, tr. 4; 1I 60.

19. For an excellent analysis of Icarian communism, see Christopher Johnson, *Utopian Communism in France* (Ithaca, N.Y., 1974).

20. Gabriel Marty, *Etienne Cabet et le procès des communistes à Toulouse en 1843* (Toulouse, 1928); A.N.: BB¹⁸1409.

21. Jean Maitron, *Dictionnaire biographique du mouvement ouvrier français*, (Paris, 1964).

22. Droulers, *Action pastorale*, p. 67.

23. A.D.: 4M63.

24. Bernard Mottez, *Systèmes de salaires et politique patronales* (Paris, 1966).

25. Karl Marx, *Capital* (New York, 1967), 1:67.

26. T. J. Markovitch, *L'Industrie française de 1789 à 1964: conclusions générales* (Paris, 1966), p. 85.

27. Idem, "Le Revenue industriel et artisanal sous la Monarchie de Juillet et le Second Empire," *Economies et Sociétés,* série AF, no. 4 (Avril 1967):85.

28.   A.M.: *Recensement de 1830*; these figures are based upon a systematic sample of every tenth individual listed in the manuscript census of 1830.

29.   A.M.: *Recensement de 1872*.

30.   A.D.: 12M32.

31.   André Armengaud, "La Fin des forges catelanes dans les Pyrénées Ariégeoises," *Annales E.S.C.* (1953): 62–68.

32.   Christopher Johnson, "Economic Change and Artisan Discontent: The Tailor's History, 1800–1848," in *Revolution and Reaction*, ed. Roger Price (New York, 1975), pp. 87–114.

33.   A.D.: 12M34, 12M32.

34.   E. Lajoulet, *Amélioration morale et matérielle de la condition du travailleur* (Toulouse, 1848).

35.   A.D.: 4M53.

36.   A.D.: 12M32.

37.   Ibid.

38.   A.N.: BB^{30}388.

39.   André Armengaud, *Les Populations de l'Est Aquitaine* (Paris, 1961), p. 176; G. Casanova, *Quelques aspects de la vie économique à Toulouse, 1856–1920* (Toulouse, 1966), pp. 58–60.

40.   A.M.: Annuaire de la Haute Garonne, 1840, 1872.

41.   Claeys, "*Le Compagnonnage à Toulouse de 1800 à 1850*," p. 162.

42.   Edmond de Planet, *Travail des enfants dans les manufactures* (Toulouse, 1867); A.M.: Secrétariat Général 137.

43.   A.N.: C953.

44.   Jules Michelet, *The People*, trans. John P. McKay (Urbana, Ill., 1973), p. 42.

45.   For an example of this tendency with respect to the history of nineteenth-century Toulouse, see Jacques Godechot, ed., *La Révolution de 1848 à Toulouse et dans la Haute Garonne* (Toulouse, 1948).

FIVE

Household and Craft in an Industrializing Economy
*The Case of the Silk Weavers of Lyons**

GEORGE J. SHERIDAN, JR.

The most striking feature of industrialization in France, as compared with the industrial revolution in Britain, was its very slow pace. Explanations of this slow pace have generally focused on the attitudes and behavior of entrepreneurs, on government policy and social organization, and on "external" economic factors, such as product markets, raw materials supply, transport networks, and availability of capital and labor in the economy as a whole.[1] The attitudes and behavior of the artisans of traditional industry, and the labor markets which these artisans entered as *employers*, have counted for little in these explanations, except as such attitudes have strengthened or weakened the monopolistic power of guilds.[2] The presence of large numbers of self-employed artisans in French industry throughout most of the nineteenth century suggests, however, that their role in retarding the onset of industrial revolution in France may have been more important than this.

In at least one major French industry, the behavior of artisans was significant in delaying "industrial revolution" and in preserving a traditional mode of manufacture for many decades after the introduction of new power techniques. This was the silk industry of Lyons. Master silk weavers of Lyons resisted mechanization and the concentration of weaving in factories by changing the social structure of their household shops. Their resistance was also a struggle for the preservation of their *urban* craft. Mechanization and

*Research for this paper was supported, in part, by grants from the Georges Lurcy Trust and the Concilium on International and Area Studies at Yale University.

factory production took place almost entirely in the countryside surrounding Lyons, where silk weaving spread throughout the second half of the nineteenth century. Since this dissemination of weaving included putting-out to rural cottages as well as the establishment of mechanized factories, the master weavers' defense of their urban trade was at the same time resistance against rural industrialization, in the more traditional sense, and resistance against "industrial revolution," in the modern sense.

While the masters' resistance did not stop either the advance of power weaving or the growth of rural cottage industry, it did share some credit for slowing down the pace of the former and for preserving urban handloom weaving for many decades despite the progress of the latter. Although the power loom had been introduced with some success in the silk industry before 1850, the number of power looms in the silk industry of the Lyons region (city and countryside) was still only 10,000 in 1877–78, out of 100,000–120,000 total looms, and only about 30,000 in 1900, out of some 86,000 looms in the region.³ Thus, after a half century of experience with the power-weaving technique, the handloom technique was still predominant. Moreover, the city of Lyons retained a sizable share of the industry throughout the century, nearly all in the form of handloom weaving, despite the dissemination of silk weaving throughout the countryside with the advance of mechanization. In 1877, for example, there were some 28,000 looms in the city—about one-fourth of the total in the industry (*fabrique*) and in 1900, about one-eighth of the looms of the industry were still within the city limits.⁴ Lyons's urban handloom trade apparently had a resilience which enabled it to defy, with some success, the advance of modern industry, even during the heyday of modern industrial growth elsewhere in Europe.

This resilience was especially notable in the 1860s. During that decade the urban fabrique faced the longest and deepest economic crisis of the century to date, threatening the very existence of urban handloom weaving. It nevertheless emerged from the crisis with most of its looms standing and active, and did not begin to decline in a serious way until after 1880. This resilience demonstrated the strength of the master weavers' resistance to industrial revolution in their trade during the 1860s. This essay will examine the nature of such resistance, explore the sources making it possible and attractive for the urban masters, and analyze the reasons it achieved some success in preserving the traditional urban household craft.

Industrial Revolution in the Silk Trade of Lyons

The industrial revolution in silk weaving was a rather complex process involving both the "industrial revolution" proper, as we normally think of it—the substitution of water and steam power in the factory for muscle power in the household or small shop—and what has been described more recently as "protoindustry"—the putting-out of silk cloths to cottages in the countryside.

Handloom weaving proliferated along with power weaving, as silk manufacture became a decentralized regional (urban and rural) industry. This proliferation was especially rapid under the Second Empire (1852–70), when the productive capacity of rural weaving, as measured by the number of looms, permanently surpassed that of urban weaving. Before 1861, the number of rural looms exceeded the number of urban looms only once in a ten-yearly reading since 1810. That was in 1840, when 52 percent of the looms in the industry were in rural areas. From 1861 on, however, the large majority of looms were in the countryside.[5] This growth of rural manufacture was shared both by handloom cottage weaving and by power factory weaving. In the Bas-Dauphiné, for example, a region of especially high concentration of rural weaving, the number of handlooms increased along with power looms, so that handlooms were not surpassed by power looms until 1900, as table 1 demonstrates:

TABLE 1

Number of Silk Looms in the Bas-Dauphiné

Year(s)	Handlooms	Power Looms
1850	3,326	500
1860–62	8,000	1,500
1877–80	12,225	4,667
1888–90	14,177	6,450
1900	12,000	15,315

SOURCE: Joseph Jouanny, *Le Tissage de la soie dans le Bas-Dauphiné* (Grenoble: Allier, 1931), p. 140.

This proliferation of rural weaving was so advanced by the 1860s that urban weavers lacked work and received low piece rates even while sales of silk cloth increased on the international market. No wonder the weavers considered themselves in the midst of an especially severe crisis, so severe, in fact, that whenever "they spoke of the *fabrique*, they said more than ever before that it was over for Lyons."[6]

This crisis was initially the result of a change in the markets for silk cloths, favoring the weaving of the simpler, nonbrocaded plain silks (*étoffes unies*) over the weaving of brocaded fancy silks (*étoffes façonnées*). Fabric markets favored sales of plain cloths largely because of changing fashion in women's dress design. Under the influence of the British-born designer Gaston Worth, cuts and folds replaced brocades in women's dress fabric. Plain silks gave the designers greater freedom of cut and fold than the brocaded fancy fabrics. Second Empire fashion also favored the fabric-hungry *crinoline* dress, and crinoline bustles were covered more cheaply by the simpler étoffes unies than by the elegant but expensive étoffes façonnées. Cost became a more important consideration than ever before, because of the price consciousness of middle-class buyers, who inundated the growing silk-fabric markets, and because of the preference of all buyers for novelty and variety of style, which could be achieved more cheaply with plains than with fancies. Moreover, the competition of other textiles (especially woolens and mixed cloths) and the growth of silk industries abroad also made low-cost production imperative. Increasing sensitivity to price differentials and growing competition together undermined the position of the fancy-silk sector. The loss of the largest market for fancy silks after 1860—namely, the United States because of the Civil War—simply underscored this decline.

Fancy-cloth weaving had been concentrated traditionally in the city of Lyons. The decline of fancy silks after 1860 therefore affected the urban trade most adversely. This would not have been too serious, had the weaving of plain silks simply replaced that of fancy cloths at the more prosperous conditions of employment and piece rates of the 1850s. Although such replacement did occur, these favorable conditions did not continue after 1860. Instead, unemployment became more frequent and piece rates fell. The demand for plain silks nevertheless continued to grow on the international market. The reason for this apparent anomaly was the growing competition of rural cottage and factory weaving for plain fabric orders. Rural weaving offered cheaper labor costs to the merchant-manufacturers of Lyons and therefore was favored by the latter over urban weaving. Rural cottage weavers accepted lower piece rates than the weavers of Lyons, largely because of lower living costs on the farms where these rural weavers grew some or all of their own food. Moreover, these weavers were able to weave the simpler étoffes unies as ably as the artisans of Lyons, so that the latter commanded no skill advantage over the former in the manufacture of these cloths. Similarly, labor for factory weaving was also more readily available in the countryside and was as capable as artisan labor for weaving the simpler fabrics.

Growing price awareness among consumers and stiffening competition encouraged the putting-out of silk cloths to the countryside even further. What gave rural weaving its strongest advantage over urban weaving, however, was the escalation of raw silk and silk thread prices in the late 1850s and 1860s. The escalation followed the outbreak of the *pébrine* silkworm disease. Beginning around 1845, this hereditary disease attacked the French herd of *Bombyx mori* silkworms. By 1855, the disease had destroyed the Cevennes race of this worm, and by 1865, nearly the entire native Mediterranean crop had been eliminated. The crop was restored by importing Japanese eggs, and Pasteur discovered a cure for the disease after 1870. But in the meantime, shortages of cocoons due to poor harvests and to adjustment to Asiatic sources kept prices of raw silk and silk thread high throughout most of the Second Empire. Such high raw materials costs focused the need for reduction of overall production costs on the labor component, for which rural weaving was relatively favored over urban weaving.

The Response of the Master Weavers

These several changes in silk fabric and raw materials markets thus favored the dissemination of silk weaving in the countryside surrounding Lyons at the expense of the traditional household industry of the city. The "crisis" of the 1860s was therefore specifically a crisis of urban household weaving, and the master silk weavers of Lyons responded accordingly by transforming their household economies—the number and type of their looms, and the number and social character of their household residents. Such transformation enabled them to resist the decline of their urban craft with some success.

Analysis of samples of silk weavers' households for two censuses—those of 1847 and 1866–reveals the manner in which masters changed their household economies to facilitate such resistance.[7] The major changes were a shift from fancy-cloth weaving to plain-cloth weaving in most of the aggregate sample, a reduction in the numbers of looms and household residents, a reduction in the proportion of residents not related to the head of the household or to his spouse, and in the proportion of nonresident workers needed to weave the active looms ("familialization"), and a reduction in the proportion of males, both kinfolk of the head or spouse and nonkin, residing in the same household ("feminization"). The changes other than the shift to plain-cloth weaving were especially evident in households with a majority of Jacquard (fancy-cloth) looms, since plain-cloth households were "traditionally" (that is, in 1847) smaller, more familial and more feminine than fancy-cloth households. Table 2 illustrates these shifts for the aggregate sample of households with silk looms in the Croix-Rousse (fourth arrondissement of Lyons after 1852), which had 42 percent of all urban looms in 1866—the largest share among all the arrondissements of Lyons in that year.[8]

The reduction in size and familialization of silk weavers' households—of fancy-cloth households in particular—tended to make these less "entrepreneurial" in 1866 than in 1847. This is true if we measure "entrepreneurship" as a positive function of the number of looms and especially as a function of the extent to which first nonresidents, then nonrelative residents, were needed to operate the active looms. This not only meant that artisan weavers operated at a smaller scale than in the past. It also meant that they were less open to outsiders, both nonresidents and nonrelatives, than they had been before. As a result, they had less contact with the labor market as employers.

Those households which remained highly "entrepreneurial" in 1866— relatively speaking and in the second sense defined above (open to outsiders)—did so in a very particular way. They hired women as resident workers, providing bed, board, and a modest monthly allotment in return for work combining both weaving (or weaving-related tasks) and domestic service.[9] This is suggested, first of all, by a testing of relationships among household characteristics by multivariate regression analysis. Suppose, for example, that an index of entrepreneurship is constructed, reflecting degrees

TABLE 2

*Summary of Changes in Social and Economic
Character of Silk Weavers' Households*

Characteristic	Year	
	1847	*1866*
Loom type		
% Fancy-loom households[a]	66.20	34.10
% Plain-loom households[b]	33.80	65.90
Numer of looms		
Average number of looms per household	2.77	2.53
Total households in sample[c]	154.00	129.00
Familialization		
% households with relatives only[d]	35.00	62.50
Feminization		
% households with females only (excepting the head)[d]	23.60	42.30
Number of persons		
Average number of persons per household	2.72	1.95
Total households in sample[e]	148.00	104.00

SOURCE: Croix-Rousse sample, 1847, 1866.

[a]Households with more fancy-cloth looms than plain-cloth looms.

[b]Households with more plain-cloth looms than fancy-cloth looms.

[c]This total does not include households with the same number of plain looms as fancy looms. The proportion of such households was a mere 1.1% of the total sample of 178 households in 1847 and a mere .7% of the total 140 households in 1866. The table total also excludes households without plain or fancy looms but with looms for weaving other kinds of silk fabrics, such as *tulles, bas* and *châles.*

[d]Familialization and feminization are here illustrated to *include* the categories "Nonrelatives = Relatives" and "Males = Females." This differs from the exclusion of such intermediate categories in the illustration of shifts in loom type. The reason for this difference is the nonnegligible share of these intermediate categories in the distribution of households by familial and feminine characteristics, in contrast to the negligible share of such categories in the loom-type distribution.

[e]The difference in sample size from that above (note c) is explained by the omission of households with *no* residents, other than the head of the household and his spouse, in the second total and the inclusion of such households in the first total. Significantly, the share of such households with no additional residents increased from 17% in 1847 (of 178 households) to 26% in 1866 (of 140 households). This increase confirms the overall impression of familialization even more.

of openness to outsiders,[10] and is regressed against variables representing respectively degrees of familialization, of feminization and of plain-cloth weaving, and age of the household head. Such a regression will indicate which relationships (if any) prevail between entrepreneurship and these other variables. A regression equation, using the data of the household samples for the Croix-Rousse, for the years 1847 and 1866, indicates a positive correlation between entrepreneurship and feminization in 1866 and no correlation between the two in 1847. (The regression equations may be found in the appendix at the end of this essay.) This suggests a tie between feminization and entrepreneurship in the latter year that did not exist in the earlier year. This tie was such that highly entrepreneurial behavior in the management of the household in 1866 may have been the consequence of relatively strong employment or presence of women in the household, whereas in 1847, the presence of women had no significant bearing on entrepreneurship. The regression equations suggest, in fact, that feminization replaced extent of plain-cloth weaving and longevity of the master (as indicated by his age) as statistically significant "determinants" of entrepreneurship between the two years.

This association between feminization and entrepreneurship suggests that women played an especially important role in preserving the traditional household economy. Contemporary literary evidence makes the same suggestion even more strongly. It confirms, first of all, the "pivotal role" of "female weavers . . . in the industry of Lyons" in the mid-1860s.[11] By 1872, "the worker called journeyman [*sic*] working on the loom of the master weaver [was] composed two-thirds of women and girls."[12] Thus women were replacing men even in the more skilled and prestigious task of weaving. Women also remained important in the task that was traditionally theirs alone—the task of *dévidage*, or rolling the warp. The special attention given these *dévideuses* by publicists and politicians during the 1860s was one sign of their continuing presence in the industry in large numbers. (Unfortunately, the census data do not permit us to specify their numbers more precisely.) As one of these observers, Jules Simon, noted in 1865, dévideuses were useful to the masters not only for their specialized work at the *dévidoir* but also for a wide range of domestic chores. The dévideuses, wrote Simon, "work long hard days for [a] modest sum, and are assigned nearly always, besides their work, all the heavy tasks of the household."[13] Thus the tasks of the dévideuse, as master weaver César Maire noted in reply to Simon, "bear much relation to those of a real servant."[14]

This condition of servitude, from which the situation of the female weaver, Maire implied, differed little,[15] suggested an importance of women in the household economy going far beyond their mere employment in larger numbers than in the past. Women workers enabled the urban household shop to survive on a lower income and therefore to compete more effectively with rural cottage and factory industry. Women weavers worked for lower wages than men, and women silk workers in general—weavers, dévideuses, and others—performed a wider range of demanding and demeaning tasks in the household than men, who worked only at their specialty. Thus, by replacing men with women, the master weaver could reduce labor costs for weaving and, at the same time, reduce general maintenance and operating costs of the household shop as well, simply by using some of the hired female labor for auxiliary tasks in the shop and for domestic chores.

Women worked for lower wages than men and assumed a wider range of responsibilities in the household not simply because they were more docile or cooperative but because they were more willing to be hired as *resident* workers, and were more readily accepted by the masters as such. As residents, they occupied an intermediate position between family labor and hired day labor. They were lodged and fed by the master, and in return performed domestic work along with their specialized shop work. They received a monetary wage besides, but this was smaller than the amount they would have received as hired day laborers. Such an intermediate position enabled the master to impose on these women a lower "real wage" simply by reducing the consumption standards of the entire resident household. Such a position also gave the master, at no extra cost to himself, a flexibility in managing the household economy, in the assignment of tasks, for instance, ordinarily confined to the management of family labor alone. The willingness of female silk workers, especially young females,[16] to assume this inter-mediate position may explain why the wages of hired women were inferior to the wages of hired men in 1868, whereas in 1865 "the female weavers"—to quote Jules Simon—"earn[ed] as much as the men."[17] "The situation of the men can still hold up despite the decline of wages," reported a police agent in 1868, "but that of the women is intolerable because their average wage hardly exceeds 1.20 [francs] per day in some privileged categories and certainly does not exceed .75 [francs] for the largest number of those employed for ordinary tasks."[18] Thus women served the interests of traditional household industry of Lyons in its struggle against rural cottage and factory weaving by offering their labor at a real wage lower than that which prevailed for men and which would have prevailed for women as well had they refused to work as residents and domestics. They helped save the traditional urban craft, in short, by offering their labor for "exploitation" by the masters.

While women served the traditional household economy in this manner, male workers other than the master (when male), including the latter's own sons, often sought better employment outside the household and even outside the weaving craft. In March 1868 the police agent reported that "if a worker is able to do other work and manages to find work for himself in this occupation, he will leave the loom without regret."[19] A year later, similar reports indicated that "master-weavers are even having their children learn other trades."[20] Such was, however, not the reaction of all male weavers—not that of most masters nor that of many skilled journeymen, notably journey-men weavers of fancy cloths. In June–July 1870, for example, more than 7,000 masters and journeymen weavers of fancy cloths threatened to strike. The journeymen organized their own strike association and carried out the threat even when the masters' enthusiasm for the strike began to wane.[21] The seemingly large numbers and militancy of journeymen fancy weavers in this strike testified to their continued presence in the urban industry. These journeymen probably wove the highly wrought dress fabrics ordered on occasion and requiring their specialized skills, and in the interim worked on simpler fabrics demanded more regularly. They worked as hired nonresidents in the master's household rather than sharing loft and kiln with the master as many had done in the past.[22] They remained associated with the domestic economy of silk weaving, in short, but in its more "modern" aspect—that involving the temporary wage contract for day labor between master and nonresident outsider.

The smaller, familial, feminized household economy could support such skilled journeymen in fancy-cloth households with exceptional work on fancy dress fabric of short duration and relatively high piece rate, such as orders for samples for the Paris Exposition of 1867.[23] Less-skilled, unspecialized resident workers were usually not able to weave these fabrics as well as the specialized skilled weavers. But because of the temporary and occasional nature of these orders, journeymen had to move from one fancy-cloth household to another in search of work, identified with no particular master but nevertheless supported by the domestic economy of urban weaving as a whole. Thus the response of urban masters to the rising competition of rural cottage and factory industry preserved a body of skilled male weavers dependent on the "exceptional" activity of each household along with a smaller, more familial, more feminized household craft for each household's "normal" activity. In this way, both masters and some skilled journeymen remained in the craft of their training and skill, resisting with some success the industrial revolution in their trade.

The Sources of Effective Resistance

What enabled these weavers to resist the industrial revolution in this manner, and why was such resistance effective enough to preserve the urban household industry for many decades after the 1860s? In other words, what were the conditions of labor supply explaining the weavers' own will to resist in this way and the availability of subordinate labor, especially female labor, permitting resistance by "exploitation"? And what were the conditions of demand for weaving labor explaining the success—or partial success—of this resistance? As will be seen shortly, mentalities and economic-environmental factors were both important for making such resistance possible and effective.

Supply. The question of labor supply, explaining how such resistance was possible, really involves two separate questions: (1) Why did master weavers choose resistance over adaptation to industrial revolution? (2) What enabled these masters to exploit family and female labor for the purpose of such resistance? The first question asks why the masters remained with an apparently declining urban fabrique instead of seeking work in one of the newer, more remunerative trades of the city during the 1860s. These abounded in Lyons during this period due to the rapid growth of the city's industry and the extensive urban renewal program begun under the Second Empire. Industrial growth opened stable and high-paying jobs in railroad transport and railroad tooling and repair shops, in machine building, in boat and barge construction, in chemical manufacture, and in thread and cloth dyeing.[24] Urban renewal required large numbers of workers for demolitions, for ditching, and for laying roadbeds. Riverbanks had to be reinforced, a new park, the Parc de la Tête d'Or, had to be laid out in the place of old marshes and woodlands, and the new Palace of Commerce had to be built.[25] All of these tasks provided much regular employment for both skilled and unskilled workers.[26] Moreover, this employment was often better paid than employment in the silk industry. In December 1866, for example, minimum daily wage rates in all cloth categories except upholstery and cloths for church use were not higher than 2.25 francs, while the minimum wages of steam-engine manufacturers and of workers in the railroad shops were 2.75 francs. Maximum wages in the highest paid cloth categories did not exceed 4.50 francs per day, while wages in the newer machine and railroad works were as high as 5.00 and 6.00 francs.[27]

From evidence cited earlier, it is clear that some weavers and weavers' sons pursued these opportunities outside their own industry. The question is why more did not do so, why many, in fact, chose to remain in the urban handloom industry despite its declining piece rates and its more frequent unemployment. Some reasons for this choice were eminently practical. One of these was the difficulty of learning a new trade or of assuming the heavy physical burdens of many of the new jobs in the city. Older masters would have found this difficulty greatest, and presumably these masters would have remained in the traditional craft in larger numbers, or at least in larger proportions, than younger masters. The available data seem to confirm this. In the 1866 sample of Croix-Rousse households, 37 percent of the masters were aged fifty-one and above, while only 13 percent of the masters in the 1847 sample were in the same age group. Another practical reason for remaining with the urban handloom was the economic and psychological cost of renouncing former training and acquired skill in silk weaving by assuming another trade. Such a cost would have been highest for the skilled fancy-cloth weavers, and it may explain the otherwise surprising persistence of journeymen in fancy-cloth weaving, despite the utter stagnation of this sector throughout the 1860s.

There were other reasons, however, for remaining in the traditional household craft that were more "ideological" than practical. These appealed to the belief that the weavers could restore their urban trade by their own efforts. Two movements at the core of what Sreten Maritch called the "social movement"[28] of the 1860s encouraged this belief. These were the cooperative movement and the resistance movement. The silk weavers of Lyons formed cooperatives and resistance societies to halt the migration of their industry to the countryside and to restore to the urban craft its traditional preeminence in determining piece rates and conditions of work. The producers' cooperative, the Association of Weavers, sought to take over urban weaving by putting out silk thread and cloth orders directly to the weavers, its members, without the intervention of the merchant-manufacturers. These weavers were exclusively urban, and they hoped to prevent the further decline of the urban craft by controlling ever larger shares of production and by favoring urban over rural weavers in the distribution of cloth orders. This was revealed by their behavior in the events of October 1866, when they threatened to demonstrate for the restriction of putting-out to the countryside. When the prefect, speaking in the name of the emperor, instead offered to approve their association as a *société anonyme* and to provide it a loan to begin business, they accepted the offer, dropping their original demand for tighter government control of their industry.[29] They readily withdrew this latter demand partly because their association, they believed, would achieve the same end. As the police reported in December 1866, the weavers of Lyons "place[d] much hope for revival of the fabrique on the establishment which is being organized under the large association of weavers."[30]

The weavers harbored the same expectations of halting the movement to the countryside and thereby reviving their industry through their organization of resistance (early trade union) societies later in the decade to enforce recently negotiated increases in piece rates. In December 1869, when the resistance movement was entering a stage of mass organization under the leadership of the plain-cloth category, the police described the movement as "a great awakening among the weavers."

> Conversations on the subject are heard everywhere, and everyone has this tremendous enthusiasm for preventing the fabrique from leaving Lyons, for bringing it back instead. They expect to attract labor from the countryside to the city—not all labor but some which left the city—and they see no other way [of achieving this] than making all the merchant-manufacturers pay the same piece rate.[31]

Thus, besides halting the emigration of the fabrique, the weavers expected their resistance societies to eliminate the worst consequences of rural competition. In particular, they expected their organization to force all piece rates up to a level determined by the collective strength of the urban weavers instead of allowing urban rates to fall to a level determined by the dispersion, lower living costs, and poverty of rural labor. In this way, the city would again dominate the labor market of silk weaving as a whole and no longer be subject to the labor market of the countryside. Although such an expectation, and the similar hope inspired by cooperation, were ill founded, many masters and some journeymen were at least persuaded to remain in their traditional household craft, at a time when the actual situation of that craft gave them more reason for despair.

The second source of labor supply was "exploitable" subordinate labor, especially female labor. Women worked readily as household residents, for lower wages than men, because alternative work, with better pay and conditions that domestic silk weaving, was hard to find, and because there were so many of them in Lyons at the time. Masters thus preferred keeping women of their own family at work on their looms, and found other, nonrelative women willing to accept a lower standard of living as resident dévideuses and journeywomen weavers.

The number of women seeking work in Lyons in the 1850s and 1860s increased from two directions. First, women migrated to Lyons in families of small-town artisans of the region who sought work in one of the many growing trades in the city. Second, women who could not find work in rural factories migrated alone to Lyons from rural villages and farms to work specifically in the silk industry. Concerning the first source, Yves Lequin demonstrated, in his book entitled *Ouvriers de la région lyonnaise (1848–1914)*, the relatively large share of artisans not native to the city who migrated to Lyons between 1851 and 1911 to preserve the craft of their fathers and of their own training and skill.[32] Some of these set up their own shoemaking, tailoring, and carpentry shops and used their wives and children for household-shop tasks much as the weavers did. But surely many were absorbed into the growing factory and public-works employment as hired labor for the many tasks requiring specialized skills of artisans. In this case, their families were without work and had to seek employment elsewhere—unless, of course, the wage earned by the artisan was adequate to support the entire family, which was not very likely.

The second source of female labor—migrations from farms and rural villages—is more difficult to explain. Such migration seems to have been motivated by a surplus of females in the countryside in relation to the work available for them, despite the increasing opportunities for employment in the rural silk industry. The reason for this surplus is still unclear. It may have been the result of a shift of weaving from a part-time farm activity to a full-time occupation, providing the only employment for the entire household. In such a case, the men in the family may have reserved weaving for themselves and for their wives, instead of leaving it to wives and daughters, as they had done in the past. As a result, the daughters would be forced to seek employment outside the village, by migrating to the "big city" to work in the low-paying tasks of domestic silk weaving, where their sex increased their chance of being hired. These reasons would explain why such young single women were, like those studied by Joan Scott and Louise Tilly, "expendable in rural . . . households, certainly more expendable than their mothers and, depending on the work of the family, their brothers."[33]

This increase in the number of women seeking work in Lyons favored the household economy of silk weaving, in particular, because of the poor conditions prevailing in other women's trades in the city. The main alternatives to working in the master weaver's household were work as dévideuses in specialized shops of dévidage, work as throwers in the larger, factory-like shops of *moulinage*, and work as seamstresses in the ready-made clothing industry. All of these were growing sectors, but most jobs in them were "sweat work." Conditions in shops of dévidage and moulinage were especially bad. Women working in these shops earned a mere 1.00–1.25 francs per day in December 1866, for example, which was lower than the minimum wage in the lowest-paying plain-cloth categories of silk weaving for the same month (1.50 francs).[34] Ernst Pariset of the Chamber of Commerce of Lyons offered this sordid picture of dévidage shops:

> Workers . . . are crammed into alcoves where the air hardly circulates and remains foul all the time; they sleep usually two in the same bed, on a straw mattress; they receive no care for personal cleanliness and do not even have the means of satisfying the basic rules of hygiene . . . The inadequacy of the food is attested by numerous complaints . . . In many shops they never eat meat, in others meat substances appear two times a week at midday meals; most of the time there is no wine to drink . . . Badly lodged, badly nourished, maltreated, our little girl ends up exhausting her physical constitution by excessive work. Whatever her age [may be], she works regularly from five in the morning until nine at night, and this fourteen-hour day is followed, when orders are brisk, by night work extending until eleven o'clock and even until midnight . . . Those who resist the longest reach the age of twenty-five before they die.[35]

When the major alternative to household weaving, even to abusive, exploitative household weaving, was such work where "all abuses meet,"[36] it is hardly surprising that women and girls did not abandon the households of master silk weavers.

The migration of women into Lyons during the 1850s and 1860s thus created a pool of female labor available for employment in urban domestic weaving, the traditional sector of the industry, to enable the latter to compete effectively with rural weaving. The contrast between this situation and that of cotton weaving in Britain during the 1830s and 1840s is instructive. In British cotton weaving, relatively cheap female and child labor was available to the growing *modern* sector of the mechanized factory. This availability was one source of the ruinous competition of the power loom against the handloom and therefore a cause of the destruction of the traditional handloom sector within a few decades. Women and children thus abetted the decline of cottage industry and improved their own earnings and status thereby.[37] In French silk weaving, by contrast, women and children enabled the cottage industry of the city to resist the wholesale ruralization and mechanization of weaving, but at the expense of their own standards of living.

Demand. The weavers' resistance to industrial revolution was thus encouraged by the ideologies of cooperation and resistance, and it was favored by an abundance of females willing to work for low wages as dependents of the household. These two factors explain why labor was supplied by the urban household economy for the purpose of resistance. Such resistance effectively prevented the sudden decline of urban domestic weaving because of factors affecting the demand for traditional household labor. Three of these factors, in particular, explained the apparent strength of urban domestic weaving: the character of technology, the cyclical nature of product demand, and the entrepreneurial attitudes and behavior of the merchant-manufacturers. Together these three factors exposed the "Achilles heel" in the evolution of demand for labor which permitted the urban weavers to defend their urban trade with some success.

Technology was the most important determinant of the relative advantage of urban handloom weaving over rural cottage weaving and over factory weaving. The chief advantages of the former over rural cottage industry were concentration and skill. Concentration permitted scale economies in the accumulation and distribution of silk thread and in the transport of woven fabric. But it especially enhanced the technical quality of urban weaving. Concentration facilitated the exchange of technical information between weavers, on the one hand, and merchant-manufacturers and their designers, on the other hand. It also allowed closer control by the merchant-manufacturer of the execution of the design by the weaver. The first advantage made design consonant with the actual technical capacities of weavers and also encouraged innovation in design and in weaving techniques by ready diffusion of new ideas. The second benefit enabled merchant-manufacturers to insure weaving of fabric of exact specification and quality. With regard to skill, urban industry fostered both a higher level and a greater variety of proficiency in weaving than rural cottage industry in any single geographical area, to be sure, and probably also than in the countryside as a whole. The high level of urban skills was partly the result of more developed "institutions" for learning such skills—such as enduring guild traditions, professors of weaving theory, and weaving families of long lineage—and partly the result of greater emulation and intensity in the practice of the trade among a relatively large number of geographically-concentrated weavers. This high level and variety of skills offered the merchant-manufacturers a pool of talent for the weaving of fabrics of excellence and of varying design.

The rural factory, whether mechanized or not, could achieve the same benefits of concentration as the city—even more efficiently in the matter of surveillance of weaving—and thus eliminate the advantage of urban weaving in this respect. But even the unmechanized factory, using the skills of handloom weavers, could not easily reduce the city's advantage of skill. The cost of reproducing in each factory, or in each geographical concentration of factories, the institutions and human incentives needed to insure an adequate supply of high-level and varied weaving skills would have been larger than the net gains of factory concentration. Only a reduction in the skill-related advantage of urban weaving over rural weaving, by a shift in product demand towards a lesser-quality silk fabric, for example, requiring less proficiency to weave, might make the factory a more efficient concentration of weaving labor than the urban household. If such an erosion of skill requirements placed silk weaving within the range of available mechanized technology as well, then the gains in labor productivity of the power loom would clearly give the margin of advantage to the factory (at least within a static framework). Only the preservation of product demand, or a component thereof, favoring silk fabric outside the range of available mechanized technique left some skill advantage to urban weaving and permitted doubt, at least, concerning the total net advantage of rural factory over the urban household. In the Lyons silk industry of the 1850s and 1860s, the preservation of demand for a medium-quality étoffe unie, requiring the skills of handloom weavers, would have had such an effect. Of course, rural cottage industry could also provide the lesser skills needed for weaving étoffes unies—even those of medium quality—and could offer such skills at lower labor cost. But this reduction in the city's former skill-related advantage over the countryside had to be matched against the advantage of concentration still held by the city.

In short, without the clear technological advantage of the mechanical loom, the net gains of rural weaving over urban weaving depended upon a balancing of factors affecting costs which varied within a short range and which could readily change as the demand for products changed. The volatility of the latter in the world of luxury fashion of the mid–nineteenth century made these gains especially uncertain in the long run. Such volatility discouraged any radical restructuring of capital investment that was irreversible, such as investment in a factory. The preservation of at least some demand for façonnées and for medium-quality unies checked, moreover, the full substitution of rural cottage industry for urban household industry. Only the latter offered the skills in adequate concentration to weave these fabrics, and the merchant-manufacturers also had some interest in preserving these skills for future growth of demand for the same quality cloths.

During the 1850s, for example, when export demand for plain cloth first "took off," stimulating more extensive dissemination of weaving into rural areas, exports of fancy silks also increased to their highest levels of the century and gave more work to skilled urban weavers as well. A large proportion of the plain-cloth demand of this period, especially that on the British market, was probably focused on plain silks of the better sort which even the new consumers seem to have preferred over the coarser velvets and mixed cloths. Demand for these more finely wrought plains would have provided more work for skilled urban weavers as well. The silk industry of Lyons, moreover, was long accustomed to cycles of prosperity and depression of short duration, to sudden "crises" following the outbreak of war, disease, poor harvests, and financial panics, and to variations in fashion styles in fabric markets. Such changes in economic conditions were "cyclical," in the sense that revivals of prosperity and former styles were anticipated and awaited as part of the structure of the silk trade. The American Civil War, responsible for the largest fall in fancy-cloth demand abroad, was clearly a temporary crisis, and even the crinoline dress style could be seen as a passing phenomenon. Pierre Dronier, for example, a journeyman weaver, regarded the crinoline style as "fortunately ephemeral like all fashion."[38] The pébrine disease may have been regarded as having more long-range effects, but high silk prices caused by poor cocoon harvests were surely considered temporary. In other words, as long as the factors responsible for the shift of demand toward the simpler silk cloths were considered passing, and a "revival" of demand and production for the better-quality silks was possible, the immediate gains of wholesale migration of the fabrique into the countryside and into the factory remained uncertain for the future. This uncertainty, in turn, discouraged wholesale ruralization and mechanization of silk weaving by individual merchant-manufacturers and gave those who chose to specialize in the finer cloths some hope for the future.

The merchant-manufacturers of Lyons were especially sensitive to such uncertainty and to its implications for long-term investment. They were especially hesitant about investing long-term capital in looms and factories which shifted the costs of adjusting to cyclical movements from the weavers to themselves. Their traditional entrepreneurial mentality was extremely averse to taking risks in production and especially concerned with preserving freedom of manipulation in the creation of design. Because of their risk aversion, they kept few inventories, produced largely on short orders (especially in the fancy fabric category), and ceased production—even to the point of refusing to accept additional orders—at the least sign of approaching crisis.[39] By responding to adversity in these ways, they simply passed on to the weavers the costs of unused capacity in the form of idle looms, unemployment, and rents on idle shops. The merchant-manufacturers of Lyons cherished, moreover, the freedom allowed them by the domestic economy for advancing new fabric styles. The domestic system enabled the merchant-manufacturer to seek out weavers with specialized skills, throwers and spinners producing specialized counts of thread, and dyers focusing on particular colors or color combinations, according to the specifications of each cloth order. It also enabled them to vary these combinations easily with changes of style and design. In this way, the merchant-manufacturer "manipulated" factors of production to create new designs and to earn the exceptionally high profits of the initiator, instead of simply receiving current styles from the market and earning large total profits from low-cost production on a large scale. "In the *soierie lyonnaise*," wrote Michel Laferrère, "it is the *collection* that matters above all."[40]

> The merchant-manufacturer of Lyons, with few inventories and with little equipment, designs in full freedom, with natural or artificial fibers, the cloth he dreams of to give value to a new *ouvraison*, to an original *armure*, a coloring combination, a design: he makes a sample and secures a reliable order for a few pieces . . . Then he must develop a market for this cloth which will prevail by its composition, its taste, its novelty, and not by its price, which is generally higher than that of a cotton or woolen fabric of the same type.[41]

Laferrère contrasted this with the behavior of the Crefeld manufacturer of silk fabrics who made his production decisions concerning the type of cloth "according to the inventories and the equipment of his factories" and then produced the article "on a large scale, insuring its sale by including designs and colors favored by current style and by setting the price at a very small margin above his unit cost."[42]

The contrast between the two modes of production is perhaps a bit overdrawn. But it probably reflects accurately enough the differing perceptions of factory weaving and urban domestic weaving by merchant-manufacturers of Lyons faced with a choice between the two modes of manufacture in the mid–nineteenth century. The factory, especially the mechanized factory, must have seemed to many merchants like the *usines* of Monsieur Haudequin, in Colette Yver's novel *Haudequin, de Lyon* (1927), which "never cease shouting in the ears of the merchant-manufacturer its terrible responsibilities"[43] and which bring to mind piles of unsold fabric lying about in "a little necropolis stacked with bins like an ossuary . . . decrepit concessions forever abandoned, . . . outmoded tulles of silk, . . . fancy satins . . . [d]iscarded, unsalable, because their flowers were too small or their tints too old-fashioned, fading away for five years, ten years, waiting for some hypothetical resurrection."[44] Those who assumed such "terrible responsibilities" seem to have been either large merchant-manufacturers (few in number) who employed rural cottage weavers along with factory hands and who often combined weaving with spinning, throwing, dyeing, or printing in their factories, or small custom manufacturers (many in number) whose factories wove thread put out to them by the merchant-manufacturers of Lyons. The large merchant-manufacturers hedged against falling profits in weaving by mechanized spinning and throwing of thread. Spinning and throwing had a more certain future, since the new Asiatic fibers used to produce most of the industry's thread after 1860 required extensive treatment. The custom manufacturers relieved their Lyons suppliers from bearing the risks of loss incurred as a result of short-term cyclical crises or changing styles. It also preserved their freedom of manipulation while allowing them to reap some of the gains of more efficient, mechanized weaving as well. Both types of factories usually specialized in particular cloth styles—such as black satins and taffetas, for which the large maison Bonnet was especially known. Such specialization tended to limit the effects of factory and mechanized enterprise in the industry as a whole. As Laferrère noted,

> most of these factories and manufactories, very little mechanized, are not organs for producing on a large scale, imposing their conditions on the entire trade by the kind of articles produced; rather they ought to be compared to sanctuaries where certain specialized products of very fine quality and limited sale, velvet, *taffetas*, fancy *satins, faille*, black plains, are wrought, or cheap articles such as scarfs, *crêpes*, mixed fabrics.[45]

This limited impact of factory industry and efforts to minimize risk even when factories were set up indicated a very weak commitment to "industrial revolution" on the part of the merchant-manufacturers of Lyons. Their preference for putting out silk orders to rural cottages when mechanization was possible and lucrative suggested a refusal to recognize the shift toward plain-cloth fashion as a permanent change. Rural cottage weaving could be "collapsed" more easily than rural factory weaving into urban household manufacture if fashion reverted back to fancy silks or to more elegant plains. Thus the risk of being encumbered with an "irreversible" long-term investment in fixed plant and machinery made the merchant-manufacturers reluctant to assume such a responsibility.

This aversion to taking risks and this unwillingness to make large long-term investments in new mechanical techniques were examples of a type of business mentality described by David Landes as "unfavorable to effective entrepreneurship" and as prevailing especially among businessmen in France, Germany, and the Low Countries.[46] This kind of business attitude placed maximization of profit per unit sold over maximization of total profits, it valued quality over quantity production, and it generally directed all decisions of the enterprise to the single goal of keeping the family patrimony intact. In this view, business was primarily a vocation, in short, a commitment to the family estate rather than a means of making money. Such a commitment demanded, first of all, protection of the reputation, capital, and familial exclusiveness of the enterprise. It therefore discouraged risking capital in the expansion of fixed productive capacity and also any extensive compromise with quality manufacture that threatened to undermine the firm's reputation for superior products.

This restrictive business mentality influenced the decisions of the merchant-manufacturers of Lyons—especially the larger, more important manufacturers—even when the prevailing economic conditions made the attainment of such ideals increasingly difficult. It explains why these merchant-manufacturers did not mechanize silk weaving more rapidly or more extensively during the 1850s and 1860s. The master weavers, for their part, took advantage of the merchants' hesitation, to resist with some success the decline of their urban household craft. Their resistance demonstrated their own immersion in an economic rationality that some would call "traditional" or "premodern." The Russian economist A. V. Chayanov best described this rationality for the case of the peasant.[47] Artisan weavers of Lyons behaved in similar fashion. Like the restrictive businessmen of the Continent, "traditional" peasant proprietors and master silk weavers directed all decisions concerning farm or household to the maintenance of the income-earning patrimony. This meant, first of all, the family itself, whose consumption needs determined the intensity of the peasant's or weaver's own work, or what Chayanov called his "degree of self-exploitation." Increasing needs generated increased self-exploitation, until the "drudgery" of work exceeded the "satisfaction" of needs and placed a limit on the exploitation of the peasant's or weaver's own labor and that of the family. What pushed this limit to its uppermost was the nonutilitarian attachment to the material, nonhuman component of the patrimony—to the land, in the case of the peasant, to loom and sometimes shop, in the case of the weaver. Because of this attachment, peasants and weavers were willing to reduce their families' levels of consumption to the barest necessities, instead of seeking alternative employment or sources of income that might weaken or destroy the household enterprise. Thus the master silk weavers of Lyons were so attached to the household mode of manufacture that they chose to resist industrial revolution in their trade by contraction of their household enterprise and by increased exploitation of its members. In so doing, they forsook more remunerative and more stable employment in other sectors of the local economy. This resistance was "adaptation" in the best traditional manner. It was favored, on the one side, by a traditional entrepreneurial mentality among the merchant-manufacturers, which discouraged their pursuing their advantage over the weavers by mechanization, and, on the other side, by a traditionally rooted willingness of large numbers of females, to engage themselves to be "exploited" along with the master's family. In this way, handloom weaving in the household shop endured as a prominent feature of the Lyons silk manufacture through the worst years of crisis of the mid-nineteenth century.

Notes

1. See, for example, David S. Landes, *The Unbound Prometheus: Technological Change and Industrial Development in Western Europe from 1750 to the Present* (Cambridge: Cambridge University Press, 1969), chap. 3; Charles P. Kindleberger, *Economic Growth in France and Britain, 1851–1950* (Cambridge: Harvard University Press, 1964); and the lucid article by François Crouzet, "Angleterre et France au XVIIIe siècle: essai d'analyse comparée de deux croissances économiques," *Annales* 21 (mars-avril 1966): 254–91.

2. E. Levasseur, *Histoire des classes ouvrières et de l'industrie en France avant 1789*, 2nd ed. (Paris: Arthur Rousseau, 1900–01) stressed the importance of guilds in France for retarding the growth of industry. According to Crouzet, op. cit., Levasseur emphasized the restrictive power of guilds a bit too much.

3. Yves Lequin, *Les Ouvriers de la région lyonnaise (1848–1914)*, vol. 1: *La Formation de la classe ouvrière régionale* (Lyon: Presses universitaires de Lyon, 1977), p. 84.

4. Lequin, *Les Ouvriers*, pp. 68, 87.

5. See Maurice Lévy-Leboyer, *Les Banques européennes et l'industrialisation internationale dans la première moitié du XIXe siècle* (Paris, 1974), p. 143; for an amplification of Lévy-Leboyer's data, see George J. Sheridan, Jr., "The Social and Economic Foundations of Association among the Silk Weavers of Lyons, 1852–1870" (Ph.D. diss., Yale University, 1978), pp. 195–96.

6. "Rapport à Monsieur Delcourt, Commissaire spécial, sur la situation de la fabrique des étoffes de soies," September 9, 1867, Archives municipales de Lyon (hereafter AML), I2–47(A), No. 305.

7. AML, *Recensement*, Croix-Rousse, 1847; Archives départmentales du Rhône (hereafter ADR) 6M-*Dénombrement*, 1866, Lyon, 4ème arrondissement, tomes XVI, XVII. The samples are stratified systematic samples of households taken for both years from the same streets of the Croix-Rousse (fourth arrondissement of Lyons after 1852)—the district of the city

with the largest share of silk weavers. Samples were originally taken from the entire population of these selected quarters, without discriminating weavers' households from households of non-weavers. But only weavers' households *with looms* were retained for the following analysis. This explains the difference in sample size between the two years. For a further discussion of content and utility of the censuses and of the utility of the samples, see Sheridan, "Social and Economic Foundations," pp. 368–71, 619–25a.

8.   M. Robin, "Situation de fabrique," June 1, 1866, in *Compte-rendu des travaux de la Chambre de Commerce de Lyon, années 1869, 1870, 1871,* p. 101.

9.   As Olwen Hufton has observed, the combination of income-earning tasks with home-making was common for married women in these small household shops. In the Lyons silk industry of the 1860s, both married and unmarried women workers, whether members of the family or not, were expected to assist with both kinds of work. See Olwen Hufton, "Women and the Family·Economy in Eighteenth-Century France," *French Historical Studies* 9 (Spring 1975):11.

10.   The construction and utility of the index of entrepreneurship (Ie) are described more thoroughly in Appendix 6 of Sheridan, "Social and Economic Foundations," pp. 626–30.

11.   Jules Simon, "L'Apprentissage," *Le Progrès* [Lyon], February 13, 1865.

12.   "Réponses de la Chambre Syndicale des Soieries de Lyon," *Enquête parlementaire sur les conditions du travail en France* (Rhône, 1872–75), Premier Questionnaire A, Observations, Archives Nationales (hereafter AN), C 3021, *Enquête sur les conditions du travail en France (1872 à 1875): Région du Sud-Est (Rhône).*

13.   Simon, "L'Apprentissage."

14.   César Maire, "A propos d'apprentissage," *Le Progrès,* February 26, 1865.

15.   Ibid. In discussing the relative conditions of female weavers and dévideuses, Maire stressed the similarity of their economic situations but implied that this similarity also extended to the position of servitude.

16.   Most observations of women's work in the silk industry of this period focused on the conditions of young female workers aged approximately fourteen through twenty-one. This suggests an especially prominent place of youth in the female labor force of the industry.

17.   Simon, "L'Apprentissage." The difficulty of interpreting wage data and comments concerning wages is illustrated by these seemingly contradictory (or rapidly changing) assessments of the relative wages of male and female weavers. According to Jules Simon, *L'Ouvrière* (Paris: Hachette, 1861), p. 32, men and women earned the same piece rate (wage per meter of cloth woven), but men earned a larger day rate because of their greater physical strength, enabling them to weave cloths of larger width. This would, of course, reconcile the seemingly contradictory assessments of relative earnings, if Simon's later statement in "L'Apprentissage" referred to piece rates rather than to daily earnings. However, the explanation is a bit too cavalier to be accepted uncritically. Moreover, the police agent's report, cited below, suggests a more systematic difference between men's and women's compensation for the same work done. This difference may have been precisely the result of the partial payment of women by bed and/or board. Their daily money wage would, therefore, have been lower than that earned by men who lodged and ate outside the household shop. Women workers who were not residents or who did not take meals with their master's family would have had to compete with resident working women rather than with nonresident working men, and their average daily wage would have been depressed thereby relative to the wage of the men. In other words, female residency would have caused, or at least strengthened, the segmentation of the labor market on the basis of sex.

18.   "Rapport adressé à Monsieur Delcourt, Commissaire spécial," September 9, 1868, AML, I2–47(A), No. 309.

19.   "Rapport à Monsieur Delcourt, Commissaire spécial, sur la situation de la fabrique des étoffes de soies," March 8, 1868, AML, ibid., No. 310.

20. "Rapport à Monsieur Delcourt, Commissaire spécial, sur la situation de la fabrique," March 6, 1869, AML, ibid., No. 312.

21. Police reports, June 21, June 25, July 13, and July 15, 1870, AML, I2–47(B); "Chronique locale," *Le Progrès*, July 15, 1870.

22. Pierre Dronier, *Essai sur la décadence actuelle de la fabrique lyonnaise* (Lyon: Nigon, 1860), pp. 6–8. (Bibliothèque du Musée des Tissus de Lyon, C.1559).

23. See report on *étoffes façonnées*, "Situation de l'industrie à Lyons," December 15, 1866, and March 15, 1867, AML, I2–47(A), Nos. 193, 196.

24. For a more thorough description of industrial expansion in Second Empire Lyons, see Michel Laferrère, *Lyon: ville industrielle* (Paris: Presses universitaires de France, 1960).

25. See Charlene-Marie Leonard, *Lyon Transformed: Public Works of the Second Empire* (Berkeley: University of California Press, 1961).

26. Report from Prefect of Rhône to Minister of Interior, July 20, 1857, AN, F^{1c} III Rhône 5, *Comptes-rendus administratifs (An III à 1870)*. See also the "Situations industrielles" from June 1859 to March 1870, AML, I2—47(A), Nos. 166–213.

27. "Situation de l'industrie à Lyon au 15 Décembre 1866," AML, ibid., No. 193.

28. Sreten Maritch, *Histoire du mouvement social sous le Second Empire à Lyon* (Paris: Rousseau, 1930).

29. "Les Reclamations des Tisseurs," *Le Progrès*, October 20, 1866; "Lettre de M. de la Valette sur le chômage lyonnais" and letter from weavers Gargnier, Chepié et al. in response, *Le Progrès*, October 28, 1866.

30. "Rapport à Monsieur Delcourt, Commissaire Spécial, sur la situation de la fabrique des étoffes de soies au 4e Trimestre Xbre [sic] 1866," December 8, 1866, AML, I2–47(A), No. 301.

31. "Rapport à Monsieur Delcourt, Commissaire Spécial, sur la situation de la fabrique de soieries," December 7, 1869, AML, I2–47(A), No. 315.

32. Lequin, *Les Ouvriers*, pp. 250–51.

33. Joan W. Scott and Louise A. Tilly, "Women's Work and the Family in Nineteenth-Century Europe," *Comparative Studies in Society and History* 17 (January 1975):52.

34. See reports on *dévidage* and *moulinage*, "Situation de l'industrie à Lyon," December 15, 1866, op. cit.

35. E. Pariset, Report to Chamber of Commerce of Lyons concerning children in industry, June 15, 1867, *Compte-rendu des travaux de la Chambre de Commerce de Lyon, années 1865, 1866, 1867, 1868*, pp. 148–50.

36. Ibid., p. 148.

37. Neil J. Smelser, *Social Change in the Industrial Revolution* (Chicago: The University of Chicago Press, 1959), pp. 208–9; B. L. Hutchins, *Women in Modern Industry* (London: G. Bell and Sons, 1915), pp. 60–61.

38. Dronier, *Essai sur la décadence actuelle*, p. 17.

39. Louis Reybaud, *Etudes sur le régime des manufactures: condition des ouvriers en soie* (Paris, 1859), p. 191.

40. Laferrère, *Lyon*, p. 107.

41. Ibid., p. 96.

42. Ibid.

43. Colette Yver, *Haudequin, de Lyon* (Paris: Calmann-Lévy, 1927), p. 8.

44. Ibid., p. 80.

45. Laferrère, *Lyon*, p. 168.

46. Landes, *The Unbound Prometheus*, p. 131.

47.   Daniel Thorner, Basile Kerblay, and R. E. F. Smith, eds., *A. V. Chayanov on the Theory of Peasant Economy* (Homewood, Ill.: Richard D. Irvin, 1966).

APPENDIX

Regression Equations

$$1847: \text{Ie} = \frac{-.56 \, \text{R}}{(64.63)} + \frac{.10 \, \text{F}}{(2.09)} - \frac{.24 \, \text{P}}{(11.19)} + \frac{.12 \text{A}}{(2.96)} - .38$$

$$r^2 = .42 \qquad F = 22.49$$
$$\text{Critical F} = 2.45$$

$$1866: \text{Ie} = \frac{-.66 \text{R}}{(62.39)} + \frac{.15 \, \text{F}}{(3.29)} - \frac{.07 \, \text{P}}{(.65)} - \frac{.03 \, \text{A}}{(.14)} - .20$$

$$r^2 = .46 \qquad F = 16.50$$
$$\text{Critical F} = 2.51$$

Ie =   Index of entrepreneurship

R   =   Proportion of relatives (i.e., relatives of the head or spouse) among all household residents exclusive of head and spouse

F   =   Proportion of females among all such residents

P   =   Proportion of plain-cloth looms among all looms

A   =   Current age of head of household

The numbers in parentheses under each variable coefficient are the calculated F-values for that coefficient. The F-value for the entire equation is given as 'F = .' Statistically significant coefficients are those with F-values equal to, or greater than, the Critical F. These are the underlined coefficients. The numbers at the far right side of each equation are the constants in the multivariate regression.

SIX

Incident at the
Statue of the Virgin Mary
The Conflict of Old and New in
*Nineteenth-Century Limoges**

JOHN M. MERRIMAN

During the bitter and violent strikes in Limoges, France, during April 1905, the butchers of the city posted armed guards to defend their statue of the Virgin Mary, which had guarded their private chapel for more than four and a half centuries, against the porcelain workers from the city's industrial faubourgs. A generation earlier, there had been more than two hundred statues of Mary and the saints in Limoges, a city once known as "Holy Limoges." Almost all were in the central city and few or none in the working-class faubourgs that had spread along the main roads into the city. During this intense period of strikes in 1905, no violent confrontation between religious butchers and anticlerical porcelain workers took place—the energies and organization of the porcelain workers were directed against the patrons and the troops and police sent to keep order. The statue survived and is still there. But almost all of the others fell victim to the forces which brought Limoges a new reputation, that of *une ville rouge.*

Limoges's reputation in the nineteenth century as a radical city began as early as the end of the Restoration, when youthful bourgeois successfully challenged the Bourbon government. Some twenty years later, the workers of the city disarmed the bourgeois National Guard two months before the June Days exploded in Paris in 1848. In 1851, Limoges *démoc-socs* went into the countryside and succeeded in organizing some resistance to the coup d'état of Louis Napoleon Bonaparte.[1] When strikes were declared legal in 1864,

*Research for this article was made possible by grants from the Whitney Griswold Fund and the Concilium on International and Area Studies, both at Yale University.

workers organized work stoppages in several trades and industries. At each major social and political challenge to the French government in the nineteenth century, Limoges was in the forefront. The end of the empire was no exception. A series of strikes followed a revival of organization by Limoges porcelain workers early in 1870. The Limoges Commune was briefly proclaimed in April 1871, after workers prevented the departure of troops sent to repress the Paris Commune. The Confédération Générale du Travail (C.G.T.) was founded in Limoges in 1895. Ten years of labor militancy culminated in the 1905 strikes (see photo insert). And between 1910 and 1914, during the years of the Nationalist revival in France, Limoges had one of the highest rates of strikes in France.[2] During the war, the deputies of Haute Vienne, Limoges's *département*, issued the first organized wartime call for peace, in the antimilitarist tradition which had developed in the city over the years.

Why was Limoges at the crest of every wave of social and political conflict in France? Beneath nearly a century of conflict lay a fundamental urban transformation which saw a commercial town become an industrial city of expanded size and altered consciousness. The city's workers emerged as contenders for political power over the course of a century, first reflecting the impact of bourgeois tutelage, or what Maurice Agulhon has aptly called "democratic patronage," and then going it alone, but often finding a strong segment of radical bourgeois as allies.[3] Beginning with the Second French Republic, the politics of the city also became those of the countryside—with the exception of *l'année terrible* of 1870–71. The allegiances of class that developed in Limoges came to set the tone of political radicalism which marked the city's metamorphosis from "Holy Limoges" to "the Rome of Socialism."

This essay contrasts the communities of butchers and porcelain workers of Limoges to illustrate the process by which urbanization and industrialization fundamentally transformed the city, the consciousness of its inhabitants, the locus of social and political conflict, and even the politics of the city's region. What factors accounted for the emergence of a relatively class-conscious community of workers which cut, to some extent, across occupational lines and which enjoyed some bourgeois support? How important was social geography in the organized quest of workers for political power in their city? How did traditional communities—like the city's butchers—with a corporate consciousness solidified by literally centuries of common experience fare in the face of rapid urban change? True, the relatively small group of butchers gathered on their own street were probably the most traditional trade in Limoges from any point of view and few comparable groups existed well into the nineteenth century. The porcelain workers, on the other hand, were the largest, most organized, militant, and geographically stable workers in the city. Yet such comparisons between social groups within the city over time may illuminate the evolution of nineteenth-century French cities, how, why, and in what ways were they reshaped, and what were the implications for urban politics and those of the city's hinterland.

The city itself—its configuration, neighborhoods, and relationship to its region—is often the neglected historical personage in the drama of social and political change when in fact it came to define and shape those changes. The impact of large-scale industrialization, the creation of a working class and the development of the labor movement cannot be divorced from its physical setting.

Emmanuel Leroy Ladurie once divided historians into parachutists and truffle hunters. We will need to be both, for the task at hand is far greater than the length and hopes of a short essay. As parachutists, we will first sketch the outlines of the city's growth as it might have been seen during a very slow descent of almost a century, beginning about 1815. We will then move from the broad outlines of the social, political, and geographic dimensions of the urbanizing experience of a single city to do some "truffle hunting," focusing on the experience of Limoges's butchers over the course of a century of life in a changing urban environment.

Limoges was one of France's fastest growing cities in the nineteenth century, with its population growing by 65 percent from 1846 to 1881, increasing from about 25,000 in 1821 to approximately 42,000 in 1851, 59,000 in 1876, 73,000 in 1891, and over 85,000 in 1911.[4] This rate of growth, while not terribly impressive by English standards, was considerable, particularly in that Limoges is the capital of the Limousin and the department of Haute Vienne, both of which were losing population. Old Limoges stood on one bank of the Vienne River, enclosed in an amphitheater-like setting in the valley of the Vienne, a plain broken by small hills that have always hindered traffic in the central city. Until the French Revolution, Limoges was really two separate walled cities that had been enemies upon occasion and once fought a war. During the One Hundred Years' War, the "cité" was destroyed by the English while the "château," the other city, survived and indeed prospered for having favored the enemy. During the Renaissance, Limoges was renowned for its enamels and began to emerge as a major commercial center, favored by its location as an axis for the roads from Paris to Toulouse and from Lyon to Bordeaux. At Limoges's three most important fairs, Bordeaux wines were traded for iron and textiles from the north, eau de vie, salt, and spices from the west, and hats made in the east. Even during the Restoration (1815–30), more tonnage of wines rattled through the city than its new product, porcelain. The 1768 discovery of kaolin, a fine white clay, near St. Yrieix, a relatively short distance from Limoges, changed the city and its region. During the course of the nineteenth century, Limoges became a major center for the production of porcelain, particularly after the arrival in 1842 of the American David Haviland, in search of porcelain to market in the United States. By 1848 the number of workers employed in the industry had jumped to about 4,000; twenty years earlier there had been 800 or 900. The dispersed and languishing textile industry was replaced as the city's premier product.[5] By 1901, despite many severe crises and setbacks, the industry employed more than 8,000 workers, many of them women, such as the *decalqueuses*, who put the decal designs on plates and had replaced many of the skilled *artistes en porcelaine* or decorators (Renoir began as one) who had hand painted the porcelain. Limoges's shoe industry expanded even more rapidly, but much later in the century. Mechanization imported from St. Louis allowed the expansion of shoemaking, which became the city's second industry during the Third Republic, but one in which the role of skilled artisans was diminished as unskilled migrants, particularly females, made up a large part of the work force.[6]

The growth of these industries altered the shape and life of Limoges. Until the Second Empire, the production of porcelain was dependent upon and largely situated near the river, where an insular community of river workers, whose wives frequently were the city's laundresses, floated the wood that fueled the fires for the *fours*. The shift to coal, which could be brought in plentiful quantities and cheaply after the railroad came to Limoges in 1856, permitted the expansion of porcelain production. At the same time, porcelain *patrons* ceased to be former skilled workers who had accumulated enough capital to begin a small operation. The new porcelain *patrons*, who required a considerable capital outlay and were more distant from the production process, were able to adopt techniques of mass production. While the *fabricant* François Alluaud earlier had constructed the first building designed as a porcelain factory near the Vienne River, the new larger factories (see photo insert) were located in the faubourgs, relatively near the railway depots built in the 1850s.

The altered industrial geography of Limoges may be seen in the maps showing the city and particularly its northern edge in 1828, 1851, and 1892 (see photo insert). This shift in the locus of industry and an expanding population encouraged population growth away from the saturated and cramped central city. Migrants, drawn from the Limousin's generally infertile land by the possibilities of work in the city, settled in the 1830s and 1840s along the roads that radiated like spokes from the center city. Most of this industrial expansion was to the north, away from the river and in the direction of the porcelain factories. The (Faubourg, then) Rue de Paris had, by 1848, five porcelain factories and eleven fabricants de porcelaine living on the street. This faubourg left the city at the Place Dauphine and began a gradual ascent away from Limoges (see photo insert). Like the nearby Faubourg Montmailler, its houses were often as crowded, poorly built, and unhealthy as those of the center city (which were justly renowned for their shocking condition); but they were considerably cheaper and sometimes offered the possibility of a small garden because of the spoke-like shape of the faubourg streets. The Rue de Paris eventually gave way to isolated houses, sometimes occupied by weavers and peasant workers, then to farms and grazing lands that came to prosper as the city grew, and finally to the chestnut groves that still contributed much to the diet of the poor in the Limousin.[7]

Horace Say, the secretary of the Paris chamber of commerce, once remarked with some surprise that as a result of the rebuilding of Paris undertaken by Louis Napoleon Bonaparte and Baron Haussmann (whom Cobb once called the "Alsatian Attila") "one did not find bourgeois families" in the suburbs where those forced from Paris by expropriation and high prices had fled.[8] The same was only somewhat less true of Limoges's northern faubourgs although they were populated as much by *campagnards* settling in Limoges as by people fleeing the center city. As early as 1848 the faubourgs were occupied by workers of the large-scale industries. On the Rue and Faubourg de Paris (48 percent) in 1848, and the Faubourg Montmailler (46 percent), porcelain workers and day laborers, most of whom worked in the porcelain industry, were by far the two largest occupational groups living on those streets. By 1905, the weavers and peasant workers who once lived at the far end of the street, had disappeared. There were now many small shops to cater to the large population (almost two-thirds of all buildings in Limoges had some sort of workshop or store on the ground floor); but porcelain workers, shoemakers and other workers predominated. Settlement became, with organization and class consciousness, linked to the organization and relative militance of the Limoges workers. By the middle of the century, the center of the city, roughly corresponding to the limits of the city at the beginning of the July Monarchy, had retained much of the classical vertical structure described in many of Balzac's novels. Working people, primarily artisans in traditional crafts and day laborers, lived in the top floors while the bottom, larger apartments were occupied by more prosperous shopkeepers and professional people. There were some important exceptions to this pattern, as several specialized quartiers survived. A number of streets were exclusively occupied by Limoges's wealthiest bourgeois, their families and servants (such as the Rues Andeix Manigne, Montant Manigne, and the relatively new quarters of the Champs de Juillet and the Rue Pétiniaud-Beaupeyrat), and the tottering remnants of the city's small group of nobles, some of whom had had to borrow money from their neighbors, the butchers, in order to emigrate during the French Revolution; and other "specialized" quarters, first, that of the butchers themselves, centering on the Rue de la Boucherie; the Naveix quartier of river workers (*flotteurs de bois*) and laundresses at the edge of the Vienne and the *ponticauds* across the river; and several streets devoted to prostitution. The differences between the faubourgs and the center city, while in no way absolute, were nonetheless important.[9]

Limoges's boundaries expanded as its population grew. Where did this new population, particularly that of the faubourgs, originate? We know that the growth of the city was due to migration, which is not surprising, as deaths exceeded births in most early and mid-nineteenth-century industrial cities.[10] For example, between 1823 and 1834, births outnumbered deaths only in

1831 and the pattern continued throughout much of the century. Limoges's range of migration was relatively short, as demonstrated by a remarkable unofficial census apparently ordered by the provisional administration just after the 1848 Revolution and discovered in the dusty attic of the town hall. Preliminary work with the census of 1906 indicates that, if anything, the range of migration became even narrower as the nineteenth century progressed and the porcelain industry developed; skilled workers, particularly the artistes en porcelain and the turners and moulders, had previously included many workers from other porcelain towns in France, particularly Villedieu (Indre), Vierzon, Paris, and Bourganeuf in the Creuse. In time, some of these skills were developed in Limoges; the artistes en porcelain themselves were reduced in number and importance because of the shift to lithographed decals as the decoration for porcelain and because plain white porcelain which was mass produced required no decoration. By 1906, porcelain workers had by far the highest percentage of workers born in Limoges. But almost half of the population as a whole continued to be migrants; and these mostly came from Limoges's relatively impoverished department of Haute Vienne, particularly from the southern region.[11] Unable to be supported by the land or by rural industry, they came to Limoges in search of work. The drying up of porcelain production in the small Haute Vienne towns of St. Yrieix, nearby Solignac, St. Brice, and St. Léonard also gave migrants from those regions with some skills in the industry cause to come to Limoges. Some of these migrants lived with kin or with others from their native villages, and relied upon them for information about jobs and assistance, a sensible arrangement demonstrated for other regions. The *montée à Limoges* was thus easier, and by no means as exciting, as the trek to the capital undertaken by migrants from the northern part of the department who went north, especially to Paris, where they worked in the building trades like their Limousin confrères.

Limoges's short range of migration may have had some consequences for the growth of the city and development of a relatively organized working class which may cause us to rethink the relationship between town and country. Alain Corbin's careful study of the Limousin stresses some fundamental tensions between Limoges and the Limousin countryside before 1885; it is echoed by Eugen Weber's stimulating book, which relies heavily on the Limousin and several similar regions to support his general argument.[12] The *villauds* hated the mythical wealthy peasant (indeed a myth in the Limousin) who hoarded his grain and drove a hard bargain when he finally did decide to market his produce. At the same time, country people feared the city, its officials, bourgeoisie, and unruly workers; French rural folk embraced Bonapartism during the Second Empire, sidestepping the influence of the *notables* and protecting themselves against the political agitations and disruptions of the city.

Within Limoges, there were tensions between the villauds and the newly arrived peasant workers, called *bicanards*. The villauds, who considered themselves the "real workers," teased their rustic coworkers about their lack of a sense of humor and joked that they still listened for the call of the rooster which could be easily heard in the morning, and not the bell of the factory.[13] Rural migrants may have sometimes been seen as competitors for jobs, unwelcome refugees from the archaic countryside. Migrants pouring into the cities should, in any case, be expected to hinder and perhaps even challenge the solidarity of the workers already in the city, particularly those who were city born. Edward Shorter and Charles Tilly have stated that "urban growth impedes solidarity and reduces the ability to act together," an argument which is anything but a restatement of the uprooting hypothesis, but one which implies that recent arrivals will not have the organizational resources or shared work experience to become organized contenders for political power.[14] Indeed a recent study shows that shoemakers, who were less organized and militant than porcelain workers in Limoges, had a much higher proportion of rural migrants.[15] But Limoges's narrow range of migration may have contributed to the broad base of support enjoyed by national, departmental, and municipal socialist leaders as well as the giant cooperative association L'Union and the Bourse du Travail by making more likely the assimilation of migrants into a community that shared a relatively similar Limousin culture. Furthermore, it certainly helps explain the marked political impact of Limoges on its hinterland.

We should not exaggerate the antagonism between town and country even before the Third Republic at the expense of understanding some essential relationships between them. The population of Limoges was linked to the countryside in several important ways. The relative proximity of the natal villages of a good number of first- and second-generation migrants enhanced contacts between the city and its region. Consider one example. During the revolutionary months of 1848 in Limoges, the porcelain workers went into the countryside to convert the rural population, first to militant republicanism and then, in 1849, to democratic socialism. They failed in 1848, and a slate of moderate and conservative candidates for the Constitutional Assembly were elected from Haute Vienne. But a year later they succeeded; the Haute Vienne returned all Montagnard representatives, establishing an electoral geography which has varied little in the region since that time. I once described this contact between urban workers and campagnards as if reporting the meeting of two totally alien worlds; as if the market place, where relations were not always happy, or the annual fair where countrywomen came to the city to sell their hair, were the sole links between town and country. My simplistic account was misleading, because relations between town and country were much more complex, subtle, and intense than I had realized.[16] Limoges's workers had many ties to the countryside, the *pays natal* for many of them. For example, many porcelain workers were originally from the small towns manufacturing the product in rural Haute Vienne, such as St. Yrieix and nearby Solignac, where they had learned some skills which served them well in Limoges. When these workers went out in 1848 carrying a political message, many were going home.

The complex relations between town and country in Limoges and elsewhere have scarcely been discussed in the literature on cities and social change. But it may not be too far fetched to suggest that Limoges's faubourgs were psychologically as well as physically contiguous. This sounds like common sense, but has frequently been ignored. Most migrants had families somewhere in the hinterland, who shared their vigorous anticlericalism. They returned home when it was possible, or necessary; they spoke the same language. Newcomers who passed the customs barrier and entered the faubourgs found people very much like themselves. If one looks closely, signs of this closeness are visible: striking or unemployed workers returning to their villages for food and work—for example to work the meager harvests; porcelain workers attempting to organize resistance to the onerous salt tax in 1860; the comings and goings of ordinary people to marriages and funerals, including their own; workers returning to the countryside, as they do today, for their favorite leisure activities—hunting, fishing, and gathering mushrooms (*cèpes*). Indeed as one historian noted in an article on the 1905 strikes, "the links between the working population of the city and the rural population were numerous, and exchanges incessant."[17] Until World War I, many workers continued to speak a patois characteristic of Limoges's region, particularly the southern part of the department. Limoges and its workers maintained an important political influence on the region which went beyond the expected relationship with the small industrial town of St. Junien. The political clash between the countryside and Limoges during the Franco-Prussian War and the Paris Commune seems to have been an aberration related to the willingness of Limoges republicans to carry the war forward, which would have necessitated military conscription from an area with a tradition of repugnance for such service, and to a number of pillaging forays of unemployed workers into the countryside. The narrow range of migration almost certainly accentuated the political influence of Limoges, its radical bourgeois element, and its growing working-class population.

At the same time, over the decades of the city's industrial growth, it is likely that Limoges's range of migration facilitated the creation of a community of workers in the faubourgs which cut, to a certain extent, across occupational lines. Although the porcelain workers were the most geographically stable group in the Limoges working class (having a significantly higher percentage born in Limoges both in 1848 and 1906 than other groups of workers) as well as the most organized and militant, they relied upon the support of other occupational groups, as did Limoges's Socialist and trade-union leaders. It seems that non–Limoges-born migrants were relatively integrated into the working-class community and the organizations that provided a framework for the emergence of workers as contenders for economic and political power, particularly the Bourse du Travail, the cooperative L'Union, and the socialist political groups. At the local level the lines between "political" and syndicalist contention were blurred by the reality of municipal politics and working-class strikes. Migrants participated in this contest for power, supporting those

Le Cordonnier. Lithograph after C. Schultz. An early nineteenth-century shoemaker's workshop. Note the picture of Napoleon on the wall. Reprinted with permission of H. Roger Viollet, Paris.

4 View of Marseille. Lithograph by Dury. A splendid panorama greets bourgeois expansion. Musée du Vieux Marseille

Dockworkers Unloading Grain in the Port by Alphonse Hovette (1876). A view of Marseille. Musée des Beaux-Arts.

Women silkworkers in nineteenth-century Lyon. Musée Historique de Lyon.

Barricade and dead horse on the Ancienne Route d'Aixe, Limoges, April 1905.

Limoges porcelain workers outside the Haviland Factory in Limoges, about 1900.

A partial view of Limoges, 1828.

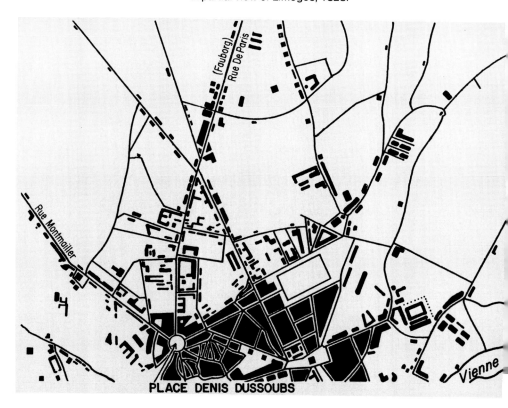

A partial view of Limoges, 1851.

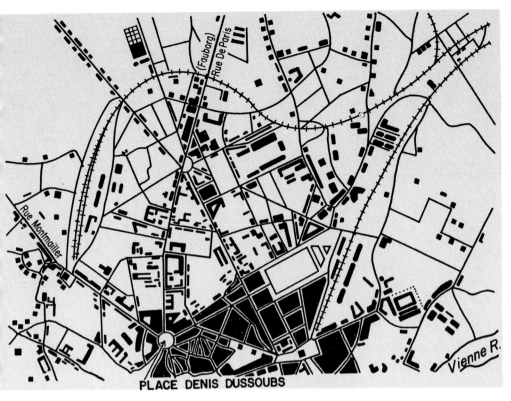

A partial view of Limoges, 1892.

The Faubourg de Paris, Limoges, about 1900.

The Place and the statue of Denis Dussoubs, Limoges, about 1900, facing the Avenue de Juillet.

The Rue de la Boucherie, Limoges, about 1900.

St-EVROULT-N.-D.-du-BOIS (Orne). - La Verrerie
Ouvriers au travail

Glassworkers and their helpers laboring under the watchful eye of a foreman in St. Evroult-Notre-Dame-du Bois (Orne) at the turn of the century.

D. D. - HARFLEUR. - ETABLISSEMENTS SCHNEIDER et Cie. - Atelier des Fusées - Machines-Outils

The Schneider Armaments Factory.

Workers leaving the factory of the Compagnie Générale d'Electricité in Ivry-sur-Seine, early twentieth century.

"We are approaching the big tunnel where there have already been three accidents since the beginning of the month." Honoré Daumier depicts an anxious moment for three bourgeois travelers.

Absinthe by Edgar Degas. Zola's central focus upon the female drinker, described with a
inimum of moral commentary, was also characteristic of paintings such as this one and
anet's *La Prune*, both of which were executed in the mid-seventies.

The scientist T. H. Huxley, a leader within the emerging community of Victorian scientists.

more organized and established groups. The fact that many still spoke patois in 1905 as in 1848 does not seem to have prevented them from participating in the politics and culture of community. Some Limoges workers protested the military conscription law on the eve of World War I in patois. Bicanards and villauds often spoke the same language of work and community, as well as patois. Work experience and residential geography were instrumental in the development of their consciousness as workers, but so too were their common geographic origins and participation in a Limousin culture which retained some of its "archaic" nature.[18]

I will cautiously suggest that by the 1880s, if not before, the customs barrier was a less significant dividing line than that between the faubourgs and the core city. One of the major markets and the Place Dauphine stood between or near where the faubourgs to the north began. The Place Dauphine, where the *diligences* once deposited weary travellers during the Restoration and the July Monarchy when Limoges extended little further than the place, was renamed the Place Denis Dussoubs during the Third Republic, in honor of the Limousin radical killed in Paris during the heroic but abbreviated resistance in the capital to the coup d'état of December 2, 1851. The statue seems to have been appropriately placed, almost guarding the entrance to the faubourgs; it was destroyed by the Germans during the occupation (see photo insert). The Third Republic developed in its own self-conscious and didactic iconography. Social conflict assumed a geography of its own in Limoges, as in Paris, Lyon, Rouen, and other cities, although this phenomenon was less marked in Limoges than in many cities. However, striking differences in voting patterns may be seen in the municipal elections held during the years that voting by section was imposed on the city. Emile Labussière, Limoges's socialist mayor and deputy, once called the second electoral district, which corresponded to the northern faubourgs, "Limoges's Belleville." The second section, together with the fourth and fifth toward the river, stood in sharp contrast to the first and third sections, which corresponded to the old central city and several new bourgeois quarters. Indeed, the second section met the first and third precisely at the Place Denis Dussoubs. Even given the location of an army barracks between the Rue de Paris and the Faubourg Montmailler, could not the placement of the workers' barricade on the latter street in April 1905 have had symbolic as well as tactical meaning? The working-class community in Limoges centered in the faubourgs, particularly, as we have seen, those to the north. When workers came en masse to the center city on May 1, it was as contenders for power to march to the Bourse du Travail after presenting petitions at the seats of national, departmental, and municipal authority, or to the large halls found only in the center city to listen to rousing speeches by Jules Guesde, Jean Jaurès, their respective lieutenants, to local labor leaders such as Edouard Treich and Jean Rougerie, or to political bosses such as Emile Labussière, or, later, Léon Betoulle. And was it more than coincidence that when the long-neglected and terribly sordid Viraclaud quarter was demolished at the turn of the century and a new prefecture built, the office for *assistance publique* faced the direction of the faubourgs?

Politics in Limoges, which were closely if not inextricably tied to the labor movement, were hardly ever triggered by wrangling party congresses or automatic imitations of events and issues in Paris. Control of the city was at stake, and despite the strength of the Guesdists, the working-class political party, a reformist municipal socialism predominated and worked in Limoges. After the violence and disappointments of 1905 led to a Radical takeover of the town hall, the socialists were once again victorious in 1912. The issues at stake set much of one class against another, but perhaps also the faubourgs and the relatively recently formed community of workers and their bourgeois allies against the traditional city.

This takes us back to the butchers and the symbolic confrontation which took place under the beatific gaze of the Virgin Mary in front of the chapel of St. Aurelien on the Rue de la Boucherie. No community was more firmly identified with the traditional city than the butchers. Their primary allegiances were to their trade and the families of their trade, their neighborhood, saints, and to a hierarchical and vertical system of political and moral authority based upon the power of father, priest, and king. In this way they resembled a good many trades in traditional French cities. In Limoges, they were perhaps most analagous to the flotteurs de bois and laundresses of the Naveix quartier along the Vienne River. Urban growth and large-scale industrialization brought, as we have seen elsewhere in this volume, a shift in solidarities and consciousness. This transformation may be traced—where it perhaps may most usefully be studied and seen today—in the stones of the city. How did the butchers fare in nineteenth-century Limoges? On that day in 1905, two communities, one old and one relatively new, with different solidarities, allegiances, and priorities, but both defined by their own work experiences and a strong sense of neighborhood, momentarily confronted each other.

In 1854, a Bordeaux visitor to Limoges had recalled his visit:

> I suddenly found myself in a street forming a horseshoe, humid, and closed tightly by relatively tall houses, which tried to hide their decay with a rather offensive whitewash. There I found only the exhalations of sweat and blood, a chaos of buildings, of muffled animal groans, and the hoarse moos of cattle; in the somber interior of the shops, nothing but ropes, hooks, and the dank smell of dead flesh . . . C'est la rue de la Boucherie.[19] [see photo insert]

In 1828, an army lieutenant, ordered to prepare an imaginary defense of the city, described the butchers as follows:

> [They] form a type of corporation . . . [and] have nothing in common with the rest of the city; their clothes, their habits, the saints who protect them, their church, their language, indeed everything is unique to them. They delight in the most excessive filth. Under no circumstances will they change their clothes . . . showing up at every gathering and public festival as though they

were going off to the most disgusting tasks of their profession ... even those people not ordinarily repelled stay far away.[20]

Thus the butchers were, during the Restoration, left alone to organize their own National Guard unit. The butchers of Limoges, first mentioned as a corporation in 1322, had received an absolute monopoly on meat slaughtered in the city in 1535; over three hundred years later that monopoly was essentially intact. Unlike any other trade or occupation, the butchers paid their customs taxes on goods brought into the city by subscription, or *abonnement*, and divided the tax among themselves. They waged war against the itinerant sellers of meat, protecting their privileges.

The center of their closed community was on the Rue de la Boucherie (see photo insert), where only butchers and their families lived. There were only six butcher clans, as there had been at the end of the seventeenth century: Plainemaison (who dated as far back as 1344), Cibot (1362), Parot (1535), Pouret (1536), Malinvaud (1561), and Juge (1575). Virtually all marriages were arranged within the families. The Revolution had only nominally ended the tradition of primogeniture on the Rue de la Boucherie, where the absolute authority of the father was passed on to the eldest son. This was a weighty charge in that many of the butchers had extremely large families: one Cibot had twenty-three children and another sent sixteen into the crowded street; there were fourteen Malinvaud children in one family and fifteen in another. No one even bothered to count the cousins; and ten Plainemaison offspring lived in the same house. The butchers retained their traditional nicknames throughout the nineteenth century, as in the sixteenth. These were even listed in the departmental almanachs as late as 1914. These names, which were necessary to differentiate the various Léonards, Martials, and Jeans (all extremely common Limousin names), had their origins in personal habits (Martial Pouret *dit* l'abbé, who was pious; Francois Cibot, *dit* le Pape, who was pious and perhaps bossy; Parot-Cherant, whose prices were high); physical characteristics (Parot-the-flat-nose, Eloi Cibot Père *dit boiteux*, the lame, whose son inherited the name but presumably not the limp); or experiences (Cibot *dit* Maisonneuve, who built a new house, Plainemaison *dit* Louis XVIII, because he had once cried out "Long live Louis XVIII!" which would have been fine except that it was at the height of the First Empire); for others we can simply guess the origins of Jean Pouret *dit* le dragon; Barthélémy Pouret *dit* Jambon; Barthélémy Cibot *dit* Sans-quartier, and so on. The patriarchs gathered each night on the corner to discuss (or rather to fix) prices, do business, and prepare for the next day's foray thirty to forty kilometers in their wagons to the markets of the region. Their dogs terrorized the adjoining streets, it was noted, "an imposing batallion like their masters, when united."[21]

The butchers were fervently religious. One visitor recalled, with horror, that on the Rue de la Boucherie, among the "hacked and hanging pieces of meat, the glistening livers and salted hams and the blue heads of dead cattle . . . punctuated with large spots of blood were niches sheltering pretty statues of saints or rich madonnas with azure coats starred with gold, before which burned religious lamps."[22] The life of the community centered, as it had for literally centuries, on the small chapel of Saint Aurelien, which had been preserved during the Revolution when two of the wealthiest butchers bought it secretly as a *bien national*, or national property, on behalf of the corporation of butchers. "Woe to those who would be bold enough to violate the sanctuary which sheltered the venerated relics of Saint Aurelien," was advice given at the Jacobin Club of Limoges, which included only one butcher, *le citoyen* Audoin Malivaud *dit let Petit*, who, it was assumed, was sent by the Corporation of Butchers to gather information. In 1827 the chapel legally became the property of the corporation.

The butchers' confraternity celebrated Limoges's annual religious festivals, particularly that of their patron saint, Aurelien, and of St. Martial, the protector of the city. The butchers maintained their ceremonial rôle in the ostensions (begun in 1515) every seven years, during which the remains of St. Martial and other saints were paraded about town in a procession which involved a total of 230 relics, in 92 reliquaires and 8 *grands chasses*, one of which cost 45,000 francs and was made in Lyon during the July Monarchy. The butchers auctioned off the right to carry the most precious relics of St. Aurelien to one of their own, escorted the relics and the bishop who, during the Restoration and the July Monarchy, was a bit of a relic himself. They fired off their muskets during the final procession as many Limogeauds cringed and entertained the clergy at a subsequent banquet.[23] The butchers' wives maintained their own confraternity, Notre Dame-des-Sept-Douleurs and celebrated the feast day known locally as Notre Dame-des-Petits-Ventres by preparing steaming plates of special tripes.

Deeply religious, the butchers were devoted monarchists throughout the nineteenth century and into the twentieth. Having suffered during the Revolution, they had little use for the Orleanists and none for Bonapartists or Republicans. They insisted on their traditional right to escort princes of royal blood into the city in 1815 and 1828; in 1845 they had to outrace the less sturdy sons of finance to greet the duke de Nemours at the entrance to the city. But soon there were no princes or princesses to escort officially. Henceforth they corresponded with royal pretenders, and even the pope, who became an honorary member of their confraternity and blessed their flag in 1887. They responded unenthusiastically when the municipal council tried to present them as a folkloric remnant to two presidents of the Republic. Marshall Pétain ultimately proved more to their taste, and it was they who offered him the keys to the city in 1942.[24] But during the Third Republic, they celebrated the feast of Jeanne d'Arc with pomp, occasionally turned out for royalist meetings, were arrested for defacing the tricolore with religious emblems, and were still mocked as "the princes of blood."

But as Limoges grew, the butchers first began to run afoul of the municipal authorities in the name of public health. The lax municipal government of the

Restoration period, ostensibly run by an incapable nobleman who preferred his countryside residence and the breeding and racing of horses to his Limoges apartment and the tedious tasks of the mairie, had tolerated an occasional dead cow floating in the Vienne River, much to the horror of the customers of the new and profitable public baths. Subsequent administrations did not. And although the butchers refused to provide meat for ten days in protest, they were forced into a municipal slaughterhouse in 1832 and could no longer slaughter in the street, as was originally required by law to protect the customers who could see, more than they probably wanted, that they were getting fresh meat. During the Second Empire, the city's limited municipal pride was stung by the barb of a slick Parisian journalist, who, sent to visit Limoges's rather modest "Exposition du Centre" in 1858, sniffed around the city and, when asked his opinion, haughtily announced, "Limoges is a sewer!"[25] Another journalist, writing in *La Presse*, claimed that a visit to the butchers' street was enough to make even a Frenchmen a vegetarian. An extensive and hurried program of public-works projects and rebuilding, as in Paris, Lyon, Marseille, and other cities, followed. The old town hall came down, replaced by one which looked suspiciously like that in the capital. But although the butchers accepted street lamps, they tried to resist the advent of public latrines on the street that another observer called "without question the most disgusting street in France." The butchers' neighbors sometimes exclaimed that "pour arranger la boucherie, il faudrait y mettre le feu." This seemed a realistic possibility in that the city, whose houses were built of wood above the ground floor, had burned to the ground several times in its history and had other serious fires. But when flames threatened the Rue de la Boucherie during the disastrous fire of 1864, the officers of the confraternity hauled out the relics of St. Martial, and the wind, so it was said, shifted as it had during the 1790 fire, sparing the ancient quarter.[26]

Unwilling to change the way they lived and thus far spared an act of God, the butchers, like the river workers and laundresses and even the prostitutes, ran into more gradual forces for change which were related to the growth and expansion of the city.

The religiosity of the butchers had been the rule in traditional Limoges. At the time of the French Revolution, Limoges had a cathedral, thirteen parish churches, two seminaries and a total of twenty-three abbeys and convents. One-tenth of the population of twenty-four thousand served as some sort of religious personnel. Many of these churches, convents, and abbeys did not survive the Revolution; the uses of some of these other buildings were drastically altered, such as one former convent whose purchaser outraged religious traditionalists by dividing the space between a masonic lodge, a café, and a public bath. But organized religion continued to be an important part of life in Limoges during the Restoration and the July Monarchy, a fact particularly noted by the military officer describing the city in 1828. The majority of the population celebrated an astonishing number of religious holidays with verve. A good number of religious confraternities were thriving, having been reconstituted during the First Empire. The most important of these were the six groups of penitents whose origins may be traced to 1598; in 1806 they had almost four thousand members and were a major force in the city during the Restoration and the July Monarchy. Nowhere outside of the Midi could one still find such a "multitude" of confraternities and regularly see, as described by the 1828 military observer, "these long lines of poorly aligned men, processional crosses covered with banderoles made from the richest cloth, lanterns placed on the end of sticks, this fantastic procession, an almost barbaric sight, this garb recalling the classic costume of magicians emerging from the shadows in China."[27] The purple penitents still accompanied the condemned to their execution, as they had for centuries, having survived the inevitable disapproval which followed what perhaps was their most charitable act, helping a condemned man escape during the 1740s. The penitents participated actively in the ostensions, which was the most significant public event in the entire region.

Signs of religious attachment were easy to spot in Limoges. Stone crosses stood at several carrefours in the city, hindering the passage of traffic. Statues of the Virgin Mary and of saints could be found in niches at almost every corner of the central city; some were the object of special quartier festivals and processions. The cult of the saints and of the magic fountains continued strong through the first half of the nineteenth century. And the poor, as they had for centuries, still could be seen going from house to house on the Fête Dieu, asking for "le part de Dieu, s'il vous plaît," their piece of the special cakes baked for the occasion.

But as the nineteenth century progressed, signs of this traditional attachment to religion gradually disappeared. The penitents declined in devotion and in number and did not survive the beginning of the Third Republic. The bourgeoisie began to turn their backs on many of the trappings of organized religion. Anticlericalism was an important theme in the growth of the political opposition to the Bourbons before the Revolution of 1830; Limoges's young bourgeois liberals protested the political power of the bishop and the arrival of the traditionalist missions. The theme of "Jesus the Montagnard" seems strikingly absent from the radical political mobilization in the city in the Second Republic, although it formed an essential part of democratic-socialist propaganda in other regions of France. The waning of religious practice in nineteenth century French cities among both the bourgeoisie and the working classes is of course well known. Large-scale industrialization, political liberalism, and ultimately the advent of socialist, anarchist, and syndicalist ideology were incompatible with the maintenance of traditional social, political, and religious allegiances.

But it is worth noting that one important reason for the decline of traditional religious adherence in Limoges may have been the character of the migrant population which accounted for the growth of the city. Those moving to Limoges seem to have been already indifferent and openly hostile to organized religion and prepared to follow municipal political leaders who shared and capitalized on their attitudes. Radicals and Socialists in France could agree on issues of religion. Limoges's hinterland, the source of much of its population, was already "dechristianized"—assuming it had *ever* been Christianized as tales of wild superstitions were common—and Haute Vienne was considered to be a missionary region by the church. Both significant delays in the baptism of the newborn and an exceptionally low level of religious vocations in rural Haute Vienne indicated a growing indifference to organized religion. The region was the despair of Limoges's bishops and the department's aged priesthood.[28] The value of the faubourgs of Limoges and, increasingly, the central city became secular, and militantly so. By the 1890s the workers' "processions"—which were not really processions but *manifestations politiques* and sometimes *cortèges révolutionnaires*—took different routes and had a significantly different agenda of stops than the city's traditional processions.[29] The organizational world of the workers came to center, after 1895, on the Bourse du Travail and the cooperative association L'Union, which grouped five thousand families of workers, and not on Limoges's rather ungraceful cathedral, which overlooked the river and around which the first settlements had been built.[30]

The changing structure and shape of the city confronted the butchers, and the symbols of their community and traditional religion. The butchers had some allies during the anticlerical heyday of the Third Republic Royalists and Social Catholics praised their corporate, familiar, and religious traditions as a social glue which could counter the disintegrating impact of godlessness. They claimed to have discovered in the butchers a "pearl of the middle ages." One Royalist compared their quarter to the faubourgs, generally feared in French cities in the nineteenth century, "populated with factories which stretch out without end."[31] Another wrote,

> If one does not go to the butchers' *quartier* to find lessons in grammar or delicate language, one does find honest work. Confined to a special quartier, they have until this time resisted the invasion of modern ideas. At the time when the existence of society is universally threatened, where the question of work is posed as the most terrible problem, would it not be useful to establish, by the example which we have under our very eyes, the condition absolutely essential to social peace?

The butchers, he went on to argue, "have shown themselves wise by abstaining from certain novelties," such as the department store.[32] He held up the butchers, these pearls of the middle ages, as models for the community of workers to imitate. But the workers, whose numerical predominance assured a tradition of socialist municipal governments after 1890 (the only exception being the tenure of Doctor Francois Chénieux, a radical), wanted to live in their own era. The butchers' wealth (which, while wildly exaggerated, was considerable) and their avarice (which apparently could not be exaggerated) were resented. No one had ever enjoyed coming all the way to the Rue de la Boucherie for expensive meat which, it was often argued, was not always

correctly weighed. As workers broke many of the statues, symbols of religious fidelity,[33] radical and then socialist municipal councils, elected by the
workers, changed the name of many of the city's streets around them. The
Avenue de la Crucifix became the Avenue Garibaldi in 1883; and today a
large number of nineteenth-century socialists are still commemorated by
street names. A municipal decree in 1876 banned the firing of muskets
during religious processions; and in 1880, the municipal council dealt a
mortal blow to the butchers' traditional religious life when it banned all
religious processions in the city, citing complaints against the butchers as one
of the reasons.[34] The "princes of blood" protested against what for them was
unthinkable—the elimination of the ostensions from the streets of Limoges.
At least once they disobeyed the law, taunting a police commissioner and
nearly initiating a riot. They continued to illuminate their street on the holy
days or on the feast days of their saints, but the lights were gradually going out
on the streets around them. In 1883, a nearby *calvaire* was knocked down to
expedite the circulation of traffic while the butchers and their dogs were on
the alert to protect their statue in front of the chapel of St. Aurelien. Finally,
during the mid-1880s, the butchers were compelled by law to transform their
corporation into a legal association, while retaining ownership of the chapel,
in order to conform to the law on associations. Their *syndicat* officially
recognized by the government in 1891, was thereafter listed in the *Almanach
Limousin* with all the other voluntary associations of the city. They had to
wait in line to file their statutes at the prefecture like every other syndicat or
leisure group.

   By the 1890s, there were even some signs of change within the butchers'
community. The appalling filth seemed to be subsiding a little in the quarter,
where, in 1887, there were still fifty butcher shops. A few second sons moved
away and set up shop outside of the Rue de la Boucherie, such as Parot,
whose store may be seen in pictures of workers following the coffin of their
slain comrade at the Place Carnot in the heart of the faubourgs in 1905. Some
sons and daughters, having more education than previously would have been
possible, married outside of the community; there were other signs of the
decline in the absolute authority of the father, a change sadly noted by the
Social Catholic writers. And very gradually the butchers began to lose the de
facto monopoly they had had for centuries, as new butchers set up shop in the
faubourgs. In 1860, only four of the sixty butchers in Limoges were not
members of the original clans. But during the next forty years the names of
other butchers appeared in the annual *Almanach Limousin*: nine in the
1860s, seven in the 1870s, fifteen in the 1880s and eighteen in the 1890s.
And in 1887 there were six new names listed as members of the butchers'
corporation. But in all, the butchers had changed remarkably little, while the
city and its population, work, consciousnesses, social organizations, and
politics had changed around them.

   The insular community of butchers had, all in all, survived remarkably
well in a city whose life and very face had been altered by large-scale

industrialization and relatively rapid population growth. Limoges in 1905 had long ceased to be a city based upon corporate and religious allegiances; over the course of more than fifty years, a community of workers developed as contenders for political power. Their allegiances were those of class. Social and political conflict developed both a geography and an iconography. As the statues of the Virgin Mary watched over the old city, the statue of the Limousin Socialist Denis Dussoubs pointed the way to the new city, its factories, and its workers. Rapid urban growth forged a community based upon work experience, class consciousness, residential patterns, and even common geographic origins. Each of these factors was important, and together they tell the story of the development of a predominantly working-class city whose politics were for the most part socialist and practical, based upon an appreciation of the local contest for power. The religiosity, craft, social and cultural values of the butchers were of a different time and a different city. If one had asked those butchers to comment upon Professor Weber's engaging argument about a single urban culture conquering the countryside between 1870 and 1914, might they not have turned the argument on its head and asked, relative to their experience and those of other traditonal groups within the city, who conquered whom?

Notes

1. See John M. Merriman, *Agony of the Republic: The Repression of the Left in Revolutionary France, 1848–51* (New Haven and London: Yale University Press, 1978).

2. Edward Shorter and Charles Tilly, *Strikes in France, 1830–1968* (Cambridge: Cambridge University Press, 1974), p. 276.

3. Maurice Agulhon, *La République au village* (Paris: Plon, 1970).

4. Limoges was one of the fastest growing cities in France, this according to Charles Pouthas, *La population française pendant la première moitié du XIXe siècle* (Paris: Presses Universitaires de France, 1956.

1806	21,757	1861	51,053
1821	24,992	1872	55,134
1826	25,612	1876	59,101
1831	27,070	1881	63,765
1836	29,706	1891	72,697
1846	38,119	1901	76,832 (84,121)[a]
1851	41,630	1906	81,685 (88,597)
1856	46,564	1911	85,173 (92,181)

SOURCE: *Almanach Limousin,* 1864, 1873, 1886, 1893; Census of 1906, etc.

[a]Unofficial population figures.

5. See particularly, Alain Corbin, *Archaïsme et modernité en Limousin au XIXe siècle, 1845–1880* (Paris, Rivière, 1975), which is the definitive study of the Limousin during the middle years of the century; Camille Grellier, *L'Industrie de la porcelaine en Limousin* (Paris, 1908). Fascinating descriptions of the city are found in the War Archives in Vincennes, in MR 1298, 1300, etc. *The Almanach Limousin*, which was published annually from 1859 to 1914, is a remarkable source for the study of Limoges. See "Limoges depuis cent ans," in the *Almanach* for 1860 ff.

6. See Kathryn Amdur, "Unity and Schism in French Labor Politics; Limoges and Saint Etienne, 1914–1922" (Ph.D. diss. Stanford University, 1978), pp. 57–60, 505, 516.

7. Gaston Ducray, *Le Travail porcelainier en Limousin* (Angers, 1940), pp. 197–98. Few studies of French cities effectively treat the relationship between the city and its suburbs; see Jean Bastié, *La Croissance de la banlieue parisienne* (Paris: Presses Universitaires de France, 1964); Robert J. Bezucha, *The Lyon Insurrection of 1834* (Cambridge: Harvard University Press, 1974); and Michael P. Hanagan, "The Logic of Solidarity: Social Structure in Le Chambon-Feugerolles, 1871–1914," *Journal of Urban History* 3 (1977): 409–26.

8. Rapport du Secrétaire de la Chambre de Commerce de Paris, June 15, 1855, exposition "Le Parisien chez lui au XIXe siècle," Archives Nationales, Nov. 26, 1976–Feb. 28, 1977.

9. This brief analysis is based upon a study of two faubourgs and a number of central city streets: the censuses of 1848 and 1906; and information provided by the *Almanach Limousin*, which I have read for the years 1859 through 1914. A large proportion of Limoges buildings housed boutiques, stores, or workshops, as noted by the Prefect of Haute Vienne in his report of May 6, 1819, in AN F 7 9711. The streets of prostitution were the center of much controversy; plans for their demolition were proposed throughout the century; see Louis Guibert, *Le Quartier Viraclaud* (Limoges, 1897).

10. Between 1820 and 1835, for example, the average number of births was 1,136 as compared with 1,200 deaths; deaths outnumbered births 15,776 to 14,330 between 1849 and 1859 (*Almanach Limousin*, 1860), there being an excess of births only in 1850 and 1853. In 1881 (actually, December to December) there were 1,600 deaths and 1,676 births (of which 148 were illegitimate); the following year there were 1,729 births and 1,692 deaths, representing a relative decline in mortality. The fact that many people from the countryside died in the Limoges hospital, charity institutions, madhouses, or jails must be taken into consideration. Between 1884 and 1893 there was an excess of births in six out of ten years with the exception of 1882 and 1890–92. Corbin lists Limoges's net migration as follows:

1846–50	4,076	1866–71	4,252
1851–55	5,526	1872–75	2,258
1856–60	4,986	1876–80	3,398
1861–65	1,029		

SOURCE: Corbin, *Archaïsme et modernité*, p. 583.

11. The remarkable unofficial census of 1848 gives place of birth and *duration de domicile* of male heads of households; it is not complete, as a number of streets were missed, probably because of the *Affaire de Limoges* of April 27. I have plotted the birthplace of all porcelain workers and day laborers who appeared in the census. The census of 1906 was also at the mairie; it has now been put in a more organized archive nearby. There were some important shifts within the porcelain industry, notably in the decline of "specialized" migrants from other porcelain cities such as Vierzon and Paris. My findings are tentative since this work is still in progress. In 1891, 56,406 of Limoges's population of 72,679 were born in Haute Vienne (2,814 in Corrèze; 2,074 in Charente; 1,947 in Dordogne; 663 in Seine; 451 in the Indre; 346 in Vienne, and so forth).

12. Eugen Weber, *Peasants into Frenchmen: The Modernization of Rural France 1870–1914* (Stanford: Stanford University Press, 1976); Theodore Zeldin, *France: Ambition, Love and Politics* (Oxford: Oxford University Press, 1976).

13. Georges-Emmanuel Clancier, *La Vie quotidienne en Limousin au XIXe siècle*. See also Clancier's novel, *Le Pain Noir*, which was serialized for French television.

14. Shorter and Tilly, *Strikes in France*, p. 276.

15. Census of 1906; Amdur "Unity and Schism," p. 516. According to the census of 1906, only slightly more than one-third of the shoemakers employed by Monteux, the largest shoe-making firm (50 Avenue Garibaldi, just up the street from Haviland porcelain), were born outside of Limoges. Amdur's sample, taken from the census of 1891, indicates that 42.4 percent of the shoemakers were born in Limoges; 41.2 percent in the department of Haute Vienne; 12.9 percent in neighboring departments; and 3.5 percent in the contiguous region. The fourteen years between the censuses is significant and indicates an increasing geographic stability in the industry, whose peak period of growth began in the 1880s.

16. John M. Merriman, "Social Conflict in France and the Limoges Revolution of April 27, 1848," *Societas* 4, no. 1 (Winter 1974): 21–38.

17. According to G. Désiré-Vuillemin, "les liens entre population ouvrière citadine et population rurale demeurent nombreux, les échanges incessants." "Une Grève révolutionnaire: les porcelainiers de Limoges en avril 1905," *Annales du Midi 83* (Jan/March 1971): 21.

18. See Amdur's summary of labor politics in Limoges in the decades before the war, "Unity and Schism," especially pp. 73–143; Désiré-Vuillemin, "Une Grève," passim; Pierre Cousteix, *Une Esquisse du mouvement ouvrier à Limoges depuis le XIXe siècle* (Angoulême, 1929). See also the following refutations of the "uprooting hypothesis": Oscar Lewis, *Anthropological Essays* (New York: Random House, 1970); Janet Abu-Lughd, *Caire: 1001 Years of the City Victorious* (Princeton: Princeton University Press, 1971); Joan W. Scott, *The Glassworkers of Carmaux* (Cambridge: Harvard University Press, 1974); Charles Tilly, "The Chaos of the Living City" in *An Urban World* ed. Charles Tilly (Boston: Little, Brown, 1974), pp. 86–108; Charles Tilly and Lynn Lees, "The People of June 1848," in *Revolution and Reaction: 1848 and the Second French Republic*, ed. R. D. Price (London: Croom Helm, 1975), pp. 170–209; Charles Tilly, Louise Tilly, Richard Tilly, *The Rebellious Century* (Cambridge: Harvard University Press, 1975).

Tensions between the center city and the faubourgs seem to have been acute in nineteenth-century French cities. Michelle Perrot, *Les Ouvriers en grève*, vol. 1 (Paris: Mouton, 1974), p. 220, has described Paris and its suburbs thusly: "La banlieue, sa réalité, ses représentations: beaux thèmes qui s'enflent en ce versant du siècle. Aux yeux des contemporains, trois traits la caractérisent: elle est misérable . . . violente et redoutable, mélange explosif de paysans déracinés, d'immigrants inadaptés, repaire des nouvelles 'classes dangereuses'; faits divers, rapports de police abondent en récits de rixes et d'agressions." Yet in some cities and in certain faubourgs, there may have been mitigating factors, such as the range of migration, availability of work, and commonality of cultural heritage.

19. *Almanach Limousin*, 1862, pp. 2–3; Louis Guibert, a Legitimist, noted that "il faut habiter longtemps notre ville pour savoir jusqu'à quel point le culte des bons saints y est pousée" (*Almanach Limousin*, 1862, pp. 2–3). See also reports in AG MR 1300.

20. AG (Ministry of War Archives), MR 1300.

21. See Adrien Delor, *La Corporation des bouchers à Limoges* (Limoges, 1877); "La Boucherie de Limoges," *Almanach Limousin*, 1862; Joseph Petit, *Une Ancienne Corporation et ses survivances* (Paris, 1906); Septime Gorceix, "La Corporation des bouchers et la confrèrie de Saint Aurelien," in *Limoges à travers les siècles* (Limoges, 1946), pp. 35–39; and M. le Marquis de Moussac, *Une Corporation d'autrefois encore vivante aujourd'hui* (Paris, 1892). The butchers' nicknames were duly noted in the *Almanach Limousin* each year, together with their addresses.

22. "Limoges depuis cent ans," *Almanach Limousin*, 1862, pp. 2–3.

23. ADHV Annex, 2V 3, reports on the ostensions; and Louis Guibert, "Les Ostensions," in the *Almanach Limousin*, 1862, pp. 63–71.

24. *Journal des Débats*, February 16, 1943.

25.   The public works in Limoges and their politics during the Second Empire may be followed in a series of articles which appeared in the yearly *Almanach Limousin*. Limoges's leading citizens were extremely sensitive about the city's bad reputation, which went back hundreds of years. A traveler wrote in 1753, "Le séjour de Limoges n'est pas agréable; les rues en sont étroites, mal percées et obscures. Les maisons, baties en bois, présentent le plus triste coup d'oeil; il n'y a pas une place décente, pas un édifice public remarquable." (Cited in *Almanach Limousin*, 1860.)

26.   "Limoges depuis cent ans," *Almanach Limousin*, 1862, pp. 29–30.

27.   AG MR 1300.

28.   Marguerite Le Saux, "Approche d'une étude de la déchristianisation: l'evolution religieuse du monde rural dans trois cantons de la Haute Vienne (Ambazac, Le Dorat, Limoges) au milieu du XIXe siècle à la première guerre mondiale" (Mémoire de Maîtrise, Université de Poitiers, 1971), which deals with only the rural communes of the canton of Limoges; anticlericalism manifested itself after the Revolution of 1830 and during the period of the 1871 Commune. See also M. Robert, *La Société limousine, 1870–1914* (Limoges, 1971), p. 125. The influence of the Revolution of 1848 and the spread of socialism in 1848–51 was also undoubtedly a factor in the weakening of religion in rural Haute Vienne, leaving little more than the superstition and the cult of the "magic fountains."

29.   See Mona Ozouf, *Fête révolutionnaire* (Paris, 1977).

30.   On L'Union coopérative, to which five thousand families belonged, see the report of the Procureur Général of Limoges, January 10, 1895, in AN BB 18 1992. I am currently studying the Bourse du Travail in Limoges.

31.   M. le Marquis de Moussac, *Une Corporation d'autrefois encore vivante aujourd'hui* (Paris, 1892), p. 81.

32.   Adrien Delor, op. cit., pp. 40–46.

33.   Paul Ducourtieux, "Les Statues de la Vièrge aux carrefours du vieux Limoges," *Limoges Illustré*, May 15, 1906. The butchers had a bad reputation in the countryside market towns. For example, they successfully boycotted the market in Laurière after preventing anyone else from buying cattle while offering only a low price and threatening local officials; 1M 142; report of the Police Commissioner, August 7, 1855. The statue mutilation was noted in the *Almanach Limousin* of 1865.

34.   This, of course, is an enormous and fascinating topic, as municipal politics in Limoges were bitter and important; the *Almanach Limousin* published yearly summaries of the meetings of the municipal councils. Much of the prewar period was dominated by the struggles of mayor and deputy Emile Labussière and his rival, the Radical Doctor Chénieux, as well as the clerical party.

SEVEN

The Three Ages
of Industrial Discipline in
Nineteenth-Century France*

MICHELLE PERROT

An industrial society implies order and rationality, at least a new kind of order, a new kind of rationality. Its emergence implies not only economic and technological changes but also the creation of new rules of the game, new forms of discipline. Industrial discipline represents only one form of discipline among others, and the factory belongs, with the school, military, penitentiary, and other systems, to a constellation of institutions which, each in its own way, contribute to the rule-making process. As a comprehensive set of considerations on power and rationalization processes, Michel Foucault's works encourage the detailed historical analysis of the increasingly tightening mesh of these networks. One of his latest books, *Discipline and Punishment*, goes beyond a mere study of the origins of the penitentiary system to research the whole configuration of interrelated phenomena.[1] It is a fascinating work, highly stimulating for an historian, provided that he does not attempt to find in it the reassuring convenience of a pattern. On the contrary, the historian should apply these often theoretical and abstract reflections to the details of concrete life, connect the various levels together, and attempt to focus on specific cases. Despite formal analogies, the factory is not a jail. Its main problem indeed has been to obtain from free people regular and prompt attendance.

Where did modern industry obtain its work force? How did farmers, craftsmen—or even vagrants—become transformed into workers? By which means? By which strategies? What were the steps of such a transformation? What were the effects of technology? What part did machines play? Did they

*Translated by Micheline Nilsen

modify the disciplinary process, and if so, how? How tenacious was resistance to this new mode of work and life-style? These are a few of the numerous questions prompted by the genesis of industrial discipline. As far as Great Britain is concerned, the works of E. J. Hobsbawm, S. Pollard, and E. P. Thompson, among others, have laid substantial groundwork.[2] French historigraphy is less abundant: the study of the workers' *movement* has polarized historians for a long time and eclipsed other problems, such as the development of the working class and its culture. However, this is changing rapidly. "Discipline" is now the order of the day![3]

In this brief essay, I would like to sketch a timing of industrial discipline as a convenient means of bringing some degree of order to apparently diverse phenomena, and to raise several questions. It goes without saying that this timing is somewhat arbitrary and is meant to be questioned.

Let us start with two preliminary remarks: first, as far as discipline is concerned, our main sources come from the dominant classes; as a discourse from the upper strata, they sometimes reflect more a plan or program than a reality. Besides, one must point out that a disciplinary system is never fully implemented. It is devised in order to deal with resistance and immediately fosters further resistance. A set of rules is always twisted to a certain extent and its reading might not provide an accurate account of daily life in the factory or workshop.

Second, evolution never occurs in a straight line. Systems overlap and coexist. A large factory could stand next to a small workshop or might itself contain several different forms of work organization. In the beginning of the twentieth century in the Lyon region, large companies contained autonomous teams of workers behind a modern facade. In 1907, the tanners in Gentilly— a small village outside of Paris—went on strike against regulations which imposed a fixed entrance and exit schedule and forbade random comings and goings, card playing and wine drinking in the shop, which the workers had been accustomed to previously, having been committed only to the completion of the assigned job. The same year, nail makers in Revin (Ardennes), who also enjoyed a great deal of freedom in terms of schedule and mobility, struck for over a hundred days against similar regulations which from then on confined them to the work place. They demanded as in the past "the right to take a break" outside as they saw fit. For them, classical factory discipline was being implemented at the very time—as we shall see—when it was becoming less rigid elsewhere.[4] Just as uneven levels of technology co-existed—as Raphaël Samuel has shown in Great Britain in a recent article[5]— varied disciplinary systems were maintained. However, prevailing types and tendencies could be found, as well as those which proved to be a sign of things to come.

The Age of Surveillance

In his famous *Panopticon* (1791), Jeremy Bentham conceives of a solution for the disciplinary problem in prisons—and, according to him, in all collective situations where monitoring presents a problem. It consists of a "simple architectural layout": from his booth located in the center of a circle, the inspector "sees without being seen" the prisoners whose barred cells surround him and are open to his viewing.[6] His mere watchful eye and the prisoner's awareness of his presence suffice to keep order.

Visiblity and observation were also the principles behind factory discipline. They coincided with a rudimentary technology based on tools rather than on machinery. Manual labor dominated and was highly divided. This division of labor was the basis for organization into various workshops and provided guidelines for spatial arrangement.

Aside from large factories, the work space was very simple and industrial architecture quite elementary. Large, often makeshift rooms grouped workers in order to save time. At first they brought their own tools—even a candle for lighting. (Later it was provided, with the cost deducted from the workers' pay, a system that remained in effect). Only raw materials were provided and control occurred at the two extremities of the production process. Preventing the theft of raw materials and assuring the quality of the finished products were the main concerns of manufacturers (*maîtres fabricants*). In large and complete factories, the system was somewhat more complex. Three principles governed spatial organization:

1. A political principle: the esthetic of the building, particularly of its facade, symbolized the king's power and the industrial privilege he granted. This aristocratic grandeur disappeared, at least for a time, from "middle-class" factories. Chaptal, for instance, cautioned owners against the investment of too much money into buildings and ostentatious display.[7]

2. A technical principle: the routing of raw materials between the various workshops in the course of production required convenience. Here one can see a first step towards the rational use of space.

3. And, lastly, the comings and goings of people and merchandise were controlled; hence a closed courtyard layout where doors served as strategic control locations.

The Manufacture Van Robais in Abbeville, established in the seventeenth century, implemented these these guidelines. Savary des Brulons described it with precision and praised "the order existing in the factory, and the large number of all kinds of workers who are gathered there." He noted particularly the magnificent and beautiful arrangement of the buildings and large workshops which they (the owners) have built."[8] The plant comprised a 1,000-square-foot enclosure located on the outskirts of the town between a road and a canal, surrounded by walls or ditches, and divided into several courtyards. It had six doors; through four of them, "workers come and go without coming into any more contact with the inhabitants of the Van Robais house than the latter care to allow. As far as these gentlemen are concerned, they can go through their house into all the workshops without being noticed."[9] The omnipresent master, who could at any time see without being seen, represented (without the visual element) the implementation of Bentham's pet idea.

Factory Discipline

The factory organized a century later by Vaucanson in Aubenas (Ardèche) also achieved this desired availability of visual control. The state factory inspector, Rodier, described it in 1758: "We walked into a 300-foot-long workshop with a tiled floor, lit by fifty windows hung with white canvas drapes. . . . In the center of this hall is an arched conduit with ajar tiles where each spinner goes, *silently*, and draws the water she needs. At first glance, this shop surprises the visitor by the large number of people employed there, by its *orderliness*, its cleanliness and the *high level of discipline* which prevails there . . . . We have counted fifty double lathes tended by one hundred spinners and as many reelers, as disciplined as armies."[10] One can easily see here the presence of two modes of discipline: religious (silence) and military (hierarchy and placement in rows).

However, the supervisory staff was relatively small. Two essential figures prevailed: the concierge or porter who controlled access, the central point of surveillance; and the piece inspector (*visiteur de pièces*) who examined finished products, particularly in the textile industry. They were key figures in discipline and keystones in matters of conflict. Neither of them had any technical training, nor did the *commis,* the employees responsible for records and accounts. Their status was equivalent to that of domestics: they received a yearly wage and sometimes wore a uniform which showed that they belonged to the employer's household. They foreshadowed the concept of "offices," distinct from the factory, where "management personnel" (*cadres*) devoted to the company would act as a buffer against worker violence if necessary.

Future "company regulations" were specifically foreseen in the Colbert-type factory where, during the eighteenth century, each new factory had its own. The placard or sign (*pancarte*) was posted for the worker to "read or have read to him." Few have been preserved.[11] They usually consisted of rather short texts (thirty-one articles at the "Manufacture Saint-Maur," eighteen at Cahors) which determined more or less strictly, schedules, breaks, holidays, modes of dismissal. They sometimes encompassed moral guidelines, forbidding fights, bringing alcohol to the work place, even the use of nicknames, and specified the nature of sanctions. These offer proof that factory regulations have extremely old roots and that a continuity exists between the "manufacture" properly speaking, relying on manual labor, and subsequent mechanized factories. As Marx demonstrated long ago, from the point of view of discipline, as from many others, the manufacture was the forerunner and training school of the mechanized factory. Industrial discipline also has its origins in the structure of society in the Old Regime.

Sanctions fell into various categories: dismissals, fines, as well as arrests and other legal action. The theft of goods, which sometimes reached considerable proportions, was considered an assault against the master-father figure and was severely repressed as such. The Napoleonic Code placed these domestic crimes under the jurisdiction of the Assize Court and made them subject to heavy penalties. In this manner, factory owners hoped to frighten workers. But on the other hand, this recourse to the state in matters relating to factory discipline had its drawbacks, and in the next developmental phase, there was less reliance on secular power. This type of discipline could be found in the Oberkampf Manufacture as it is described by Serge Chassagne and his collaborators at the beginning of the nineteenth century.[12]

The Disciplinary Function of the Family

The process of work itself remained mostly in the hands of workers and their families, the disciplinary influence of which must be stressed. As the economic unit of the domestic system, the family was a dominant force behind child labor, which tended to increase during periods of preindustrialization, as Hans Medick has demonstrated.[13] This type of apprenticeship—the mother and father teaching the children to work—continued well into the nineteenth century, wherever cottage industries, especially weaving, remained active. In his studies of the family, Le Play, who was obviously attracted by this social system, gave numerous examples of these arrangements.[14] It would be interesting for our purposes to know the respective roles the mother and father played, particularly as Medick's attractive hypothesis maintains that this system favored interchangeable roles and therefore fostered sex equality.

The first factories, whether mechanized or not, were generally located in the country, as close as possible to the labor force. One must indeed recognize the uniqueness of the French model of industrialization, woven into the rhythms of an agriculture which remained the base of the economy, a gradual transformation which occurred as a "shifting without a drastic break."[15] Here again the family unit was the core of the system. Manufacturers sought to employ the *whole* family in order to ensure the recruiting and devotion of the work force. Each member of the family was put to work according to his or her strength and status. As is the case with the domestic system, the father undertook the training and disciplining and, in some cases, the remuneration of his children. "In the spinning mills, children belong to the adult workers who are employed there," wrote Ducpétiaux; "in the spinning mills when the spinner has a family, he finds it to his material advantage to choose helpers among his children."[16] The most typical case was indeed the work team consisting of a spinner and his helpers. Mothers as well used daughters and very young children as helpers: iconography often takes us back to a time when the family unit served as a work team in workshops. Parents were thus responsible for the work and discipline of their children.

They maintained this control by the means of the *livret*, which legally could not be given to children under age and was thus entrusted by the employer to the parents, who ensured their children's punctuality and diligence. In this manner, industrialization, far from destroying the family, as one often believed, sometimes tended to strengthen it, to adopt it for its own ends, but not without increasing its contradictions and internal tensions[17]—the eventual rebellion of young people against the factory also became a revolt against the father.

On the other hand, the family unit became the basis for the first type of industrial "management," usually referred to as *paternalism*. Its history and functioning are noteworthy. In my understanding, it was characterized by three main features:

1. The physical presence of the employer at the production place—an arrangement extolled by such early industrialists as Bergery[18]—as evidenced in the layout of numerous factories of the first generation, which were built as rural enterprises with the master's house as the center.[19] After industries became concentrated (e.g., following the economic depression at the end of the nineteenth century), the employer removed himself from the work place and thus contributed to the collapse of the paternalistic system.

2. The social aspect of labor relationships was based on the family pattern. This could be seen in the language of the company family, where the employer was the father and the workers the "children"; in the existence of some form of welfare; in the expectation that the employer must provide work for his workers. It was also evident in the daily practice of patronage, noticeable on some holidays, connected with such events in the master's family as the marriage of his children. Although the existence of some welfare provisions was not always a necessary condition, in some instances it indicated the onset of another type of industrial relations.

3. Workers accepted this form of integration and even considered it a privilege. They identified in speech and spirit with the "house" and were proud to belong to it.

This acceptance by workers of paternalism was much more frequent than is generally believed. Numerous examples of this system can be found until the end of the nineteenth century and no doubt considerably later, even today. This enables us to understand why, in the end, many companies have not been affected by strikes, which are by definition unthinkable in a paternalistic system. It is obvious that repression is quite insufficient to explain the absence of rebellious spirit on the part of some workers.[20] Obviously, the workers' dedication is absolutely essential to the functioning of the paternalistic system. When it ceases to exist, paternalism collapses and must be replaced by another system of industrial relations. As it stands, paternalism is a rather subtle management system which needs to be appreciated from all its angles—sociological, political, and symbolic. For example, a study could be made of how the Fascists exploited persisting paternalism in German industrial society.

Workers' Autonomy

The preceding remarks mostly apply to the *textile* industry, keystone of the first industrial revolution. In the metal industry, the workers' autonomy was even more prevalent. Steelworkers were protected by their professional skills, which they defended fiercely through the practice of the *trade secret*, often passed on through the system of family apprenticeship.[21] Work was often subcontracted to family groups or professional teams, under various forms of collective contractual financial agreements. These contractual arrangements could also be found in the mines. The steward or work-team leader paid his fellow workers himself; however, he was neither a foreman nor a pieceworker. This mode of production lasted until major technical changes in the steel industry in the 1870s and 1880s considerably increased the role of engineers. In some sectors it survived much longer. However, the era of the puddlers or flatteners (*lamineurs*)—skilled industrial workers who retained real job control—did not survive the First World War.[22]

These modes of industrial management and discipline offered substantial advantages: they were cheap and appropriate for the weak control mechanisms of the first generation of capitalist entrepreneurs. These early industrialists, thus freed from a whole series of tasks, could manage with a minimal supervisory staff and devote the main part of their investment to productive operations. But on the other hand, these systems suffered from a certain amount of rigidity—they favored the status quo rather than growth. Indeed, skilled workers, because of their know-how, were capable of bringing about a constant slowdown in the production process. This was especially true at the beginning of the nineteenth century when French workers—as no doubt all workers at the onset of industrialization[23]—totally lacked the capitalist spirit. According to many witnesses, they "lack foresight and eagerness to work," preferring leisure to additional income. How could they be put to work?

Finally, family discipline had two types of critics. For some, the working-class family was quite incapable of disciplining its own children who played hookey from the factory, preferring to be vagabonds and live off odd jobs or pilfering. Large cities favored this emancipation of workers' children.[24] Others, including doctors and hygienists (as Villermé, or Ducpétiaux in Belgium) were concerned for the future of a race they feared would be affected by degeneration. They feared the ill effects of fathers, who were often the worst foremen. Out of greed or need, they demanded that employers hire their children very young, protested regulations restricting work, objected to mandatory schooling, and exerted a very strict discipline. Ducpétiaux reported that "if a child is mistreated, it is almost always by his father or brother."[25] It thus became necessary for someone else to step in. The factory had to develop its own discipline.

The Classical Age of Factory Discipline

First Managers

During the first half of the nineteenth century in France, theoretical thinking on work organization was relatively minimal[26] compared to the development of technological writing.[27] A systematic search of industrial journals, for example the *Annales de l'industrie nationale*, published under various titles from 1820 to 1849 under the direction of J. G. V. Moléon, might yield many surprises. Graduates from the Ecole Polytechnique, such as Charles Dupin and Claude-Lucien Bergery, were very aware of labor-related problems. Bergery's *Economie industrielle ou science de l'industrie*, published between 1829 and 1831 is of great interest for our purpose.[28] The third volume was devoted to the "management of a factory" and offered advice on "the organization of work." Recommendations included carefully calculated division of labor ("the duration of each basic operation must be carefully appraised") and suggestions on the "policing of workshops." Bergery demanded cleanliness, silence, obedience, and most of all, punctuality: he recommended the dismissal of those who were absent mornings, the "plague of our national industry."[29] He insisted on the attentiveness of supervisors, whose devotion must be purchased with high wages: "Nothing can be expected from the best policies without a constant surveillance. Do not attempt to save on the wages of the men you deem capable of policing well; they would have to be paid quite highly indeed for these costs not to be worth the price." Along with these standard procedures, he advocated a judicious division of the workshop, the segregation of sexes and separation of the production processes and particularly piecework, which links wages and production: "After all, you do have a very simple means to avoid problems and to obtain with certainty and without any supervision the optimal performance out of every worker: by paying him for piecework. The desire to increase their wages will prompt all your workers to supervise themselves. . . . The worker paid according to the work accomplished and not the time spent at work keeps working without wasting an instant for as many hours as his strength will allow him; he lengthens his work day until rest becomes absolutely necessary." By appealing to the psychology of individual interest and connecting wages with productivity, Bergery outlined more modern forms of labor management.[30] However, it is difficult to determine whether these suggestions had any actual bearing on the practices of employers.

These practices remained largely theoretical, a specialized technical staff played a part mostly in state-owned factories such as weapons or tobacco, or in semipublic companies such as mines and, later, railroads. Large concerns, which also employed such technicians, were still few and far between in the middle of the nineteenth century.

Architecture

The new factories were enclosures with their own regulations and watchmen. After the first generation of factories, often established in old convents put to different uses after the French Revolution, the new factories were built according to two main plans: "elevated" to take better advantage of the driving power of rivers (textile factories along the water); or at ground level, often built around a closed courtyard. The gate once again became the sensitive spot for surveillance; a bell or clock often was placed on top of it, as workers were only gradually beginning to own their own watches in the nineteenth century.[31] The question of the opening and closing of the gates became crucial in conflicts and workers' demands; the departure from the factory was a special moment in the daily routine, so much so that it became, between 1880 and 1914, the subject of group photographs which may be seen today on old postcards.[32] With the increased regimentation of the clock, the control at the gates became stricter. On the other hand, until the implementation of work inspection and its official reorganization in 1892,[33] employers enjoyed a form of extraterritoriality. Even today the factory remains a secluded place, and investigators as well as filmmakers know how difficult it is to enter a French factory.

Regulations

The factory regulations formed the basis of the system.[34] The Revolution had abolished the principle of regulations, but the practice remained in effect, leaving a state of disorder favorable to worker insubordination. This explains Chaptal's attempt to take things in hand at the time of the Consulat: he entrusted Louis Costaz, the founder of the Société pour l'encouragement de l'industrie nationale, with the responsibility for drawing up a set of general regulations. This project failed and the employer retained the right to draw up his own factory rules as he saw fit. The only constraint was the necessity of posting or reading the regulations to the workers (for instance, when hiring a worker) and the obligation to deposit a copy with the justice of the peace who, in principle, oversaw them. The regulations were thus the expression of the employer's will, in which workers had no part.

Regulations multiplied throughout the nineteenth century. Every factory of importance had its own set, more or less influenced by current models. They were relatively short and simple in the beginning of the century and became longer and more specific as time passed. The regulations of the Compagnie des Forges de Champagne de Saint-Dizier included more than 60 articles; those of the Industrie Textile (Roubaix-Tourcoing, 1900) 167 items! At first, regulations determined schedules and penalty-fine rates; they particularly included moral prescriptions. Provisions considering wages were added—often at the request of the workers themselves, concerned about arbitrary decisions—as well as hygiene and safety rules necessitated both by the presence of new machines and national legislation. This included the requirement of advance notice (in order to avoid a rapid turnover of workers), more specific prohibitions against circulation within the factory itself as it expanded, and even dress codes. During the Second Empire, a working woman in Aubusson was fined quite heavily for coming to the factory wearing sabots. Factory regulations followed the same pattern as the nineteenth-century legal code: as they become more and more complex and tyrannical, they become less and less enforceable. Hence the crisis at the end of the century.

Regulations included sanctions, usually fines, for a variety of transgressions, including absenteeism, tardiness, poor work quality, damage to equipment, brawling within or outside the factory, improperly extinguished pipes, drinking bouts (*ribotes*), "quarrels, rudeness, scurrilous language, indecent behavior," drunkenness, chattering, moving outside of the work area, rudeness towards supervisors, graffiti, and so on.[35] These regulations suggest a double purpose, at once economic but also fundamentally political, as patrons, through their hired staff, sought to discipline the body, the gestures, and behavior of the unsubmissive worker.

Fines for insubordination were often very high. As a rule, they were deposited in a special fund for collective use. For example, at the Thiriez factory in Lille, the fines were to be used for the celebration of the weavers' "Broquelet" festival. Elsewhere, they provided relief funds, but in any case their management was totally out of the workers' hands and therefore became increasingly resented. For this reason large factories were the first to abandon this source of conflict and favor a dismissal system inspired by military and school procedures. Thus at the Schneider plant in Le Creusot, the sequence was as follows: warning, temporary suspension (from a few hours to several days), and as a last resort, dismissal.

Supervisory Staff

In order to exert such control, the *patronat* came to be concerned with the necessity of creating a staff of overseers (see photo insert). At first it made use of the traditional managerial institutions, the military and the church. After the end of the Napoleonic Wars, many retired officers *demi-soldes)* were hired as foremen. Later the patronat turned as well to retired noncommissioned officers, who also served as overseers in department stores. Today companies such as Michelin or Citroën still resort to this type of supervisory staff. The church, traditionally devoted to children and women, provided personnel for living-in factories organized primarily in the silk industry of the Lyon region (Jujurieux and La Seauve were the two most famous factories) which employed either country girls or "repenting girls." The religious order of Recoubeau was even created especially for that purpose. The almost convent-like discipline of these institutions brought numerous conflicts, especially after the Revolution of 1848 and in 1880.[36] In a general way, the direct or indirect influence of organized religion on French factories was not negligible. In northern France, the clericalism of the patronat accounted for the long maintenance of fines against blasphemy. In almost every area, moralizing statements on workshop walls reminded the workers of their duties.

The introduction and development of machines brought new needs, including the necessity of competent technical overseeing personnel. At the beginning of the nineteenth century, British workers were imported for this purpose; there were approximately fifteen thousand of them in France in 1822.[37] However, their relations were poor both with the management, who resented their demands and mobility, as well as with the French workers, who detected in them the advance guard of industrial modernization, a threatening prospect for workers. Progressively, through the organization of courses or through direct promotion, French foremen were trained. Dupin and Bergery, graduates of the Ecole Polytechnique and the Société pour l'encouragement de l'industrie nationale, were pioneers in this domain. The role, social origin, and ratio of the foremen to the workers varied according to the various branches of industry, and this influenced the nature of their relationship with the workers. All foremen were not slave drivers—on the contrary, some of them exerted a representative function for their group of workers. However, employers did all in their power to ensure the foremen's allegiance and separated them from the mass of workers, using material benefits such as better wages, paid monthly, as well as symbolic and honorary privileges. During the 1880s, poor relations between foremen and workers were the rule. The workers mocked the incompetent and sneaky "little bosses" who acted as a real screen between themselves and employers. The rejection of the "running dogs of capitalism" and the "bosses' cops" was such that many union regulations required the exclusion of any member who was promoted to the rank of foreman.

The foremen developed a double role. First they maintained the traditional position of overseer. This function was particularly fraught with tension in the textile industry, where women workers protested against the foremen's familiarity and sexual demands. Workers' newspapers were filled with complaints of this nature, as some foremen could virtually use the promise of favor to blackmail workers. On the other hand, the foreman's role became increasingly technical. He had to watch and often adjust machines and thus became involved in the production process itself, which was increasingly beyond the workers' control. The foreman, as a result of his understanding of the various operations of the machine, could even determine the rhythm of work. The machine thus indirectly introduced a more subtle type of discipline. It also restricted the worker's mobility by literally fastening him to his seat in the workshop. Little by little, the machine came to impose its own rhythm, becoming the master of the game and gradually even replacing the foreman. With the machine, surveillance became unnecessary.

The Politics of Large Factories

Large companies did not limit their control to the perimeter of the factory. They attempted to extend control over the daily life of their workers through a set of institutions and a use of space which extended as far as building industrial housing (*cités industrielles*). These factory towns were not built merely to enforce work discipline but rather to guarantee a stable work force whose employment and, indeed, whose reproduction could be maintained as economically as possible. We might even speak in terms of the eugenics of industrial populations.[38] The origin of factory towns had its roots in the resistance to industrialization of rural populations, which only accepted the factory as a secondary—and unreliable—source of income. Rolande Trempé (within the single occupation of mining) and Yves Lequin (within the area of Lyon and its surrounding region) have demonstrated the intensity of this resistance, the history of which still remains to be written.[39] Here it suffices to point out that disciplinary systems are almost always responses to such resistance.

Housing, factory stores (called "cooperatives"), welfare funds to protect against accident and illness, schools, sometimes retirement funds, and leisure associations such as philharmonic, gymnastics, or sport societies were the main benefits provided by employers. Only large companies offered a complete range of benefits. At the Schneider operations in Le Creusot (Saône-et-Loire), such a system was fully implemented.[40] In exchange for their discipline, Schneider offered its factory workers job security as well as numerous social benefits and genuine opportunities for promotion, made possible by strict economic management based on the systematic reinvestment of capital gains. In spite of the employer's power—visible in every aspect of life—the Schneider system was not merely paternalistic. (Schneider, in fact, expressed his rejection of the Le Play version of paternalism.) Rather, Schneider established a policy of material profit and security that foreshadowed the large companies of modern capitalism.[41] However, its political despotism belonged to the classical age of industrial discipline. The great strike of 1899 at Le Creusot and Montceau-les-Mines was to show its limitations.

The Crisis of Discipline and the Reorganization of Work

Devised to put an irregular and restive work force to work, this discipline was very unpopular. The factory became a penitentiary where workers drudged and slaved like convicts under the iron rod of task masters. Between 1883 and 1890, several workers' newspapers in the Nord adopted the convict image: *The Convict (Le Forçat), The Convict's Cry (Le Cri du Forçat), The Revenge of the Convict (La Revanche du Forçat).*[42] These papers, like the majority of workers' newspapers of the time, printed an "abuse column" or "jail review." These columns often included letters from workers who denounced in no uncertain terms excessively strict work schedules, unduly high fines, and above all, incompetent, tyrannical, fussy, and lewd foremen. Many other signs indicated resistance against the factory, including chronic absenteeism and a high turnover ratio, especially among young workers. Recruiting workers was very difficult in some industrial sectors, such as mining, where people remained only when no other alternative was available. Personnel books, studied by Rolande Trempé in the Aveyron, reveal a great deal of instability. At the beginning of the century, the ironworks at Decazeville had to hire five workers to keep one, the zinc works at La Vielle Montagne, nine for one, and in 1907, the mines in Carmaux, thirty for one![43]

Collective protest against industrial discipline increased at the beginning of the twentieth century, as indicated by global strike statistics as well as local studies. In 1907, for example, regulations and fines were central issues in 78 strikes which mobilized over 20,000 workers in 277 factories. In the companies of the Lyon area, described by Yves Lequin, incidents with managing or supervising staff (concièrges or timekeepers) became increasingly frequent. Workers rebelled against these "little bosses," demanded the withdrawal of moralizing statements hung on the workshop walls, and would no longer tolerate insults or arbitrary treatment. In short, they expected to be treated with dignity.[44] Even large companies like Schneider at Le Creusot, where the system appeared to have been successful, had their share of unexpected conflicts. During the massive strikes in 1899–1900 in Montceau-les-Mines, and then in Le Creusot, which progressed with surprising momentum, the workers demanded above all the freedom of assembly and association, the right to unionize, and the acceptance of worker representatives by the patronat, a new factor to which we shall return.[45]

This resistance was reenforced by the support of young people from all milieux, rebelling against the traditional forms of discipline. At school, in the army, or in reform institutions for young delinquents, incidents and sometimes riots occurred. Contrary to traditional societies, the industrial society denies its young people a specific role and ironically causes them to become conscious of themselves. In the working class, many adolescents rejected the work ethic preached by family and school, and attempted to escape the dismal world of the factory. The Apaches, in Paris at the turn of the century, constituted one of the first youth gangs, envied and admired by their peers who believed they were the "knights of the modern city."[46] With time, workers' demands came to assume a more qualitative nature. They insisted on the need for free time and more control over their work. May 1, 1906 became the date of the ultimatum for the eight-hour workday: "From May 1st 1906 on, we will not work more than eight hours a day," proclaimed the CGT (Confedération Générale du Travail) posters.[47] As we know, the attempt failed, but it did result in a decrease in the level of production and an increase of the old slowdown tactic as a means of opposing the acceleration of the work rhythm, a common trend in industrial societies at the beginning of the twentieth century. Max Weber, the prophet of rationalization, described this process in 1909 in a celebrated article. The enduring fear of over-production and unemployment, as well an intense taste for daily leisure, led workers to this daily "loafing" which Taylor considered the main obstacle to economic growth.

On the other hand, workers who were now being deprived of control over the production process by mechanization sought to resist and demanded more institutionalized modes of control such as factory councils and delegates of factory personnel. This "job control" movement was quite generalized, as has been demonstrated in the recent works of David Montgomery (United States), James Hinton (Great Britain) and Patrick Fridenson (France).[48] One can speculate on its significance, interpreting it as a defensive move of dispossessed skilled workers or, on the contrary, as the beginning of a new vision of the workers' power. It nevertheless testifies to the acuteness of problems in the organization of work at the turn of the century and to the obsolescence of prior forms of discipline.

A New Work Discipline: Incipient Stages

Confronted with these problems, the French patronat, taken aback, hesi-tated. At times they seemed ready to give in: in 1899, Schneider accepted unions and workers' delegates; Louis Renault followed in 1912; and between 1905 and 1910, several factories in the Nord permitted workers' committees with some representative power. Take, for example, the regulations of a large soap factory in Lille. The first article stated that "workers are grouped in sec-tions, each with a foreman. Between January 5 and 10, each section will elect, by secret vote, two representatives whose mandates will last for a year. They are responsible for discussing with the employers the interests of the personnel in their section and for defending the rights of delinquent workers."[49] But in most cases, employers held on to their authority and absolutely refused any concessions in terms of sharing power; once the immediate peril seemed to have passed, they rescinded their concessions or attempted to co-opt the delegate mechanism. Schneider incorporated its "delegate workers," reluc-tantly accepted under Waldeck-Rousseau's pressure during the first days of the strike, into the management. These "delegate workers" became part of the new 1900 factory regulations, and were to act as the only channel for all worker demands, to the exclusion of the unions, which Schneider refused to recognize. Given a choice, most employers preferred to deal with "home" delegates rather than outside, independent unions. These unions remained the worst threat to employers who attempted to retaliate by creating company unions. Acting as a substitute for declining paternalism, company unions enjoyed substantial success, and seemed to suggest the possibility of a corporate structure, before meeting with failure.[50] By the eve of the war, employers had stiffened their resistance and resorted once again to the usual coercive arsenal: lockouts and massive dismissals in case of strikes (four hundred workers at Renault in 1913).[51] The factory remained a fortress.

Innovative measures were to be found elsewhere: in wage procedures (the development of a bonus system), in a socially minded technical reorganization which preceded and prepared the way for Taylorism.[52] The increasing intervention of the state and of specialized engineers were two sources of a "new factory" and of a "contractual" and "scientific" discipline.

The role of the radical and socialist left in the advent of industrial democracy was considerable and goes beyond our immediate scope. Commissions of inquiry such as the Office du Travail, created in 1890, and social legislation—the rudiments of a social security system which provided accident and retirement coverage and fostered social stability—were the work of a handful of politicians and administrators who claimed an allegiance to positivism[53] or to "solidarism," an organic social philosophy which deserves examination. Men such as Millerand, Briand, Waldeck-Rousseau, Léon Bourgeois, Arthur Fontaine, and Albert Thomas, whose importance has not yet been given proper credit, were very consicous of the need to make the factory more accessible in order to normalize social interaction. They wanted to mediate in relations between employers and workers both to prevent dangerous conflicts and to manage the work force at the national level. During the 1899 strike at Le Creusot, Millerand offered to mediate, suggesting the implementation of worker delegates. In November 1900 he proposed a "Project for the amicable settlement of conflicts related to working conditions," introducing joint planning boards and strike regulations.[54] Requirements governing industrial hygiene became more specific and led to the development of a new form of industrial architecture which provided for "neutral" spaces including locker rooms, refectories, rest rooms, and so on. From this point of view, the factories built between 1910 and 1914 are quite interesting. A new mode of control can be detected in them and the creation of an appropriate environment played a part in this control.

These politics of mediation and integration met with opposition from employers and from the major part of the workers' movement, which feared the interference of the state and the concomitant increase of control mechanisms. On the eve of the war, all of the problems of industrial democracy had thus been posed.

The Science of Work

The desire to create a "science of work" was the other avenue for change. On the one hand, the worker's body became the object of study and care. Physicists and hygienists studied movement in order to achieve a better utilization of the "human machine."[55] At the "Station du Parc des Princes," Marey, a colleague of Gilbreth (*The Motion Study*, 1911) pursued his fundamental research on continuous motion with the help of time-lapse photography. His associate, Demeny, intended to derive a harmonious and "rational form of gynmastics" from his observations, offering a contrast with the brutal and syncopated methods of military exercise. He hoped to develop "the ability to accomplish a large amount of mechanical labor in a given time," with as little fatigue as possible. The body became the focus of the production apparatus, less for its strength, which the machine rendered less and less essential, than for its ability to resist mental attrition. The study of fatigue (*ergonomie*) had become a scientific pursuit.

On the other hand, the work space, cluttered and irrational, became a subject of concern for engineers. Taylorism, which A. Moutet has called the ideology of engineers, was the outcome. It became the most visible element of a rationalization process which affected all industrialized countries and was accelerated by the World War.[56] These developments are well known and we are here only interested in their implications for work dicipline. Discipline is at the heart of the problem since one of its main objectives was a triumph over the workers' idleness (*flânerie*) and laziness. Several means were used to this end, including the replacement of old tools, still often owned by the workers themselves, with modern standardized tools provided by the company;[57] and the scientific measure of work. In addition the linking of wages and productivity was no longer by the old piecework system, with its approximate wage structure demands, but by the unquestionable rule of a minimal standard of work. Only beyond a specifically defined workload remunerated by a minimal wage was the worker's efforts to be rewarded by a "bonus." In another respect, worker initiative was considerably restricted. They now had to obey orders—the famous company memo established by the planning office. Workers were reduced to merely carrying out instructions conceived of and sent down from above.

This type of discipline completed the process of dispossessing the skilled worker of his expertise and consequently of his power. It reduced the danger of conflicts with foremen whose role was considerably diminished. The loudmouth drill sergeants were replaced by the cold exactness of timekeepers in white coats. The new discipline was conceived of as scientific and therefore even less open to question.

Just before the war, all of this had only reached preliminary stages in France. (In spite of the well-known strike in protest against the timing of work [*chronométrage*] at the Renault factory in 1912 and again in 1913, it is estimated that only 1 percent of the workers were concerned by Taylorism itself.) The disciplinary landscape was extraordinarily varied. All the various types of discipline which we have described could be found. Extreme differences existed according to geographical areas and industrial sectors. Some industries still operated at the age of simple surveillance while others were being influenced by changes brought from America and Germany.

We must carry this survey through until the present. What changes have taken place since the Second World War! Automation has introduced an ever more efficient organization of work, which has further reduced the initiative of the worker (indeed the "operative" has replaced the worker) and at the same time the need for surveillance. The watchful eye of the master has now become that of the computer. It has the force of mathematical logic matched to its quiet violence.

The penetration of the human sciences, notably of psychology, into industrial relations has considerably mediated authority relationships. Experts, with their measures and their tests, have taken the place of concierges and fines. Their judgment has the stamp of science.

Ever more invisible and further removed, discipline has also become increasingly internalized. Through education, in the largest sense of the word, the values of utility and work have molded the consciences of men who are defined by their place in the work process. The confusion of the unemployed (workers or *cadres* notably) in the face of unemployment, demonstrates how it is sometimes difficult (and not only for material reasons) to live with free time. The workers of the beginning of the nineteenth century were bewildered by work; we, on the other hand, find ourselves bewildered by freedom! Today, our conscience is our foreman. We can, under these conditions, ask ourselves if *autogestion*, as appealing as it may be, constitutes perhaps only the ultimate ruse of reason.

But at the same time, at least in developed societies, where the problem is no longer shortage but that of surplus and waste, production ceases to be the major imperative. The obligations of industrial work are no longer at the heart of social problems. For the same reason, industrial discipline as a standard no longer has the priority that it had in other times, as in France from 1850 to 1950. In certain regards, even if many workers find themselves thrown together at the factory, industrial discipline already belongs to our past. Its history has the virtues of historical experiences which are relatively complete. Such a history permits us to understand the causes and effects of the process of rationaliztion in one of its most fundamental and spectacular developments.

Notes

1. Michel Foucault, *Surveiller et punir: naissance de la prison* (Paris: Gallimard, 1975). *Discipline and Punishment: The Birth of the Prison*, trans. Alan Sheridan (New York: Pantheon, 1977).

2. S. Pollard, *The Genesis of Modern Management* (London, 1965); idem, "Factory Discipline in the Industrial Revolution," *Economic History Review* 16, no. 2 (December 1963): 254–71; E. J. Hobsbawm, "The Machine Breakers," *Past and Present* 1 (February 1952): 57–70; E. P. Thompson, "Time, Work-discipline and Industrial Capitalism," *Past and Present*, 38 (December 1967): 56–97; D. A. Reid, "The Decline of Saint-Monday, 1766–1876," *Past and Present* 71 (May 1976): 76–101.

3. See, for example, Rolande Trempé, *Les Mineurs de Carmaux (1848–1914)* (Paris: Editions Ouvrières, 1971); "Naissance de la classe ouvrière en France" [special issue of *Le*

Mouvement social 97 (octobre-décembre 1976)]; Lion Murard and Patrick Zylberman, eds., *Le Petit Travailleur infatigable* [special issue of *Recherches* 25 (November 1976)]; *Le Soldat du travail, guerre, fascisme, et Taylorisme* [special issue of *Recherches* 32 (September 1978)]; Yves Lequin, *Les Ouvriers de la région lyonnaise (1848–1914)* (Lyon: Presses Universitaires de Lyon, 1977).

4.   Thierry Baudouin, "Grèves et luttes urbaines" (Doctorat de 3e cycle, Université de Paris VIII-Vincennes, 1978).

5.   R. Samuel, "Steam Power and Hand Technology in Mid-Victorian Britain," *History Workshop* 3 (1977):6–72.

6.   Jeremy Bentham, *Le Panoptique ou l'oeil du pouvoir*, with a preface by Michel Foucault (Paris: Belfond, 1977).

7.   Cf. Jean-Antoine Chaptal, De l'industrie française, vol. 2 (Paris: Renouard, 1819), p. 232: "Another factor which has an unfavorable influence on companies in France is the craze for building."

8.   Jacques Savary des Brulons, *Dictionnaire universel du commerce* (Geneva, 1750), vol. 3, p. 739.

9.   Ibid., p. 742.

10.   A. Doyon and L. Liaigre, *Jacques Vaucanson, mécanicien de génie* (Paris: Presses Universitaires de France, 1966), p. 296 (emphasis in original).

11.   Emile Levasseur, "Police intérieure de la manufacture de Saint-Maur," in *Histoire des classes ouvrières et de l'industrie en France avant 1789*, vol. 2 (Paris, 1900–1901), p. 520; D. Ligou, "Un règlement de manufacture à la fin du 18e siècle," *Revue de'historie économique et sociale* 31, no. 3 (1953): 272–75.

12.   Serge Chassagne, Alain Dewerpe, and Yves Gaulupeau, "Les Ouvriers de la manufacture des toiles imprimées d'Oberkampf à Jouy-en-Josas (1760–1815) [special issue: "Naissance de la classe ouvrière en France," *Le Mouvement social* 97 (octobre-décembre 1976)].

13.   H. Medick, "The Proto-Industrial Family Economy: The Structural Function of Household and Family during the Transition from Peasant Society to Industrial Capitalism," *Social History* 3 (1976): 291–315.

14.   Pierre Guillaume Frédéric LePlay, *Les Ouvriers des deux mondes* (Paris, 1857–62).

15.   Pierre Caspard, "La Fabrique au village," *Le Mouvement social* 97 (octobre-décembre, 1976):15–37; discusses the factory in Cortaillod.

16.   E. Ducpétiaux, *De la condition physique et morale des jeunes ouvriers et des moyens de l'améliorer*, vol. 1 (Brussels: Meline, 1843): 22.

17.   Cf., in the American context, Tamar K. Hareven's work entitled "The Dynamics of Kin in an Industrial Community (Manchester, New Hampshire, 1880–1930)," *The American Journal of Sociology* 84 Supplement (1978): S151–82; idem, *Family Time and Industrial Time*, forthcoming; see also Joan Scott and Louise Tilly, "Women's Work and the Family in Nineteenth-Century Europe," *Comparative Studies in Society and History* 17, (1975): 36–64; diem, *Women, Work and Family* (New York: Holt, Rinehart, and Winston, 1978).

18.   According to C. L. Bergery, *Economie industrielle ou science de l'industrie*, 3 vols. (Metz, 1829–31), 3: 63; "The master is the chief of his workers, since he commands them; he is their father, as he provides for them."

19.   On industrial architecture, see *L'Usine, Travail, Architecture* [special issue of *Architecture, Mouvement, Continuité* 30 (1973)]; *Le Bâtiment à usage industriel aux 18e et 19e siècles en France* (Paris: Centre de documentation d'histoire des techniques, 1978). This situation existed mostly for textile factories; in the old ironworks and glassworks, on the other hand, the owner's house was most often at a distance. Spatial organization was and is at the same time a production arrangement and a symbol of social relationships.

20.   M. Perrot, *Les Ouvriers en grève (France, 1871–1890)* (Paris: Mouton, 1974); I have not sufficiently considered this problem.

21.   J. Vial, *L'Industrialisation de la sidérurgie française (1814–1864)* (Paris: La Haye, Mouton, 1967), pp. 144–65 and 344–73; J. P. Courtheoux, "Observations et ides économiques de Réaumur," *Revue d'histoire économique et sociale* 35, no. 4 (1957): 347–69; idem, "Privilèges et misères d'un métier sidérurgique au XIXe siècle: le puddleur," *Revue d'Histoire économique et sociale* 37, no. 2 (1959): 161–84.

22.   Courtheoux, "Privilèges et misères"; M. Verry, *Les Laminoirs ardennais: déclin d'une aristocratie professionnelle* (Paris: Presses Universitaires de France, 1955).

23.   See Paul Mantoux, *La Révolution industrielle en Angleterre* (Paris: Colin, 1928).

24.   J. Donzelot, *La Police des familles* (Paris: Minuit, 1977); K. Lynch, "The Problem of Child Labor and the Working-Class Family in France during the July Monarchy," *Proceedings of the Western Society for French History* 5 (1977): 228–36.

25.   Ducpétiaux, *De la condition,* p. 29.

26.   Perrot, "Les Ouvriers et les machines en France dans la premier moitié du 19e siècle," *Le Soldat du travail,* pp. 347–75.

27.   "Les Commencements de la technologie" [special issue of *Thalès* (1966)].

28.   Perrot, "Travailler et produire: Claude-Lucien Bergery et les débuts du management en France," *Mélanges d'historie sociale offerts à Jean Maitron* (Paris: Editions Ouvrières, 1976), pp. 177–90.

29.   Bergery, *Economie industrielle,* Vol. 3, pp. 40–63; he estimated that two million workers were Monday absentees "and therefore two million francs were lost for France each week."

30.   Ibid., pp. 45–46, 57. See also B. Mottez, *Systèmes de salaire et politiques patronales: essai sur l'évolution des pratiques et des idéologies patronales* (Paris: C.N.R.S., 1966).

31.   See Le Play's studies; few watches are to be found in the detailed inventories of the clothing and furniture of the working-class family in the nineteenth century. A fascinating history remains to be written.

32.   A certain number of these may be seen in a book of photographs by M. Perrot and D. Schulman, *Trimer en 1900* (Paris: Le Seuil), forthcoming.

33.   Twenty-one labor inspectors were established by the Law of 1874, 92 in 1892, and 110 in 1902. It was mostly because of accidents, the Law of 1898, and strikes that the factory became a concern for the administration.

34.   A. Melucci, "Action patronale, pouvoir, organisation: règlements d'usine et contrôle de la main-d'oeuvre au 19e siècle," *Le Mouvement social* 97 (octobre-décembre 1976): 139–56 (which should be modified on some points); numerous legal theses on this topic were prepared at the beginning of the twentieth century because of the legislative debates at that time; some quote complete texts. See, for example, the useful studies by L. Godart, *Les Règlements de travail à Lille* (Lille, 1910), and H. Gazin, *De la nature juridique des règlements de travail* (Paris, 1913).

35.   Regulations of the Thiriez factory (1840), in *Les Règlements,* p. 29.

36.   See, for example, L. Struminger,"Les Canutes de Lyon," *Le Mouvement social* 105 (octobre-décembre, 1978): 58–87, and D. Vanoli, "Les Couvents soyeux," *Révoltes logiques,* no. 2 (1976).

37.   "Des ouvriers et des machines en France," *Revue Britannique* 1 (1825), (referring to English workers and machines), mentions fourteen hundred. Other sources estimate that sixteen thousand English workers arrived in France about 1822.

38.   Murard and Zylberman, *Le Petit Travailleur infatigable,* examine the patronat's housing policies as well as other topics.

39.   Trempé, *Les Mineurs*; Lequin, *Les Ouvriers*; Perrot, "La Formation de la classe

ouvrière lyonnaise: une naissance difficile," *Annales, E.S.C.* 233 (juillet-août, 1978): 830–37, comments on Lequin's book.

40.   A visit to Le Creusot (Saône-et-Loire) is mandatory for anyone interested in these problems. The *Ecomusée du Creusot* is located in the old Schneider château and offers essential documents for the history of this company.

41.   On the originality of the Schneider system, see Emile Cheysson, *Oeuvres choisies* (Paris: Rousseau, 1911), pp. 24ff. Cheysson was a civil engineer, a follower of Le Play, a prominent statistician, an advocate of social hygiene, and director at Le Creusot during the crucial period from 1871 to 1874.

42.   Perrot, "L'Usine et sa discipline," *Les Ouvriers en grève*, pp. 295ff.

43.   Trempé, "L'Utilisation des archives d'entreprise: le fichier du personnel," *Mélanges ... Maitron*, p. 262; Trempé, *Les Mineurs de Carmaux*, p. 186.

44.   Lequin, *Les Ouvriers de la région lyonnaise*, 2, p. 151. An increase in new types of demands was noticeable after 1900: "All, or almost all of them, deal with human relations, either individual or collective, within the company"; on the increase of incidents with management after 1880, see pp. 154–55.

45.   "Au pays de Schneider: prolétariat et militants ouvriers de la Commune à nos jours" [special issue of *Le Mouvement social* (avril–juin 1977)]: pp. 25, 98.

46.   Perrot, "Dans la France de la Belle Epoque: 'Les Apaches,' premières bandes de jeunes" [special issue of *Cahiers Jussieu: Les Marginaux et les exclus dans l'histoire* (Paris: L'Union Générale d'Editions, 1978).]

47.   Helene Oecònomo, "Le Premier Mai 1906 à Paris" (Master's thesis, Université de Paris VII-Jussieu, 1978).

48.   Patrick Fridenson's article, "France–Etats-Unis: genèse de l'usine nouvelle," *Le Soldat du travail: recherches* 32 (September 1978), treats the question for the period 1900–1920. Note that the expression "the new factory" is, apparently, that of Albert Thomas writing in 1917.

49.   Godart, *Les Règlements*, pp. 157–58 (1905 regulations).

50.   On company unions, see Z. Sternhell, *La Droite révolutionnaire (1880–1914): les origines françaises du fascisme* (Paris: Seuil, 1978), pp. 245–318.

51.   Peter Stearns, "Against the Strike Threat: Employer Policy towards Labor Agitation in France (1900–1914)," *Journal of Modern History* 40 (1968): 474–500.

52.   See B. Mottez, *Systèmes*, and P. Fridenson, "France—Etats-Unis," p. 385.

53.   On the importance of positivists as pressure and liaison groups between the state and the workers' movement, see Perrot, "Note sur le positivisme ouvrier" in *Le Positivisme* [special issue of *Romantisme*], forthcoming.

54.   P. Pic, *Les Lois ouvrières* (Paris: Rousseau, 1902), pp. 976ff.

55.   J. Amar, *Le Rendement de la machine humaine* (Paris, 1909); idem, *Le Moteur humain: les bases scientifiques de travail professionnel* (Paris, 1914).

56.   A. Moutet, "Patronat français et systéme Taylor (1907–1914)," *Le Mouvement social* 93 (octobre-décembre, 1975): 15–49; idem, "La Politique de rationalisation de l'industrie française au lendemain de la première guerre mondiale," *Le Soldat du travail*, op. cit., pp. 433–49.

57.   This marked the end of the tool-box era; the tool box had been indispensible for old professional workers and was the instrument as well as the symbol of their independence. On this subject, see the recent testimony by Robert Linhart, *L'Etabli* (Paris: Editions de Minuit, 1978).

EIGHT

Getting and Spending
The Family Budgets of English Industrial Workers in 1890

LYNN HOLLEN LEES

Although social stratification is a characteristic of any industrial society, the experience of social class for individuals and families changes over time as society changes. Between the beginning and the end of the nineteenth century, England became a highly urbanized, industrialized country. By 1900, many more workers had jobs in factories and large plants; real wages approximately doubled between 1850 and the end of the century; a majority of the population had moved into cities and towns. Moreover, the introduction of compulsory schooling and the growth of a cheap popular press vastly increased workers' access to education. Then too, the spread of music halls, workers' clubs, theaters, and team sports made new leisure activities more available. At the same time, the widened suffrage along with the rising number of trade unions, Socialist groups, and party organizations brought greater opportunities for political action. How much impact had this changed environment had by 1890 on the life-styles and class experiences of English industrial workers?

There have been relatively few studies of English workers in the decades just preceding the First World War. Although the class experiences of London artisans and casual laborers have been analyzed by Gareth Stedman Jones and Geoffrey Crossick, those of northern industrial workers after 1850 have been largely ignored by historians, who have concentrated their attention on the conditions and relationships of the 1830s and 1840s.[1] In addition, most research neglects important familial and industrial influences on social class, emphasizing instead the specific occupations and skill levels of male household heads. But class experience depends upon far more than the relationship to the means of production. People's perceptions of and

responses to social position are shaped and reshaped by economic conditions, ideologies, and cultural norms. Moreover, the structure of the local
community and the family mediates between individuals and the labor
market. Studies of class experience should therefore range much more widely
than analyses of male occupations. Unfortunately, few workers left detailed
accounts of their social relationships, much less commentaries on class. The
historian must therefore turn to indirect sources.

Although much of the minutiae of ordinary social life are never recorded,
clear traces of regular choices and restrictions survive in the form of family
budgets. Indeed, Charles Booth, Benjamin Seebohm Rowntree, Mrs. Pember
Reeves, and Lady Bell, among others, used budgets extensively to illustrate
their perceptive commentaries on working-class life in late Victorian and
Edwardian England.[2] Although the work of these social investigators is
familiar, the results of a similar, more extensive American survey of British
and European workers are not. In order to provide information for American
congressmen about to debate the McKinley tariff, the United States Department of Labor carried out in 1889 and 1890 an international survey of
production costs in nine protected industries, primarily iron, steel, coal, and
textiles.[3] Carroll D. Wright, a pioneering statistician and former United
States Commissioner of Labor, directed the inquiry and also chose to include
material on the condition of workers' families. As a result, his investigators
collected itemized yearly budgets and demographic data on 8,544 households
from the United States, Great Britain, France, Belgium, Germany, and
Switzerland.[4] The result was a wealth of information on workers' consumption patterns in a wide sample of occupations. In this essay, I shall examine
the budgets collected by Wright's investigators in England in 1890 in order to
explore the nature of industrial workers' life-styles at the end of the nineteenth
century.

The 777 English families surveyed by the U.S. Department of Labor
worked in the cotton, wool, steel, pig iron, bar iron, bituminous coal, coke,
and glass trades and were chosen from among the employees of firms
cooperating in the project. They are divided very unequally among industries,
52 percent being employed in cotton or wool; skilled workers predominate in
the sample. Unfortunately, the exact details of the families' selection were not
recorded; the official report merely states that the Department of Labor
attempted to collect budgets from: "a representative number of employees of
the establishments covered" and from those families "whose surroundings
and conditions made them representative of the whole body of employees in
any particular establishment."[5] The head of the travelling commissioners
later said that employers supplied wage data and that home visits to workers
were made in the company of trusted local people to ask for information when
regular accounts were not kept. Henry Higgs, a contemporary admirer and
analyst of these budgets, guessed therefore that yearly totals of income and
expenditure were estimated from data on short periods of time.[6] That the
investigators were concerned to collect accounts from a wide sample of

workers is clear, but we can only speculate upon their success in securing what they viewed as "representativeness." A present-day statistician would certainly not use that term to describe their procedures. It is clear, moreover, that investigators introduced a variety of biases into the data. Some workers chosen were, they admit, either unwilling or unable to give the figures requested, for only the more precise and steadily employed person would have kept accounts or met the investigators. In any case the workers were not picked randomly but from among family heads in selected but unidentified firms. And because the budgets cannot be linked to particular cities, regions, or companies, the characteristics of firms and places included cannot be compared with those excluded. The extent and nature of biases cannot be checked, therefore.

Nevertheless, the sample has several compensating features. It is very large, and the families in it are identified according to the industry, specific occupation, age, and sex of the head. Internal comparisons can be made that avoid some of the pitfalls of aggregation. Moreover, the sample is drawn from the most important sectors of the English industrial economy, although it excludes newer, fast-growing trades, such as engineering. By 1890, 23 percent of the English industrial labor force was employed in textiles, mining, or the production of metals and machines, trades located predominantly in northern and midland areas.[7] Since most of the family budgets with which historians are familiar come from London, nonindustrial market towns, or rural areas, this American data refers to a portion of the English labor force whose standard of living has not been adequately charted by the work of Booth and Rowntree. The timing of the survey is also noteworthy. Not only were 1889 and 1890 years of high industrial production marked by an upturn in the business cycle, but the level of unemployment was moderate.[8] The budgets therefore record the life-styles of industrial workers during a period of relative prosperity, one in which the effects of long-term increases in real wages should have been readily apparent. The survey deals, then, with a specific sort of English working-class family probably living in the most highly industrialized regions. Drawn from important sectors of the English industrial economy, and coming primarily from the ranks of the semiskilled and skilled workers, they represent, I would guess, the stable labor force of the larger, better established firms. While the sample is clearly biased away from the unskilled, from the transient, the irregularly employed, and the youngest workers, it clearly reaches far beyond an aristocracy of labor. It looks at a large segment of the British labor force, one underrepresented in all other analyses of workers' standards of living in the late nineteenth century.

The Family Incomes of English Industrial Workers

The English industrial families surveyed by the U.S. Department of Labor earned on the average $515 per year (converted into U.S. currency, of course), an amount 25 percent lower than American families employed in the same trades.[9] But substantial differences existed among the industries examined. Families whose heads worked in bar iron, coal, and glass had the highest total incomes, earning far more than employees of textile, coke, or pig iron firms (see table 1). Unequal family sizes largely compensated for these inequalities in total earnings. Although the average household head in the coke industry supported only 3.6 people, a coal miner or steel worker had 5.5 members in his family. As a result, per capita income among miners and steel workers' families was relatively low; among textile workers, the combination of large families and only moderately high wages also lowered per capita incomes. Only the employees of glass firms combined high earnings with smaller than average family sizes (see table 1).

TABLE 1

Mean Family Incomes and Family Sizes of English Industrial Workers, 1889–1890

Industry	Family Income	Family Size	Income per Person
Steel (N = 45)	$484	5.5	88
Bar Iron (N = 91)	537	4.8	111
Pig Iron (N = 21)	434	4.2	103
Glass (N = 26)	503	4.0	125
Coal (N = 124)	512	5.5	93
Coke (N = 12)	343	3.6	96
Wool (N = 117)	436	4.9	89
Cotton (N = 341)	554	4.7	117

SOURCE: U.S. Congress, House of Representatives, *Sixth and Seventh Annual Reports of the Commissioner of Labor (1890 and 1891).*

These total incomes represent the combined earnings of parents and children who together constituted a family economy, within which money and services were shared to ensure survival. Not surprisingly, the budgets reflect a division of labor widespread in England, North America, and Europe during the nineteenth century: normally husbands contributed wages while wives ran the household. Yet this generalization tells only part of the story. Because male wages did not change in harmony with household needs, others beside the husband and father regularly had to enter the labor force. If the budgets are divided according to the ages of household head and children and if we assume that no major changes in labor force participation took place during the adjoining decades, these financial records simulate those of households as they changed over time, as families grew and different members took paying jobs. When treated in this way, the budgets reveal a regular pattern of wage earning, based upon local employment opportunities and a family's developmental cycle.

Despite the insecurities of the labor market, a male household head provided at least half of the financial support for his family during all stages of its development. For the first ten to fifteen years after marriage, he earned virtually the entire money income of the household. But this pattern, if continued, would have produced a regular decrease in financial resources, because a manual worker's wages usually reached their peak when he was between the ages of thirty and forty and then declined.[10] Moreover, his family's needs continued to increase as more children were born and lived to adolescence. In order to insulate families at least partially from regular decreases in their standard of living, children were expected to enter the labor force when they left school, to live at home, and to contribute earnings to their family for as long as they were willing to postpone marriage or moving elsewhere. After the age of thirty, a father could usually count upon a growing contribution to income from children's wages. In fact, by the time fathers were over fifty, children earned an average of 38 percent of total family income among wool and coal workers, 36 percent among those in cotton, and 29 and 25 percent respectively for those in steel and bar iron. The early entry of children into the labor force was still a normal part of working class social life in 1890. Of the families sampled in the woollen industry who had children ten years of age or older, 83 percent had working children, and only among families in industries where the total sample was small (coke, pig iron) did the proportion for families with children ten or older who worked drop to 40 percent or below. Far more children than wives worked in every industry surveyed (see table 2).

TABLE 2

Supplementary Wage Earners in the English Family Economy

Industry	%Families with Working Wives	%Families with Children, Age Ten or More, Whose Children Worked	%Families with Boarders
Cotton (N = 340)	11	77	6
Wool (N = 116)	11	83	9
Steel (N = 45)	0	59	0
Bar Iron (N = 91)	0	60	4
Pig Iron (N = 21)	0	33	5
Coal (N = 123)	1	59	1
Glass (N = 25)	0	71	0
Coke (N = 12)	0	38	0

SOURCE: U.S. Congress, House of Representatives, *Sixth and Seventh Annual Reports of the Commissioner of Labor (1890 and 1891).*

In contrast to the earning roles of husband and older children, wives and mothers took on a different series of tasks. Louise Tilly has written elsewhere of the choice for females between production and reproduction.[11] In the families of English industrial workers, the vast majority of married women clearly opted for reproduction and associated tasks (see table 2). Only among families whose head was employed in the textile trades, which had many jobs for women, did many wives work (11 percent of both cotton and woollen workers' wives), and most of these had no young children. Women left the labor force when they married and began to have families. Even the number who took in boarders was small. Only 6 percent of the cotton workers' families sampled in 1890 had lodgers: contrast this with the 23 percent found by Michael Anderson among the residents of Preston, a Lancashire cotton town, in 1851.[12] Since mid-century, industrial workers' wives had retreated even more to non-income-producing tasks except in times of emergency and male unemployment. Not only did they care for their several children, but most baked all of the family's bread and some made their children's clothing. In addition, wives managed the family's cash, buying food and clothes as well as paying the rent. It was their responsibility to make incomes stretch to cover necessities and to generate extra resources in the form of credit when they fell short. The work of several family members outside the home was made possible, therefore, by the work within the home of an adult female who made sure that all were fed, clothed, and nurtured in proportion to her resources and abilities.

The patterns of both female and child labor revealed in the budgets of 1890 illustrate changes that had taken place in the preceding half century as a result of rising incomes and of parliamentary legislation. While in 1840 many children had worked as early as parents could find something for them to do, the building of a state school system coupled with laws restricting child labor and enacting compulsory primary education effectively removed most children under twelve from the labor force by the late 1870s. By 1890, English industrial workers sent their children to school for between six and nine years, removing them after age twelve according to their need for extra income and the level of local demand for child labor. The opportunity to send children to work early was greatest for textile workers who lived in towns where jobs in the mills were widely available; it was lowest for families employed in heavy industry (see table 2). Parents responded according to the nature of their local labor market. Of the co-residing children aged ten to fourteen, 94 percent in iron workers' families, 90 percent of those in steelworkers' families, 76 percent in woollen workers' families, but only 51 percent of the children of cotton workers were still in school.[13] The sons and daughters of steel, coal, and iron workers normally stayed in school until age fourteen, after which about 75 percent of them went to work, and 25 percent, mostly daughters, remained outside the labor force but lived at home for a few years. Then as they reached twenty, exodus began: most left home by the age of twenty-five. The children of textile workers, in contrast, not only left school earlier, around the age of twelve, but also entered the labor force in larger numbers, and they remained at home longer. For example, over 90 percent of the co-residing children over fourteen of cotton and woollen workers had paying jobs in

1890. In addition, the relatively greater opportunities for female labor in the textile trades delayed the withdrawal of daughters from their households of origin. Although virtually all sons of cotton workers had left their parents' households by the age of twenty, daughters age twenty-five and over constituted 16 percent of the co-residing children older than fourteen in cotton spinners' households. Although the children of workers in both heavy and light industry entered the labor force soon after leaving school, their sex and the nature of local labor demands influenced the length and timing of their years as contributing members of their natal family economies and the amount of education allowed them.

The needs of their families for supplementary income was the major factor influencing the early entry of children into the labor force. Using the entire sample of European and American budgets, Michael Haines has shown that the tendency to send children to work increased as fathers' incomes decreased and as the number of preschool children became larger. On the other hand, the entry of children into the labor force was slowed in families where wives took in boarders or had paying jobs.[14]

The total earnings of a household varied greatly as the age structure and composition of the nuclear family changed; it also obviously depended on a worker's skill level and industry. A look at average family incomes among both skilled and unskilled iron, steel, and cotton workers at several points over the life cycle will illustrate the differences that existed (see fig. 1).

Laborers in both heavy and light industry normally earned far less than men in the most highly skilled jobs, but the wide availability of employment for children in textile areas meant that cotton laborers' families could increase earnings much more than their counterparts in steel and iron during the years when adolescent children remained at home. In fact, the mean family income of cotton laborers in life-cylce stage three (family with youngest child aged 5–13) was more than double that of families in life-cycle stage two (family with youngest child aged 0–4), while those of steel and iron laborers decreased slightly as they moved along this part of their developmental cycles. The earnings curves of skilled workers in these same industries resemble those of the laborers. Cotton spinners regularly increased family incomes through all stages of the life cycle until their children left home, but puddlers and rollers working in iron and steel plants reached their maximum family income while they still had preschool children. Cotton workers therefore reached their highest incomes much later in the life cycle than did workers in heavy industry. Also, the gap between the best and worst paid employees was much greater in the metal than the textile trades. Although the mean family incomes of the cotton spinners and laborers sampled differed by only $72 per year, puddlers and rollers earned on the average $217 more per year than laborers in the same firms. While many spinners and cotton laborers would have enjoyed a similar standard of living during the middle stages of their families' developmental cycles, the elite of steel and iron always had incomes at least 43 percent higher than laborers in their trades in

FIGURE 1

*Changes in Total Earnings during the Life Cycle of
Male-Headed Families in Selected Occupations*

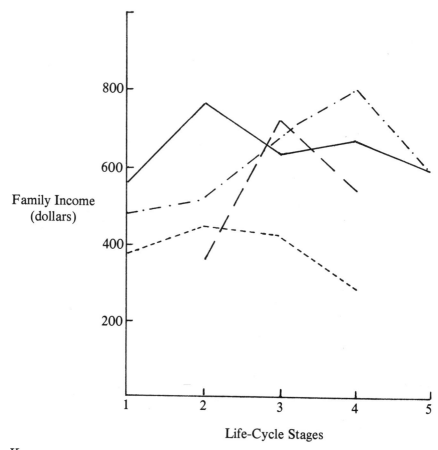

Life-Cycle Stages

 Key

—·— ·   Cotton Spinners
— — —   Cotton Laborers
————   Iron and Steel Puddlers and Rollers
------   Iron and Steel Laborers

Life-Cycle Stages: 1. Married, no children, wife under 45 years
2. Youngest child, 0–4 years
3. Youngest child, 5–13 years
4. Youngest child, over 14 years
5. Children gone, wife over 45 years

all stages of their life cycles. The economic stratification of workers in heavy industry was therefore much more rigid and unchanging than in textiles, where children's and wives' wages could produce roughly equal average total incomes among high- and low-skilled workers during the middle point of a family's developmental cycle. As a result, standards of living were more similar among textile workers than among those in heavy industry.[15] To be sure, equality of income does not imply equality of experience. The wives who had to earn a living and keep house simultaneously and the children who left school earlier made substantial sacrifices for the extra money and led different lives from their unemployed peers. The pressures leading families to send added members into the labor force are clear: workers' incomes were still sufficiently low and irregular for extra wages to be needed to secure a decent standard of living and, if possible, savings to insulate them from the unavoidable calamities of illness, loss of work, and old age.

Consumption Patterns and Life-Styles

The consumption patterns derivable from family budgets mirror both communal norms and individual needs. Moreover, comparative levels of purchasing provide clues to differences in life styles. I will examine first the cost of subsistence through workers' expenditures for food, rent, and clothes, and then turn to the purchase of such discretionary items as books, insurance, and entertainment in order to show how preferences varied among industries and occupations.

Rent required only a modest share of industrial workers' incomes. Among both laborers and the highly skilled, housing costs ranged between 6 and 13 percent of total income (see table 3). This sum purchased, however, what was at the time considered to be an adequate amount of space although the dwelling itself might have been in appalling condition. While almost none of the families owned their own home, the vast majority lived in four or more rooms, which in northern industrial towns meant a separate house with two rooms upstairs and two downstairs. In model company towns such as Saltaire, workers were rented clean dwellings provided with gas and water, but in most places, the absence of regulatory codes and philanthropists' involvement meant that workers' housing was badly constructed, lit, and ventilated. While the condition of their homes was probably no better, workers in the largest English towns regularly spent more money for less space. Most of the laborers' families in South London interviewed by Mrs. Pember Reeves in 1912 lived in two or three uncomfortable rooms and paid between 20 and 33 percent of their income for the privilege. In York, laborers' families spent 18 percent of weekly income on rent, while foremen and clerks allotted 13 percent. Among the Liverpool and Manchester workers' families investigated by the Economic Club in 1893, around 20 percent of income was most commonly allotted to rent; only a few households paid as little as 12 percent of income, and several allotted as much as 35 percent.[16] The industrial workers of the Labor Department survey, therefore, had a double advantage when compared to workers in the largest towns. Not only could they live in a separate dwelling, but they paid substantially less for housing than counterparts in London and Manchester, leaving them more disposable income for food, clothes, and extras.

TABLE 3

The Division of Family Income for Laborers and the Skilled Elite

Industry	Mean Expenditures as Percentage of Family Income			
	Food	Rent	Clothes	Other
Cotton Spinners (N = 149)	45	9	14	32
Cotton Laborers (N = 14)	50	8	14	28
Iron and Steel Puddlers and Rollers (N = 28)	38	8	15	39
Iron and Steel Laborers (N = 13)	65	12	15	8

SOURCE: U.S. Congress, House of Representatives, *Sixth and Seventh Annual Reports of the Commissioner of Labor (1890 and 1891).*

In 1890, food constituted by far the largest expenditure in workers' family budgets requiring on the average for each industrial group between 40 and 52 percent of total income. Only among laborers in heavy industry was this proportion exceeded (see table 3). In general, laborers and those in the lowest paying industries allocated more income to food than did skilled workers and those in higher paying trades; yet even in a good year, almost half of a skilled worker's family earnings went for the purchase of food. Moreover, the families surveyed, with the exception of the iron and steel laborers, held a relatively advantaged position when compared to the subjects of all other published late nineteenth-century budgets, who spent on the average 58 percent of total incomes on food.[17] Since this second group was drawn primarily from craftsmen and laborers' families in London, Edinburgh, York, and smaller provincial towns, the evidence points toward a higher standard of living in 1890 among textile and skilled metal workers in the north and midlands than among workers in less mechanized and capitalized trades in the metropolis or in nonindustrial regions.

The industrial workers surveyed purchased a diet based heavily upon bread, potatoes, tea, sugar, and either butter or margarine. Occasional additions of milk, eggs, cheese, fish, and meat provided their protein, iron, and calcium, as well as some relief from monotony, but little was spent on either fruit or vegetables. The study does not report enough detail to permit analysis of nutritional values, but a contemporary study of industrial workers' diets in similar trades and regions is available. In 1894, Dr. Thomas Oliver, a doctor in Newcastle-upon-Tyne, investigated the normal menus of northern miners, metal workers, and textile workers and computed their adequacy in terms of carbon and nitrogen content. Using data on Durham and Northumberland, he judged that "coal miners, as a class . . . feed well; . . . they believe in the necessity of taking every day a fairly large quantity of animal food, particularly beef." Similarly, textile spinners and iron and steel workers had a sufficient intake of calories and protein. He also found the diets of Bradford woollen spinners generally adequate. Wages were good enough, he said, among the spinners and skilled iron and steel workers for them to buy "substantial food." His analysis also shows, however, that the semiskilled and unskilled workers in these same sectors and in other less well paid trades ate badly and were below his standard of sufficiency.[18] Benjamin Seebohm Rowntree comes to similar conclusions about York workers' families. The artisans' and foremen's households he studied had an "adequate" food supply, as long as they spent little money on alcohol. Their protein intake was under his standard, however. The rest of York's workers were "seriously underfed." In fact, the laborers' families on whom he based his conclusion consumed a diet that had 17 percent fewer calories and 28 percent less protein per week than he considered necessary.[19]

Much of this difference among the various strata and industries of the working class can be linked to meat intake. D. J. Oddy has shown that as incomes rose so did a worker's consumption of meat and milk, while other purchases varied much less.[20] Families with higher incomes added bacon or sausage to breakfasts, sometimes ham, sausage, or fish to teas and suppers, and bits of beef, pork, or mutton to their midday meals of potatoes, bread, and pudding. Laborers who could purchase less of these additions were consequently much less well nourished. In the U.S. Department of Labor study, the better paid families spent more on meat. Coal miners, for example, spent $96 a year on meat, but coal laborers allotted only $75 per year on this item. There also were systematic differences in meat consumption among industries; workers in coal, iron, and steel ate more meat than those in textiles, and this held true for the unskilled. Despite the fact that their average incomes were over $100 per year higher than those of iron and steel laborers, textile laborers bought only $54 worth of meat in a year (25 percent of their food budget) in comparison to the $61 per year (37 percent of their food budget) spent by unskilled workers in heavy industry. The obvious need of men who spent their days in strenuous physical labor for a nutritious diet influenced therefore the type of food purchased. It also produced an unequal allocation of the most nourishing items. The collectors of family budgets all agreed that fathers got by far the largest share of meat, and sometimes were given all of it when the amount bought was small.[21] In order to keep up their strength and morale, fathers were given chops and sausages, while children and sometimes wives ate bread and drippings. The long-term results of such practices were to be predicted: malnourished women and children, lowered resistance to diseases, high infant and maternal mortality rates.

Clothing constituted the third major expenditure of English workers' families, absorbing an average of 17 percent of income among those sampled in heavy industry and 14 percent among those in cotton textiles. These families had moved beyond the stage where every clothing purchase represented a luxury and diverted money from the food budget. The allocation of this money tells us a bit about needs and values of these families. Parents usually spent more on their children than they did upon themselves, but the comparative share given to wives varied among industries. In well over half the families sampled among miners and iron workers, men took more money for clothes than did their wives, while in textile areas, this allocation of funds was reversed. The clothing needs of men in heavy industry probably exceeded those of textile workers, but the aspirations and bargaining power of wives in textiles and in heavy industry probably differed too. In textile towns local standards of female dress were higher than in mining towns. Besides, more wives of textile workers contributed money to their families by taking in boarders and occasionally going to work in a factory. In contrast, the women in coal or iron towns had fewer chances to earn. Moreover, the example of single working women who could live with parents and divert a comparatively high share of income into dress was largely absent. Women who helped or who had helped at some stage to earn, as well as to bake, the family bread might well have been entitled to a greater share of income than those whose role in the family economy was less easily measurable in cash.

Once most of these families had paid for rent, food, and clothing, a substantial share of income remained for all but laborers in heavy industry to be divided among a variety of expenses including fuel, household goods, entertainment, alcohol, books, as well as savings; Wright's survey catalogued all these expenses. Almost all of these industrial workers had a surplus that could be spent in many ways depending upon a family's preferences. We know little about how these decisions were made, although the control over expenditures differed among family members. The day-to-day allocation of funds was done primarily by adult women. Husbands either turned over their entire pay packets to their wives, receiving back a small amount of pocket money to be spent as they chose, or they gave wives a fixed amount with which to run the household and kept the rest. Both patterns were common, and it is impossible to estimate their incidence. Since the 1880s and early 1890s were a period of declining prices and rising real wages, housewives could make do under both systems as long as husbands restrained their demands for personal funds. Since the bulk of a family's cash came first into the hands of the male wage earner, he had substantial power over the family standard of living. In contrast, children had little direct influence over household spending. Their consumption needs were met by parents, and young children who earned generally put all their wages into family coffers.

Only when they reached adolescence and began to look toward marriage did they assume greater control over their own wages, sometimes paying just room and board to parents. The expectation that they would contribute to family funds remained, however, for at least as long as they lived at home.

These workers valued future security as well as present consumption, and balanced involvement in the community with individual leisure pursuits. Virtually all the workers thought it necessary to buy life insurance, probably for both adults and children, and to join "sick clubs," which paid benefits when husbands could not work because of illness. These were the major forms of savings chosen by the sampled families. The combination of high mortality rates, clear communal norms regarding the "proper" sort of funeral, and incomes inadequate to pay undertakers' fees encouraged families to pay several pennies a week for protection against the heavy financial and social burden of death. Both skilled workers and laborers responded to this pressure: at least 75 percent of the families in each of the industries and skill levels surveyed bought some form of insurance, and most of the rest probably purchased it indirectly through the friendly societies to which many belonged.[22] By late in the nineteenth century, this kind of prudential saving had become a staple of workers' life-styles in England. Faced with high levels of insecurity and no government help except the despised workhouse, most families responded by attempts to cushion themselves. Yet the protection gained was modest, for payments usually only covered funeral expenses; sums received during illness did not cover the wages lost and usually lapsed after a fixed number of weeks.

The benefits provided by insurance clubs, friendly societies, and unions were much more than financial ones, for they also brought male workers membership in a lively social world. Such groups as the Foresters or the Oddfellows held monthly meetings to collect contributions and provided yearly or half-yearly dinners and other social events.[23] Belonging to them gave a worker entry into a local community of men with similar needs and expectations. Trades unions fulfilled similar functions, in addition to their economic ones, and their appeal was strong among the families surveyed by the U.S. Department of Labor. Indeed, 67 percent of the cotton workers, 59 percent of those in wool and coal, 41 percent in bar iron, and 33 percent of the steelworkers gave money to a union. The figures reflect relative differences in the extent of industrial unionization in 1890. It is significant, too, that while skilled workers were more likely to have been organized than the laborers, over half of the unskilled in textiles and mining had also joined. For example, 85 percent of the cotton spinners and 57 percent of the cotton laborers interviewed by the U.S. Department of Labor supported a union in 1890. These are very high proportions, for Sidney and Beatrice Webb estimated that in England in 1892, there were 1.5 million trade unionists, who comprised only 20 percent of the total adult-male employed population, although their incidence was higher in the northern industrialized counties.[24] The workers surveyed, therefore, belonged to a relatively privileged section of the

English working class: unionized, insured, and probably adequately fed, they had several advantages denied to many of their peers.

In addition, this sample of industrial workers could spend a considerable sum yearly on leisure. At least two-thirds of the families in every industry except steel and coke could allot money for trips and entertainment; even laborers' families could spare an average of $31 in 1890 for these items. Textile laborers, for example, allotted 3.5 percent of yearly income on entertainment, although those with children working spent much more than those with infants or school-age children. The budgets do not tell how the money was allocated, but several possibilities are most likely. By 1890, cheap family trips to resorts by rail or steamboat were a popular summer activity, and industrial towns had a variety of professional sporting events, cheap theaters, and music halls. Highly commercialized forms of recreation were widespread by the late nineteenth century.[25]

Entertainment, particularly for males, usually included drinking and smoking; pubs and working men's clubs provided a congenial setting for both activities, which remained important in working-class culture, despite pressure from temperance advocates. Those employed in heavy industry were more likely than those in textiles to purchase alcohol or tobacco. While in the budgets 96 percent of the miners, 82 percent of the steelworkers, and 77 percent of the bar iron workers spent money on these items, only 52 percent of those in textiles did so. The unskilled textile workers mirrored the general pattern of their industry, while iron and steel laborers, perhaps because of poverty, were far less likely to drink than puddlers and rollers (see cols. 3 and 4 in table 4).

TABLE 4

Comparative Consumption Patterns for Laborers and the Skilled Elite: Mean Expenditures on Alcohol and Printed Matter

Industry	Family Income	Expenditure on alcohol	% spending alcohol	Expenditure on printed matter	% spending on printed matter
Cotton Spinner	$566	$21	50	$6	80
Cotton Laborer	494	24	57	5	79
Iron and Steel Rollers and Puddlers	602	27	79	8	96
Iron and Steel Laborers	387	11	46	2	69

SOURCE: U.S. Congress, House of Representatives, *Sixth and Seventh Annual Reports of the Commissioner of Labor (1890 and 1891).*

Teetotalism seems to have been more prevalent in textile communities than among miners or metal workers, where the proportion of nondrinkers was small and to be found almost exclusively among the churchgoing population. The chapel and the pub appealed therefore to different segments of the working-class community.

In contrast to the widespread disaffection of urban workers with formal religion reported by commentators in the late nineteenth century, a substantial minority of these industrial families maintained ties to either the Anglican church or to a sect.[26] About one-third of those in cotton, steel, pig iron, and coke donated money to a church or chapel; the ratio increased to one-half among coal and bar iron workers. Within each trade, the skilled worker was somewhat more likely than the laborer to spend money in this way. But how belief and observance are linked to financial support is unclear; we should be careful not to infer too much. Donations to a church tell us about institutional ties, not mentalities.

The number of contributors within the sample indicates a minimum proportion of industrial families who maintained a link in some form to a local religious community, perhaps by sending children to Sunday school or by attending special ceremonies or services. These ties might well have been weak ones; yet religious beliefs can exist apart from participation in a particular church's rituals. The use by trade unionists of religious forms and references and the ability of new sects such as the Salvation Army to attract thousands of adherents in the late nineteenth century testify to the continuing appeal of religion to English workers.[27]

Another clue to the mental world of families examined by the U.S. Department of Labor is provided by the fact that almost all had family members who were literate. At least 80 percent of those interviewed in every industry (and over 90 percent in coal, iron, coke, wool, and glass) bought books and newspapers. These proportions apply to both laborers and the highly skilled in textiles, although in heavy industry the unskilled were less likely to read and spent smaller sums on books (see cols. 5 and 6 in table 4). Very few families allocated, however, more than seven or eight dollars a year for printed matter, an amount that would buy little beyond a daily and Sunday newspaper, although free lending libraries were available in most towns to supplement purchases. This extensive, but limited taste for reading is confirmed by Lady Bell's interviews of Middlesborough workers around 1900. Of 200 families she interviewed, only 15 percent did not care to read or had no reading member. Yet most chose just newspapers and light novels. A small but culturally significant minority (13 percent) read biographies, histories, travellers' accounts, or the better contemporary fiction.[28] The literary world of most workers therefore mixed sports, crime, and general news with romantic or sensationalist fiction, and virtually all had contact with a wider cultural world through the commercial press.

By 1890, a complex and relatively self-enclosed working-class culture had developed in English industrial communities. People in the major branches of manufacturing participated in its rituals and institutions, although their ability to do so varied with a family's developmental cycle and with income and occupation. Increasing real wages provided the basis for their inclusion in this social world, which brought the beginnings of a consumers' culture to their doorsteps. But industrial workers did not apportion added income equally among competing temptations. Very little was spent, for example, on either housing or household goods. These industrial workers chose to use cash in ways other than the improvement of their physical surroundings. To be sure, many were trapped by the stock of local housing into damp, nasty dwellings and therefore had only limited options. Yet if workers' families had wanted to divert money from their entertainment budget, they could have purchased many more material possessions. Instead, they bought themselves Sunday suits and dresses in which to visit music halls and seaside resorts; they joined clubs, unions, and churches, keeping alive ties to a local community and placing their loyalties, security, and aspirations within the groups of which they were a part. Privatized forms of leisure and entertainment were less popular than public ones.

The growing diffusion of literacy, the enforcement of compulsory education, and the availability of cheap national newspapers helped to decrease regional and occupational differences at a time when urbanization and improved transportation continued to break down the separateness of working-class communities and the divisions among workers of different skill levels. This process had gone farthest in the textile industry. By 1890, skilled and unskilled cotton and woollen workers lived in the same cultural and material world. They ate the same foods; they read similar newspapers and magazines. Where jobs for women and children were more easily available, laborers' families could attain a relatively high income during the middle stages of their life cycles and, therefore, consume and participate in the community at levels analogous to those of spinners. In contrast, laborers in heavy industry lived in much more straitened circumstances, in large part because of the different employment prospects of their children. Not only were they less likely to read or to be unionized, but they had far less money to spend on clubs, pubs, and entertainment, the staples of working-class social life. They remained relatively isolated from their more affluent colleagues. The nexus of family and industry helped to define the class experiences of English workers in the late nineteenth century.

Notes

1. Gareth Stedman Jones, *Outcast London: A Study in the Relationship between Classes in Victorian Society* (Oxford, 1972); Geoffrey Crossick, *An Artisan Elite in Victorian Society: Kentish London, 1840–1880* (London, 1978); Standish Meacham, *A Life Apart: The English Working Class, 1890–1914* (Cambridge, Mass., 1977); Peter N. Stearns, *Lives of Labor:*

Work in a Maturing Industrial Society (London and New York, 1975). On the earlier period, see for example, E. P. Thompson, *The Making of the English Working Class* (New York and London, 1963); John Foster, *Class Struggle and the Industrial Revolution* (London, 1974); John and Barbara Hammond, *The Town Labourer, 1760–1832: The New Civilization* (London, 1925).

2.   Benjamin Seebohm Rowntree, *Poverty: A Study of Town Life* (London, 1922); Charles Booth, *Life and Labour of the People of London*, series 1: *Poverty*, 4 vols. (London, 1902); Mrs. Pember Reeves, *Round About a Pound a Week* (London, 1913); Lady Bell, *At the Works: A Study of a Manufacturing Town* (London, 1907).

3.   U.S. Congress, House of Representatives, *Sixth Annual Report of the Commissioner of Labor, 1890*, Part 3: "Cost of Living," House Executive Document 265, 51st Congress, First Session, 1891; U.S. Congress, House of Representatives, *Seventh Annual Report of the Commissioner of Labor, 1891*, Part 3: "Cost of Living," House Executive Document, 52nd Congress, 1st Session, 1892, All data describing family budgets in this essay, unless otherwise identified, are drawn from these two reports.

4.   This collection of budgets has begun to attract scholarly attention in recent years. John Modell has analyzed the American families in the sample; see "Patterns of Consumption, Acculturation, and Family Income Strategies in Late Nineteenth-Century America," in *Family and Population in Nineteenth-Century America*, ed. by Tamara K. Hareven and Maris A. Vinovskis (Princeton, 1978). Michael Haines has worked on the demographic characteristics and the life-cycle composition of income for the entire sample; see his "Industrial Work and the Family Life Cycle, 1889–1890," Cornell University, Economics Department Pamphlet 111 (May 1976). [A revised and expanded version is contained in *Research in Economic History* 4, in press.]

5.   U.S. Congress, *Sixth Annual Report, 1890*, pp. 610–11.

6.   Henry Higgs, "Workmen's Budgets," *Journal of the Royal Statistical Society* 56 (1893): 260; Carroll Wright also discusses the procedures of the report and stresses reliance on personal interviews; see "A Basis for Statistics of Cost of Production," *Proceedings of the American Statistical Association* 2 (1890–91): 157–77, 261.

7.   B. R. Mitchell and Phyllis Deane, *Abstract of British Historical Statistics* (Cambridge, Eng., 1962), p. 60.

8.   Derek H. Aldcroft and Peter Fearon, eds., *British Economic Fluctuations, 1790–1939* (London, 1972), pp. 9, 12, 78, 88; Mitchell and Deane, *Abstract*, p. 64.

9.   Data on the average incomes and earning patterns of American industrial workers can be found in Haines, "Industrial Work," pp. 43, 46.

10.   Ibid., p. 9.

11.   Louise Tilly, "The Family Wage Economy in a French Textile City, Roubaix, 1872–1906," *Journal of Family History*, in press.

12.   Michael Anderson, *Family Structure in Nineteenth-Century Lancashire* (Cambridge, Eng., 1973), p. 46.

13.   To derive these percentages from the U.S. Department of Labor survey, I combined the separate listings for each family of children's ages and the numbers at work and in school, making the assumption that the oldest children would be those at work and that no children aged three or under would be at school.

14.   Haines, "Industrial Work," pp. 14, 20.

15.   This result is not merely a statistical artifact produced by calculating average incomes. While the range of incomes within each industry was wide, most incomes clustered close to the mean; within most life-cycle stages there were few atypical incomes. Cotton spinners (stage 3) and iron and steel puddlers (stage 2) showed the most extensive range of variation.

16.   Reeves, *Round About*, p. 26; Rowntree, *Poverty*, pp. 288, 293, 338–341; The Economic Club, *Family Budgets: Being the Income and Expenses of Twenty-Eight British Households, 1891–1894* (London, 1896), Appendix D.

17.   D. J. Oddy, "Working-Class Diets in Late Nineteenth-Century Britain," *Economic History Review*, second series, 23, no. 2 (August 1970): 322.

18.   Thomas Oliver, "The Diet of Toil," *The Lancet*, June 29, 1895, pp. 1632–35.

19.   Rowntree, *Poverty*, pp. 279, 297.

20.   Oddy, "Working-Class Diets," p. 318–20.

21.   Ibid., pp. 320–21; Reeves, *Round About*, pp. 97–107; Rowntree, *Poverty*, pp. 83–86; Economic Club, *Family Budgets*, pp. 58, 61.

22.   P. H. J. H. Gosden, *Self-Help: Voluntary Associations in the Nineteenth Century* (London, 1973), p. 91.

23.   Ibid., p. 22.

24.   Sidney and Beatrice Webb, *The History of Trade Unionism* (London, 1902), p. 413; Mitchell and Deane, *Abstract*, p. 60.

25.   Peter Bailey, *Leisure and Class in Victorian England: Rational Recreation and the Contest for Control, 1830–1885* (London, 1978).

26.   Charles Booth, *Life and Labour of the People of London; Third Series: Religious Influences*, 7 vols. (London, 1903), 7:399; Hugh McLeod, *Class and Religion in the Late Victorian City* (London, 1974), p. 28; Economic Club, *Family Budgets*, p. 54.

27.   Eric J. Hobsbawm, *Labouring Men: Studies in the History of Labour* (London, 1964), pp. 373–77; Alan D. Gilbert, *Religion and Society in Industrial England: Church, Chapel and Social Change, 1740–1914* (London and New York, 1976), pp. 42–43.

28.   Bell, *At the Works*, p. 162.

NINE

On the Bourgeoisie
A Psychological Interpretation

PETER GAY

I want to consider anxiety and guilt among the nineteenth-century bourgeoisie. This proposal, I know, crowds two provoking ideas into a single sentence. To begin with, we may doubt that that collective term, "nineteenth-century bourgeoisie," is a fine enough sieve to separate out all the distinct middle classes that populated Europe in the age of Tocqueville and Marx. It is only too obvious that the configuration of traits defining any individual—his character—emerges from the complex, in part unpredictable confluence, and clash, of personal endowment, family constellation, social status, historical circumstances, ethnic and religious and regional loyalties. And among these, status and historical circumstances—the relative position of the individual not only against other classes but within his own class and the experience of groups within the middle classes with the state and with one another—significantly differentiate one type of bourgeois from others. Nor need I here discover the varieties of nineteenth-century bourgeois experience; in addition to the expected individual idiosyncrasies, we find group characteristics, marked and carefully observed, differences in power, wealth, traditions, and location. And there were massive, in fact astonishing, structural changes across time, as documented by that extraordinary growth of what sociologists would come to call the "new" bourgeoisie—the office clerk, the middle manager. Bourgeois sported many cultural styles; I have elsewhere contrasted middle-class attitudes in the court-capital of Munich to those of the commercial center of Manchester, and other distinctions await their historian. The "bourgeoisie" also displayed a certain coherence of response—enough of a unity to induce Adeline Daumard to reach for a portrait of what she calls the "bourgeois soul."[1] I have called that unity a response because it was at least in part imposed from without; it was a way of coping in common with the pretensions of the privileged and the threats of the underprivileged.

But guilt and anxiety?

That hypermodern discipline, psychohistory, has acquired, rightly I think, a most dubious reputation. It cannot be my intention, nor would I have the time, to defend psychohistory here. It is, as it is now being practiced, a most ungainly, often a vulgar enterprise.[2] Let me therefore preface my exploration with a disclaimer. Among the many criticisms that historians employing the psychoanalytic dispensation have had to confront, that of reductionism is the most irritated, the most weighty and, I think, the most justified. But while I would hope that my reflections will compel some adjustment in the way you see the nineteenth-century past, many of them will be complementary to other explanations, rather than in conflict with them. However deeply ideas, actions, and institutions may be rooted in the needs of the psyche, however derivative, in other words, ideas, actions, and institutions may turn out to be, the social—the historical—process enforces what I call an emancipation of derivatives: they acquire a momentum of their own, a kind of urge for life and self-perpetuation that gives our accustomed sociological, economic, and political interpretations their right to persist, and indeed much work to do.

"The principal function of the mental mechanism," Freud wrote in 1913, "is to relieve the individual from the tensions created in him by his needs. One part of this task can be achieved by extracting satisfaction from the external world; and for this purpose it is essential to have control over the real world." Psychoanalysis has much to say about the commerce of the individual with the real world, but in any event, the full explanation of that commerce continues to require the cooperation of the several social sciences. None of Freud's programmatic pronouncements can in any way discredit the claim of such disciplines on the historian's attention; nor were they intended to do so.

But anxiety and guilt will wait no longer. Anxiety is, it would seem, a ubiquitous affect, ranging all across the centuries and the whole social scale. I do not propose to argue that the nineteenth-century bourgeoisie was uniquely susceptible to it; nor, for that matter, that this so-called "bourgeois century" is a candidate for that troubling title, "Age of Anxiety." In a fine (as yet unpublished) paper, William Bouwsma has persuasively nominated the time of the High Renaissance and of the Reformation as an Age of Anxiety; and the claims of our own century, of course, have been put forward by W. H. Auden, for good and sufficient reasons. It is, indeed, from our particular perspective as citizens in an Age of Anxiety that we have discovered, and celebrate, the Cassandras of the nineteenth century, its Kierkegaards and Ruskins, its Morrises and Dostoevskys and Nietzsches. They have more resonance for us than they had for their contemporaries. But as historians we must note that they speak more in the voices of *our* time, than in that of their own; they were prophets, not representatives. It was, rather, Prince Albert addressing the Lord Mayor's banquet in 1850 who typified his age. "Nobody who has paid any attention to the peculiar features of the present era," he said, apostrophizing the forthcoming Great Exhibition, "will doubt for a moment that we are living at a period of most wonderful transition, which tends rapidly to accomplish that great end, to which, indeed, all history points—the realization of the unity of mankind . . . Knowledge acquired becomes at once the property of the community at large . . . So man is approaching a more complete fulfillment of that great and sacred mission he has to perform in this world."[3] We recognize, in these rousing, somewhat self-satisfied tones, the dominant strain of the age. It is the voice of energy. I dispute none of this. All I want to say is that this confidence, this heartiness, this optimism, were shadowed by an admixture of uneasiness, of discontent, of a vague fear, or their derivatives, strong enough to color the moods, and affect the actions, of the middle classes. Even the most successful bourgeois sensed this anxiety, making it a presence worth studying yet so far little studied.

There is, in fact, one aspect of this phenomenon, nervousness, that has received the attention of some historians, including myself. In his recent volume on modern France, Theodore Zeldin calls "personal anxiety" an "uncharted territory," but some mapmakers have been busy.[4] I find it significant that the old term *nervous*, which used to mean vigorous and sinewy, began to acquire a new and pejorative meaning around the beginning of the nineteenth century. For decades, the old meaning coexisted with the new, until the innovation gradually monopolized the field of discourse. Nervous came to mean "irritable, tense, agitated." And it came to be associated with such unwelcome qualities as effeminacy among men and valetudinarianism among women, if not with downright invalidism. Thus, Basil Ransom, Henry James' spokesman for old-fashioned Southern manliness in *The Bostonians*, speaks for more than his region and his reactionary social views when he rants, in a splendid phillipic, against his "feminine, nervous, hysterical, chattering, canting age."

The tempo of self-denunciation in and about this "nervous century" markedly increased in the 1880s and 1890s. There was, before 1900, a great deal of nervousness about nervousness. And however vehemently schools of psychologists and pedagogues might debate all else, they agreed that nervousness was a specifically modern—*the* specifically modern—disease and that its incidence had reached alarming proportions in the last hundred years or so. The diagnoses that flooded the scientific journals in England, on the Continent, and in the United States, and from about 1890 onward, the popular periodical press everywhere, essentially held that it had been the rapidity and the intensity of change that had somehow generated this epidemic of anxiety. Thus in 1901, the alert economist and social critic J. A. Hobson described the rise of neurasthenia as a response to the overwhelming mass of experiences that were swamping modern man, virtually drowning him in too large a number and too great a variety of impulses and impressions. It was, Hobson wrote, "the strain of adaptation [to] complex changes of external environment," that had become so "grave as to impose a nervous wear and tear which is quite apparent in the features of a town population"—a *town* population as opposed to the slower-changing and hence healthier-minded countryside. And Hobson was certain that "neurotic diseases" were particularly prevalent "in every nation which has proceeded far in modern industrialism."[5] The Germans published whole bibliographies on neurasthenia, while the French discovered its symptoms mainly in the middle orders. They were familiar symptoms: fear of failure, lack of leisure, search for pleasure, neglect of exercise, obsessive work, pathological thrift. "It is time," wrote Dr. Proust, "to move on to the gospel of relaxation." (His son, I might note parenthetically, did not take that advice).[6] Not even Sigmund Freud, though he offered a characteristically original explanation of the phenomenon,[7] doubted for a moment that nervousness was greatly on the increase.

It is tempting to ask: How did they know? Quantitative assertions about the growth of nervousness could never be verified; the most circumspect estimate could only be highly impressionistic. Perhaps cases diagnosed as neurasthenia reflected a heightened awareness of the malady which was, therefore, being more fully reported than before: perhaps the invention of diagnostic tools, or at least terms, separating out neurasthenic from other disorders, had given it a new visibility; perhaps the secularization of diagnosis has translated what had been possession by the devil in earlier centuries into nervous weakness. Or they might reflect (as Alex Comfort has suggested)[8] the anxieties of medical men, of the very profession called to alleviate them.

All this may be so. It is very likely. But I have come to think that this nervousness about nervousness can actually supply some revealing clues about the century in which it flourished. Even if this anxiety was not the cure for the disease it named and saw everywhere but rather a symptom—and it was more than that—all the more profitable for the historian. For that alone would reveal the contours of a culture in which such alertness became possible, even necessary. It suggests, to me, the strength of the undercurrent of anxiety in the confident bourgeois century.

I am speaking, of course, about anxiety among adults, though worried pedagogues discovered alarming instances of it among secondary-school children. But it is to early childhood that we must turn for a proper definition. Anxiety is an often quite unspecific feeling of apprehensiveness or vigilance, sometimes but not always accompanied by bodily sensations, signalizing danger. It arises, like most affects, in a "social" situation: the repeated encounter between the infant and its mother. There seems to be an innate "predisposition to anxiety,"[9] part of the armamentarium of human nature. And there are patterns of very early anxiety behavior, notably what René Spitz has called the "eighth month anxiety," that appear to be so general as to constitute a phase through which human beings must pass, to be preserved in memory and reactivated through later experiences.[10]

"Reactivated"—I must dwell on this point for a moment. The anxiety of the adult is in the main a reenactment of earlier anxieties. The infant lays down memory traces, and begins to mobilize defensive measures around moments of delay in feeding, around the absent mother, around internally generated, and overpowering, feelings of love or rage, and it is the revival of this infantile helplessness before such looming, if vaguely apprehended, dangers of starvation or punishment or confusion that provides the anxiety of the adult with its charge.

This sense of lost bearings, intermittent but powerful, is the heritage of humanity. With all its diversity, humanity is a brotherhood in anxiety. Yet it is a brotherhood fatally divided. Anxiety implies a sense of hope, normally a chance for relief; it differs, dramatically, from the realistic fear of tangible misery. In the nineteenth century, and beyond, there were many, the poor, who could literally not afford anxiety, or take the time to be anxious about it when they did feel it. To quote from Robert Roberts' *The Classic Slum*, a little masterpiece about the working class in Salford in Edwardian times:

> Under the common bustle crouched fear. In children—fear of parents, teachers, the Church, the police and authority of any sort; in adults—fear of petty chargehands, foremen, managers and employers of labour. Men harboured a dread of sickness, debt, loss of status; above all, of losing a job, which could bring all other evils fast in train. Most people in the undermass worked not, as is fondly asserted now, because they possessed an antique integrity which compelled "a fair day's work for a fair day's pay" (whatever that means); they toiled on through mortal fear of getting the sack. Fear was the *leitmotif* of their lives, dulled only now and then by the Dutch courage gained from drunkenness.[11]

That fear—fear of getting the sack and all the others—was realistic, objective, present fear, not anxiety recalled. But in saying this I am not suggesting that anxiety is always remote from reality. It is important to remember—and this applies to guilt quite as much as to anxiety, and to the defenses mobilized against both—that from the psychologist's, as from the historian's perspective, these mental experiences take many forms and invite many verdicts. Anxiety may be realistic or irrational, appropriate or excessive, drawn from facts or fantasies, right for the stage in a person's life or out of phase. The decision which of these it is must await the appraisal of each particular situation. Moreover, what may be adaptive to the individual, reducing pain and easing accommodation, may be maladaptive to his culture or, far more frequently, the other way about: the most poignant psychological suffering of the individual—a sign that his defenses have somehow failed—may be precisely the quality that society requires to exploit its resources or guarantee its survival. I recall only Max Weber's capitalist, scrimping, saving, postponing and denying himself pleasures, so that his business and, with that, his social system, might thrive.

In all these instances, reality plays at least some part in the creation of anxiety. It does so, also, in the erecting of defenses. Even for the neurotic, who retreats from the intolerable harshness of the real world, reality remains the great teacher. Indeed, the most efficacious defenses against anxiety—routine, habit, regularity—originate almost wholly in the child's traffic with the outside world. The anxiety over separation from the mother, which is the prototype of later anxieties, can yield, or be appeased, by the rhythmic alternation of the mother's departure and return, by the regular brief interval between hunger and its satisfaction. The child builds up a repertory of expectations permitting him to put anxiety-producing dangers into perspective, to accept reassurances, to discriminate, however roughly, between disaster and "normal" deprivation, between permanent desertion and temporary absence. In short, it learns to inhabit a structured, stable little world that gives it a measure of security.

The repertory of expectations of which I am speaking grows with the child until it acquires a storehouse of values, and of appraisals; until it knows what brings applause or censure, and can predict what is likely to happen in that uninhabited, fearful space ahead, the future. The notorious capacity of children for repeating games, jokes, or verbal messages, is part of the process of internalizing family routines and social mores until they become, almost literally, a second nature. The experiments that small children perform (such as covering their eyes, or running away or tentatively saying no) are the obverse of the same learning process. By mapping out areas of freedom, and gambling for modest stakes, the child tests the security of the cage of constraints in which it learns to live.

These modest rehearsals of autonomy are, at the same time, adaptive devices helping the child to cope with the inescapable disruptions that invade that structured, stable little world: the arrival of a sibling, the illness of its mother, a change of residence, and the trials of growth itself which, presenting it with new capacities and new excitations, threaten that ultimate realistic defense against anxiety, habit. And it is not only disaster—or what is experienced as such—or the emergence of new conflicts produced by increasing awareness of one's sexuality and aggressiveness, but also gratifying, even longed-for innovations that arouse anxiety, often while they give pleasure at the same time. What triggers anxiety is unpredictability, suddenness, a call for readjusting expectations, anything that invalidates, or confuses, the guidelines so laboriously built up. The notorious conservatism of children, their symptomatic timidity before the very experiences for which they have been clamoring, illustrates this crucial point to perfection. There is no question in my mind: if children had the vote, Tories would rule the world forever.

That change itself—good news as much as bad—should generate anxiety is a discovery of the greatest importance, and it is not, I think, an accident, that it should have been a great nineteenth-century psychologist in spite of himself, Emile Durkheim, who built that discovery into his famous analysis of social anxiety, which he called anomie. Nor is it an accident that his contemporary diagnosticians of nervousness, that most expressive form of anxiety, regularly included the process of change, and change for the better, in their diagnosis just as much as its results.

No one will deny that the nineteenth century was a time of dramatic change. It was the century in which that evocative phrase for traditionalism, "the cake of custom," was coined, at the very time that the cake was being rapidly nibbled away. It is, I know, a commonplace that all history is the record of change; the wheel of fortune, whose turns indeed constitute what we mean by history, has at times slowed down but never stood quite still. But in decisive respects, there was so much more of nineteenth-century change that here quantity was practically transposed into quality. And with it, the quality of anxiety probably changed as well. In antiquity, and down through the ages, anxiety was recurrent, seasonal, tied to the vagaries of bountiful or stingy nature. Thus in classical Greece, E. R. Dodds tells us, popular religion was tied to the anxieties of the farmer's year. "It is a pattern of anxiety punctuated by relief, and it repeats itself every year in much the same form. The anxiety is always there, but every year it mounts to a crisis at certain crucial periods," at seedtime and in the spring. And later, when Roman pagans confronted Roman Christians, Dodds writes elsewhere, anxiety was the pervasive sense of impending, uncontrollable catastrophes—a sense similar to the one that Bouwsma discerns in the fifteenth and sixteenth centuries.[12] To all these ages, change meant expected disaster, unanticipated good fortune, the rise and fall of a ruling dynasty. Nineteenth-century change, in contrast, was exhilarating and depressing, it was surprising, accelerating, profound; above all, it was irreversible. That is precisely why there were so many intense reactionaries trying to reverse it. The life of Metternich, a notable and instructive nineteenth-century career, is a tribute to the changes he attempted to arrest, if not undo, until they undid him.

I need not belabor the details. The resounding abstractions of the textbooks—industrialization, urbanization, secularization, professionalization, migration, and that most significant term of them all, mobility—say everything, or almost everything. Let me merely add a few glosses to these once evocative, by now tired, global words. Industrialization, urbanization, and the rest sum up massive quantities of human experiences, usually of a profoundly troubling, or at least unsettling, sort. And they traumatized, not merely the victims of progress, but its beneficiaries as well.

There is abundant and persuasive evidence that alert contemporaries, even those indifferent to nervousness, perceived the nineteenth century to be an age of profound innovation. Those who lamented the rise of industrial civilization and those who celebrated it agreed on that. It was an age of movement, of physical, social, religious, economic, political, artistic—and psychological—movement. The very term *movement*, with its derivation from motion, came to be used in place of more static terms like *school* or *sect*; in the same way, long-familiar names for social divisions, like *estates*, or *orders*, or, even more graphically, *Stände*—all of which implied a rooted permanence—now gave way to more dynamic names suggesting divisions and, with that, a possibility of, or perhaps a need for, drastic readjustment of the social landscape: *classes* or *parties*, or, later in the century, interest groups. Even the arts, which, however restless and divided, had always looked to the past for instruction, witnessed, as Henry James put it at the end of the nineteenth century, a "grand collapse of all the forms." Looking back at the decades just past, Holbrook Jackson[13] characterized the 1890s as a time when novelty became an incantation, with books called *The New Hedonism* and *The New Fiction*, and with movements—they were, of course, movements—calling themselves the New Paganism, and the New Voluptuousness, and in obvious reaction, the New Remorse, but also the New Spirit, the New Humor, the New Realism, the New Drama, to say nothing of the New Unionism and the New Woman. Indeed, shortly after 1890, the Austrian critic and essayist Hermann Bahr noted the repeated emergence of "young" schools of art and literature everywhere, even, he added, of "youngest" schools. "Every day," he wrote, "sees the appearance of a new aesthetic of the future. Everyone offers his particular formula for the novel. Everywhere, schools are being founded, but no one wants to be a disciple. The old formulas have served their turn, there is an irresistible thirst after the new."[14]

One might qualify this as superficial attitudinizing in a restless decade. But it was more. It went deeper and was older than the aesthetes of the 1890s. "The world," said Charles Péguy in 1913, "has changed less since Jesus Christ than in the last thirty years," and Péguy here meant more than painting or poetry.[15] And, indeed, observers had noted the ubiquity and the depth of change long before the 1890s. Thus, in 1873 Walter Bagehot wrote, in the opening paragraph of his book, *Physics and Politics*, that "one peculiarity of this age is the sudden acquisition of much physical knowledge. There is scarcely a department of science or art which is the same, or at all the same, as it was fifty years ago. A new world of inventions—of railways and of telegraphs—has grown up around us which we cannot help seeing; a new world of ideas is in the air and affects us, though we do not see it."

Bagehot articulated, with his usual acuity, what many others dimly sensed. Yet even he could not be wholly specific, so profound was the transformation he was witnessing: "A new world of ideas is in the air and affects us, though we do not see it." This is precisely my point. Whether we study railroads—that symbol of the new—from the perspective of the avid promoter, the angry reformer, the trained engineer, or the ambivalent traveler, we discover men bewildered and overwhelmed by the avalanche of invention and innovation. And the railroad was only the most spectacular product of that dizzying time. Wherever men looked, whatever men did, however men lived, they had to fashion new responses to meet new opportunities or new threats—the psychological effect, we know, was the same whether it was the one or the other. Routine, custom, structures of expectation—"iterative experiences," René Spitz has called them—seemed all equally obsolete and equally irrelevant. There was, even among the profiteers, then, much ground for anxiety.

This formulation gives me an opportunity to offer, before I turn to guilt, yet another disclaimer. Nothing I am saying should be taken as exculpation of exploiters, of sweaters, of stock manipulators. It is no apology for their conduct that they had anxiety attacks all the way to the bank. The purpose of psychoanalytic history cannot be to serve as a substitute for moral judgments, but only as a substitute for primitive psychologizing.

Guilt, another defining quality of nineteenth-century middle-class psychology, is much like anxiety; it is, really, a special and late kind of anxiety. Like anxiety, guilt is partly conscious and partly unconscious; it is both a patent and a concealed spur to action, and a prodigious generator of defenses. Like anxiety, too, guilt emerges from the confluence and the conflict of external pressures and internal needs. And like anxiety, guilt is unpleasurable but may prove adaptive either to the individual or to society, or to both. Finally, like anxiety, guilt was the monopoly neither of the nineteenth century nor of the bourgeoisie; an ancient and very general human experience, it merely took a particular form of special interest to the historian, in the bourgeois cetury. I would describe that form, a little portentously perhaps, as the privatization of guilt.

In part, guilt is difficult to define because it so closely resembles another prevalent psychological mechanism: shame. The two are sometimes indistinguishable from one another, may parade in one another's garments, or give rise to each other in a reciprocal action.

Certainly, shame had its place in the bourgeois mental economy, especially in such reaction formations as fanatical cleanliness, or sexual gentility. But in general, shame seems to have been the inner policeman of the working class far more than that of the middle classes. For guilt (and here, too, it resembles anxiety) presupposes hope and care; it grows particularly poignant in the guise of bitter self-reproach for having offended—or merely having *wished* to offend—loving and beloved parents. The nineteenth-century bourgeoisie invented neither the nuclear family nor parental affection, but it made more of both than other classes in its time, and than its own ancestors had made before them. Middle-class nineteenth-century families enjoyed—and suffered—closer intimacy than others; for all the rigidity of their controls, they also permitted themselves to cherish their children. Hence it was precisely this kind of family that proved the most fertile soil for the potent self-criticism we call the sense of guilt. It produced some exquisite superegos. The superego is formed by a variety of agencies, by teachers, friends, siblings, priests; but it arises first in the intimate triangle, the child with his parents. And guilt is not plain fear—the calculating fear of being found out by others. It is, rather, fear overstrained, unrealistic, wholly self-referential, the fear of being found out by oneself. The superego is canny, incorruptible, and merciless. The man driven by a sense of guilt is wicked criminal, brilliant prosecutor, and hanging judge at the same time.

That is why—and this type was well known in the bourgeois century—the most innocent person, the best behaved and most moral, often had the most exigent and inexorable guilt feelings of them all. The degree of his docility only testifies to the severity of his self-criticism; he was so good because he thought himself so bad. The notorious contempt that most "normal" children feel for the "goody-goody," the Little Lord Fauntleroy, a contempt that many adults, however unconsciously, share, is better grounded than they know.

Of course, the sense of guilt was, as I have insisted, not an invention of the nineteenth-century bourgeoisie. It informs, even dominates, most religions.

Christianity, after all, is an enormously elaborate system for explaining and placing guilt: God the Father, though the dispenser of all misery, is absolved from responsibility for evil, since guilt for transgression falls upon man, his creature. "In Adam's Fall we sinned all." But Christianity also drew the sting of this doctrine by prescribing the recovery of innocence. While, throughout two millennia, thoughtful and guilt-ridden Christians tried to restore psychological weight to the dogma of human depravity, the church institutionalized it with confession and penance, with cleansing rituals like baptism and communion, and appointed agents—secular priests, monks, nuns—to go the way, and do the work, of holiness. Most dramatically, Jesus, son of God, himself free of all sin, took mankind's guilt upon himself in sacrificing his life. Nor were these religious defense mechanisms, which provide immense psychological relief to believers, confined to Roman Catholicism. "A succession of Victorian clergymen," Brian Harrison has written of Protestants, "ensured that reform was as frequently inspired by upper-class guilt as by working-class anger."[16]

It would be a mistake to treat such guilt as instances of pharisaism or masks for hypocrisy. For all the much-publicized secularizing inroads made by students of geology, the higher criticism, positivist philosophy, atheist socialism, and of course, Darwin, the nineteenth century was a deeply religious time; especially among the bourgeoisie, the churches regained ground lost in the century before. When Karl Marx called religion the opium of the masses he was, for his own time, quite wrong; it was the opium of the middle classes, and a potent drug with varied side effects, of which beneficence is only the best known.

Nor was guilt simply a response to religion. What I have called the privatization of guilt can best be observed, perhaps, among those untouched by the revival of evangelicalism or the emergence of Social Catholicism. "There was a rather mysterious movement," G. Kitson Clark has written of the early nineteenth century, "which if often confounded with the revival of religion but seems to have affected many who were outside the main areas of religious ferment, an ever-increasing sense of moral responsibility and a growing sensitivity to the challenge of human suffering and the suffering of animals."[17] There were, in the nineteenth century, not merely abundant opportunities for feeling uncomfortable with oneself, but many bourgeois who took the opportunity. Priests, pastors, and social critics did not produce guilt so much as to keep alive, and give direction to, the guilt feelings generated in loving middle-class families.

One way, then, of suitably complicating our experience of nineteenth-century bourgeois life is to discover the impulses of anxiety and guilt in middle-class sentiment and conduct. But, as you may expect, affects so painful as these do not often reach the level of public notice unedited, unmediated. Man's mind, Freud taught us long ago, tries to evade or, if possible, to erase them by employing a variety of defensive strategies. And while the defenses only rarely eliminate the actuating causes of such miseries, they manage to ward them off by compromises, by disguises. These defenses are of particular interest to the historian, for they are the public face of private suffering—public not merely in their expression but also in their consequences, and public also in their choice of forms, for each culture and each subculture has its favored set of defenses.

There is a dizzying variety of such strategies. Most recently, Susan Sontag has called photography, among other things, a defense against anxiety. Here I want to list, and briefly discuss, only four of them. Note that they can be utilized singly or in combinations, serve anxiety and guilt alike, and differ in their relation to reality, as well as in their intensity. They may be sensible or irrational, moderate or convulsive.

The defenses of greatest interest to us are, I think, these:

1. *Denial*: I feel anxious, but there is nothing to be anxious about. Or: I feel guilty, but there is, in fact, nothing to be guilty about.

2. *Projection*: I feel anxious, but that is because others have made me feel that way. Or: I feel guilty, but I am not guilty; whatever there is to be guilty about is the fault of others.

3. *Regression*: I feel anxious or guilty, and I can only manage these discomforts by seeking refuge in earlier, simpler stages of mental organization.

4. *Reaction formation*: I feel anxious and I must control it by presenting to the world the very opposite kind of behavior. Or: I feel guilty and compelled to assuage my guilt by conduct the reverse of my guilt feelings.

Denial.   Nineteenth-century denial took the traditional form of a programmatic hedonism, more or less desperate, a clinging to pleasures designed to shut out of awareness the terrible dislocations produced by the industrial revolution. Such hedonism amounted to a constriction of affect, or even of perception, to the familial or (in extreme narcissistic behavior) the personal sphere. Drinking, sports, gambling, and related ways of prolonging, or restoring, childhood were favorite ways of evading reality in the bourgeois century, and they were not confined to noblemen, peasants, and working men.

Two interesting, if still debated, arenas for such denials are the nineteenth-century city and family. Cities, as David Pinkney and other urban historians have noted, were increasingly segmented among particular social groupings, so that many people lived among, and experienced, only a modest segment on the scale of reality. At the same time, the new metropolis housed the most variegated populations, thus providing inviting alternatives to inherited, humdrum but stable modes of conduct. And the nineteenth-century bourgeois family, jealously guarding its privacy and resenting intrusion, professed to serve as a bastion against the ugly realities of commercial, industrial, and political life. These defenses are, as I said, still debated, for we all have evidence to contradict them: the Parisian five-story apartment building that housed a cross-section of most strata of the Parisian population; or the open-handed hospitality that graced the bourgeois style—here and there. However ambiguous the evidence, however ambivalent the middle-class attitudes it reveals, I have no doubt that both residential segregation and familial privacy had their place among the defensive strategies of the nineteenth-century middle classes.

One popular way of denying realities was to invent a largely imaginary class: the poor who did not suffer; Standish Meacham has noted that English manufacturers often made themselves believe that their "hands" were a grosser breed than they, and thus not very sensitive to monotony, unending labor, deprivation, and dirt.[18] Here the wish was father to the belief. However convenient such perceptions may appear, they are not "hypocritical"; the hypocrite professes one belief while actually believing something else, or consciously acts in a way incompatible with his professions. This invention of the happy poor was actually a distortion of vision, all the more cherished, no doubt, for being so profitable, but a defensive distortion nonetheless.

Not surprisingly, Marx and Engels made sport of this sort of denial. In his *Condition of the Working Class in England in 1844*, Engels reproduces, from the *Manchester Guardian*, an irate letter to the editor, primly signed "A Lady," which complains about "swarms of beggars 'haunting' our main streets, 'who' try to awaken the pity of the passers-by in a most shameless and annoying manner, by exposing their tattered clothing, sickly aspect, and disgusting wounds and deformities." She plaintively inquires if those who, like herself, pay the poor rates and contribute generously to charitable institutions had not earned the right "to be spared such disagreeable and impertinent molestations."[19]

Of course, Engels and Marx also diagnosed more philosophical forms of denial by exposing what they called "reification," the treatment of relations among people as though they were relations among things, thus concealing their exploitative character. And certainly the nineteenth century saw some notable attempts to raise denial to the level of theory, to develop systems in which evil and misery became necessary elements in the greater good, or the inevitable price of progress. While the classical economists have been rather maligned, it remains true that versions of their doctrines, like contemporary theories of progress and, later, of Social Darwinism, were self-satisfied rationalizations in which the facts of social life paled before, or wholly disappeared behind, the ponderous abstractions of the system. Such "philo-sophical" forms of denial achieved their aim in two ways: they subsumed real injustices and suffering under imaginary benefits, and they fled the concrete experiences that this suffering entailed.

Projection.   For its part, projection is closely related to denial, since it often conceals, behind its facade, a kind of defensive rage. Tacitus observed long ago that we never forgive those we have injured, and nineteenth-century public debate, letters to the newspapers, or statements to boards of directors abound in such self-serving reproaches: it is the improvidence and the intemperance of the poor that keeps them poor, not the harshness and the acquisitiveness of their masters.

Projection, though, goes beyond this kind of apologetic aggressiveness. It is a way of mastering one's own disreputable impulses and wishes—oral greed, anal rage, and genital lust—by ascribing them to others: to foreigners, Jews, Freemasons, radical agitators. Such projective activity offers significant secondary gains, such as group solidarity, for (as Adam Ferguson had already pointed out in the eighteenth century) there is nothing that cements friendships and alliances more solidly than a common enemy. Projection, of course, was, like all the other defenses, no nineteenth-century innovation. But in tribal societies, and in the Christian centuries, permissible hatred had been institutionalized; it was licensed, as it were, by the authorities: the heretic was only one example of the officially designated enemy. In the bourgeois century, projections of this sort, as they emerged in chauvinism or anti-Semitism or class hatred, were rather looser, publicly formulated but privately chosen. For in that century a series of daring principles and practices—free trade, free enterprise, careers open to talents, religious toleration greater than ever before—broke through the centuries-old division of the world into good and evil. A competitor, whether at home or abroad, was less wicked, less suitable a target for aggression than the old outsiders had been. The nineteenth century invited complex perceptions, and feared them. Where, then, could aggressive feelings go? One could always hate one's neighbor as oneself, of course, but society also supplied a variety of possible hateful objects. Hence projection was constantly at war with more pacific ideals.

Regression.   The categorical way of simplifying experience links projection to regression. For regression (if I may baldly summarize a complicated phenomenon) is a psychological retreat from advanced rational perceptions to earlier, more primitive modes of grasping the world—the mode of the child. Pediatricians, child psychoanalysts, and indeed observant parents know that troubles and anxieties bring regression in their wake, invite a return to stages presumably outgrown but continuing to lurk in the unconscious. The liberal culture of the nineteenth century, however incomplete and imperfect, demanded a certain mental maturity. It implied tolerating (at least a little) ambiguous situations; conceding (to some degree) one's ambivalence about important persons; acknowledging (if reluctantly) the complexity of life or the good points of a rival. True enough: many, even in the nineteenth century, never reached this kind of independence. But the point is that many who had reached it would withdraw to the far safer, essentially infantile position of pitting friend against enemy, of magnifying trivial incidents into portentous events, as soon as the routine of their existence, the predictable course of their expectations, had been somehow disturbed.

An instructive instance of such regression is Matthew Arnold's vehement outburst against the so-called "Hyde Park rioters." On July 23, 1866, the respectable, overwhelmingly middle-class Reform League, an organization pushing for parliamentary reform, held a public rally in Hyde Park. Finding themselves barred on government orders, some exasperated demonstrators then broke (or were shoved, thus breaking) the railings, causing much general milling about but no violence or injuries. But the breaking of the barriers seemed a symbolic violation of boundaries, and aroused keen anxiety in Matthew Arnold and his like; in *Culture and Anarchy*, Arnold found adjectives worthy of a minor revolution in describing the incident: "[The] Hyde Park rough," Arnold wrote, "has not yet found his groove and settled down to his work, and so he is just asserting his personal liberty a little, going where he likes, assembling where he likes, bawling as he likes, hustling as he likes." This is irrational talk from a rational man who took pride in trying to see things as they were. Actually, Arnold saw things from the perspective of one he himself had been many years before.

Leaving aside all discussion of specific policies, I would add extreme forms of conservatism to the list of regressions. It is a search for stable foundations in an insecure, forever-changing world. Here, as elsewhere, we can see defenses coordinating their work until they become practically indistinguishable from one another. Thus, Henry James lamented, in a brilliant analysis, the reluctance of novelists to treat sexual matters in their fiction; this reluctance joins denial to regression in the childlike incredulity that one's parents actually perform intercourse. James noted that there were "many sources of interest neglected—whole categories of manners . . . unvisited"; instead, writers made do with shopworn substitutes for the real thing, "mistakenly" taking it "for granted that safety lies in all the loose and thin material that keeps reappearing in forms at once ready-made and sadly worse for wear."[20] The search in all these defenses is, as James so shrewdly recognized, for safety.

Reaction formation.   But not all safety lies in evasion. There is also what the Germans so picturesquely call "Flucht nach vorn," the flight into action, into life. I have reached the last of the defenses I want to discuss: reaction formation. This strategy is, as the name suggests, the attempt to mask and master unacceptable wishes and frightening affects by means of contrary feelings and conduct: by shame to cover exhibitionism, by disgust, coprophilia. Again I must insist that reaction formation has nothing to do with hypocrisy, nor is it pathological unless, of course, it lapses into the caricature that is fanaticism, into what Charles Dickens sarcastically called "telescopic philanthropy." A striking real-life counterpart to this caricature is that familiar nineteenth-century reformer, the passionate, single-minded, intolerant antivivisectionist. The inappropriate, artificial,and often curiously dated refinement of the parvenu, so often a source of ridicule and somewhat snobbish contempt, is really a defense by the newcomer in an anxiety-producing situation. Those egregious Veneerings (to return to Dickens once again), with their "bran-new" house, "bran-new" furnishings, "bran-new" everything, may be thoroughly distasteful, but they are also, just as thoroughly, anxious underneath their glittering, "bran-new" veneer. Books of etiquette, which virtually swamped the middle-class reading public in the nineteenth century, in Germany and France quite as much as in England, are reminders that Dickens' observation of the social climber was keen, if a little unfeeling.

But not all reaction formation, as I have said, tips the scale of excess. Far more moderate, responsive in part to real issues and in part to inner demons, were the periodic bouts of middle-class self-abasement, those fits of morality which Macaulay found so ridiculous. Some of them, to be sure, amounted to what Anna Freud has called "identification with the aggressor,"[21] accepting the judgment of the enemy as true. But the contingent of nineteenth-century self-lacerators—from Gustave Flaubert to William Morris, and from John Ruskin to Friedrich Nietzche—were not simply translating psychopathology into social criticism. With them, reaction formation did the work of civilization; it belongs, as Mrs. Humphry Ward wrote, among "those fundamental rules which human nature has worked out, with such infinite difficulty and pain, for the protection of its own weakness."[22]

Sometimes, in fact, those fundamental rules and the weakness they attempted to protect, did combat so openly, so intensely, that the struggle invaded consciousness. The Christian Socialists, Catholic and Protestant alike, and the philosophical reformers were perfectly aware that their passion for reform was an effusion of guilt. In a much-quoted 1883 lecture, Arnold Toynbee said:

> We—the middle classes I mean, not merely the very rich—we have neglected you; instead of justice we have offered you charity, and instead of sympathy we have offered you hard and unreal advice. ... You have to forgive us, for we have wronged you, we have sinned against you grievously—not knowingly always, but still we have sinned, and let us confess it; but if you will forgive us— nay, whether you will forgive us or not—we will serve you, we will devote our lives to your service, and we cannot do more.[23]

Commenting on this overpowering wish to undo wrongs, Beatrice Webb perceptively noted that "the origin of the ferment is to be discovered in a new consciousness of sin among men of intellect and men of property. ... The consciousness of sin was a collective or class consciousness."[24] This was a productive flight into reality, the very opposite of Dickens' Gradgrind, who defended himself against *his* feelings by fleeing into his constricted, cold, affectless reality, into facts, facts, facts.

I conclude with a reminder and an observation: everything I have said should be taken as experiment, nothing as dogma. I do not offer the psychological mechanisms I have discussed as the sole—or even as the principal— causes in the history of the nineteenth-century bourgeoisie. I have not forgotten the complexity of human affairs; in fact, I am undertaking these studies in the conviction that they are even more complex than most historians have been willing to believe.

And I want to observe that while I intended these remarks as suggestions for new ways of looking at familiar phenomena, a significant part of the task ahead is to establish facts before we make interpretations. I should conjecture, for example, that we would find particularly poignant anxieties, to say nothing of guilt, plaguing those at the *edge* of bourgeois life, prosperous and ambitious artisans ready to claim bourgeois status without being able to shed their craftsman's origins. And I also believe that the interplay of social forces within the bourgeoisie, the working out of aggressive, envious, and submissive feelings produced, in the nineteenth century, some striking instances of ambivalence. There is, I think, much research to be done into the behavior of the nineteenth-century middle classes.

I have tried to demonstrate elsewhere that the bourgeoisie was, in fact, less genteel, which is to say, far less defensive, than has usually been thought. And there are other similar factual issues aching to be explored. But that is another essay.

Notes

1. Daumard, *Les Bourgeois de Paris au XIXe siècle* (Paris, 1970), pp. 319–44. True, Werner Sombart's once famous book, *Der Bourgeois*, published in 1913, attempted a unified definition, but the work is shallow and unrevealing, typical of that imaginative, opportunistic, and unscrupulous academic entrepreneur.

2. For a brief critique of the field, see Peter Gay, "Introduction: Dimensions of Cause," *Art and Act: On Causes in History—Manet, Gropius, Mondrian* (New York, 1976), pp. 1–32.

3. Quoted in Sir Nikolaus Pevsner, *High Victorian Design* (London, 1951), p. 16.

4. See Zeldin, *France, 1848–1945*, vol. 2: *Intellect, Taste and Anxiety* (Oxford, 1977), part 3, passim.

5. Hobson, *The Psychology of Jingoism* (London, 1901).

6. See Zeldin, *France 1848–1945*, 2:841–43.

7. See Freud's essay, " 'Civilized' Sexual Morality and Modern Nervous Illness" (1908), in *The Standard Edition of the Complete Psychological Works of Sigmund Freud*, ed. James Strachey et al., vol. 9 (London, 1959), pp. 177–204.

8. Comfort, *The Anxiety Makers: Some Curious Preoccupations of the Medical Profession* (London, 1967).

9. See Phyllis Greenacre, "The Predisposition to Anxiety" [1941], in *Trauma, Growth, and Personality* (London, 1952), pp. 27–82.

10. *See Spitz, The First Year of Life* (New York, 1965).

11. Roberts, *The Classic Slum: Salford Life in the First Quarter of the Century* (Manchester, 1973), p. 88.

12. Of Dodds' works from which I have learned immensely and on which I have leaned heavily, most relevant here are *The Greeks and the Irrational* (Berkeley, 1951), *Pagan and Christian in an Age of Anxiety: Some Aspects of Religious Experience From Marcus Aurelius to Constantine* (Oxford, 1965); and "The Religion of the Ordinary Man in Classical Greece," in *The American Concept of Progress* (Oxford, 1973), pp. 140–55.

13. Jackson, *The Eighteen Nineties: A Review of Art and Ideas at the Close of the Nineteenth Century* (New York, 1913), passim.

14. Ruth Gay has called attention to the conjunction of youth and novelty in the versions of Art Nouveau, which was called Jugendstil in Germany.

15. Quoted in Roger Shattuck, *The Banquet Years: The Origins of the Avant-Garde in France, 1885 to World War I* (New York, 1955), p. 1.

16. Harrison, "For Church, Queen and Family: The Girls' Friendly Society, 1874–1920," *Past and Present*, no. 61 (1973): 115.

17. Clark, *Churchmen and the Condition of England, 1832–1885* (London, 1973), pp. xv-xvi.

18. Meacham, *A Life Apart: The English Working Class, 1890–1914* (London, 1977), p. 133.

19. Engels, *Condition of the Working Class in England in 1844* (London 1892 [orig. edn. 1845]), pp. 278–9.

20. James, "The Future of the Novel" [1899] in *Selected Literary Criticism*, by Henry James, ed. Morris Shapera (Harmondsworth, 1963), pp. 187–8.

21. See Anna Freud, *The Ego and the Mechanisms of Defence* (London, 1937), pp. 117–31.

22. Quoted in William S. Peterson, *Victorian Heretic: Mrs. Humphry Ward's "Robert Elsmere"* (Leicester, 1976), p. 5.

23. Quoted in Peter d'Alroy Jones, *The Christian Socialist Revival, 1877–1914: Religion, Class, and Social Conscience in Late-Victorian England* (Princeton, 1968), pp. 85–86n.

24. Webb, *My Apprenticeship* (London, 1926), pp. 179–80.

TEN

After the Commune
Alcoholism, Temperance, and Literature in the Early Third Republic

SUSANNA BARROWS

In the spring of 1871, Jean-Baptiste Barth's house was burned to the ground. "His heart bursting with shame and rage," Dr. Barth was horrified by the "filthy and monstrous orgies" of the Commune, which had cost him his residence and his peace of mind. When the fighting ceased, he determined to attack what he regarded as the root cause of French decadence. He set about organizing a temperance society.[1]

As Dr. Barth's traumatic experience suggests, the terrible year of 1870–71 triggered an immediate and dramatic shift in the perception of drink. Before 1870 the subject of drunkenness and alcoholism had aroused little interest in France; after the French defeat and the bloody uprising in Paris, it preoccupied the medical profession, legislators, men of property, and government officials. The adoption of the new paradigm of alcoholism in France owed less to scientific research than to psychological factors—anger, fear, humiliation, and guilt. As men like Barth surveyed the wreckage of life and property strewn about Paris in 1871, they sought desperately to explain the apparent "mad" decadence of the Commune, to alleviate their own burden of guilt for its violent end, and to prevent any reoccurrence of such "insane" attacks upon the social order. They thus embarked upon a sacred crusade—the moral reform of the working classes.

Within five years of the Commune, the French temperance movement had emerged as an influential private arm of public repression. Gathering several hundred distinguished gentlemen into their fold, temperance leaders propagated a new myth of alcoholism and championed the passage of a law against public drunkenness. So persuasive was their propaganda, and so vigilant the government's censorship, that scarcely anyone dared question in print the new official view of drink. Scarcely anyone, that is, but Emile Zola. Far from reflecting the new paradigm of working-class alcoholism, Zola's journalism and his fiction reveal him to be one of its sharpest and most persistent critics.[2] By placing Zola's writings on drink in the specific context of French temperance, one can map more fully the underlying mental geography of class perceptions and the boundaries of social criticism in the wake of the Commune.

Throughout most of the nineteenth century, public opinion in France held that alcoholism was a disorder wholly alien to its soil. In 1852 Magnus Huss had baptised the disease of drink as "alcoholism"; French physicians had been quick to praise his pioneering work, yet reluctant to apply his findings to their contemporaries. "There may be a good many drunkards in France," conceded one French doctor during the Second Empire, "but happily there are no alcoholics."[3] Most of his colleagues could agree. Although a medical paradigm for the disease of drink had been established by Huss and discovered by French doctors among French patients long before the Commune, medical interest in the physiological disorders caused by drink was scant before 1871. Between 1843 and 1866 only seven articles on alcoholism were published in the *Annales médicos-psychologiques*, and despite research which had isolated ten different maladies associated with excessive use of spirits between 1813 and 1852, the *Catalogue générale de la bibliographie française* listed a mere five books on alcoholism published in French between 1840 and 1870. Drunkenness, be it in its transitory (*ivresse*) or chronic (*ivrognerie*) forms, was the preferred term of mid-nineteenth-century physicians.

Such nonchalance was reflected—even after the Commune—in the conventional wisdom of French encyclopedias. As late as 1875 *La Grande Dictionnaire du XIXe siècle* informed its readers that "in our country, although drunkenness is not unknown, it is far from having a character as repellent and as nefarious as in England and in America."[4] The disparity between French moderation and Anglo-American dipsomania was attributed to race. In the opinion of the *Grande Dictionnaire*, temperance movements, so common in England, Germany, and America, served to "moderate the hereditary ardor of the Teutonic race and the Anglo-Saxon race for alcoholic spirits."[5] Since the French did not spring from that unfortunate family tree, they had no need for temperance.

The *Grande Dictionnaire* had made a grievous error. In echoing the mid–nineteenth-century view of alcoholism, it had confused national concern with national consumption. Throughout the nineteenth century, temperance was a broader-based reform movement in America than in France, but that did *not* mean that Americans drank more than French men and women. It simply meant that French crusades for temperance before 1871 had all come to rapid and unsuccessful ends. The first, a Société de sobriété based in Amiens, disappeared almost immediately after its formation in 1835. The next and equally ephemeral pleas for moral reform were heard in Aix, Rouen, and Versailles as the Second Republic was being dismantled in 1851. Toward the end of the Second Empire, scattered organizations for the "extinction of drunkenness" were founded in the Vendée and the Finistère. But as even late nineteenth-century temperance leaders had to admit, these associations were "absolutely barren and isolated attempts" to reform popular drinking habits.[6]

The failure of such temperance organizations, however, should not suggest that chronic drunkenness was diminishing of its own accord. Between 1820 and 1869, government statistics indicated that the amount of pure alcohol consumed in France nearly tripled, rising from 350,000 to 978,000 hecto-liters; per capita consumption of both wine and distilled spirits climbed during the same period by at least 50 percent.[7] Disturbed by the wastefulness and "demoralization" of urban and industrial workers, a handful of social theorists and reformers—notably Jules Simon and Frédéric Le Play—decried the chronic inebriation they believed was blighting the French working classes.[8] They pushed for government reform, but they accomplished nothing.

Until the seventies, the simple state of drunkenness, however offensive to the passerby, did not constitute a violation of French law. Discussing the wisdom of that prerogative in 1861, the French senate had upheld the right of any individual to become as besotted as he might choose. Twice prompted by legislators' inquiries in the sixties, the government asked prefects to comment upon proposed sanctions against drunks. But in 1861, as in 1868, the ministries of Napoleon III determined that such a measure was both unwarranted and an unnecessary abridgement of individual liberty.[9]

The Second Empire, to be sure, had not always been so mindful of libertarian principles. On December 29, 1851, shortly after the coup d'état, Louis Napoleon Bonaparte had issued a decree which threatened every cabaret in France. Prefects were given the discretionary right to close down any existing cabaret, cafe, or *débit de boisson* in their department, to reject any application to open such an establishment, and to subject any *cabaretier* to fines and/or imprisonment. As the decree itself indicated, the future Napoleon III's motives were frankly political; he held cabarets—especially those in the countryside—responsible for "disorders," "demoralization," the "rise of secret societies," and for the "progress of despicable passions."[10] The decree proved an extremely useful political weapon, at least for the first ten years of the Second Empire. Cabarets, *auberges*, and *chambrées* had often served as meeting places during the Second Republic for workers, as schools and libraries for educating and radicalizing laborers and peasants, as centers for organizing political protest.[11] In Balzac's phrase, they were the "parliament of the people;" by 1855 the number of such potentially subversive forums had been cut from 350,424 to 291,244. In the sixties, during the so-called liberal phase of the empire, few prefects actually used the law, although it remained within their rights to do so.

Once the repression was moderated, both the per capita consumption of alcohol and the numbers of cafes and cabarets surpassed any earlier recorded figures for the nineteenth century. Despite the resurgence of cabarets, totalling nearly 366,000 in 1869, Napoleon III's ministries chose, in the end, not to curb their number.[12] The Second Empire worried less about the quantity and kind of drink than the political circumstances in which such drinking transpired. The official record of indifference to the abuse of alcohol was scarcely called into question, even by its most iconoclastic artists and writers. Before the Commune, poets like Charles Baudelaire described alcohol as the *via poetica* to the kingdom of the unfettered imagination or the balm of the dipossessed.[13] When Edouard Manet depicted the absinthe drinker in 1859, his central figure—a sinister male whose dark cape blended ominously into the shadows—belonged more to the early nineteenth-century urban picaresque tradition described by Louis Chevalier than to the Paris of Baron Haussmann.[14] The artist's fascination with the world of drink as part of the exotic subculture of the city was reflected as well in dictionaries of working-class slang, in guidebooks to cabarets and bistros, and in descriptions of popular neighborhoods.[15] Throughout the Second Empire, artists and *hommes des lettres*, like most physicians or government officials, paid less attention to the abuse of alcohol than to the specific settings of its use.

The insouciance of the prewar years was rendered totally inappropriate by the nightmare of the *année terrible*, 1870–71. From the anguish of foreign and civil war emerged the myth, sturdy and none too subtle, of the habitually drunken, politically dangerous commoner. During both the siege of Paris and the Commune, when food was scarce and spirits cheap in comparison, the well-to-do often bemoaned the prodigious amount of wine and liquor consumed by the National Guard and the Communards. Determined to stem the "ravages of intemperance," and to "raise and fortify national vitality," a group composed largely of titled men and women founded the Société patriotique de tempérance one month after German troops had encircled Paris.[16] Working-class observers and soldiers were offered memberships at the reduced rate of two francs, but few apparently chose to join.

The experience of the Commune enlarged the sphere of public concern about alcoholism far beyond the ranks of titled patriots. After 1871 much of the bourgeoisie used alcoholism as a code word for working-class irrationality and as an overarching explanation for the French defeat. Echoing the sentiments of Dr. Barth, the conservative bellelettrist Maxime Du Camp described the Communards as the "chevaliers of debauchery, the apostles of absinthe," and claimed that the Parisian rebels wallowed in wine, eau-de-vie, and other poisonous spirits.[17] A wave of medical research soon lent scientific respectability to such literary insults. Between 1871 and 1873 Doctors Lunier, Bouchereau, Magnan, and Laborde published accounts in the important medical journal *Annales médicos-psychologiques* purporting to prove the pathology of the Commune, with lengthy columns of statistics on the admissions of alcoholic ex-Communards into mental hospitals, or detailed family trees of the debauched ancestry of armed children seized at the end of the uprising.[18]

Having amply documented the diseased nature of the Communards,

French physicians moved rapidly to a categorical condemnation of revolution in general. In the spring of 1871, concluded one doctor, a "wind of madness" had blown through the capital of France; the eye of the storm was drink.[19] The perceived relationship between alcoholism and the Commune led another physician to write, in a somewhat more prosaic manner,

> Now one can understand the bestial and savage faces of the workers in the uprising, the thefts, the massacres, and the arson; the insanity, imbecility and idiocy which affected such a large number of them; their vicious instincts, their lack of morality, their laziness, their tendancy toward crime, and in the long run, their reproductive impotence. In short, it is not surprising to see that each new revolution brings an increase of atrocities and degeneration![20]

As the hyperbolic rhetoric indicates, the new myth of the alcoholic revolutionary was a highly charged subject, and the admixture of science with politics would have far-reaching consequences for both moralists and the supposed victims of the disease. By equating revolution with alcoholism, Thiers' defenders could bypass entirely any painful discussion of the social and economic causes which had triggered the revolt, and they could dismiss the Communards' vision of social justice as the wild hallucinations of a dipsomaniac. The bloodletting which finally ended the rebellion could be justified as a necessary operation in the interest of national health. Both on a conscious and unconscious level, the new myth of the proletarian drunkard provided comforting resolutions to the anxieties of men of order. It alleviated their guilt and shame, allowed them to project their rage and disgust upon the "degenerate" worker, and to rationalize severe measures of political and social repression.

The implications of the new myth of proletarian alcoholism were not lost upon the few socialists and members of the working classes who were not purged or silenced by the government. Regarding any criticism of working-class life as slanderous and reactionary mud-slinging, defenders of the proletariat hotly denied the accusations of their adversaries. Victorine Brocher, who fought first for the defense of Paris, later for the Commune, contrasted "poor Paris," true patriots used as cannon fodder, with the champagne-drinking "rich Paris," who thought: "Jacques Bonhomme is a drunkard, a lazy bum, he is delighted to have the opportunity to get himself killed, he prefers that to work."[21] Indignantly defending the moral probity of the poor, Brocher observed that she had "never seen a drunken Communard," and that cognac was used only to fortify the wounded and dying.[22]

As class antagonisms sharpened in the seventies, attitudes towards drink polarized, each side refusing to admit that alcoholism was a disease which could cross class lines. But the debate was weighted against the Left and the working classes, since the political repression made broad criticism of the government impossible. Lacking physicians and laboratories, lacking statistical experts and noted savants, the Left could not hope to refute the charges of their adversaries, at least not on "scientific" terms. Almost immediately after the Commune, the very subject of alcoholism had become suspect, if not taboo, within working-class and leftist circles. Against the avalanche of exposés on proletarian drinking, "poor" Paris defended itself with sullen silence. For at least a generation, the discussion of drink was a dialogue of the deaf bourgeoisie with the mute working classes.

Having satisfied themselves that the French working class was mired in alcoholic debauchery, bourgeois reformers predictably redoubled their efforts to salvage as many errant souls as possible. The institutionalization of the myth, in other words, was a revitalized temperance movement which ably complemented the religious and secular moralism of the seventies. In popular attitudes, just as in politics, this was the decade of *l'ordre moral*.

Before the end of 1871, two new organizations joined the Société patriotique de tempérance's crusade against drunkenness. In both cases, most of the leadership and the rhetoric were derived from the medical profession. The Association française contre l'abus de tabac, which had been founded by the alienist Dr. Henri Jolly in 1868 to combat that "scourge of the century"— smoking—now decided that two scourges were ravaging France. When they appended "et boissons alcooliques" to their title, the fledgling Société contre l'abus de l'alcool decided somewhat reluctantly to adopt the English-sounding rubric of the Société française de tempérance.[23]

Temperance, yes, but in the French mode. Deferring to the wine, cider, and beer interests, French temperance societies attacked not the use, but the abuse, of alcoholic beverages. Singling out distilled spirits as the enemy, they uged French men to consume instead such "healthy" and "hygienic" drinks as wine, cider, coffee, tea and beer.[24] In order to change popular tastes, temperance leaders relied heavily upon the written word and the moral example. They sponsored essay competitions, subsidized the publication of instructive books, brochures, and almanacs. Other funds were set aside to award prizes to worthy workers and educators, to hold conferences on the evils of intemperance, to encourage the establishment of special libraries, temperance *cercles,* and hygienic drink cooperatives for workers. Skirting utterly any discussion of alcoholism among the well-to-do, the society focused exclusively upon the dangers of drink among the working classes.[25] But the society's actual contact with the proletariat or the rural poor was slight; in the first year of the sobriety awards, not a single worker came forth to accept a prize.

Unlike its Anglo-American counterparts, the Société française de tempérance was not a mass organization, nor did it seek to become such. At the outset, the society offered two categories of membership; "sponsors" paid twenty francs a year dues, while "adherents" contributed half that sum. Throughout the seventies, recruits to the cause remained small in number, socially select, and overwhelmingly Parisian.[26] Over a third were physicians; other frequently cited professions included law, academics, administration, business, letters, and the clergy. Their political affiliations and their actual commitment to the movement were by no means homogeneous.[27] Considered as a group, they shared one characteristic—fame; almost to a man, they were regarded as distinguished leaders in their particular fields.[28]

So exclusive, indeed, was the roster that the *British Medical Times* accused the Société in 1874 of deliberately setting their dues above the means of the very classes they were trying to reform.[29] The Société thereupon decided to widen the circle. They admitted women to full membership and established a third-class category for workers. By paying one franc a year, workers could become "affiliates" of the society but were not entitled to receive its periodical, *La Tempérance.* Until the organization offered medals and saving accounts to those males designated as models of sobriety, few ordinary folk bothered to join. Thereafter, new affiliates were generally recruited from those who already received prizes. During the mid-seventies, the society solicited potential prizewinners by writing the heads of large industries; in 1877 they delighted in awarding 405 medals to particularly sober workers, 60 percent of whom later became affiliates. But the regular membership remained small and select.[30]

The modesty of the society's size, however, should not suggest that the French temperance society was a marginal and ineffectual organization. Like many other moralistic associations of the nineteenth century, French temperance circles chose to "lobby at the top."[31] Within two years of the Commune, they had generated considerable medical interest in the subject of alcoholism, and perhaps more important, they had championed a national crusade to outlaw public drunkenness.

Immediately after the suppression of the Paris Commune, members of the National Assembly asked the Ministry of the Interior to enforce the decree of December 29, 1851, and to shut down large numbers of cabarets. But the Thiers government refused, claiming that such an action would constitute an assault on private property—that is, on the liquor trade in general—and counseled its prefects to clamp down only on those establishments which "posed a danger to morality or public order."[32]

In place of the cabaret, the National Assembly now focused upon a new villain, "the public drunk." Deputies committed to temperance proposed legislation which made public inebriation a crime, and any offender subject to fines, imprisonment, even the loss of voting privileges.[33] Describing drunkenness as a "social scourge, the shame of the present and one of the great dangers of the future," the legislative committee, headed by Dr. Théophile Roussel, asked their fellow deputies to take action against the "ever growing number of drunks" with whom they were forced to share the streets.[34] Moreover, they held the public drunk responsible for the failure of the defense of Paris in the fall and winter of 1870–71, for the rising incidence of suicide and insanity, for the demoralization of the family and, last but hardly least, for what they obliquely termed "the events which followed the end of the war."[35] Swayed by the committee's report, the National Assembly debated the law on three occasions in 1872 and at the beginning of 1873; it was promulgated on February 3.

The "loi Roussel," as it came to be known, was by no means the harshest set of restrictions placed upon French citizens in the wake of the Commune. The loss of the liberty to besot oneself in public, and the penalties for disobeying the law were, after all, minor compared with the draconian measures imposed for participation in the Commune, membership in the First International, organizing a strike or a trade union, even for singing a few bars of the Marseillaise or waving a tricolore on Bastille Day. Although it fell outside the realm of overt political repression, the loi Roussel in effect extended governmental surveillance to include the everyday activities of France's ordinary people. The law thus aimed at a kind of total control over individual and collective behavior which might have been unthinkable before the Commune. Such moral legislation would remain in the legal code long after the Republicans had secured control of the government.

No one criticized the law more vehemently than Emile Zola. As a correspondent for the newspapers *La Cloche* and *Le Corsaire*, Zola regularly reported on the deliberations of the National Assembly in Versailles. Far more than the events of 1870–71, the massive repression following the Commune pushed Zola's social perspective to the Left. And as the deputies discussed drink, his anger mounted. Regarding their discussion of the loi Roussel as an act of collective hypocrisy, Zola underscored the parliamentarians' bald self-interest. He faulted the deputies for refusing to raise taxes on absinthe or other alcoholic beverages.[36] When they allowed the government to increase taxes on tobacco, a public monopoly, Zola became infuriated. Whenever private interests were at stake, he concluded, French deputies refused to interfere: "I believe that if French farmers and businessmen grew and marketed arsenic, they would defend the cause of arsenic and claim that any restriction placed upon it would constitute an attack on private property."[37]

Like the National Assembly, Zola believed that alcoholism was blighting France, but he doubted that fines or prisons would cause drunkards to mend their ways. The loi Roussel would be ineffectual in stemming alcoholism and selective in its victims. "I would like to know," he asked sarcastically, "if copies of the law will be sent to the Maison d'Or and the Café Anglais," two of Paris's most luxurious cafes. "I have been told that they occasionally see tipsy types. Pure lies, perhaps, spread by Belleville's *marchands de vin*."[38]

Throughout the summer and fall of 1872, Zola's frontal attacks on the government became increasingly acerbic. On December 16 a secret police report described workers' great interest and delight in Zola's most recent denunciation of the upper classes and for his "vigorous" and truthful defense of the proletariat.[39] That article, entitled "Le Cabaret," contained Zola's most scathing denunciation of the National Assembly's vision of drink: "The cabaret has become their supreme insult, their decisive argument, the swear word with which they insult and condemn the people. To listen to them, it would appear that the revolutionary spirit escapes from a badly corked bottle, and that the great legal victories of '89 have been distilled from the slops of the counter."[40] In Zola's view, overwork, misery, and fatigue pushed the common laborer to drink wine, while the hypocritical rich wallowed in more sordid and expensive vices—gluttonous addiction to fine wines and absinthe, gambling, and the callous seduction of innocent girls and young dancers.[41]

Five days after his exposé on drink, Zola again pilloried the ruling classes. Shifting his focus from wine to bread, Zola published an article in *Le Corsaire* which accused rich, titled ministers of deliverate indifference to the plight of hungry and jobless Parisian laborers. Zola had gone too far; he had accused French ministers by name. *Le Corsaire* was immediately shut down; Zola was fortunate to escape prosecution.[42]

For the next three years Zola's social criticism moved underground; his articles on politics and the social question carried no byline. Devoting most of his energies to fiction, Zola wrote three more novels in the Rougon-Macquart series, including one on parliamentary corruption, and supplemented his income as a critic of literature and the arts. But his concern for the problem of drink had not evaporated, and in the spring of 1876 the Republican newspaper *Le Bien public* began serializing *L'Assommoir*, Zola's seventh novel on the Rougon-Macquart family. It was his first "proletarian" novel in the series, one that Zola had included in his preliminary outline of 1868.

By 1875, when Zola began work on the novel, bourgeois perceptions of the problem of drink had been dramatically reshaped and the myth of the inebriated, subversive worker had been rooted in the law of the land. Highly critical of the new bourgeois attitudes towards drink, Zola recast his original designs for the novel in important and controversial ways. In 1868 Zola had planned to treat all aspects of working-class life in a single work of fiction. Cognizant of the new psychological association of alcoholism with radical politics, Zola now determined to focus first upon daily life and to save proletarian politics for a later novel. If his earliest plans gave no hint of the sex of his central character, by the mid-seventies Zola had chosen a woman. Surely Zola realized that the very mention of female drinking would horrify the respectable reader. Since the official literature on alcoholism after the Commune was richly sprinkled with moralistic pronouncements, Zola, like the avant-garde painters Degas and Manet (see photo insert), intentionally steered clear of the picturesque, melodramatic, and didactic point of view. Within the novel itself Zola adopted a stance—rarely encountered elsewhere in his writings—of strict moral neutrality.[43] While spokesmen for temperance resorted to hyperbolic prose and dwelled upon the most gory *faits divers*, Zola sought to reconstruct "the simple life of Gervaise Macquart." To that end, he scrapped an earlier note which indicated that his heroine would be stabbed in the stairwell of her apartment building. By avoiding the exceptional event, Zola hoped to throw in sharper relief the real causes of proletarian drinking—urban squalor and poverty.

As early as 1868, Zola had viewed the popularity of the cabaret as the result, not the cause, of working-class demoralization and indigence. Describing the crowds of laborers huddled in the cabarets of Saint-Ouen for readers of *La Tribune*, Zola noted that

> it is a simple question of milieu. Workers are suffocating in cramped and miry neighborhoods, . . . the black alleys adjacent to the rue Saint-Antoine, the pestilential holes of the rue Mouffetard. It is not for them that the city is being cleaned up . . . When Sunday comes, not knowing where to go to breathe a bit of fresh air, they install themselves in cabarets. . . . Their decline is inevitable. . . . Work requires recreation and when money is short, when the horizon is closed, one grasps at available pleasure.[44]

After the Commune, Zola reiterated his analysis of why workers resorted to drink; treated like cogs in a machine, overworked, underpaid, laborers turned to the only solace at hand—alcohol. For such a state of affairs, the ruling classes had only themselves to blame. Drunkenness in the faubourgs, Zola admonished his fellow bourgeois, "is your fault."[45]

Zola's accusation passed unnoticed by reformer and industrialist alike. When he transposed his analysis of drink into fictional form, Zola, the self-avowed "dignified bourgeois," challenged his social equals to reexamine their simple-minded view of working-class morality. Zola's intended audience was the bourgeoisie, but his attack upon the myth of alcoholism was couched in a language the supposed victims could understand—the frank and colorful slang of the faubourgs. In both idea and form, *L'Assommoir* attempted to reopen the broken dialogue on drink. But with public opinion so polarized, Zola's intentions were misread.

Zola had expected that conservative critics would take offense at his replication of the earthy argot of workers which he had distilled from Denis Poulot's *Le Sublime* and Alfred Delvau's exhaustive *Dictionnaire de la langue verte*. Writing on behalf of the working classes, Zola was determined that his characters speak in their own vernacular, even if his novel would offend respectable standards of literary decorum. Zola surely anticipated critics' complaints that *L'Assommoir* "isn't realism, it's smut; it isn't crude, it's pornographic," or that "it stinks to high heaven." Imagine, however, his surprise when he found his work being praised by "diehard reactionaries and enemies of the Republic," who used the novel's characters as splendid examples of working-class debauchery or as proof of the folly of universal suffrage.[46]

The controversy over the message of *L'Assommoir* was further tangled when Zola found himself attacked most sharply from unexpected quarters— from Republicans, Socialists, and proclaimed spokesmen for the working classes. Charles Floquet, a Gambettist deputy from the poor eleventh arrondissement, rented a hall to blast the novel as the "unhealthy garbage of Zola, who vilifies the people and demoralizes the public."[47] Feminist Maria Desraimes criticized Zola for besmirching the reputation of proletarian women and for implying that the wives of drunkards eventually came to share their spouses' "filthy passion."[48] Her attack on Zola for misplaced emphasis was echoed by the Socialist Mlle. B. Gendre, who faulted the naturalist for reproducing "only a tiny nook" of life in the faubourgs.[49] Most baffling of all, Zola's work was ignored by the very organization which led the crusade against drink—the French temperance movement.[50]

Not that they were indifferent to the instructive value of fiction. In 1873 the Société française de tempérance had offered five hundred francs to "the author of a work—be it in the form of a novella, narrative, maxim, or illustration—which presents the most gripping tableau of the dangers of alcoholism." Among the sixteen entries considered worthy of discussion were a "map of the State of Drunkenness across the cantons of Misery, Crime, Insanity, and Illnesses," maxims for student dictations, a rambling poem about a drunken worker who kills his wife, and an assortment of violent tales of proletarian drunkards who sink to murder, suicide, crime, or insanity. These fictional drinkers were without exception male; only one came from a genteel family. The prize committee's reaction to particular novels sheds light on the standards for moralizing literature in the seventies and on the uproar over *L'Assommoir*. They rejected one entry because it advocated total abstinence, which, they claimed, "runs counter to our aims," another because its language was vulgar. Still others were downgraded for lacking the proper balance of literary skill and a firm moral underpining. The committee expected authors to delineate the *causes* of alcoholism, but neither the writers nor their judges included any of the factors Zola had outlined as early as 1868—poverty, inhumane and excessive labor, lack of alternative forms of leisure, dismal housing, closed horizons for the future.[51]

The combination of avoidance, anger, and prudish indignation which characterized the reception of *L'Assommoir* forced Zola into the uncomfortable position of explaining his intentions—both artistic and ideological. For the first time since the general introduction to the Rougon-Macquart series, Zola felt constrained to append a preface defending his work as "pure morality," realism, or "pure philology."[52] To the newspaper *Le Bien public*, which had stopped installments of the novel once the critics began to rail, Zola affirmed the integrity of his fiction and the progressive nature of his politics:

> If I were forced to draw a conclusion, I would say close the cabarets, open the schools. . . . And I would add: clean up the faubourgs and raise salaries. The question of lodging is capital: smelly streets, sordid stairways, narrow rooms stuffed with fathers and daughters . . . are the great cause of the depravity of the faubourgs. And for this state of affairs we have only our society to blame.[53]

But despite his repeated entreaties, Zola's attempt to reopen the dialogue on drink came to nothing. For at least a generation, public attitudes toward drink remained bitterly divided along class lines. Not until the nineties was either side willing to regard alcoholism in a more dispassionate and nuanced manner, willing to admit that this disease could affect all sectors of society. In science and literature, as in politics, the legacy of the Commune was bitter and perhaps even more enduring.

Notes

1. *La Tempérance* 2 (1878): 51. Barth's influence in the medical profession was considerable. He served as president of the Académie de Medécine and counted among his patients Adolphe Thiers.

2. As an illustration of the commonly held view that *L'Assommoir* replicates the "bourgeois" discourse on drink, see Jacques Dubois, *L'Assommoir de Zola* (Paris: Larousse, 1973), pp. 10–15, 73–106. The historian Michael Marrus, on the other hand, has claimed that "there was still no substantial body of opinion on the subject when Emile Zola published *L'Assommoir.*" "Social Drinking in the Belle Epoque," *Journal of Social History* 7, no. 2 (Winter 1974):115–41.

3. Cited in Marrus, "Social Drinking," p. 117.

4. *La Grande Dictionnaire du XIXe siècle* (Paris, 1875 ed.), p. 1579.

5. Ibid.

6. Dr. L. Lunier, "De l'origine et de la propagation des sociétés de tempérance," *La Tempérance* 1 (1873):1–23.

7. For a thorough discussion of those statistics, see Marrus, "Social Drinking," pp. 120–27.

8. Jules Simon, *L'Ouvrière* (Paris: Hachette, 1861), pp. 125–45. For an excellent analysis of the perception of drink during the Second Empire, see Georges Duveau, *La Vie ouvrière en France sous le Second Empire* (Paris: Gallimard, 1946), pp. 498–537.

9. Archives de la Préfecture de Police de Paris (hereafter cited as APP), DB 174, circular of the Ministry of the Interior to prefects, October 14, 1861, and Archives Départementales du Nord, M 193.12.

10. APP, DB 174, decree of December 29, 1851.

11. See Maurice Agulhon, *La République au village* (Paris: Plon, 1970), and John M. Merriman, *The Agony of the Republic* (New Haven: Yale University Press, 1978), esp. pp. 96–101.

12. APP, DP 175, Reinach, *Rapport*, p. 31.

13. See the collection of poems entitled "Le Vin" in *Les Fleurs du mal* by Charles Baudelaire (Paris: José Corti, 1968), pp. 205–16.

14. For a discussion of fictional representations of the working classes in the early and mid–nineteenth century, see Louis Chevalier, *Laboring Classes and Dangerous Classes in Paris* (New York: Howard Fertig, 1973).

15. See, for instance, Alfred Delvau, *Dictionnaire de la langue verte* (Paris: Dentu, 1866); Denis Poulot, *Question sociale: le sublime* (Paris: Librairie internationale, Lacroix et Verboeckhoven, 1870).

16. Archives Nationales (hereafter cited as AN), F^7 12377. In 1875 the society was renamed the Société patriotique et internationale de tempérance.

17. Maxime Du Camp, *Les Convulsions de Paris* (Paris: Hachette, 1881), 1:vii; 4:115.

18. Dr. Lunier, "De l'influence des grandes commotions politiques et sociales sur le développement des maladies mentales," *Annales médicos-psychologiques*, 5e sér., 9 (1873):

241–80, 427–68; 10 (1873): 22–72, 237–65, 430–63; idem, "L'Histoire des événements de 1870–1871," 5e sér., 8 (1872): 161–84; Drs. Bouchereau and Magnan, "Statistique des alcooliques entrés au bureau d'admission à Sainte-Anne pendant les mois de mars, avril, mai, juin 1870 et les mois correspondants de 1871," 5e sér., 7 (1872): 51–58; Dr. Laborde, *Les Hommes et les actes de l'insurrection de Paris devant la psychologie morbide* (Paris, 1872). For a late nineteenth-century summary of such literature, see Edmond Toulouse, *Les Causes de la folie* (Paris: Société d'Editions Scientifiques, 1896).

19. Bouchereau and Magnan, "Statistique," p. 58.

20. Dr. A. Brière de Boismont, "De la proportion toujours croissante de l'aliénation mentale sous l'influence de l'alcool," *Bulletin de l'association française contre l'abus du tabac et des boissons alcooliques* 4, no. 1 (1872):18.

21. Victorine B[rocher], *Souvenirs d'une morte vivante* (Paris: François Maspero, 1977), p. 110.

22. Ibid., pp. 159, 168.

23. AN, F⁷12377.

24. Ibid.

25. In the first ten years of its publication, *La Tempérance* did not publish a single article on alcoholism among the well-to-do. In "Moyens pratiques de substituer dans les habitudes des populations des boissons salutaires telles que le café, le thé aux boissons alcooliques," *La Tempérance* 1 (1873):400–480, the pharmacist M. Leclerc described the bourgeoisie as "the most sober and disciplined" of all classes in their drinking. Defending the bourgeois bachelor's visits to the cafe as a reasonable means of relaxation, Lunier claimed that workers went to their own cafes because they were lazy, intemperate, or in order to forget their domestic problems.

26. Over 80 percent of the original members lived in Paris, another 5 percent in Neuilly or Versailles. Of the 302 Parisian members, 89 percent resided in the expensive areas of the capital: first, second, fifth, sixth, eighth, ninth, and sixteenth arrondissements being the best represented. None lived in the poorer sections of Paris—the thirteenth, nineteenth, or twentieth arrondissements. *La Tempérance* 1 (1873): 111–56.

27. The following list provides an indication of the political perspectives of the members: Baron Haussman, Victor Duruy, the Duc de Broglie, François Guizot, the temperance leader Roussel, Richard Wallace, Alphonse Bertillon, and Claude Bernard.

28. The membership list included thirty-seven members of the *Institut*, forty-eight members of the Académie de Médecine, forty-one deputies, seven members of the Académie Française, and twenty-two titled gentlemen. *La Tempérance* 1 (1873):111–56 lists the names, professions, and addresses of the original members.

29. See the indignant response in *La Tempérance* 1 (1873):23.

30. In the seventies, regular membership hovered around 500, 446 of whom joined by 1873.

31. See Robert J. Bezucha's pioneering article, "The Moralization of Society: The Enemies of Popular Culture in the Nineteenth Century," in *The Wolf and the Lamb: Popular Culture in France*, ed. Jacques Beauroy et al. (Saratoga, Calif.: Anma Libri, 1977), pp. 175–87.

32. *Journal officiel*, séance of January 8, 1872, p. 923.

33. Ibid., p. 890.

34. Ibid., p. 891.

35. Ibid.

36. Emile Zola, "Les Droits sur l'absinthe," *La Cloche*, March 28, 1872; reprinted in *Oeuvres complètes* (Paris: Cercle du Précieux, 1969), 13:934–35.

37. Zola, "L'Import sur le tabac," *La Cloche*, March 2, 1872; reprinted in *Oeuvres complètes*, 13:882–83.

38.   Zola, "Le Projet sur l'ivresse," *La Cloche*, April 26, 1872; reprinted in *Oeuvres complètes*, 13:957–59.

39.   APP BA 1302, report of no. 12, December 16, 1872. The newspaper appeared a day in advance of its dateline.

40.   Zola, "Le Cabaret," *Le Corsaire*, December 17, 1872; reprinted in *Oeuvres complètes*, 14:199–202.

41.   Ibid., p. 201.

42.   Zola, "Le Lendemain de la crise," *Le Corsaire*, December 22, 1872; reprinted in *Oeuvres complètes*, 14:206–10. On the censorship of Zola's articles, see F. W. J. Hemmings, *Emile Zola* (Oxford: Oxford University Press, 1966), and Henri Mitterand's introductory notes to the *Oeuvres complètes*, vols. 13, 14.

43.   See Leon Deffoux, *La Publication de l'Assommoir* (Paris: Malfère, 1931), and Henri Massis, *Comment Zola composait ses romans* (Paris: Fasquelle, 1906).

44.   Cited in Emile Zola, *Les Rougon-Macquart* (Paris: Gallimard, 1961), 2:1539–40.

45.   Zola, "Le Cabaret", p. 200.

46.   Deffoux, *La Publication de l'Assommoir,* passim; and Zola, *Les Rougnon-Macquart,* 2:1556–68.

47.   Deffoux, *La Publication de l'Assommoir,* p. 131.

48.   Maria Deraismes, *Epidémie Naturaliste* (Paris: E. Dentu, n.d.), p. 64.

49.   B. Gendre, *Etudes sociales* (Paris, 1886), pp. 124–28.

50.   I could find no mention of either Zola or *L'Assommoir* by name in *La Temperárance* from 1876 to 1881.

51.   *La Tempérance* 1 (1837): 298–306.

52.   Zola, *Les Rougnon-Macquart,* 2:373–74.

53.   Zola, "Au Directeur du *Bien Public*," February 13, 1877; reprinted in Zola, *Correspondance* (Paris: François Bernouard, 1927), pp. 465–71.

54.   For the workers' view of *l'Assommoir* in the 1890s, see Henri Leyret, *En Plein Faubourg* (Paris, 1895), pp. 54–56. For one of the first articles on alcoholism among the well-to-do, see Michel Peter, "L'alcoolisme chez les gens du monde," *Premier Congrès National Contre l'Alcoolisme* (Paris, 1904), pp. 550–57.

ELEVEN

The Victorian Conflict between Science and Religion
*A Professional Dimension**

FRANK M. TURNER

Was there a conflict between science and religion in late Victorian England? T. H. Huxley, Bishop Wilberforce, John Tyndall, Francis Galton, W. K. Clifford, and William Gladstone certainly thought so. Other contemporaries, such as Lord Tennyson, E. B. Pusey, Frederick Temple, Frederic Harrison, and Herbert Spencer, feared so but hoped not. Sermons criticizing the arrogance of scientists and articles decrying the ignorance of clergy as well as books such as John Draper's *History of the Conflict between Religion and Science* (1874) and that of his fellow American Andrew White, *The Warfare of Science* (1876), with a preface by British physicist John Tyndall, suggested a bitter controversy between spokesman for religion and science. Early twentieth-century writers, including J. M. Robertson, J. B. Bury, Bertrand Russell, and Arthur Balfour, assumed that a conflict had raged over the subject a generation or so earlier.[1]

Later commentators have been less certain about the existence of the struggle, its dimensions, and even its issues. Robert Ensor regarded it parenthetically as "real enough at the time."[2] Charles Raven contended the debate over science and religion amounted to little more than "a storm in a Victorian tea-cup."[3] R. K. Webb explained that the number of people whose religious faith was shaken by scientific discoveries was "probably fairly small" but consisted of "people whose opinions counted for much."[4] Owen Chadwick drew the important distinction "between science when it was against religion and the scientists when they were against religion."[5] The

*This essay first appeared in *Isis*, 69, no. 248 (1978): 356–76, and is here reprinted by kind permission.

220 *Frank M. Turner*

discoveries and theories of science might cast doubt on the accuracy of the Bible, but a scientist could also use a scientific theory to attack the Bible or to discredit the clergy for reasons that had little or no intrinsic relationship to theory. Considerable validity attaches to each of these assessments, particularly that of Chadwick. Yet to reduce the proportions of the dispute, while useful for achieving better perspective, still fails to account for its character, causes, or significance. Those problems—the brew in Canon Raven's teacup—remain.

The most common approach to the substantial issues of the debate has assumed the existence of an enduring and probably necessary conflict between scientific and religious modes of perceiving the world. Antagonism may arise because the naturalistic explanations of science dispense with the metaphysical presuppositions of theology, or because particular scientific theories contradict the literal reading of passages in the Bible, or because religious dogma and authority interfere with scientific research.[6] George Gaylord Simpson succinctly outlined the major features of this interpretation:

> The conflict between science and religion has a single and simple cause. It is the designation as religiously canonical of any conception of the material world open to scientific investigation. . . . The religious canon . . . demands absolute acceptance not subject to test or revision. Science necessarily rejects certainty and predicates acceptance on objective testing and the possibility of continual revision. As a matter of fact, most of the dogmatic religions have exhibited a perverse talent for taking the wrong side on the most important concepts of the material universe, from the structure of the solar system to the origin of man. The result has been constant turmoil for many centuries, and the turmoil will continue as long as religious canons prejudice scientific questions.[7]

There can be no doubt that such disputes arising from epistemological differences over the role of theology as an intellectual authority were major issues at the center of the Victorian conflict between science and religion. By the second quarter of the nineteenth century, substantial developments in geology, physics, biology, physiological psychology, and philosophy of science challenged or cast into doubt theological assumptions and portions of the Bible. During those years both Charles Lyell and Charles Darwin complained about the hindrance to scientific advance raised by metaphysics and theology. After mid-century Huxley (see photo insert), Tyndall, Joseph Dalton Hooker, Henry Maudsley, and others continued to press against the influence on scientific work of metaphysical and religious categories of thought and to urge the authority of critical reason and empirical verification against the authority of the Bible and natural religion.[8]

However, without questioning the presence, validity, or significance of the epistemological disagreements, it is possible to question the adequacy of the enduring conflict approach as a wholly satisfactory historical interpretation of the Victorian conflict between science and religion. This interpretation, if not further supplemented, takes too much at face value the statements of polemical interchange. The epistemological dichotomy, proclaimed at the time in such phrases as G. H. Lewes's "Religion and Science,—the two mightiest antagonists," was an integral part of the debate and has come by default to provide an explanation for it.[9] While defending Darwin's *Origin of Species*, Huxley might declare, "Extinguished theologians lie about the cradle of every science as the strangled snakes beside that of Hercules."[10] But the history of science has been more complex and problematical.

Statements such as Huxley's emerge from an ideology of science as well as from an attempt to account for disagreements between religious and scientific spokesmen. To pursue this track is to posit historically concrete forms for the theological and positive stages of Comte or for the mytho-poetic and critical-rational epistemological dichotomy so brilliantly delineated by Ernst Cassirer. So far as the internal development of modern science is concerned, this juxtaposition of good progressive science against evil retrogressive metaphysics and theology fails to account for false starts on the part of scientists, their adherence to incorrect theory, the overlooking of evidence that might have led to further discovery, and the enduring influence of metaphysics and religion on scientific work that continued well into the nineteenth century. Moreover, the progressionist ideology also ignores the frequent hostility of scientific authorities and the scientific community, as well as that of theologians and clergymen, to new theories that challenge existing paradigms and reputations.[11]

To penetrate other levels of the Victorian conflict of religion and science, it is necessary to recognize that the epistemological redefinition of science to mean critical research based on empirical verification constituted only one element in a broader redefinition of the entire scientific enterprise in Great Britain. The debates over particular theories and methods were part of a broader ongoing discussion about the character of the Victorian scientific community, its function in society, and the values by which it judged the work of its members. These latter issues largely determined why spokesmen for religion and science clashed when they did and as they did.

In 1873 physicist James Clerk Maxwell inquired rhethorically about the condition of British science and replied: "It is simply this, that while the numbers of our professors and their emoluments are increasing, while the number of students is increasing, while practical instruction is being introduced and text-books multiplied, while the number and calibre of popular lecturers and popular writers in Science is increasing, original research, the fountain-head of a nation's wealth, is decreasing. . . ."[12] Maxwell's concern about the paucity of research was widely shared at the time. But for the purposes of this essay the activity he did observe was more significant. The expansion in the numbers of professional scientists and the widespread dispersion of scientific ideas on the popular level and within institutions of education meant science was forging ahead in British society if not necessarily in British laboratories. The result of this process, according to A. W. Benn, who witnessed it, was "a transfer of authority from religious to naturalistic belief." In turn, as naturalistic belief grew, "a great part of the reverence once given to priests and to their stories of an unseen universe has been transferred to the astronomer, the geologist, the physician, and the engineer."[13] It was this shift of authority and prestige, noted by numerous other contemporaries, from one part of the intellectual nation to another that caused the Victorian conflict betwen religious and scientific spokesmen. Recognition of this development may explain why the Cambridge philosopher Henry Sidgwick termed the debate "a great and prominent *social* fact of the present age."[14]

The primary motivating force behind this shift in social and intellectual authority, which deeply involved the epistemological controversy, was activity within the scientific community that displayed most of the major features associated with nascent professionalism. As characterized by Bernard Barber, these include

> a high degree of generalized and systematic knowledge; primary orientation to the community interest rather than to individual self-interest; a high degree of self-control of behavior through codes of ethics internalized in the process of work socialization and through voluntary associations organized and operated by the work specialists themselves; and a system of rewards (monetary and honorary) that is primarily a set of symbols of work achievement and thus ends in themselves, not means to some end of individual self-interest.[15]

During the early stages of professionalism, an elite from the emerging professional group attempts to project a new public image by formulating codes of ethics, strengthening professional organizations, establishing professional schools, penetrating existing educational institutions, and dispersing information to the general public. These leaders may simply be seeking to improve their social or economic position rather than self-consciously attempting to organize a profession. But to the extent that they are successful in improving their condition through these kinds of activities, their occupational group will assume to a greater or lesser degree the features of a profession.

Normally, pursuit of these ends requires the professionalizing elite to engage in conflict with persons inside and outside the existing occupational or amateur group. Within they must raise standards of competence, foster a common bond of purpose, and subject practitioners to the judgment of peers rather than external social or intellectual authorities. Outside they must establish the independence of the would-be professional group, its right of self-definition, and its self-generating role in the social order. Consequently, there are usually disputes between professionals and amateurs and between professionals and outsiders who wish to impose their own definition on the group or who presently carry out the social function that the professionalizing group wishes to share or to claim as its own exclusive domain. The mid-Victorian scientific community experienced such pangs of professionalization, and the conflict of science and religion was one of the by-products.

During the first half of the nineteenth century, amateurism, aristocratic patronage, miniscule government support, limited employment opportunities, and peripheral inclusion within the clerically dominated universities and secondary schools were the major characteristics of British science. The Royal Society was little more than a fashionable club as befitted a normally amateur occupation of gentlemen. In 1851 Charles Babbage complained, "Science in England is not a profession: its cultivators are scarcely recognized even as a class. Our language itself contains no *single* term by which their occupation can be expressed."[16] Rev. William Whewell, the Cambridge mathematician and philosopher of science, had invented the term *scientist* in 1834 and reasserted its usefulness in 1840, but the term enjoyed little currency until very late in the century. Even the Devonshire Commission in the seventies found it necessary to define the term *science* to mean physical rather than moral science. Except for Babbage, other spokesmen in the "Declinist" controversy, and Sir Robert Peel, all-too-few people within or without the scientific world related the advancement of physical science to national health, physical well-being, military security, or economic strength.[17]

Although before mid-century the utility of science for manufacturing, agriculture, and improvement of the working class received attention in the Mechanics Institutes, the Society for the Diffusion of Useful Knowledge, and University College London, still scientific knowledge as a buttress of natural theology figured most prominently among the justifications for its pursuit. Many scientists considered the moral and metaphysical imperatives of natural theology as a proper and integral part of their vocation and not as an intrusion of extraneous categories imposed by outside institutions.[18] Early presidents of the British Association repeatedly urged the interdependent relationship of science and theology. For example, in 1849 Rev. Thomas Romney Robinson, an astronomer, reminded the association that

> science is not necessarily wisdom. To know, is not the sole nor even the highest office of the intellect; and it loses all its glory unless it act in furtherance of the great end of man's life. That end is, as both reason and revelation unite in telling us, to acquire the feelings and habits that will lead us to love and seek what is good in all its forms, and guide us by following its traces to the first Great Cause of all, where only we find it pure and unclouded. If science be cultivated in congruity with this, it is the most precious possession we can have—the most divine endowment. But if it be perverted to minister to any wicked or ignoble purpose—if it even be permitted to take too absolute a hold of the mind, or overshadow that which should be paramount over all, the perception of right, the sense of Duty—if it does not increase in use the consciousness of an Almighty and All-beneficent presence—it lowers instead of raising us in the great scale of existence.[19]

Such convictions were not mere rhetorical window dressing. They influenced the behavior of men of science in their capacity as practicing scientists, defined the scope and intellectual context of scientific work, and frequently determined the kinds of questions and conclusions deemed appropriate or inappropriate for research.

Natural theology, whether derivative of the mechanical reasoning of Paley and the *Bridgewater Treatises* or the idealist metaphysics of Richard Owen, could pose a major intellectual barrier to the further advance of critical empirical theory in science. A thoroughly naturalistic approach to the investigation of the universe was thwarted by considerations that had no intrinsic relationship to the undertaking. By mid-century many scientists had come to question or to reject the epistemological limitations established by regard for natural theology; yet those influences remained present throughout much of the scientific community. This division of opinion about the method and scope of science displayed itself in the debates over geology, natural selection, and the place of humankind in nature. However, as Robinson's statement indicates, the impact of religion extended beyond the strictly intellectual issue of epistemology. Scientific research stood subordinate to moral values, a concept of God, and a view of human nature that had been formulated by clergy and religious writers. Certain questions, areas of inquiry, methods of research, and conclusions were discouraged or proscribed because they carried the implication of impiety, immorality, or blasphemy. These limitations reflected the social context of early nineteenth-century science in which clergy and laymen with strong religious convictions controlled access to much scientific patronage and employment. On more than one occasion practitioners of science, such as Charles Lyell and William Lawrence, had curbed or modified expression of their opinions for fear of offending both clerical and scientific colleagues.[20] The pervasive influence of natural theology and the derivative influence of the clergy meant the early Victorian scientific community was not yet self-defining in regard to its own function.

From the 1840s onward the size, character, structure, ideology, and leadership of the Victorian scientific world underwent considerable transformation. It eventually possessed most of the characteristics associated with a modern scientific community.[21] Between 1850 and 1880 the memberships of all the major scientific societies markedly increased, with many of them doubling their numbers. Total memberships during that period grew from 4,597 to 12,314. Even allowing for multiple memberships there can be little doubt that the numbers of scientists rose considerably during the third quarter of the century. This increase in the size of the scientific community finds further confirmation in the expansion of the physics and chemistry faculties. In 1850 there were seventeen physics professors and two other faculty members teaching physics in the United Kingdom. By 1880 the figures had risen to twenty-eight and twenty-two, respectively. The number of chemistry professors in 1850 was eleven with four other chemistry faculty members. By 1880 the university chemistry faculties had expanded to twenty-five professors and thirty-four other instructors. When calculated, figures for the other sciences will probably reveal similar magnitudes of expansion.[22]

Directly tied to the growth of the scientific community was a new direction and character in its leadership. In 1847 the rules for membership in the Royal

Society were reformed to favor the future inclusion of men whose achievements were scientific rather than social. That reform also included provisions for reducing the size of the society by limiting new memberships to fifteen annually. The long term result would be a smaller society composed of practicing men of science. The year of the Royal Society reforms also saw the formation of the Philosophical Club, whose membership was limited to forty-seven persons, each of whom had to be a researching and publishing scientist.[23] From the 1850s onward a group of newly arrived scientists whom Leonard Huxley later called "the young guard of science" took up the public championship of professionalized science from the hands of persons such as Charles Babbage and the jurist William Grove.[24] The "young guard" included as its chief spokesmen T. H. Huxley, John Tyndall, Joseph Dalton Hooker, George Busk, Edward Frankland, Thomas Archer Hirst, John Lubbock, William Spottiswoode, and Herbert Spencer, all of whom composed the X-Club, and Henry Cole, Norman Lockyer, Francis Galton, and Lyon Playfair.[25]

By the 1870s these men—in terms of editorships, professorships, and offices in the major societies—had established themselves as a major segment of the elite of the Victorian scientific world. Lockyer was the chief editor of *Nature* from its founding in 1869 until 1919. Hooker, Spottiswoode, and Huxley occupied the presidency of the Royal Society from 1873 until 1885. At one time or another between 1850 and 1900, one or more of this coterie served as presidents of the British Association for the Advancement of Science, the Anthropological Society, the Chemical Society, the Royal College of Surgeons, the Institute of Chemistry, the Ethnological Society, the Geological Society, and the Mathematical Society. They also held key positions in the Royal School of Mines, the Royal Institution, University College London, the Róyal Botanical Gardens at Kew, the Royal Naval College, and the Solar Physics Observatory. They were also frequently consulted by the government on issues of scientific research, industry, and education.[26]

Such achievements had not been easy. These scientists had generally grown up on the peripheries of the English intellectual establishment. With a few exceptions they had not been educated in the English universities, but in their Scottish counterparts or London medical schools, the civil service, the military, or in provincial dissenting communities. Although gifted and often brilliant, they had possessed no ready access to the higher echelons of Victorian society. There were all-too-few jobs that depended on merit rather than patronage. Neither public opinion nor government policy at mid-century generally recognized their social utility as scientists. The key to their own future social and financial security was the establishment of a greater public appreciation for science and its contribution to the welfare of the nation.

As expressed in 1868 in the prospectus of a short-lived journal called *Scientific Opinion*, such ambitious young scientists needed to advocate "the cause of Science and the interests of scientific men in England, to enforce . . . the claims of science upon the general public, to secure her followers their proper need of recompense and social distinction and to help them in their daily pursuits."[27] To those professionalizing ends "the young protagonists in science"[28] both individually and on occasion collectively participated in the Royal Society, the Philosophical Club, the British Association, and more specialized societies; delivered popular lectures to a variety of audiences; wrote textbooks; were active in the establishment of the unsuccessful *Reader* and the spectacularly successful *Nature*; served on and testified before government commissions for furthering scientific education; campaigned for the national endowment of research; and attempted to protect future physiological and medical research by doing battle with the antivivisectionists.[29] They repeatedly sought to relate the advance of science and of its practitioners to the physical, economic, and military security of the nation; to the alleviation of social injustice; to the Carlylean injunction for a new aristocracy of merit; and to the cult of the expert inherited from their utilitarian forerunners.[30]

Championship of the "vigilant verification" of the empirical method and of a thoroughly naturalistic approach to science was integrally related to these professionalizing efforts.[31] The positivist epistemology constituted both a cause and a weapon. The "young guard" agreed among themselves that science should be pursued without regard for religious dogma, natural theology, or the opinions of religious authorities. But neither such critical science nor its practitioners could flourish where the religious beliefs of clergy and other scientists could and did directly influence evaluation of work, patronage of research, and appointments in scientific institutions, the universities, and the public schools. By claiming their own epistemology as the exclusive foundation for legitimate science and as the correct model for knowledge generally, the professionalizing scientists sought to undermine the intellectual legitimacy of alternative modes of scientific thought and practice. Positivist epistemology provided an intellectual solvent to cleanse contemporary science of metaphysical and theological survivals. By excluding the kinds of questions as well as the answers that might arise from theological concerns, it also served to discredit the wider cultural influence of organized religion. Intellectual and social advance went hand in hand. For as the advocates of professional and critical science came to enjoy greater social prestige, their view of the purpose and character of science became more widely accepted, though not necessarily for philosophical or scientific reasons.

The drive to organize a more professionally oriented scientific community and to define science in a more critical fashion brought the crusading scientists into conflict with two groups of people. The first were supporters of organized religion who wished to maintain a large measure of control over education and to retain religion as the source of moral and social values. The second group was the religiously minded sector of the preprofessional scientific community which included both clergymen and laymen. The debate within the scientific world deserves prior consideration because much of the harshest rhetoric stemmed from the determination of the aggressive, professionally minded scientists to exorcise from their ranks clergymen-scientists and lay scientists who regarded the study of physical nature as serving natural theology or as standing subordinate to theology and religious authority.

Since the seventeenth century the parson-naturalist and the academic clergyman-scientist had played a major and by no means inglorious role in British science, as the names of John Ray, Joseph Priestley, John Stevens Henslow, Adam Sedgwick, and William Whewell attest. Such scientists were often contributing members of the Royal Society and in some cases recipients of high awards for their work. During the 1830s the clerical scientists had joined the effort to found the British Association for the Advancement of Science and had served as its officers. For them natural science and natural theology, the clerical and the scientific callings, were not simply compatible, but complementary. From at least the 1840s onward, however, their position had become increasingly difficult. The naturalistic bent of theories in geology, biology, and physiological psychology drove deep wedges into existing reconciliations of scientific theory with revelation or theology. The faith that the truth of revelation and the truth of science must be the same had become severely strained. The place of humankind in nature particularly raised difficulties. Fewer lay scientists remained concerned with meshing science and religion.[32]

Besides urging a completely naturalistic view of nature and banishment of religious purposes and categories from scientific work, the drive by young lay scientists toward professionalization struck the clerical scientists on two other levels. The first was that of the degree of expertise that might qualify a person and his work for professional recognition and monetary support. In 1859 Huxley told Hooker, in regard to a proposed research fund,

> If there is to be any fund raised at all, I am quite of your mind that it should be a scientific fund and not a mere naturalists' fund. . . . For the word "Naturalist" unfortunately includes a far lower order of men than chemist, physicist, or mathematician. You don't call a man a mathematician because he has spent his life in getting as far as quadratics; but every fool who can make bad species and worse genera is a "Naturalist."[33]

Here was the cutting edge of the professionalizing spirit before which, as much as before the edge of objectivity, the amateur parson-naturalist fell. With or without the impact of Darwin and other new theories, the amateur's day as a "man of science" was drawing to a close. As persons of Huxley's opinion and ambitions came to control the meager research funds administered by the Royal Society, the British Association, and other professional scientific societies, amateur scientists with marginal training and expertise could expect both less support and less recognition.

Second, the clerical scientists stood accused of dual loyalties that were incompatible with the pursuit of thoroughly naturalistic science according to which theological, teleological, and metaphysical concerns stood banned both as matters for investigation and as principles of explanation. The emerging professional coterie considered "scientifical-geological-theologians" such as Hugh Miller and Adam Sedgwick, who continued to attempt to reconcile science and revelation, as public embarrassments who resembled "asses between bundles of hay, distorting their consciences to meet the double-call of their public profession."[34] In the professional scientific community there would be little or no room for the person of two callings. Science and the scientist must serve the profession or community at large but not some particular religious doctrine, sect, or church to which scientific activity was subordinate. In this respect Philip Gosse and the Victoria Institute were as much a conclave of amateurs surviving into the dawn of the professional era as they were a group of orthodox theologians.

The professionalizers were not content merely to note or to ridicule the intellectual problems of the clerical scientist. In some cases they set out to prove that no clergyman could be a genuine man of science. Such an argument provided a secondary theme for Francis Galton's *English Men of Science: Their Nature and Nurture* (1872). This book was both a pioneering work of statistical inquiry and a professional manifesto that contended, "The pursuit of science is uncongenial to the priestly character,"[35] To support this contention Galton noted that very few men whom he defined as scientists came from clerical homes. His own experience on scientific councils, he believed, confirmed his view of the incapacity of clergymen for serious scientific work. He explained that between 1850 and 1870 clergymen had occupied only 16 out of 660 positions on the councils of the major scientific societies, "and they have in nearly every case been attached to those subdivisions of science which have the fewest salient points to scratch or jar against dogma."[36] He quickly added, "There is not a single biologist among them."[37]

Galton's tactic was the commonplace one within emerging professional groups of edging out marginal members on the grounds of alleged indifference or incompetence. His real charge against the clergymen-scientists was that they were clergymen first, scientists second, and thus could not be good professionals as he and others had begun to define the term. Galton hoped to persuade his readers that since clergymen by virtue of their theological vocation could not be genuine scientists and could not honestly teach science, professional men of science seeking to serve the material needs of the entire community should occupy those positions of research and teaching in the universities and public schools presently occupied by clergy or persons appointed and controlled by clergy. The message was also relevant to the managers of the new school-board schools. Galton hoped those teaching positions as well as employment in government agencies would eventually "give rise to the establishment of a sort of scientific priesthood throughout the kingdom, whose high duties would have reference to the health and well-being of the nation in its broadest sense, and whose emoluments would be made commensurate with the importance and variety of their functions."[38] Banishment of clergymen from positions of influence in the scientific world and the abolishment of clerically dominated education were essential to that goal.

For inclusion in his data Galton had defined a "man of science" with his professionalizing aims in mind. To qualify, a person had to have been elected to the Royal Society after 1850, that is, three years after the important membership reforms. Second, the scientist must have earned a medal for his work, presided over a learned society or section of the British Association, have been elected to the Council of the Royal Society, or occupied a professorship in an important college or university. These distinctly professional criteria effectively excluded both amateur aristocratic practitioners of science and the more notable of the clerical scientists most of whom had been elected to the Royal Society prior to the reforms of 1847. Consequently, no matter what the quality of the work of the clerical scientists or the number of scientific honors and offices achieved, those people had almost no impact on Galton's data. Had he not so skewed his numbers by choosing the date of 1850, more clergymen would have been included. Moreover, some of those investigators would have been deeply involved with geology during a period when that science did indeed jar against dogma.[39]

Galton's handling of his evidence in effect made prescriptive a steady decrease in the number of clergymen-scientists occupying significant positions in the scientific community. This process of clerical withdrawal from the world of science commenced in the third quarter of the century and is quite apparent in the figures recording the number of Anglican clergymen who were members of the Royal Society at various intervals during the last half of the century.[40]

TABLE 1

Anglican Clergymen Members of the Royal Society, 1849–99

Year	Total Membership	Anglican Clergy	Clerical Percentage of Total Membership
1849	741	72	9.7
1859	636	57	8.96
1869	544	44	8.1
1879	488	27	5.5
1889	466	17	3.6
1899	449	14	3.1

SOURCE: Royal Society membership lists, *The Royal Society.*

During the entire lifetime of the Philosophical Club (1847–1901), the professionally oriented offshoot of the Royal Society, only two clergymen-scientists, Adam Sedgwick and Baden-Powell, ever graced the membership roll.[41]

The figures for major participation by Anglican clergy in the British Association are equally striking. They are also perhaps even more indicative because the standards of the association were less rigorous than those of the Royal Society.[42] From 1831 to 1865, the first thirty-five years of the association's history, nine clergymen held the office of president. The last one did so in 1862. During the second thirty-five years of the association's existence no clergyman was president. Prior to 1865 a total of fifty-two Anglican clergymen served in the rather honorary post of one of the association's several vice-presidencies. From 1866 to 1900 the number fell to nineteen. A similar pattern occurred among the local secretaries of the association who helped with the local arrangements for the annual meetings. during the first forty years (1831–70), twenty-one clergymen attended to this task. Between 1871 and 1900 only five clergymen did so. The number of Anglican clergymen presiding over the individual sections of the association repeated the picture of clerical departure. In each case, clergymen gave way to lay professionals.

TABLE 2

Anglican Clergymen Presiding over Sections of the British Association for the Advancement of Science

	1831–1865	1866–1900
Mathematics	15	2
Chemistry	4	0
Geology	6	0
Biology	8	1
Mechanical	8	0

SOURCE: *Report of the Seventy-First Meeting of the British Association for the Advancement of Science.*

This gradual severance of Anglican clergy from the world of British science reflected changes in the religious community as well as the harassment of the professionalizing scientists and the dispersion of theories incompatible with the Bible and natural theology. When early Victorian clerical scientists of stature such as Sedgwick, Powell, and Whewell died, there were few replacements from the ranks of the clergy. Many young clergymen not unnaturally had come to regard science as the enemy rather than the helpmate of religion. But reasons unrelated to developments in the scientific community also shaped this new attitude. A considerable body of clergy influenced by the Oxford Movement wanted the Anglican Church itself to become more autonomous from extraecclesiastical and extratheological influences and to define its mission and character in terms of its own peculiar institutional and theological values. Most prominently they sought to liberate the Church of England from domination by the secular state. This movement also contained an intellectual component. The Bible and church tradition were to define doctrine and serve as the foundation for religious truth and practice. Adjustment of theology for compatibility with science, such as had occurred in England since the age of Newton, implied a surrender of part of the intellectual and theological autonomy of the church to nonreligious authority. Science, especially as defined by the professional man of science and as accepted by the contemporary liberal or Broad-Church theologians, was part and parcel of the liberalism rejected by the Tractarians and their followers.

As these clergymen—probably the most dynamic element in the mid-century Church—defined the priesthood in distinctly clerical, theological, and devotional terms, it became increasingly difficult for men who might wish to combine the priesthood and the scientific calling to do so. For professional scientists that double vocation seemed retrogressive, but for the high church clergy it seemed too progressive and potentially rationalizing. Consequently, within the Church of England a clergyman-scientist confronted the choice of perpetuating traditional natural theology and risking ridicule by scientists or attempting further rationalization of theology in accord with science and encountering persecution by fellow clergymen.[43] The new rising clericalism in the Church of England gave further credibility to the stereotyped clergyman who disliked science and progressive thought generally.[44] The growing absence of clerical scientists seemed to prove that clergymen could not be scientists. Reform of the universities, removal of religious tests, and new opportunities for employment of scientifically trained persons in the government, school-board schools, the civic universities, and sometimes in industry meant that the Church and ecclesiastical patronage were no longer paths to the scientific career. By the third quarter of the century it had become increasingly clear that to be a scientist was one vocation and to be a clergyman was another. The professionalizing scientists seized upon these developments, not wholly of their own making, to effect an intellectual and social reorientation of the scientific community.

Yet fewer clergy in the ranks of the scientific world solved only part of the professional problem. Lay scientists, such as the powerful and much disliked Richard Owen, still retained active religious convictions, curried favors of the ecclesiastical hierarchy, and subordinated their intellectual enterprise to theological values.[45] This traditional and preprofessional outlook manifested itself in several British Association presidential addresses during the 1860s and early seventies and in the famous "Scientists' Declaration" of 1865.[46] So long as this reverent spirit did not measurably interfere with a person's teaching, research, or peer evaluation, there was minimal professional difficulty. For example, despite his compromising with ecclesiastical authorities, his regular church attendance, and his reluctance to accept the antiquity of man and natural selection, no one really doubted Charles Lyell's professional loyalty. Nor did James Clerk Maxwell's theistic speculations based on the nature of molecules raise questions. The same was true of W. B. Carpenter, a distinguished Unitarian physiologist, who hoped that science might still provide some grounds for a personal theism. His faith was not professionally pernicious, and he stood more than ready to do battle with spiritualists and the antivivisectionists. All of these men generally succeeded in separating their religious faith from a critical approach to scientific research.[47]

There were, however, other more harmful cases of scientific allegiance to traditional religion. In 1875 P. G. Tait and Balfour Stewart published *The Unseen Universe*, in which they attempted to prove the validity of the Christian doctrine of immortality. These writers were answered and their speculations thoroughly criticized.[48] But the more significant target was any lay scientist who actually employed his scientific expertise to reconcile science with the doctrines of an ecclesiastical organization. Such a person had to be attacked frontally, for he was a remnant of those earlier scientific men who were, in Huxley's words, "citizens of two states, in which mutually unintelligible languages were spoken and mutually incompatible laws were enforced."[49] Professionally minded scientists would not tolerate persons who employed or seemed to employ science for ecclesiastical ends or in hope of ecclesiastical commendation.

St. George Jackson Mivart, a Roman Catholic biologist, was just such a professional apostate who proved an irresistible and necessary target for professionalizing wrath. He had been a Huxley student, an adherent to natural selction, and a peripheral member of the Darwin circle. But in the late 1860s, Mivart came to entertain doubts (as did others at the time) about the sufficiency of natural selection alone to determine species. In the *Genesis of Species* (1871) he expressed his newly found scepticism and set forth supplementary explanations. The same year he also criticized an article on marriage and divorce written by George Darwin and did so in such a manner as to cast aspersions on the younger Darwin's moral character.[50] Each of these factors invited attack, but what particularly aroused Huxley and re-quired detailed refutation was Mivart's contention that evolution was perfect-ly compatible with the Church fathers and later Roman Catholic theologians. After numerous references to Augustine and Suarez, Mivart had declared, "It is then evident that ancient and most venerable theological authorities dis-tinctly assert *derivative* creation and thus harmonize with all that modern science can possibly require. . . . The various extracts given show clearly how far 'evolution' is from any necessary opposition to the most orthodox theology."[51] In this fashion Mivart hoped to reconcile the Roman Catholic Church of Pius IX to the general doctrines of modern science.

Mivart's immediate reward was perhaps the most scathing review essay ever to come from Huxley's pen. The proposed reconciliation might have saved evolution for the church, but it would have directly undercut arguments for the pursuit of science oriented toward the profession and the community rather than toward the approval of ecclesiastical authorities. Mivart was also in effect suggesting that little difference separated religious and scientific epistemology. If sustained, Mivart's analysis would have perpetuated the dual citizenship in scientific work that Huxley and others of his opinion abhorred. To those of Huxley's professional persuasion, it was essential that evolution not be embraced by the Roman Catholic Church.

Consequently, Huxley spent several hours in an Edinburgh library reading Augustine and Suarez to assure himself and later the readers of "Mr. Darwin's Critics" (1871) that the teaching of the Church was absolutely irreconcilable with evolution. Huxley also warned that no one should imagine that "he is, or can be, both a true son of the Church and a loyal soldier of science."[52] That opinion came as a severe shock to the beleaguered Mivart who replied that, "it is not . . . without surprise that I learned my one unpardonable sin . . . the one great offense disqualifying me from being 'a loyal soldier of science'—was my attempt to show that there is no real antagonism between the Christian religion and evolution."[53] Mivart, like most of the historians after him, assumed the antagonism of science and religion related primarily to ideas, when it was also profoundly involved with men and institutions. In good Baconian fashion still regarding physical science as intimately related to natural theology, he had quite understandably failed to perceive that the issue at stake was not only the substance of theory but also the character of the scientific community and the right of its members to set the parameters of their thought, education, epistemology, employment, and social utility independent of considerations for religious doctrine or ecclesiastical organization.

Outside the boundaries of the scientific community the professionally minded scientists confronted further obstacles to their redefinition of the direction and role of science. As Peter Marsh has rightly observed, "Above Victorian England's nagging doubts, there was a thick layer of organized activity among all Christian denominations, thicker than at any time since the Civil War."[54] This activity constituted the religious counterpart to the popular diffusion of science previously described by Clerk Maxwell. Between 1850 and 1880 ten new Anglican theological colleges were founded, and the number of priests rose from 17,320 in 1851 to 21,663 in 1881. From 1868 to 1880 approximately seventy new urban parishes were organized annually. In 1888 a spokesman at the Anglican Church Congress reported that between 1860 and 1885 over 80.5 million pounds had been expended on building and restoring churches, missions, charities, and education. The ritualist movement and the restoration of Anglican conventional life continued to revitalize Anglo-Catholicism. In 1878 the Lambeth conference approved reinstitution of auricular confession on a voluntary basis. Beginning in the late 1850s and culminating in the 1870s with the visit of Moody and Sankey, revivals took place throughout the nation. Nonconformists and their preachers, such as Charles Spurgeon, were reaching the height of their influence. Under the leadership of Cardinal Manning, English Roman Catholicism made considerable headway among the poor. The third quarter of the century also witnessed a broad Roman Catholic religious revival in Ireland. These developments, as well as the launching of the Salvation Army, the intrusion of Spiritualism from America, and the spectacle of the miracle of Lourdes in

France, proved fundamental to the scientists' perception of their situation in the general society and intellectual nation.[55] John Morley was not alone in his conviction that "our age of science is also the age of deepening superstition and reviving sacerdotalism."[56]

This climate of aggressive corporate and devotional religious revival, as much as their own naturalistic theories, brought the scientists into conflict with the clergy. Because of their friendships with liberal churchmen and their mutual resistance to theological excesses, unorthodox men of science have sometimes been portrayed as holding a position "in which theological dogma was being attacked not for the sake of undercutting religious faith, but as a means of freeing that faith for what were regarded as nobler and more adequate forms in which it could find expression."[57] This interpretation is largely, if not wholly, incorrect. It ignores the frequent disagreements between liberal theologians and advocates of science and obscures the social and professional goals of the professionalizing scientists.[58] The latter sought to reform religion for the sake not of purifying religious life but of improving the lot of science in Victorian society. The intellectual authority frequently ascribed to the clergy, the Bible, and theological concepts such as divine providence exerted a pernicious influence on the practical affairs of everyday life. Traditional religious authority provided the justification for sabbatarianism, restrictive marriage laws, prayers to change the weather and to prevent disease, religiously dominated education, and other social practices that inhibited the discovery, diffusion, and application of scientific truth.[59] So long as that authority and those practices continued, the scientists could not achieve the cultural and social influence necessary for the establishment and improvement of their professional position.

Education provided the major arena for confrontation and conflict. In the mid-1860s liberal Bishop Connop Thirlwall shrewdly observed that much of the hostility between scientists and clergymen arose because "Science is debarred its rightful share of influence in the education of the national mind."[60] Penetration of the educational system at both the secondary and university levels would insure the dispersion of scientific knowledge and eventually lead to broader applications throughout the society. Achievement of a larger share of educational influence also meant to the professional scientific elite attainment of social legitimacy and prestige and of new areas of employment for students of science. The scientists' assault on the educational system necessarily required confrontation with the religious groups who controlled it and guided its curriculum. Acquiring professional inclusion in the major educational institutions involved attacking the sufficiency of strictly literary training, calling for removal of theological tests in the universities and informal requirements in the public schools, opposing denominational control of the school boards after the Education Act of 1870, and demanding that the science taught be science as defined by professional scientists. This process involved more frequent clashes with Roman Catholics and Anglicans than with Protestant Nonconformists who in the seventies were themselves frequently calling for nonsectarian education.

A large measure of the scientists' complaint against religious influence over education and culture generally was reserved for Roman Catholicism, which Huxley described as "our great antagonist" and "that damnable perverter of mankind."[61] Linking the advance of science to anti-Catholicism allowed the cause of the professional scientists to benefit from the widespread popular antipapist sentiment in Britain.[62] But much more was involved than anti-Catholicism. Under the pontificate of Pius IX the Roman Catholic Church epitomized the most extreme mode of religious authority and clerical pretension for control of intellectual life. The Church had specifically condemned the theory, methods, conclusions, and practice of modern science. However, as much as the general condemnation in the *Syllabus of Errors* (1864), the role of the Roman Catholic Church in Ireland accounted for the intense antipathy of the scientists. So long as Catholicism permeated Ireland and its hierarchy dominated the Catholic University, science and its practitioners could play no effective role in that nation. Ireland stood as an object lesson in the potential ecclesiastical blight of a nation, and the scientists, who were generally unionists, regarded Ireland as an integral part of Britain.[63]

It was against Irish Catholicism and more particularly against its impact on education that John Tyndall directed his notorious Belfast Address of 1874. In the course of his presidential address to the British Association, Tyndall declared that men of science "claim, and . . . shall wrest from theology, the entire domain of cosmological theory. All schemes and systems which infringe upon the domain of science must, in so far as they do this, submit to its control, and relinquish all thought of controlling it."[64] Probably no single incident in the conflict of religion and science raised so much furor. Most contemporaries interpreted Tyndall's remarks as applying to all churches. However, a careful reading of the address and of Tyndall's later "Apology for the Belfast Address" (1874) reveals that by theology he meant Roman Catholicism in particular. A few months earlier the Irish Catholic hierarchy had refused the request of the laity for inclusion of physical science in the curriculum of the Catholic University. To a scientist with eyes to see, ecclesiasticism was alive, well, and prospering across the Irish Sea. Tyndall, who was an Anglo-Irishman, used his presidential address to chastise the Irish Catholic religious authorities.[65] But the widespread hostile criticism of the address throughout the British religious community suggested that Irish Catholic bishops were not the only religious authorities who aspired to limit the cosmological speculations of their flocks.

Within England the scientists were fighting a similar battle although against a weaker mode of ecclesiasticism. Since the late thirties, provision of education for the nation had constituted the chief claim of the Church of England to social utility. Although the Education Act of 1870 destroyed the Anglican pretension to monopoly in that area, the Church continued to exercise widespread educational influence. Indeed the provisions of the Education Act served to stir new Anglican activity to avoid imposition of school-board schools.[66] However, probably at no time in modern history did the Anglican Church appear to be less of a *national* establishment. The ritualist controversy persuaded many people that the church harbored potential or secret Roman Catholic clergy. The hostile reaction to *Essays and Reviews* discouraged hopes that the Church might become more liberal from within. The judicial actions taken against both the reviewers and the ritualists cast the Church of England in the role of a persecutor. In 1867 J. R. Green, the historian, complained, "At present the breadth of the Church is brought sharply out against the narrowness of the clergy. They do not even represent the Church. What then do they represent? Not the educated laity—not the intelligence of England—but its unintelligence."[67] Throughout the third quarter of the century the Anglican clergy appeared to the general public to be pursuing party goals within the church and denominational ascendancy within the nation.

Such an institution in the eyes of many citizens seemed unfit to be the schoolmaster of the nation. Later the Church had to oppose raising standards of scientific education because the added cost would harm already tight budgets.[68] All of these conditions permitted the professional scientists not only to compare their rationalism with the faith of the clergy but also to contrast both implicitly and explicitly their own enlightened, practical, and unselfish goals with the apparently narrow, vested, dysfunctional, and denominational interests of the clergy. In opposition to Irish Catholic and Anglican ecclesiastical authorities who spurned the inclusion of science and other practical subjects favored by middle class parents, the scientists emerged as the educational party of national efficiency and imperial vision whose concerns and self-interest were at one with the medical, economic, military, and industrial requirements of the nation.

The internal ideology of much, though certainly not all, early Victorian science had been related to tracing the presence of the Creator in the creation. But that of the more nearly professionalized science in the second half of the century became the glorification and strengthening of the nation and its wealth. In 1870, during the Franco-Prussian War, Norman Lockyer argued:

> As there is little doubt that a scientific training for the young officer means large capabilities for combination and administration when that officer comes to command, we must not be surprised if the organization of our army, if it is to do its work with the minimum of science, will, at some future time, again break down as effectually as it did in the Crimea, or that our troops will find themselves over-matched should the time ever come when they will be matched with a foe who knows how to profit to the utmost from scientific aids.[69]

During the same period Henry Cole repeatedly pointed to the necessity for better scientific education as the key to Britain's continued economic supremacy. Edition after edition of *Nature* carried the same message. In

1875 the Devonshire Commission on which Huxley served and for which Lockyer was secretary declared that "considering the increasing importance of Science to the Material Interests of the Country, we cannot but regard its almost total exclusion from the training of the upper and middle classes as little less than a national misfortune."[70] The linking of the fortunes of science with the fate of the nation climaxed at the turn of the century when the elderly Lockyer lectured the British Association on "The Influence of Brain Power in History" (1903), and as Karl Pearson in a whole series of books and articles proclaimed the necessity for scientists to advise the government and for politicians to pursue scientific policies and procedures in all areas of national life.[71] These were the arguments of concerned, patriotic Englishmen. But they were also the arguments of persons who understood that only by connecting in the public mind the future of their emerging profession with the welfare of the nation could they attain the financial support, employment prestige, and public influence they desired.

Commenting in the mid-1920s on J. W. Draper's *The Conflict between Religion and Science*, Arthur Balfour observed, "It is not perhaps surprising that the most interesting characteristic of Dr. Draper's volume of 1873 is its total want of interest for readers in 1925."[72] That development had not, however, come about because of any genuine intellectual reconciliation of science and religion. As David Lack has argued, "The basic conflict is unresolved."[73] Rather the social and professional context of science in Britain had changed. By World War I most Christian theologians had abandoned natural theology, and clergy no longer seriously sought either to rival or complement scientists as interpretors of physical nature. From the standpoint of the scientists, their efforts to carve out for themselves an independent social and intellectual sphere had largely succeeded. The scientific community had become self-defining. Scientists had established themselves firmly throughout the educational system and could pursue research and teaching free of ecclesiastical interference. Science, as defined by the profession rather than for the profession, had become a part of national life. Politicians such as Balfour and Haldane, though theists and authors of books on religious philosophy, no longer defended the Bible as had Gladstone. Rather, they joined the chorus of spokesmen urging the national and imperial significance of science in light of the German economic and military threat.[74]

Asa Briggs once wrote, "The conflict between science and religion petered out, giving way to new debates about the nature not of the Universe but of society."[75] However, at its center much of the debate including consideration of epistemological and scientific theory had involved controversy about the social structure of the intellectual nation as well as about the structure of knowledge and of the universe. When the former set of issues had been resolved, many of the latter no longer furnished grounds for continued dispute. In this regard the Victorian conflict of science and religion represents one chapter in the still-to-be-written intellectual and social history of the emergence of the professionalized society in the West.

Notes

1. T. H. Huxley, *Collected Essays* (London: Macmillan, 1894), vols. 4 and 5; E. B. Pusey, *Un-science, Not Science, Adverse to Faith* (London: J. Parker, 1878); Frederick Temple, *The Relations between Religion and Science* (New York: Macmillan, 1884); Herbert Spencer, *First Principles*, 4th ed. (New York: D. Appleton, 1896), pp. 3–136; J. W. Draper, *History of the Conflict between Religion and Science* (New York: D. Appleton, 1874); Andrew Dickson White, *The Warfare of Science* (London: Henry King, 1876). White's book eventually grew to two volumes entitled *A History of the Warfare of Science with Theology in Christendom.* Standish Meachem, *My Lord Bishop: The Life of Samuel Wilberforce, 1805–1873* (Cambridge, Mass.: Harvard University Press, 1970), pp. 207–34; J. M. Robertson, *History of Freethought in the Nineteenth Century* (London: Watts, 1929), 1:313–42; J. B. Bury, *History of Freedom of Thought* (London: Oxford University Press, 1957; rpt. of 1913 edn.), pp. 141–85; Bertrand Russell, *Religion and Science* (New York: Holt, 1935); Lord Balfour, Introduction, in *Science, Religion, and Reality,* ed. Joseph Needham (New York: Macmillan, 1928), pp. 1–18.

2. Robert K. Ensor, *England, 1870–1914* (Oxford: The Clarendon Press, 1936), p. 162.

3. Charles E. Raven, *Science, Religion, and the Future* (Cambridge: Cambridge University Press, 1943; rpt. 1968), p. 33.

4. R. K. Webb, *Modern England from the 18th Century to the Present* (New York: Dodd, Mead, 1970), p. 413.

5. Owen Chadwick. *The Victorian Church* (New York: Oxford University Press, 1970), 2:3.

6. Chadwick, ibid., 2:1–9; William H. Brock and Roy M. MacLeod, "The 'Scientists' Declaration': Reflections on Science and Belief in the Wake of Essays and Reviews, 1864–5," *British Journal for the History of Science* 9 (1976):60.

7. George Gaylord Simpson, *This View of Life: The World of an Evolutionist* (New York: Harcourt, Brace and World 1964), p. 214.

8. Charles Lyell, *Principles of Geology,* (London: John Murray, 1830), 1:1–91; *Life, Letters and Journals of Sir Charles Lyell, Bart., edited by his sister-in-law, Mrs. Lyell* (London: John Murray, 1881), 1:263, 316–17, 445–46; Charles Darwin, *The Origin of Species* and *The Descent of Man* (New York: Modern Library, n.d.), pp. 122, 135, 319–24, 367–74; Huxley, *Collected Essays,* 1:18–41; Joseph Dalton Hooker, "Presidential Address," *Report of the Thirty-eighth Meeting of the British Association for the Advancement of Science,* (London, 1869), pp. lxxiii–lxxv; Henry Maudsley, *Body and Mind* (New York: D. Appleton, 1875), p. 275; Charles Coulston Gillispie, *Genesis and Geology: A Study in the Relations of Scientific Thought, Natural Theology and Social Opinion in Great Britain, 1790–1850* (New York: Harper & Row-Harper Torchbook, 1959), pp. 217–28; Frank Miller Turner, *Between Science and Religion: The Reaction to Scientific Naturalism in Late Victorian England* (New Haven: Yale University Press, 1974), pp. 217–28.

9. G. H. Lewes, *Problems of Life and Mind, First Series* (Boston: Osgood, 1874), 1:2.

10. T. H. Huxley, *Collected Essays,* 2:52.

11. Ernst Cassirer, *Language and Myth* (New York: Dover, 1946), idem, *The Philosophy of Symbolic Forms,* 3 vols. (New Haven: Yale University Press, 1953–57); T. S. Kuhn, *The Copernican Revolution* (Cambridge, Mass.: Harvard University Press, 1957) and, idem, *The Structure of Scientific Revolutions* (Chicago: University of Chicago Press, 1962); Stephen Toulmin, *Human Understanding* (Princeton: Princeton University Press, 1972); Jerome R. Ravetz, *Scientific Knowledge and Its Social Problems* (Oxford: Clarendon Press, 1971), pp. 11–74; Bernard Barber, "Resistance by Scientists to Scientific Discovery," *Science* 134 (1961): 594–602; James Friday, "A Microscopic Incident in a Monumental Struggle: Huxley and Antibiosis in 1875," *The British Journal for the History of Science* 7 (1974): 64–71.

12. W. D. Niven, ed., *The Scientific Papers of James Clerk Maxwell* (New York: Dover, 1965), 2:356.

13. A. W. Benn, *A History of English Rationalism in the Nineteenth Century* (London: Longmans, Green, 1906), 1:198.

14. Henry Sidgwick, "Presidential Address to the Society for Psychical Research, July 16, 1888." in *Presidential Addresses to the Society for Psychical Research* (Glasgow: Society for Psychical Research, 1912), p. 35 (emphasis in original).

15. Bernard Barber, "Some Problems in the Sociology of the Professions," *Daedalus* 92 (1963):672. See also J. A. Jackson, ed., *Professions and Professionalization* (Cambridge: Cambridge University Press, 1970); E. Mendelsohn, "The Emergence of Science as a Profession in Nineteenth-Century Europe," in *The Management of Scientists*, ed. K. Hill (Boston: Beacon Press, 1964), pp. 3–48.

16. Charles Babbage, *The Exposition of 1851, or Views of the Industry, the Science, and the Government of England* (London: John Murray, 1851), p. 189.

17. Sydney Ross, " 'Scientists': The Story of a Word," *Annals of Science* 18 (1962):65–86; *Third Report of the Royal Commission on Scientific Instruction and the Advancement of Science* [1873], in *British Parliamentary Papers, Education: Science and Technology* (Shannon: Irish University Press, 1970), 4:15; G. A. Foote, "The Place of Science in British Reform, 1830–1850," *Isis* 42 (1951):192–208.

18. Gillispie, *Genesis and Geology*, pp. 3–49, 184–228; David L. Hull, *Darwin and His Critics: The Reception of Darwin's Theory of Evolution by the Scientific Community* (Cambridge, Mass.: Harvard University Press, 1973), pp. 37–67; Arnold Thackray, "The Industrial Revolution and the Image of Science," in Arnold Thackray and Everett Mendelsohn, *Science and Values: Patterns of Tradition and Change* (New York: Humanities Press, 1974), pp. 3–20; Arnold Thackray, "Natural Knowledge in Cultural Context: The Manchester Model," *American Historical Review* 79 (1974):672–709; David Layton, *Science for the People: The Origins of the School Science Curriculum in England* (New York: Science History Publications, 1973); George Foote, "Science and its Functions in Early Nineteenth Century England," *Osiris* 11 (1954): 438–54; see also the annual reports of the British Association.

19. *Report of the Nineteenth Meeting of the British Association for the Advancement of Science* (London, 1850), pp. xliii–xliv.

20. Leonard G. Wilson, *Charles Lyell, the Years to 1841: The Revolution in Geology* (New Haven: Yale University Press, 1972), pp. 310–15; Peter G. Mudford, "William Lawrence and the Natural History of Man," *Journal of the History of Ideas* 29 (1968):430–36.

21. According to Steven Shapin and Arnold Thackray, "... the 'scientist' is himself a social construct of the last hundred years or so. And, as usually understood, so are 'science', 'the scientific community,' and 'the scientific career.' " "Prosopography as a Research Tool in the History of Science: The British Scientific Community, 1700–1900," *History of Science* 12 (1974):3.

22. Dr. Roy M. McLeod has very generously furnished me with these figures. The membership figures include the following societies: Chemical, Geological, Royal Anthropological, Royal Astronomical, Royal Entomological, Royal Microscopical, Royal Statistical, and Zoological.

23. Henry Lyon, *The Royal Society, 1660–1940* (Cambridge: Cambridge University Press, 1944), pp. 260–63, 282–83; T. G. Bonney, *Annals of the Philosophical Club* (London: Macmillan, 1919), pp. 1–3.

24. Leonard Huxley, *Life and Letters of Sir Joseph Dalton Hooker* (London: J. Murray, 1918), 1:541.

25. Other names, such as that of John S. Burdon-Sanderson, might obviously be added to this group. Three of the persons included may seem problematical. Galton held no professional offices, but he worked consistently for the practical application of science and for its professional

organization. Henry Cole was not a scientist, but as Secretary of the Department of Science and Art he was one of the persons most vocal in calling for links between science and industry. Herbert Spencer was also not a scientist, but he was treated by his contemporaries as a scientific figure and constituted a strong voice in the advancement of science.

26. Consult the relevant articles in the *Dictionary of National Biography* and the *Dictionary of Scientific Biography*. See also D. S. L. Cardwell, *The Organization of Science in England*, rev. ed. (London: Heineman, 1972), pp. 84–98, and the following series of important articles by Roy M. MacLeod: "The Alkali Acts Administration, 1863–1884: The Emergence of the Civil Scientist," *Victorian Studies* 9 (1965):85–112; "Science and Government in Victorian England: Lighthouse Illumination and the Board of Trade, 1866–1886," *Isis* 60 (1969): 4–38; "The X-Club: A Social Network of Science in Late-Victorian England." *Notes and Records of the Royal Society of London* 24 (1970): 305–22; "Of Medals and Men: A Reward System in Victorian Science," *Notes and Records of the Royal Society of London* 26 (1971): 81–105; "The Support of Victorian Science: The Endowment of Research Movement in Great Britain, 1868–1900," *Minerva* 9 (1971): 197–230.

27. Quoted in *Nature* 224 (1969):435.

28. Huxley, *Life and Letters of Sir Joseph Dalton Hooker*, 2:54.

29. John Francis Byrne, *The Reader: A Review of Literature, Science, and the Arts, 1863–1867* (Ann Arbor: University Microfilms; 1965); Arthur Jack Meadows, *Science and Controversy: A Biography of Sir Norman Lockyer* (Cambridge, Mass.: MIT Press, 1972), pp. 1–38; Richard D. French, *Antivivisection and Medical Science in Victorian Society* (Princeton: Princeton University Press, 1975), pp. 60–111.

30. Roy M. MacLeod, "The Support of Victorian Science: The Endowment of Research Movement in Great Britain, 1868–1900," *Minerva* 9 (1971):197–230; idem, "The Ayrton Incident: A Commentary on the Relations of Science and Government in England, 1870–73," in *Science and Values; Patterns of Tradition and Change,* ed. Arnold Thackray and Everett Mendelsohn, pp. 45–80; Frank M. Turner, "Victorian Scientific Naturalism and Thomas Carlyle," *Victorian Studies* 18 (1975):325–43.

31. Lewes, *History of Philosophy from Thales to Comte,* 4th ed. (London: Longmans, Green, 1871), 1:xxxix. For a further discussion of the character and function of this empirical epistemology, see Hull, *Darwin and His Critics*, pp. 37–67, and Turner, *Between Science and Religion*, pp. 17–23.

32. Richard Westfall, *Science and Religion in Seventeenth-Century England* (New Haven: Yale University Press, 1958); Gillispie, *Genesis and Geology*, passim; Walter F. Cannon, "Scientists and Broad Churchmen: An Early Victorian Intellectual Network," *Journal of British Studies* 4 (1964):65–88; Michael Ruse, "The Relationship between Science and Religion in Britain, 1830–1870," *Church History* 44 (1975):505–22; Milton Millhauser, "The Scriptural Geologists: An Episode in the History of Opinion," *Osiris* 11 (1954):65–86; Robert M. Young, "The Impact of Darwin on Conventional Thought," in *The Victorian Crisis of Faith,* ed. Anthony Symondson (London: The Society for Promoting Christian Knowledge, 1970), pp. 13–36.

33. Leonard Huxley, *The Life and Letters of Thomas Henry Huxley* (New York: D. Appleton, 1900), 1:177.

34. Huxley, *Life and Letters of Sir Joseph Dalton Hooker*, 1:520.

35. Francis Galton, *English Men of Science: Their Nature and Nurture* 2nd ed. (London: Frank Cass 1970), p. 24. See also Victor L. Hilts, *A Guide to Francis Galton's English Men of Science* (Philadelphia: Transactions of the American Philosophical Society, 1975), N.S. 65, p. 5.

36. Galton, ibid., p. 26.

37. Ibid., p. 26. For this polemical passage Galton was compelled to fall back on his own experience with clergymen and scientists because the respondents to his questionnaire had

overwhelminghly insisted that the religious training of their youth and even their present religious convictions did not interfere with their scientific work. See Galton, *English Men of Science*, pp. 126–201, and Hilts, *A Guide to Francis Galton's English Men of Science*, pp. 29–31.

38. Galton, *English Men of Science*, p. 260.

39. Ibid., p. 4. In one case, namely, that of Rev. John Stevens Henslow, Galton actually solicited information on a clergyman-scientist. Henslow was dead, but his son provided information. The reasons for Galton's decision in this case are not known. See Hilts, *A Guide to Francis Galton's English Men of Science*, pp. 13–14.

40. The figures for this table have been calculated from the Royal Society membership lists, published annually during the nineteenth century under the title of *The Royal Society*.

41. See the membership lists and biographical sketches in Bonney, *Annals of the Philosophical Club*.

42. These figures have been calculated from the officer lists published in the *Report of the Seventy-first Meeting of the British Association for the Advancement of Science* (London, 1901), pp. xl–lxxxiii.

43. See note 32 and Chadwick, *The Victorian Church*, 1:309–24, 455–68, 476–80, 487–91; Kenneth A. Thompson, *Bureaucracy and Church Reform: The Organizational Response of the Church of England to Social Change, 1800–1965* (Oxford: Clarendon Press, 1970), pp. 26–55, 117–21; M. A. Crowther, *Church Embattled: Religious Controversy in Mid-Victorian England* (Hamden, Conn.: Archon Books, 1970), pp. 13–39, 138–240; Mecham, *Lord Bishop*, pp. 207–34; F. W. Farrar, "The Church and Her Younger Members," *Authorized Report of the Church Congress Held at Dublin* (Dublin: Hodges, Smith, and Foster, 1868), pp. 143–47. In regard to the changing character of the Anglican clergy during the third quarter of the century, I wish to acknowledge information gleaned from conversations with Professor Josef Atholz of the University of Minnesota.

44. To cite J. R. Green, "The clergy have their ideal conception of men of science, and men of science have an equally ideal notion of the clergy. The ordinary parson creates an imaginary being bent on destroying the fact of a revelation, the truths of religion, and the difference between a man and a brute. This imaginary being he christens Professor Huxley. On the other hand, the man of science constructs an equally imaginary being who resists every step of physical research, who is blind to the most obvious facts, who had no sense of truth, and who is laboring to make others as blind and as untruthful as himself. This imaginary being he styles the English Parson." "Professor Huxley on Science and the Clergy," *The Saturday Review* 24 (1867):692. Such mutually distorting appeals to stereotypes are a common occurrence during struggles over professionalization.

45. Roy M. MacLeod, "Evolutionism and Richard Owen, 1830–1868: An Episode in Darwin's Century," *Isis* 56 (1965):259–80.

46. William H. Brock and Roy M. MacLeod, "The 'Scientists' Declaration': Reflections on Science and Belief in the Wake of Essays and Reviews, 1864–5," *British Journal for the History of Science* 9 (1976):39–66.

47. Wilson, *Charles Lyell, the Years to 1841*, pp. 310–15; W. B. Carpenter, "On Mind and Will in Nature," *Contemporary Review* 20 (1872):738–62; idem, *Mesmerism, Spiritualism, etc., Historically & Scientifically Considered* (New York: D. Appleton, 1877); James Clerk Maxwell, *Matter and Motion* (London: Society for Promoting Christian Knowledge, 1876); idem, "Molecule," *Encyclopedia Britannica*, 9th ed.; Lewis Campbell and William Garnet, *The Life of James Clerk Maxwell* (London: Macmillan, 1882), pp. 321–22, 338–40, 393, 404.

48. P. G. Tait and Balfour Stewart, *The Unseen Universe; or Physical Speculations on a Future State* (London: Macmillan, 1875); W. K. Clifford, *Lectures and Essays*, ed. Leslie Stephen and Frederick Pollock (London: Macmillan, 1901), 1:268–300; P. M. Heimann, "*The Unseen Universe*: Physics and the Philosophy of Nature in Victorian Britain," *British Journal for the History of Science* 6 (1972):73–79.

49.   T. H. Huxley, "Past and Present," *Nature* 51 (1894):1.

50.   Jacob W. Gruber, *A Conscience in Conflict: The Life of St. George Jackson Mivart* (New York: Columbia University Press, 1960), pp. 52–114.

51.   St. George Jackson Mivart, *The Genesis of Species* (New York: D. Appleton, 1871), p. 283.

52.   T. H. Huxley, *Collected Essays*, 2:149.

53.   St. George Jackson Mivart, *Essays and Criticisms* (London: James R. Osgood, McIlvaine 1892), 2:60.

54.   P. T. Marsh, *The Victorian Church in Decline* (London: Routledge and Kegan Paul, 1969), p. 66.

55.   Kenneth Inglis, *The Churches and the Working Classes in Victorian England* (London: Routledge and Kegan Paul, 1964), pp. 27–28, 41; George Kitson Clark, *The Making of Victorian England* (New York: Atheneum, 1971), pp. 169–71; J. Edwin Orr, *The Second Evangelical Awakening in Britain* (London: Marshall, Morgan, and Scott, 1949); Ralph W. Sockman, *The Revival of Conventional Life in the Church of England in the Nineteenth Century* (New York: W. D. Gray, 1917); Marsh, *The Victorian Church in Decline*, pp. 132–33; Emmet Larkin, "The Devotional Revival in Ireland, 1850–1875," *American Historical Review* 77 (1972):625–52.

56.   John Morley, *The Struggle for National Education*, 2nd. ed. (London: Chapman and Hall, 1873), p. 63.

57.   Maurice Mandelbaum, *History, Man and Reason: A Study in Nineteenth-Century Thought* (Baltimore: The Johns Hopkins Press, 1971), p. 30. For variations of this theme, see Walter Houghton, *The Victorian Frame of Mind, 1830–1870* (New Haven; Yale University Press, 1957), pp. 48–53, 70–71; William Irvine, *Apes, Angels, and Victorians: The Story of Darwin, Huxley, and Evolution* (New York: McGraw Hill, 1955), pp. 127–134, 339–41; Robert Young "The Impact of Darwin on Conventional Thought," in *The Victorian Crisis of Faith*, pp. 13–36.

58.   During the 1830s and 1840s certain scientists did see their work as leading to a higher, more rational conception of the deity. However, by the 1860s and later this impulse had become much more rare. Unorthodox scientists such as Huxley, Tyndall, Galton, and Spencer did repeatedly protest that they opposed ecclesiasticism and particular theological doctrines rather than religion itself; and they also allowed a limited role in personal life for inner emotional experiences which they, like contemporary religious liberals, classified as "religious." Such adherence to vague modes of liberal religion proved existentially useful to some of these scientists and also separated them from less respectable working-class atheists and secularists. But the critical scientists adamantly opposed religion as it was generally defined by religious authorities and spokesmen in their culture. Moreover, late Victorian religious liberals such as Benjamin Jowett, James Martineau, and R. H. Hutton understood that scientific naturalism was basically antithetical to both traditional and liberal Christianity. As the Broad-Church impulse came to have less and less influence within the church, the scientists made fewer and fewer accommodations. See note 32 and Huxley, *The Life and Letters of Thomas Henry Huxley*, 1:233–39; 2:9; Huxley, *The Life and Letters of Sir Joseph Dalton Hooker*, 2:54–58; Tyndall, *Fragments of Science,* 6th ed. (New York: D. Appleton, 1892) 2:198–201; Karl Pearson, *The Life, Letters, and Labours of Francis Galton* (Cambridge: Cambridge University Press, 1930), 3B:471–72; Herbert Spencer, *First Principles* (New York: P. F. Collier and Sons, n.d.), pp. 1–38; Evelyn Abbott and Lewis Campbell, eds., *Letters of Benjamin Jowett* (New York: E. P. Dutton, 1899), p. 190; James Martineau, *Essays, Reviews, and Addresses* (London: Longmans, Green, 1891), 3:185–218; 4:165–268; Richard Holt Hutton, *Aspects of Religious and Scientific Thought*, ed. Elizabeth M. Roscoe (London: Macmillan, 1899).

59.   Frank M. Turner, "Rainfall, Plagues, and the Prince of Wales: A Chapter in the Conflict of Religion and Science," *Journal of British Studies* 8 (1974):46–65.

60. Connop Thirlwall, *Essays, Speeches, and Sermons*, ed. J. J. Stewart Perowne (London: Richard Bently and Sons, 1880), p. 287. Thirlwall drew his distinction between literary men and scientists rather than between clergy and scientists, but from the essay it is clear that by literary men he meant clergy educated for their calling in the classics. For a direct challenge by a scientist to clerical educators, see John Tyndall, *Heat Considered as a Mode of Motion* (New York: D. Appleton 1864), p. vi.

61. T. H. Huxley, *Science and Education* (New York: D. Appleton, 1898), p. 120; Huxley, *Life and Letters of Thomas Henry Huxley*, 2:242. During one session of the London School Board, Huxley seems clearly to have used an appeal to anti-Catholicism to consolidate his position among other members who were otherwise somewhat unsympathetic to his general point of view. See *The Times*, October 28, 1871, p. 11. Anti-Catholicism permeated the writings of the scientists and their allies. For examples of this sentiment, consult Edward B. Tylor, *Anahuac: or Mexico and the Mexicans, Ancient and Modern* (London: Longman, Green, Longman and Roberts, 1861), pp. 20, 126, 289; and W. K. Clifford, *Lectures and Essays* 2:233–34. In Draper's *History of the Conflict between Religion and Science* as well as in the various editions of White's *Warfare of Science and Theology in Christendom* the religion and theology in question were primarily Roman Catholicism. Apparently outside Catholic journals few commentators noticed the anti-Catholic bias of the scientists. Three exceptions were: Robert Buchanan, "Lucretius and Modern Materialism," *New Quarterly Review* 6 (1876):18; J. R. Seeley, *Natural Religion* (Boston: Roberts Brothers, 1882), passim; and T. W. Marshall, *My Clerical Friends and Their Relations to Modern Thought* (London, 1873), pp. 263–70. Owen Chadwick noted in passing the problem of Catholicism for the scientists but did not emphasize it. However, a newspaper article which he cites as an example of interest in the conflict refers only to the problems of science with Roman Catholicism. Chadwick, *The Victorian Church*, 2:2–3; *The Times*, May 25, 1864, pp. 8–9.

62. G. F. A. Best, "Popular Protestantism," in *Ideas and Institutions of Victorian England*, ed. Robert Robson (London: Bell, 1967), pp. 115–42, and E. R. Norman, *Anti-Catholicism in Victorian England* (New York: Barnes and Noble, 1968).

63. Gladstone's policy of Irish Home Rule and resentment over the fate of General Gordon were among the reasons for Huxley's debating Gladstone over Genesis. Huxley later explained, "It was most important at that moment to shake him in the minds of sensible men." Huxley, *Life and Letters of Thomas Henry Huxley*, 2:450; see also 2:124, 130. Tyndall also attacked Gladstone on the Home Rule issue; see John Tyndall, *Mr. Gladstone and Home Rule* 2nd ed. (Edinburgh and London: William Blackwood and Sons, 1887).

64. Tyndall, *Fragments of Science*, 2:197.

65. Ibid., 2:196–97, 210–18. On the petition of the Irish Catholic laity, see *The Times*, Dec. 2, 1873, p. 7. Tyndall renewed his advice to Roman Catholics in the "Prefatory Note" (1876) to White, *The Warfare of Science* (1876 ed.), pp. iii–iv.

66. Marsh, *The Victorian Church in Decline*, pp. 72–81.

67. Leslie Stephen, ed., *The Letters of J. R. Green* (New York: Macmillan, 1901), p. 142. About the same time Joseph Dalton Hooker told a correspondent, "The worst of it is that the present condition of things prevents the rising talent and candid thinkers from entering the Church at all, and we shall be bepastored with fools, knaves, or imbeciles." Huxley, *Life and Letters of Sir Joseph Dalton Hooker*, 2:57.

68. Marsh, *The Victorian Church in Decline*, pp. 79–81.

69. Norman Lockyer, *Education and National Progress: Essays and Addresses, 1870–1905* (London: Macmillan, 1906), p. 4.

70. *Sixth Report of the Royal Commission on Scientific Instruction and the Advancement of Science* [1875] in *British Parliamentary Papers, Education: Science and Technical*, 4:24.

71. Lockyer, *Education and National Progress*, pp. 172–215. Karl Pearson, *The Ethic of Freethought* (London: T. F. Unwin, 1888), pp. 115–34; *National Life from the Standpoint of*

Science (London: A. and C. Black, 1901); *The Grammar of Science* (London: J. M. Dent and Sons, 1951), pp. 7–18; Bernard Semmel, *Imperialism and Social Reform: English Social-Imperial Thought, 1895–1914* (Garden City, N.Y.: Doubleday, 1968), pp. 24–42.

72.   Lord Balfour, Introduction, in *Science, Religion, and Reality,* p. 4. Balfour alludes to Draper's Preface of 1873; the book appeared in 1874.

73.   David Lack, *Evolutionary Theory and Christian Belief* (London: Methuen, 1957), p. 9.

74.   Cardwell, *The Organization of Science in England*, pp. 156–87; George Haines, *Essays on German Influence upon English Education and Science, 1850–1919* (Hamden, Conn.: Shoe String Press–Archon Books, 1969), pp. 47–87, 122–66; G. R. Searle, *The Quest for National Efficiency: A Study in British Politics and Political Thought, 1899–1914* (Oxford: Basil Blackwell, 1971), pp. 1–107.

75.   Asa Briggs, *The Age of Improvement, 1783–1867* (New York: David McKay, 1964), p. 488.

Selected Bibliography

Agulhon, Maurice, *La République au village*. Paris: Plon. 1970.
Anderson, Michael. *Family Structure in Nineteenth-Century Lancashire*. Cambridge: Cambridge University Press, 1971.
Ariès, Philippe. *Centuries of Childhood*. New York: Vintage books, 1962.
――――. *Histoire des populations françaises*. Paris: Seuil, 1971.
Armengaud, André. *Les Populations de l'Est-Aquitain au début de l'époque contemporaine*. Paris: Mouton, 1961.
Artola, Miguel. *La burguesiá revolucionaria, 1808–1874*. Madrid: Alianza Editorial, 1973.
――――. *Partidos y programas políticos, 1808–1936*. Madrind: Aguilar, 1974–75.
Bairoch, Paul, ed. *La Population active et sa structure*. Brussels: Institut de Sociologie, Université Libre de Bruxelles, 1968.
Banks, J. A., and Olive Banks. *Feminism and Family Planning in Victorian England*. Liverpool: Liverpool University Press, 1964.
Berend, Iván T., and György Ránki. *Economic Development in East-Central Europe in the Nineteenth and Twentieth Centuries*. New York: Columbia University Press, 1974.
Bernaldo de Quirós y Pérez, Constancio. *El bandolerismo Andaluz*. Madrid: Ediciones Turner, 1973.
Best, Geoffrey. *Mid-Victorian Britain, 1851–75*. New York: Schocken Books, 1971.
Bezucha, Robert J. *The Lyon Uprising of 1834*. Cambridge, Mass.: Harvard University Press, 1974.
Blok, Anton. *The Mafia of a Sicilian Village, 1860–1960*. New York: Harper & Row, 1974.
Blum, Jerome. *The End of the Old Order in Rural Europe*. Princeton: Princeton University Press, 1978.
Braun, Rudolf. *Industrialisierung und Volksleben*. Zurich: Rentsch, 1960.
――――. *Sozialer und kultureller Wandel in einem landlichen Industriegebiet*. Zurich: Rentsch, 1965.
Briggs, Asa. *Victorian Cities*. Harmondsworth: Penguin Books, 1968.
――――. *Victorian People*. Chicago: University of Chicago Press, 1970.

Burnett, John. *Plenty and Want: A Social History of Diet in England from 1815 to the Present Day*. London: Nelson, 1966.

Cameron, Rondo. *France and the Economic Development of Europe, 1800–1914*. Princeton: Princeton University Press, 1961.

Carr, Raymond. *Spain, 1808–1939*. Oxford: Oxford University Press, 1966.

Casares, Gabriel Tortella. *Los orígenes del capitalismo en España: banca, industria y ferrocarria en el siglo XIX*. Madrid: Editorial Ternos, 1973.

Cherry, Gordon E. *Urban Change and Planning*. Henley-on-Thames: G. T. Foulis, 1972.

Chevalier, Louis. *Classes laborieuses et classes dangereuses*. Paris: Plon, 1958.

Clark, T. J. *The Absolute Bourgeois*. London: Thames and Hudson, 1973.

Cobb, Richard. *The Police and the People*. Oxford: Oxford University Press, 1970.

Corbin, Alain. *Archaïsme et modernité en Limousin, 1845–1880*. 2 vols. Paris: Marcel Rivière, 1975.

Dahrendorf, Ralf D. *Class and Class Conflict in an Industrial Society*. Stanford: Stanford University Press, 1959.

Daumard, Adeline. *Les Bourgeois de Paris au XIXe siècle*. Paris: Flammarion, 1970.

Del Carria, Renzo. *Proletari senza rivoluzione: storia delle classe subalterne italiane dal 1860 al 1954*. 2 vols. Milan: Oriente, 1966.

Diaz del Moral, Juan. *Historia de las agitaciones Andaluzas*. Madrid: Alianza, 1969.

Duveau, Georges. *La Vie ouvrière en France sous le Second Empire*. Paris: Gallimard, 1946.

Dyos, H. J. *Victorian Suburb: A Study of the Growth of Camberwell*. Leicester: Leicester University Press, 1961.

———, and Michael Wolff. *The Victorian City*. Vol. 1. London: Routledge and Kegan Paul, 1973.

Edwards, Stewart. *The Paris Commune, 1871*. New York: Quadrangle Books, 1971.

Engelsing, Rolf. *Zur Sozialgeschichte deutscher Mittel—und Unterschichten*. 2nd ed. Göttingen: Vandenhoeck & Ruprecht, 1978.

Fox, Edward W. *History in Geographic Perspective: The Other France*. New York: W. W. Norton, 1971.

Gay, Peter. *Art and Act*. New York: Harper & Row, 1976.

Gellatey, Robert. *The Politics of Economic Despair: Shopkeepers and German Politics, 1890–1914*. Beverly Hills, Calif.: Sage, 1975.

Hamerow, Theodore S. *Restoration, Revolution, and Reaction*. Princeton: Princeton University Press, 1958.

Hemmings, F. W. J. *Culture and Society in France, 1848–1898* New York: Scribner 1971.

Hobsbawm, E. J. *The Age of Capital, 1848–1875*. New York: Scribners, 1975.

——. *The Age of Revolution: Europe, 1789–1848*. London: Weidenfeld and Nicholson, 1962.

——, and George Rudé. *Captain Swing*. London: Lawrence and Wishart, 1969.

——. *Primitive Rebels*. Manchester: Manchester University Press, 1962.

Johnson, Christopher H. *Utopian Communism in France*. Ithaca: Cornell University Press, 1974.

Jones, Gareth Stedman. *Outcast London: A Study in the Relationship between Classes in Victorian Society*. Harmondsworth: Penguin Books, 1976.

Kaplan, Temma. *The Anarchists of Andalusia, 1868–1903*. Princeton: Princeton University Press, 1977.

Köllmann, Wolfgang. *Bevölkerung in der industriellen Revolution*. Göttingen: Vandenhoeck & Ruprecht, 1974.

——. *Sozialgeschichte der Stadt Barmen im 19. Jahrhundert*. Tübingen: J. C. B. Mohr, 1960.

Koselleck, R. *Preussen zwischen Reform und Revolution*. Stuttgart: Kleit, 1967.

Landes, David. *The Unbound Prometheus*. Cambridge: Cambridge University Press, 1968.

Lequin, Yves. *Les Ouvriers de la région lyonnaise (1848–1914)*. 2 vols. Lyon: Presses Universitaires de Lyon, 1977.

Levine, David. *Family Formation in an Age of Nascent Capitalism*. New York: Academic Press, 1977.

Lhomme, Jean. *La Grande Bourgeoisie au pouvoir (1830–1880)*. Paris: Presses Universitaires de France, 1960.

Mack Smith, Denis. *Italy*. Ann Arbor: University of Michigan Press, 1969.

Malefakis, Edward E. *Agrarian Reform and Peasant Revolution in Spain*. New Haven: Yale University Press, 1970.

Marsh, David C. *The Changing Social Structure of England and Wales, 1871–1951*. London: Routledge and Kegan Paul, 1958.

Martinez. Cuadrado, Miguel. *La burguesia conservadora (1874–1931)*. Madrid: Alianza Editorial, 1973.

Merriman, John M. *Agony of the Republic: The Repression of the Left in Revolutionary France, 1848–51*. New Haven: Yale University Press, 1978.

——, ed. *1830 in France*. New York: Franklin Watts, 1975.

Milward, Alan S., and S. B. Saul. *The Economic Development of Continental Europe, 1780–1870*. London: George Allen & Unwin, 1973.

Moore, Barrington, Jr. *Social Origins of Dictatorship and Democracy*. Boston: Beacon Press, 1966.

Moss, Bernard H. *The Origins of the French Labor Movement*. Berkeley: University of California Press, 1976.

Mumford, Lewis. *The City in History*. New York: Harcourt, Brace and World, 1961.

Murard, Lion, and Patrick Zylberman. *L'Haleine des faubourgs*. Fontenay-sous-Bois: Recherche, 1978.

Nipperdey, Thomas. *Gesellschaft, Kultur, Theorie*. Göttingen: Vandenhoeck & Ruprecht, 1976.

Noyes, P. H. *Organization and Revolution: Working-Class Associations in the German Revolutions of 1848–49*. Princeton: Princeton University Press, 1966.

Obermann, K. *Die deutsche Arbeiter in der Revolution von 1848*. Berlin: Dietz, 1953.

Oberschall, Anthony. *Social Conflicts and Social Movements*. Englewood Cliffs, N.J.: Prentice-Hall, 1973.

Payne, Stanley G. *The Spanish Revolution*. New York: W. W. Norton, 1970.

Perkin, Harold. *Origins of Modern English Society, 1780–1880*. London: Routledge and Kegan Paul, 1969.

Perrot, Michelle. *Les Ouvriers en grève*. 2 vols. Paris: Mouton, 1974.

Pierrard, Pierre. *La Vie ouvrière à Lille sous le Second Empire*. Paris: Bloud et Gay, 1965.

Pinkney, David H. *The French Revolution of 1830*. Princeton: Princeton University Press, 1972.

———. *Napoleon III and the Rebuilding of Paris*. Princeton: Princeton University Press, 1958.

Price, Roger, *The Second French Republic*. Ithaca: Cornell University Press, 1972.

———, ed. *Revolution and Reaction: 1848 and the Second French Republic*. London: Croom Helm, 1975.

Quazza, Guido. *La lotta sociale nel Risorgimento: classe e governi della Restaurazione all'Unità (1815–1861)*. Turin: 1951.

Ritter, Gerhard Albert. *Die Arbeiterbewegung im wilhelminischen Reich, 1890–1900*. Berlin: Colloquium, 1959.

Roberts, Robert. *The Classic Slum*. Manchester: Manchester University Press, 1971.

Roth, Guenther. *Social Democrats in Imperial Germany*. Totowa, N.J., Bedminster Press, 1963.

Rudé, George. *The Crowd in History*. New York: Wiley, 1964.

Schneider, Jane, and Peter Schneider. *Culture and Political Economy in Western Sicily*. New York: Academic Press, 1976.

Scott, Joan W. *The Glassworkers of Carmaux*. Cambridge, Mass.: Harvard University Press, 1974.

———, and Louise Tilly. *Women, Work and Family*. New York: Holt, Reinhart and Winston, 1978.

Shorter, Edward. *The Making of the Modern Family*. New York: Basic Books, 1975.

——, and Charles Tilly. *Strikes in France, 1830–1968.* New York and London: Cambridge University Press, 1974.

Smelser, Neil J. *Social Change in the Industrial Revolution.* London: Routledge and Kegan Paul, 1959.

Stadelmann, Rudolf. *Soziale und politische Geschichte der Revolution 1848.* Munich: Münchner Verlag, 1948.

Stearns, Peter. *European Society in Upheaval: Social History since 1750.* 2nd edn. New York: Maxmillan, 1975.

Strauss, Rudolf. *Die Lage und die Bewegung der Chemnitzer Arbeiter in der ersten Hälfte des 19. Jahrhunderts* Berlin: Akademie, 1960.

Suger, Peter F. *Industrialization of Bosnia-Hercegovina, 1878–1918.* Seattle: University of Washington Press, 1963.

Thompson, E. P. *The Making of the English Working Class.* New York: Vintage Books, 1963.

Thompson, F. M. L. *English Landed Society in the Nineteenth Century.* London: Routledge and Kegan Paul, 1963.

Tilly, Charles. *The Vendée.* Cambridge, Mass.: Harvard University Press, 1964.

——, ed. *The Formation of National States in Western Europe.* Princeton: Princeton University Press, 1975.

——, Louise Tilly, and Richard Tilly. *The Rebellious Century.* Cambridge, Mass.: Harvard University Press, 1975.

Trempé, Rolande. *Les Mineurs de Carmaux.* 2 vols. Paris: Les Editions Ouvrières, 1971.

Tudesq, André-Jean. *Les Grands Notables en France.* 2 vols. Paris: Presses Universitaires de France, 1964.

Tuñon de Lara, Manuel. *El movimiento obreso en la historia de España.* Madrid: Taurus, 1972.

——. *La España del siglo XIX, 1808–1914.* Paris: Club del Libro Espanol, 1961.

Ullman, Joan Connelly. *The Tragic Week: A Study of Anticlericalism in Spain, 1875–1912.* Cambridge: Cambridge University Press, 1968.

van de Walle, Etienne. *The Female Population of France in the Nineteenth Century. A Reconstruction of 82 Departments.* Princeton: Princeton University Press, 1974.

Vetterli, Rudolf. *Industriearbeit, Arbeiterbewusstsein und gewerkschaftliche Organization.* Göttingen: Vandenhoeck & Ruprecht, 1978.

Vicens Vives, Jaime. *An Economic History of Spain.* Princeton: Princeton University Press, 1969.

Vigier, François. *Change and Apathy: Liverpool and Manchester during the Industrial Revolution.* Cambridge, Mass.: MIT Press, 1970.

Vigier, Philippe. *La Seconde République dans la région alpine.* 2 vols. Paris: Presses Universitaires de France, 1963.

Walker, Mack. *German Home Towns.* Ithaca: Cornell University Press, 1971.

Warriner, Doreen, ed. *Contrasts in Emerging Societies: Readings in the Social and Economic History of South-Eastern Europe in the Nineteenth Century*. Bloomington: Indiana University Press, 1965.

Weber, Adna Ferrin. *The Growth of Cities in the Nineteenth Century*. Ithaca: Cornell University Press, 1967.

Weber, Eugen. *Peasants into Frenchmen: The Modernization of Rural France, 1870–1914*. Stanford: Stanford University Press, 1976.

Wehler, Hans-Ulrich, ed. *Moderne deutsche Sozialgeschichte*. Köln: Kiepenheuer und Witsch, 1966.

Wright, Gordon. *Rural Revolution in France*. Stanford: Stanford University Press, 1964.

Wrigley, E. A. *Population and History*. New York: McGraw-Hill, 1969.

Zeldin, Theodore. *France, 1848–1945: Ambition, Love and Politics*. Oxford: Clarendon Press, 1973.

———. *France, 1848–1945: Intellect, Taste and Anxiety*. Oxford: Clarendon Press, 1977.

Notes on Contributors

RONALD AMINZADE teaches sociology at the University of Wisconsin. He is the author of "Breaking the Chains of Dependency: From Patronage to Class Politics, Toulouse, France, 1830–1872," which appeared in the *Journal of Urban History* 2 (Summer 1977).

SUSANNA I. BARROWS is Assistant Professor of History at Mt. Holyoke College.

PETER GAY is Durfee Professor of History at Yale University. His many books include *The Enlightenment: The Rise of Modern Paganism; The Science of Freedom; Weimar Culture; Style in History; Art and Act;* and *Freud, Jews Other Germans.*

CHRISTOPHER JOHNSON teaches at Wayne State University. He is the author of *Utopian Communism in France: Cabet and the Icarians, 1839–1851,* and has published a number of articles.

LYNN HOLLEN LEES teaches at the University of Pennsylvania. She is the author of *Exiles of Erin* and coeditor, with Andrew Lees, of *Nineteenth-Century Cities.*

JOHN M. MERRIMAN is Associate Professor of History at Yale University and Chairman of the Council on West European Studies. He has edited *1830 in France* and is the author of *The Agony of the Republic: The Repression of the Left in Revolutionary France, 1848–51.*

MICHELLE PERROT teaches history at the University of Paris VII (Jussieu). She is the author of *Les Ouvriers en grève.*

WILLIAM H. SEWELL, JR., is a Fellow at the Institute for Advanced Study at Princeton University. He is the author of "La Classe ouvrière de Marseille sous la Seconde République: structure sociale et comportement politique," which appeared in *Mouvement Social* 76 (1971). His forthcoming book, *Labor and Revolution in France, 1789–1848: From Corporative Community to Socialist Republic,* is to be published by Cambridge University Press.

GEORGE SHERIDAN, JR., is Assistant Professor of History at the University of Oregon. He has published several articles on the silk industry of Lyon.

CHARLES TILLY is Professor of Sociology and History at the University of Michigan. He is the author of *The Vendée, From Mobilization to Revolution, The Rebellious Century: 1830–1930* (with Louise Tilly and Richard Tilly), *Strikes in France, 1930–1968* (with Edward Shorter), and has edited *The Formation of National States in Western Europe.*

FRANK M. TURNER is Associate Professor of History at Yale University. He is the author of *Between Science and Religion* and coauthor, with Donald Kagan and Stephen Ozment, of a recent textbook entitled *The Western Heritage since 1648.*

Index

Index